Literature of Mystery and Detection

MEMOIRS

OF

VIDOCQ

[Eugène François Vidocq]

Volumes I and II

ARNO PRESS
A New York Times Company
1976

Editorial Supervision: EVE NELSON

Reprint Edition 1976 by Arno Press Inc.

Reprinted from copies in
  The University of Illinois Library

LITERATURE OF MYSTERY AND DETECTION
ISBN for complete set: 0-405-07860-9
See last pages of this volume for titles.

Manufactured in the United States of America

Library of Congress Cataloging in Publication Data

Vidocq, Eugène François, 1775-1857.
    Memoirs of Vidocq.

    (Literature of mystery and detection)
    Translation of Mémoires.
    Reprint of the 1828-29 ed. issued as v. 25-28
of Autobiography, a collection of the most instructive and amusing lives ever published. Vol. 1-2
printed for Hunt and Clarke, London; v. 3-4 published by Whittaker, Treacher, and Arnot, London.
    1. Vidocq, Eugène François, 1775-1857.
2. Police--France--Correspondence, reminiscences,
etc. I. Title. II. Series. III. Series:
Autobiography; a collection of the most instructive
and amusing lives ever published ; v. 25-28.
HV7911.V4713 1976   363.2'092'4 [B]   75-32789
ISBN 0-405-07903-6

MEMOIRS

OF

VIDOCQ

VIDOCQ.

London, Pub. by Whittaker & C? Ave Maria Lane, 1829.

MEMOIRS

OF

VIDOCQ,

PRINCIPAL AGENT OF THE FRENCH POLICE

UNTIL 1827:

AND NOW PROPRIETOR OF

THE PAPER MANUFACTORY AT ST MANDE.

WRITTEN BY HIMSELF.

TRANSLATED FROM THE FRENCH.

" Le plus grand fleau est l'homme qui provoque. Quand il n'y a
point de provocateurs ce sont les forts qui commettent les crimes,
parceque ce ne sont que les forts qui les conçoivent. En pólice, il
vaut mieux ne pas faire d'affaire que d'en créer."
MEMOIRES, VOL. I. ·

IN FOUR VOLUMES.

VOL. I.

LONDON, 1828 :

PRINTED FOR HUNT AND CLARKE,

YORK STREET, COVENT GARDEN.

INTRODUCTION.

To attempt an analysis of the Memoirs now laid before the public would be utterly impossible, so romantic are the narratives, so thrilling the horrors, so powerful the descriptions, so continuous the thread of its history. As a piece of Autobiography, it has many and singular characteristics, which stamp it at once as one of the most interesting and peculiar narratives ever penned, replete with astonishing incident and instructive moral. In these days, when the hand of improvement, so called, (God save the mark!) macadamizes the hoary relics of antiquity to smoothen the path along which civilization progresses; when the age of chivalry is gone; and daring deeds and adventurous

exploits are superseded by mere common-places
and matter-of-fact details; it is a thing of mar-
vel to read the incidents of a life so full of
romance, so teeming with the wild and wonderful. To the light reader, who but skims over
the surface of a book, and enjoys the tale merely
as one of passing amusement, forgotten soon
as read, these Memoirs offer all that the most
fastidious can desire of the piquant and attractive : to the reflective reader, who, not content
with the mere detail of events, inquires into
causes, searches out motives, and philosophizes,
en passant, on the wit or weakness, power or
puerility, of the human mind, herein will be found
ample scope and verge enough for his most
meditative musings.

As a work of fiction, it would be said, and
with apparent justice, that the Author had drawn
too largely on his inventive powers, that he had
exceeded the bounds of possibility, and set no
limits to the excursions of his fancy; but " *le
vrai n'est pas toujours le vraisemblable ;*" and independently of the assertions of Vidocq himself
as to the veracity of his Memoirs, we have other

powerful inducements to credit his statements. Many of the persons whom he has handled with severity, and spoken of in no very measured terms, are still living, and would doubtless be too happy to refute the charges alleged, did not truth forbid denial. Of his wonderful and multiplied escapes from " durance vile," we are equally assured, as no man in his senses would give fictitious descriptions of what could be readily disproved if false; and a similar argument may be applied to other seemingly over-wrought narrations; but so many of them tell *against* our hero, that their truth cannot be impugned. Perhaps no man in his time ever assumed so many parts in life's drama, and so frequently on the very shortest possible notice, as EUGENE FRANÇOIS VIDOCQ. But too early initiated in deception, he soon became an adept in dissimulation, and expert in disguising his person or his intentions. Endued with a mind powerful but perverted, a temper careless but impetuous, and feelings kindly but irritable, he, by the early association with depraved companions, rendered himself, by one false step, induced by a too ready compliance, an outcast, excluded from the pale of orderly society, and condemned to herd with the very refuse of mankind. Much may be urged in his defence, who, suffering under the penalty of a sentence, the result of perjured evidence, sought to escape the contamination which beset him in the recesses of his prison only to establish himself respectably; who, having lost caste amongst his fellow citizens, sought eagerly the means of re-instatement. But no sooner were respectable connexions formed, credit established, affections nourished, or hopes entertained, than some fortuitous and evil occurrence dashed the cup of anticipated happiness and security from his lips, leaving but the bitterness of the dregs to swallow, and thus again was he

————— Like ocean weed uptorn,
And loose along the world of waters borne;
Thus cast companionless from wave to wave
On life's rough sea.

With a mind not naturally vicious, he was again and again condemned to mate with the most abandoned; with feelings not callous, he was compelled to harbour with the most hardened; with a yearning after a life of honest labour, he was coupled with villains whose conduct was one tissue of impious blasphemy, atrocious rascality, and unutterable bestiality. To escape this there was but one only course open to him, and that he adopted. He offered his services to the police, who, aware of his talent, acuteness, activity, and courage, accepted his proferred aid. This did not result from a fear of danger or a spirit of treachery; the urgent motives that led VIDOCQ to this measure, were the desire of avoiding the perpetual contact with the vile scum with with whom his lot was cast, and the knowledge that he could benefit his country, and thus pay recompense for past misconduct. Above all he could then enjoy liberty and have before him the encouraging prospect of a re-instatement in society, which, lost to him by one early and precipitous step, was to be recovered by years of suffering and daring, open obloquy and secret approval. Much was ventured, for much was to be achieved.

We shall give a brief narrative of our hero,

and leave our readers to form their own decision
on his eventful life.

EUGENE FRANÇOIS VIDOCQ was a native of
Arras, where his father was a baker : and from
early associations he fell into courses of excess
which led to the necessity of his flying from the
paternal roof. After various, rapid, and unex-
ampled events in the romance of real life, in
which he was everything by turns and nothing
long, he was liberated from prison, and became
the principal and most active agent of police.
He was made Chief of the Police de Sureté
under Messrs Delavau and Franchet, and continued in that capacity from the year 1810 till
1827, during which period he extirpated the
most formidable of those ruffians and villains to
whom the excesses of the revolution and subsequent events had given full scope for the perpetration of the most daring robberies and iniqui-
tous excesses. Removed from employment,
in which he had accumulated a handsome independence, he could not determine on leading a
life of ease, for which his career of perpetual vigilance and adventure had unfitted him, and he built

a paper-manufactory at St Mandé, about two leagues from Paris, where he employs from forty to fifty persons,—principally, it is asserted, liberated convicts, who having passed through the term of their sentence, are cast upon society without home, shelter, or character, and would be compelled to resort to dishonest practices did not this asylum offer them its protection and afford them opportunity of earning an honest living by industrious labour.

One additional point of interest in the present volumes is, that the author is still living. The criticism on autobiography falls harmless when the hand that penned it is mouldering with its kindred dust; and in the present instance the shafts of severe comment will be blunted on the shield of candid and contrite avowal.

PREFACE.

IT was in the month of January 1828, that I
finished these Memoirs, of which it was my wish
to direct the publication personally. Unfortunately, in the month of February I broke my
right arm; and as it was fractured in five places,
it was thought that amputation must ensue.
For more than six weeks my life was in danger,
and I was in the most racking agonies. In this
distressing situation I was scarcely in condition
to re-write my manuscript, and give it the
finishing touches : but I had sold it, and the
bookseller was anxious to publish, and offered
me a reviser. Deceived by the recommendation
of a writer well spoken of in the literary world,
to perform a work, which under no other circumstances would I have trusted to other hands,
he introduced to me one of those pretended men
of letters, whose excessive impudence conceals
their stupidity, and who had no other object in
view than to make money. This pretended
literatus boasted so much of his individual

b

merits, that I was somewhat suspicious; but he was backed by so respectable an introduction, that I rejected all suspicion as unjust, and agreed to avail myself of his aid until I was convalescent. This worthy ran over the manuscript; and, after a superficial glance to show his ability, he declared, according to custom, that there was a great deal to revise and correct. The bookseller also, according to custom, believed his assertion, and I was persuaded of this truth also; and, like so many others who do not boast of it, I had got hold of a botcher.

Certainly there was much to alter in my style: I knew nothing of the forms of literary style, but yet I had some method; I knew that tautology was to be avoided; and if I was not so good a grammarian as Vaugelas, either by intuitiveness or by habit, I could always avoid bad orthography. Vidocq writing at all correctly was perhaps an unlikelihood in the eyes of my censor, I know not, but this is the case :—

In July last, I went to Douai, to get a confirmation of the pardon granted me in 1818, and on my return I asked for the printed proofs of my Memoirs; and as my restoration to the rights of a citizen did not allow of my fearing any arbitrary injunctions from the authorities, I had proposed revising my manuscript, and including all relative to the police, so as to complete the information till then kept back.

What was my astonishment when, on reading the first volume and part of the second, I found that my compilation had been entirely altered;

and that, instead of a narrative developing perpetually the sallies, vivacity, and energy of my
character, another had been foisted in, totally
deprived of all life, colouring, or promptitude.
With few alterations, the facts were nearly the
same; but all that was casual, involuntary, and
spontaneous, in a turbulent career, was given as
the long premeditation of evil intent. The
necessity that impelled me was altogether passed
over; I was made the scoundrel of the age, or
rather a Compere Mathieu, without one redeem-
ing point of sensibility, conscience, remorse, or
repentance. To crown my disgrace, the only
motives that can justify some avowals of a
candour somewhat uncommon, were not allowed
to appear; I was only a shameless villain, who
unblushingly united with the immorality of some
of his actions the desire of narrating them. To
lessen me still more, a language was attributed
to me of the most puerile sort. I really felt
myself humiliated with the details which the
press had produced, and which I should certainly
have obliterated, had I not relied on the revision
of a man of judgment. I was shocked at the
multitude of vicious conversations, long circum-
locution, and prolix phrases, in which the ear,
good sense, and syntax, were equally offended.
I could not conceive how, with the total deficiency of talent, any person could assume the
title of a literary man. But suspicions quickly
arose, and in the suppression of certain names,
which I was surprised not to find (that of my
successor, Coco-Lacour, for instance), I thought
I could trace the finger of the retired police, and

the traces of a transaction which my bookseller
and myself had no wish should appear. Apparently, Delavau and Franchet, informed of my
sad accident, which precluded me from super-
intending a publication which must disquiet them,
had profited by the circumstance, to garble my
Memoirs in such a way as to paralyze beforehand the effect of those discoveries on which
they would have little cause for self-gratulation.
All conjecture was fair : and I could only accuse
the incapacity of my reviser; and as without vanity,
I was more satisfied with my own prose than his,
I begged him to terminate his labours.

It would seem that he had no objection,—but
could he leave his post? He stated his bargain,
and the commencement of his labours, by virtue
of which he assumed a privilege of mutilating me
at his pleasure, and to do what he pleased with
me as long as he chose, if he received his " consideration." I had a much greater right to ask
him for damages and recompense; but where
there is neither cash nor honesty, what avails
any demand of this nature? To lose no time in
useless debate, I had back my manuscript, and
payed its ransom under certain reservations,
which I kept " in petto."

From this moment, I determined to destroy
the pages in which my life and various adventures were mentioned without apology. A complete destruction was the surest method of overturning an intrigue, of which the plot was easily
decyphered; but the first volume was ready,
and the second far advanced. A total suppression would have been too considerable a sacrifice

for the bookseller ; and, on the other hand, by a
culpable breach of confidence, the pirate traf-
ficking in a fraudulent manner, sold my Memoirs
in London ; and, inserted by extracts in the news-
papers, they soon reached Paris, where they were
given as translations. The theft was audacious ;
I do not hesitate to point out the author. I
might prosecute him ; his deeds shall not go unpunished. In the mean time, I thought it best to
publish with all speed, to secure the bookseller,
and that he might not be anticipated by a robbery unheard of in the literary world. Such an
inducement was necessary to urge me to sacrifice
all personal feeling : and it is because the consideration has been all powerful with me, that,
contrary to my own interest and to satisfy the
public impatience, I accept now as my own, a
production which, at first, I would have rejected.
In this text all is true ; only the truth, as far as
regards me, is told with too little carefulness,
and without any of those precautions which a
general confession requires, and by which every
one will pass judgment on me. The principal
defect is in a too careless disposition, for which
I alone can complain. Some alterations have
appeared indispensable, and I have made them.
This explains the difference of tone which may
be observed in comparing some parts of these
Memoirs ; but after my entering amongst the
corsairs at Boulogne, it will be perceived that I
have no longer an interpreter ; no one has thence
meddled or shall hereafter meddle with the task
I have imposed on myself, of unfolding to the
public all that can interest them. I speak, and

will speak, without reserve, without restriction,
and with all the frankness of a man who has no
longer cause for fear; and who, at last restored
to the fulness of those rights of which he was
unjustly deprived, aspires to the fullest exercise
of them.   If any doubts be created as to the
reality of this intention, it is only necessary to
refer my reader to the last chapter of my second
volume, when he will have ample proof that
I have the will and the power of keeping my
word.

CONTENTS.

CHAPTER I.

Page

My birth—Precocious disposition—I become a journeyman baker—The first theft—The false key—The accusing fowls—The stolen plate—Prison—Maternal
clemency—My father's eyes opened—The finishing
stroke—Departure from Arras—I seek a ship—The
shipbroker—The danger of idleness—The trumpet calls
—M. Comus, first physician in the world—The preceptor of general Jaquot—The rope-dancers—I enter
the company—Lessons of the Little Devil—The savage
of the South Seas—Punch and the Theatre of Amusing Varieties—A scene of jealousy, or the serjeant in
the eye—I go into the service of a quack doctor—
Return to my father's house—Acquaintance with an
actress—Another chace—My departure in a regiment
—The rash companion—Desertion—The raw Picardy
soldier and the assignats—I go over to the enemy—A
flogging—I return to my old standard—A domestic
robbery, and the housekeeper of an old worthy—Two
duels a day—I am wounded—My father a public
functionary—I join the war—Change of regiment—
Residence at Arras........................... 1

CHAPTER II.

Joseph Lebon—The orchestra of the guillotine, and the
reading of the bulletin—The aristocrat parrot—Citizeness Lebon—Address to the Sans Culottes—The
apple-woman—New amours—I am imprisoned—The
jailor Beaupré—The verification of the broth—M. de
Bethune—I get my liberty—The sister of my liberator

Page.

—I am made an officer—The quarters of St Sylvestre Capelle—The revolutionary army—The retaking of a vessel—My betrothed—A disguise—The pretended pregnancy—I marry—I am content without being beaten—Another stay at the Baudets—My emancipation 24

CHAPTER III.

Residence at Brussels—Coffee-houses—The gastronomic gendarmes—A forger—The roving army—The baroness and the baker-boy—The disappointment—Arrival at Paris—A gay lady—Mystification.......... 38

CHAPTER IV.

The gypsies—A Flemish fair—Return to Lille—Another acquaintance—The Bull's-eye—The sentence of punishment—St Peter's tower—The prisoners—A forgery 55

CHAPTER V.

Three escapes—The *Chauffeurs*—The suicide—The interrogatory—Vidocq accused of assassination—Sent back on a complaint—Fresh escape—Departure for Ostend—The smugglers—Vidocq retaken 68

CHAPTER VI.

The pewter keys—The quacks—Vidocq an hussar—He is retaken—The siege of the dungeon—Sentence—Condemnation 88

CHAPTER VII.

Page

Departure from Douai—The prisoners revolt in the forest
of Compeigne—Residence at the Bicêtre—Prison
customs—The madhouse 113

CHAPTER VIII.

The departure of the chain—Captain Viez and his
lieutenant Thierry—The complaint of the galley-
slaves—The visit from Paris—Humanity of the galley-serjeants—They encourage plundering—The loaf
converted into a portmanteau—Useless attempt to
escape—The Bagne at Brest—The benedictions 126

CHAPTER IX.

Of the colonization of the convicts................. 137

CHAPTER X.

The pursuit after the galley-slave—The village mayor—
The voice of blood—The hospital—Sister Françoise—
Faublas the second—The mother of robbers........ 150

CHAPTER XI.

The market-place at Cholet—Arrival at Paris—History
of captain Villedieu 165

CHAPTER XII.

Journey to Arras—Father Lambert—Vidocq a schoolmaster—Departure for Holland—The "sellers of souls"
—The mutiny—The corsair—Catastrophe.......... 181

CHAPTER XIII.

Page

I see Francine again—My re-establishment in the prison
of Douai—Am I, or am I not, Duval?—The magistrates embarrassed—I confess that I am Vidocq—
Another residence at Bicêtre—I find captain Labbre
there—Departure for Toulon—Jossas, the famous robber—His interview with a great lady—A tempest on
the Rhone—The marquis of St Armand—The executioner of the Bagne—The plunderers of the wardrobe—
A family of Chauffeurs 193

CHAPTER XIV.

Father Mathieu—I enter on a new line of business—
Ruin of my establishment—I am supposed to be
paralyzed in my limbs—I am assistant major—Ecce
Homo, or the psalm-seller—A disguise—Stop him!
he is a fugitive convict—I am added to the double
chain—The kindness of the commissary—I tell him
a made-up tale—My best contrived escape—The lady
of the town and the burial—I know not what—Critical situation—A band of robbers—I detect a thief—
I get my dismissal—I promise secrecy 220

MEMOIRS OF VIDOCQ.

CHAPTER I.

My birth—Precocious disposition—I become a journeyman baker
—The first theft—The false key—The accusing fowls—The
stolen plate—Prison—Maternal clemency—My father's eyes
opened—The finishing stroke—Departure from Arras—I seek
a ship—The ship broker—The danger of idleness—The trumpet
calls—M. Comus, first physician in the world—The preceptor
of general Jacquot—The rope dancers—I enter the company—
Lessons of the Little Devil—The savage of the South Seas—
Punch and the Theatre of Amusing Varieties—A scene of jealousy, or the serjeant in the eye—I go into the service of a
quack doctor—Return to my father's house—Acquaintance with
an actor—Another chace—My departure in a regiment—The
rash companion—Desertion—The raw Picardy soldier and the
assignats—I go over to the enemy—A flogging—I return to
my old standard—A domestic robbery, and the housekeeper
of an old worthy—Two duels a day—I am wounded—My father
a public functionary—I join the war—Change of regiment—Residence at Arras.

I WAS born at Arras; my continual disguises, the
flexibility of my features, and a singular power of gri-
macing, having cast some doubt concerning my age,
it will not be deemed superfluous to declare here, that
I was brought into the world on the 23d of July 1775,
in a house adjoining that in which Robespierre was
born sixteen years before. It was night; the rain fell
in torrents; the thunder growled; a relation, who
combined the functions of midwife and fortune-teller,
predicted that my career would be a stormy one.
There were even then in the world some good people
who believed in prognostications; now that the world

has become more enlightened, how many men, and those far from being old women, would bet on the infallibility of Miss Lenormand !

However that may be, we will presume that the sky was not troubled on my special account; and although there is always something very attractive in the marvellous, I am far from thinking that the turbulence of the elements had much reference to my birth. I had a most robust constitution, and there was plenty of me, so that as soon as I was born they took me for a child of two years of age; and I gave tokens of that athletic figure, that colossal form, which have since struck terror into the most hardened and powerful ruffians. My father's house being situated in the Place d'Armes, the constant resort of all the blackguards of the vicinity, I had my muscular powers early called into action, in regularly thrashing my comrades, whose parents were regularly complaining of me to my father and mother. At home nothing was talked of but torn ears, black eyes and rent garments; at eight years of age, I was the terror of all the dogs, cats, and children of the neighbourhood; at thirteen I handled a foil sufficiently well not to be defeated in an attack. My father perceiving that I associated chiefly with the military of the garrison, was alarmed for me, and desired me to prepare myself for the first receiving of the communion : two devotees undertook to prepare me for this solemn duty. God knows what fruit I have gathered from their lessons. I began at the same time to learn the trade of a baker, which was my father's business, in which he intended that I should succeed him, although I had an elder brother.

My employment principally consisted in carrying bread through the city. During my rounds I made frequent visits to the fencing-rooms, of which my parents were not long in ignorance; but the cooks all gave such testimony of my politeness and punctuality that they winked at this trifling prank. This went on until they discovered a deficiency in the till, of which they never took away the key. My brother, who visited it in the same manner as myself, was detected in the very act, and sent off in a hurry to a baker at Lille. The day after this event, which had not been explained to me, I was about to explore, according to custom, the convenient drawer, when I perceived that it was carefully closed. The same day my father desired me to use more alacrity in my rounds, and to return at a certain hour. It was then evident that from this day forward I should be equally deprived of liberty and money. I bewailed this twofold calamity, and hastened to impart it to a comrade named Poyant, older than myself. As a hole was cut in the counter to drop the money through, he first advised me to introduce a feather dipped in glue; but this ingenious expedient only produced me very small pieces of money, and it became necessary for me to employ a false key, which was made for me by a blacksmith's son. I then dipped again into the chest, and we spent together the fruits of these pilferings at a public-house where we had established our head quarters. There assembled, attracted by the master of the house, a great many well-known rogues, and some unfortunate young fellows, who, to get replenished pockets, used the same expedient as myself. I soon joined the society of the most abandoned vagabonds of the country, Boudou, Delcroix, Hedon, Franchison, Basserie, &c., who initiated me into all their villanies. Such was the honourable society in the bosom of which I spent my leisure hours, until one day my father surprised me, as he had done my brother, took away my key, heartily thrashed me, and took such precautions as totally cut off all my hopes of ever again getting a dividend from the receipts therein deposited.

My only resource was now to take my tithes from the bakings. Occasionally I pilfered a loaf or two; but as in disposing of them I was compelled to sell

them very cheaply, I scarcely by their sale obtained
sufficient to regale myself with tarts and honey.
Necessity makes us active; I had an eye for everything; all was agreeable to me, wine, sugar, coffee,
and liquors. My mother had never known her
provisions to disappear so quickly, and perhaps
would not have discovered so soon, but two chickens
which I had resolved on disposing of to my own
peculiar profit raised their voices to accuse me.
Hid in my breeches pocket, and concealed by
my baker's apron, they thrust out their heads and
crowed; and my mother thus informed of their intended fate, came out to prevent it. She gave me
several cuffs of the head, and sent me supperless to
bed. I did not sleep a wink, and it was, I think, the
evil spirit that kept me awake; all I know is, that I
rose with the determination to lay hands on all the
plate. One thing alone gave me uneasiness. On
each piece the name of VIDOCQ was engraved in large
letters. Poyant, to whom I broached the matter,
overruled all difficulties; and the same day, at dinner
time, I swept off ten forks and as many coffee spoons.
Twenty minutes afterwards the whole was pawned,
and the next day I had not a farthing left of the
hundred and fifty francs which they lent me on them.

I did not return home for three days, and on the
third evening I was arrested by two police officers,
who conveyed me to the Baudets, a place in which
mad persons are confined, together with those committed for trial, and the rogues of the district. I was
kept in a dungeon for ten days without being told the
cause of my arrest, and then the jailor told me that I
had been imprisoned at the desire of my father. This
information a little composed me: it was a paternal
correction that was inflicted on me, and I accordingly
judged that its continuance would not be rigorous.
My mother came to see me the next day, and I was
pardoned. Four days afterwards I was set at liberty,
and I returned to work with a determination and

promise of henceforward conducting myself irreproachably. Vain resolve! I soon resumed my
old habits, except extravagance; and I had excellent
reasons for no more playing the prodigal, for my
father, who had before been rather careless and re-
gardless, now exercised a vigilance that would have
done credit to the commandant of an advanced guard.
If he left the post at the counter, my mother relieved
guard; it was impossible for me to approach it,
although I was constantly on the look out. This
put me in despair. At last one of my tavern companions took pity on me; it was Poyant again, that
thorough rogue, of whose abilities in this way the
citizens of Arras may still preserve the memory. I
confided my sorrows to his friendly bosom. " What,"
said he, " you are a precious fool to remain thus; and
what a thing it is that a lad of your age should be
ever short a farthing. Ah! were I in your place, I
know what I should do."—" Well, what?"—" Your
parents are rich, and a thousand crowns, more or less,
would not hurt them. The old misers! they are fair
game, and we must carry it off."—" I understand, we
must grasp at once what we cannot get in detail."
—" You're right; and then we will be off, neither
seen nor known."—" Yes, but the police."—" Hold
your tongue; are you not their son? and your mother
is too fond for that." This consideration of my
mother's love, united to the remembrance of her indulgence after my late freaks, was powerfully per-
suasive; I blindly adopted a project which smiled on
my audacity; it only remained to put it in execution,
and an opportunity was not long wanting.

One evening whilst my mother was at home alone,
a confidant of Poyant came kindly to tell her, that
engaged in a debauch with some girls, I was fighting
everybody, and breaking and destroying everything in
the house, and that if I were not stopped there would
be at least a hundred francs to pay for the damage
done.

At this moment my mother was seated in her chair knitting; the stocking dropped from her hand, she arose with haste, and ran with great alarm to the place of the pretended affray, which had been fixed on at the extremity of the city. Her absence could not be of long continuance, and we hastened to profit by it. A key which I had stolen from the old lady procured us admittance into the shop. The till was closed; I was almost glad to meet with this obstacle. I recalled the memory of my mother's love for me, not as an inducement to commit the act with impunity, but as exciting feelings of coming remorse. I was going to retire; Poyant held me, his infernal eloquence made me blush for what he called my weakness; and when he presented me with a crowbar, with which he had the precaution to provide himself, I seized it almost with enthusiasm; the chest was forced; it contained nearly 2,000 francs (upwards of 80*l.*) which we shared, and half an hour afterwards I was alone on the road to Lille. In the trouble which this affair threw me into, I walked at first very quickly, so that when I reached Lens I was much fatigued. A return chaise passed, into which I got, and in less than three hours arrived at the capital of French Flanders, whence I immediately started for Dunkirk, being excessively anxious to place myself beyond the reach of pursuit.

I had resolved on visiting the new world. My fate forbade this project. The port of Dunkirk was empty. I reached Calais, intending to embark immediately, but they asked me more than the whole sum in my possession. I was induced to hope that at Ostend the fare would be less; and on going there found the captains not more reasonable than at Calais. Thus disappointed I fell into that adventurous disposition which induces us to throw ourselves voluntarily into the arms of the first enterprize that offers; and, I scarcely know why, I expected to meet with some good fellow who would take me on board his vessel

without being paid, or at least would make a considerable reduction in favour of my good appearance,
and the interest which a young man always inspires.
Whilst I was walking, full of this idea, I was accosted
by a person whose benevolent appearance induced a
belief that my vision was about to be realized. The
first words he addressed to me were questions. He
had learnt that I was a stranger; he told me that he
was a ship-broker; and when he learnt the cause
of my coming to Ostend, he offered his services.
" Your countenance pleases me," said he, " I like an
open face; there is in your features the air of frankness and joviality which I like, and I will prove it to
you by procuring for you a passage for almost nothing."
I spoke of my gratitude. " No thanks, my friend,
that will be soon enough when your business is completed, which I hope will be soon; but surely you will
be tired of waiting about in this manner?" I said
that certainly I was not very much amused. " If you
will accompany me to Blakemberg, we will sup there
together, with some jolly fellows, who are very fond of
Frenchmen." The broker was so polite, and asked
me so cordially, that I thought it would be ungentle-
manly to refuse, and therefore accepted his invitation.
He conducted me to a house where some very agreeable ladies welcomed us with all that ancient hospitality which did not confine itself only to feasting.
At midnight, probably—I say probably, for we took
no account of hours—my head became heavy, and
my legs would no longer support me; there was around
me a complete chaos, and things whirled in such a
manner, that without perceiving that they had undressed me, I thought I was stripped to my shirt in
the same bed with one of the Blakembergian nymphs;
it might be true, but all that I know is, that I soon
fell soundly asleep. On waking I found myself cold;
instead of the large green curtains which had appeared
to me in my sleep, my heavy eyes only gazed on a
forest of masts, and I heard the watchful cry which

only echoes in the sea-ports. I endeavoured to rise, and my hand touched a heap of cordage against which I was leaning. Did I dream, then, or had I dreamt the previous evening? I felt about, I got up, and when on my feet I found that I did not dream, and what was worse, that I was not one of the small number of those personages whom fortune favours whilst sleeping. I was half naked, and except two crowns and six livres, which I found in one of my breeches pockets, I was pennyless. It was then but too clear to me, as the broker had said, " my business had soon been done." I was greatly enraged, but what did that avail me? I was even unable to point out the spot where I had been thus plundered. I made up my mind and returned to the inn, where I had some clothes which remedied the deficiencies of my attire. I had no occasion to tell my misfortune to the land-lord. " Ah, ah!" said he to me, as far off as he could see me, " here comes another. Do you know, young man, that you have got off well? You return with all your limbs, which is lucky when one gets into such a hornet's nest; you now know what a land shark is; they were certainly beautiful syrens! All pirates are not on the sea, you observe, nor all the sharks within it; I will wager that they have not left you a farthing." I drew my two crowns from my pocket to show them to the inn-keeper. " That will be," said he, " just enough to pay your bill," which he then presented. I paid it and took leave of him, without however quitting the city.

Assuredly, my voyage to America was deferred till the Greek calends, and the old continent was to be my lot; I was about to be reduced to the level of the lowest degrees of degraded civilization, and my future lot was the more uncertain and disquieting, as I had no present resources. At home I never wanted bread; and this inspired regret for my paternal roof; the oven, said I to myself, was always heated for me as well as for others. After these regrets, I ran over mentally

all that crowd of moral reflexions which people have
thought to strengthen by clothing them in the garb of
superstition :—" A bad action brings no good luck:
ill acquired gains profit us nothing." For the first time I
acknowledged from experience a mine of truth in these
prophetic sentences, which perpetual predictions were
more sure than the admirable Centuries of Michael Nos-
tradamus. I was in the repenting mood, as may be
believed from my situation. I calculated the consequences of my flight and its aggravating sequel, but
these were but ephemeral feelings: it was written that
I should not so soon be placed in the right way. The
sea was open to me as a profession, and I resolved to
betrothe myself to it, at the risk of breaking my neck
thirty times a day, by climbing, for eleven francs a
month, up the rigging of a ship. I was ready to enter
like a novice, when the sound of a trumpet suddenly
arrested my attention ; it was not that of a regiment,
but of Paillasse (Merry-Andrew) and his master, who,
in front of a show bedecked with the emblems of an
itinerant menagerie, was awaiting the mob, which never
hisses the vulgar exhibitions. I saw the beginning ;
and whilst a large crowd was testifying its gratification
by loud shouts of laughter, it occurred to me that the
master of Paillasse might give me employment.
Paillasse appeared to me a good fellow, and I was desirous of securing his protection; and as I knew that
one good turn deserves another, when he got down
from his platform, on saying " *follow the crowd,*" thinking that he might be thirsty, I devoted my last shilling
in offering him half a pint of gin. Paillasse, sensible
of this politeness, promised instantly to speak for me,
and as soon as our pint was finished, he presented me
to the director. He was the famous Cotte-Comus ;
he called himself the first physician of the world, and
in traversing the country, had united his talents to
those of the naturalist Garnier, the learned preceptor
of general Jacquot, whom all Paris saw in the square
of the Fountains before and after the revolution. These

gentlemen had with them a troop of rope dancers,
Comus, as soon as I appeared before him, asked me
what I could do. " Nothing," said I. " In that case,"
said he, " they will teach you: there are greater fools
than you, and then besides, you have not a clumsy
appearance. We shall see if you have a taste for the
stage; then I will engage you for two years; the first
six months you shall be well fed, and clothed; at the
end of that time you shall have a sixteenth of the
profits; and the year following, if you are bright, I will
give you a share like the others; in the mean time, my
friend, I will find occupation for you."

Thus was I introduced, and then went to partake of
the flock-bed of the obliging merry-andrew. At the
break of day we were awakened by the sonorous voice
of our master, who leading me to a kind of small room,
said, whilst showing me the lamps and wooden chan-
deliers—" There is your employment, you must clean
these and put them in proper order; do you understand? And afterwards you must clean out the cages
of the animals, and brush the floors." I went about
my job, which did not greatly please me: the tallow
disgusted me, and I was not quite at my ease with the
monkeys, who enraged to see a fool to whom they
were not accustomed, made inconceivable efforts to
tear my eyes out. But I yielded to iron necessity. My
duty performed, I appeared before the director, who
said that I was an apt pupil, and that if I was assiduous
he would do something for me. I rose early, and was
very hungry; it was ten o'clock, but no signs of breakfast were visible, and yet it was agreed that I should
have bed and board. I was sinking from want, when
they gave me a piece of brown bread, so hard, that
being unable to get through with it, although gifted
with sharp teeth and a famous appetite, I threw the
greater portion amongst the animals. I was obliged to
light up in the evening, and as, from want of practice,
I did not evince in my occupation all possible dispatch, the director, who was a brute, administered to

me a slight correction, which he renewed the next and following days. A month had not elapsed before I was in a wretched condition; my clothes, spotted with grease and torn by the monkeys, were in rags; I was devoured by vermin; hard diet had made me so thin that no one would have recognised me; and then it was that there arose in all imaginable bitterness the regrets for my paternal home, where good food, soft bed, and excellent clothing were mine, and when I had no monkeys to make clean and feed.

I was in this mood, when one morning Comus told me that after due consideration he was convinced that I should make an admirable tumbler. He then placed me under the tuition of sieur Balmate, called the " little devil," with orders to train me. My master just escaped breaking my loins at the first bend which he compelled me to make. I took two or three lessons daily. In less than three weeks, I was able to execute with much skill the monkey's leap, the drunkard's leap, the coward's leap, &c. My teacher, delighted at my progress, took pains to forward me; a hundred times I thought that in developing my powers, he would dislocate my limbs. At length we reached the difficulties of the art, which became more and more complicated. At my first attempt at the grand fling I nearly split myself in two; and in the chair-leap I broke my nose. Bruised, maimed and tired of so perilous a business, I determined on telling Comus that I had no desire to become a vaulter. " Oh you do not like it," said he; and without objecting to my refusal gave me a sound thumping. I then left Balmate entirely and returned to my lamps.

Comus had given me up, and it was now for Garnier to give me a turn. One day, after having beaten me more than usual (for he shared that pleasing office with Comus) Garnier, measuring me from head to foot, and viewing with a marked delight the dilapidation of my doublet, through which my flesh was visible, said to me, " I like you; you have reached the point that

pleases me. Now, if you are obedient it remains with
yourself to be happy: from to day you must let your
nails grow; your hair is already of a sufficient length;
you are nearly naked, and a decoction of walnut-tree
leaves will do the rest." I did not understand what
Garnier meant, when he called my friend Paillasse and
desired him to bring the tiger skin and club. Paillasse
obeyed—" Now," said Garnier, " we will go through
the performance. You are a young savage from the
South Seas, and moreover a cannibal; you eat raw
flesh, the sight of blood puts you in a fury, and when
you are thirsty, you introduce into your mouth flints
which you crack; you utter only broken and shrill
sounds, you open your eyes widely, your motions are
violent; you only move with leaps and bounds: finally,
take for your model the ourang-outang who is in cage
number one." During this lesson, a jar full of small
stones quite round was placed at my feet, and near it a
cock which was tired with having its legs tied together;
Garnier took it, and offered it to me, saying " Gnaw
away at this." I would not bite it; he threatened me.
I rebelled, and demanded to be released; to which he
replied by a dozen cuffs of the ear. But he did not
get off scot-free: irritated at this usage, I seized a stake,
and should assuredly have knocked the naturalist on
the head, if the whole troop had not fallen on me,
and thrust me out at the door with a shower of blows
from the fist and kicks of the feet.

Some days afterwards, I was at the same public
house with a showman and his wife who exhibited
puppets in the open street. We made acquaintance,
and I found that I had inspired them with some feelings of interest. The husband pitied me for having
been condemned to what he termed the society of
beasts. He compared me with Daniel in the lions' den.
We may see that he was learned, and intended for
something better than to play ' Punch.' At a later
period he superintended a provincial theatrical company, and perhaps superintends it still. I shall conceal

his name. The embryo manager was very witty, though his wife did not perceive it; he was very ugly, which she plainly perceived. She was one of those smart brunettes with long eyelashes, whose hearts are of most inflammable material, which deserve a better destiny than to light a fire of straw. I was young and so was the lady: she was only sixteen, her husband thirty-five. As soon as I found myself out of place, I went to seek this couple; it struck me that they would advise me correctly. They gave me some dinner and congratulated me in having dared to free myself from the despotic yoke of Garnier. "Since you are your own master," said the husband to me, " you had better accompany us : you will assist us ; at least, when we are three in number we shall have no lost time between the acts ; you will move the actors whilst Eliza goes round with the hat; thus the public will be attracted and not go off, and our profits will be more abundant. What say you, Eliza ?" Eliza answered, that she would do in this respect all he might desire, and besides she entirely agreed with him ; and at the same time gave me a look which bespoke that she was not displeased, and that we should soon understand each other. I accepted the new employ with gratitude, and at the next representation I was installed to my office. The situation was infinitely superior to that at Garnier's. Eliza, who, despite my leanness, had discovered that I was not so badly made as I was clothed, made a thousand secret advances, to which I was not backward in reply : at the end of three days she said she loved me. I was not ungrateful; we were happy and constantly together. At home, we only laughed, played and joked. Eliza's husband took all that for child's sport; when at work we were side by side under a narrow cabin, formed of four cloth rags, dignified by the splendid title of " Theatre of Amusing Varieties." Eliza was on the right of her husband, and I on her right hand, and filled her place when she was not there to superintend the exits and entrances. One Sunday the

c

play was in full representation, and there was a crowded audience round the stage. Punch had beaten everybody, and our master, having nothing more to do with one of his personages (the Serjeant of the Watch) wished it to be removed, and called for his assistant. We heard him not. " Assistant, assistant," he repeated with impatience, and at the third time turning round he saw us enfolding each other in a close embrace. Eliza, surprised, sought for an excuse, but the husband without listening cried out again, " Assistant," and thrust against his eye the hook which served to suspend the serjeant. At the same moment the blood flowed, the representation was interrupted, and a battle ensued between the two married people; the show was overturned, and we were exposed in the midst of a numerous crowd of spectators, from whom this scene drew a lengthened peal of applause and laughter.

This disaster again threw me on the wide world, without a home to shelter my head. If I had had a decent appearance I might have procured a situation in a respectable family, but my appearance was so wretched that no one would have anything to say to me. In my situation I had but one resource, that of returning to Arras: but then how to exist on the road? I was a prey to these perplexities, when a person passed near me whom I took by his appearance to be a pedlar. I entered into conversation with him, and he told me that he was going to Lille; that he sold powders, opiates, and elixirs, cut corns, relieved bunnions, and sometimes extracted teeth. " It is a good trade," added he, " but I am getting old, and want somebody to carry my pack; it is a stiff-backed fellow like you that I need, with a firm foot, and steady eye; so if you like we will tramp it together."—" Willingly," was my reply, and without any further stipulation, we went on our way together. After an eight hours' walk, night drew on, and we could scarcely see our way, when we halted before a wretched village inn."—" Here it is." said the itinerant doctor, knocking at the door.—" Who

is there ?" cried a hoarse voice. "Father Godard with his
pack," answered my guide ; and the door immediately
opening, we found ourselves in the midst of a crowd
of pedlars, tinkers, quack-doctors, umbrella-venders,
showmen, &c. who hailed my new master, and ordered
a plate to be brought for him. I thought they would
do me equal honor, and I was about to seat myself
at table, when the host, striking me familiarly on the
shoulder, asked me if I was not the mountebank of
father Godard. "Who do you call a mountebank ?"
said I with astonishment. "The merry-andrew, then."
I confess that, despite of the recent reminiscences of
the menagerie, and the Theatre of Amusing Varieties, I
felt mortified at such an appellation. But I had a devil
of an appetite, and as I thought that supper would
follow the interrogatory, and that, after all, my situation
with father Godard had not been accurately defined,
I consented to pass for his mountebank. On my answering, the host led me at once to a neighbouring
spot, a sort of barn, where a dozen of fellows were
smoking, drinking, and playing at cards. He said that
they would send me in something to eat. Soon afterwards, a stout wench brought me in a mess in a
wooden bowl, on which I feed with the utmost avidity.
A loin of mutton was swimming in a sea of pot liquor
with stringy turnips: I cleared the whole up in a
twinkling. This done, I laid myself down with the
other packmen's valets, on some piles of straw, which
we shared with a camel, two muzzled bears, and a
crowd of learned dogs. The vicinity of such bed-
fellows was not the most pleasing; but it was necessary to put up with it. I did not close my eyes, whilst
all the others snored away most gloriously.

Father Godard paid for all, and however bad were the
beds and the fare, as we drew near Arras, it was necessary that I should not quit him. At length we reached
Lille, which we entered on a market day. By way of
losing no time, father Godard went straight to the
principal square, and desired me to arrange his table,

his chest, his vials and packets, and then proposed that I should go and announce his arrival round the place. I had made a good breakfast, and the proposition disgusted me : I could put up with acting with a dromedary, and carrying his baggage from Ostend to Lille, but to go round in parade, at ten leagues from Arras—No! I bade adieu to father Godard, and then set out towards my native city, of which the clock soon became visible. Having reached the foot of the ramparts, before the closing of the gates, I trembled at the idea of the reception I should meet with: one moment I was tempted to beat a retreat, but fatigue and hunger could not allow that; rest and food were vitally necessary : I wavered no longer, and ran towards my paternal roof. My mother was alone in the shop : I entered, and throwing myself at her feet, wept whilst I intreated her forgiveness. The poor old woman, who hardly recognised me, so greatly was I altered, was softened. She had not power to repulse me, and even appeared to have forgotten all. She reinstated me in my old chamber, after having supplied all my wants. But it was necessary to tell my father of my return. She did not feel courage to face his first bursts of anger : a priest of her acquaintance, the almoner of the regiment of Anjou, garrisoned at Arras, undertook to be the bearer of the words of peace; and my father, after having vowed fire and flames, consented to pardon me. I trembled lest he should prove inexorable, and when I learnt that he had yielded, I jumped for joy. The almoner brought the news to me, and followed it up with a moral application, which was no doubt very touching, but I do not remember a word of it; I only recollect that he quoted the parable of the Prodigal Son, which was in truth a history similar to my own.

My adventures had made some noise in the city; everybody was anxious to hear them from my own lips. But no one, except one actress of the Arras company, took more interest in them than two milliners of

the Rue de Trois Visages : I paid them frequent visits.
However, the actress soon obtained the exclusive
privilege of my attention, and an intrigue followed, in
which, disguised as a young girl, I renewed at her
house some scenes from the romance of Faublas. A
sudden journey to Lille with my conquest, her husband, and a very pretty little maid servant, who passed
me off for her sister, proved to my father that I had soon
forgotten the troubles of my first campaign. My absence was not of long continuance : three weeks had
scarcely elapsed, when, from want of money, the actress
refused any longer to allow me to form part of the
baggage. I returned quietly to Arras, and my father
was confounded at the straightforward way with
which I asked his consent to enter the army. The
best he could do was to comply, which he did;
and the next day I was clad in the uniform of the
Bourbon regiment. My height, good figure, and skill
in arms, procured for me an appointment in a company
of chasseurs. Some old veterans took offence at it,
and I sent two to the hospital in consequence, when
I soon joined them myself, on being wounded by one of
their comrades. This commencement gave me notoriety,
and they took a malicious pleasure in reviewing my
past adventures ; so that at the end of six months,
Reckless,—for they bestowed that name on me,—had
killed two men and fought fifteen duels. In other
respects I enjoyed all the pleasures of a garrison life.
I mounted guard at the cost of some good shopkeepers,
whose daughters took on themselves the charge of
making me as comfortable as possible. My mother
added to these liberalities, and my father made me an
allowance ; and besides I found means to run in debt:
thus I really cut a figure, and scarcely felt anything of
the troubles of discipline. Once only I was sentenced
to a fortnight's imprisonment because I had not answered to three summonses. I underwent my punishment in a dungeon beneath one of the bastions, where
one of my comrades was shut up with me, a soldier

in the same regiment. He was accused of various robberies, which he had confessed.   Scarcely were we
alone when he told me the grounds of his detention.
Doubtlessly the regiment would give him up, and this
idea, joined to the dread of dishonouring his family,
threw him into dispair.   I pitied him, and seeing no
remedy for so deplorable a case, I counselled him to
evade punishment either by escape or suicide. He determined to try the former ere he resolved on the
latter; and, aided by a young friend who came to visit
me, I prepared all for his flight.   At midnight two
bars of iron were broken, and we conducted the prisoner to the ramparts, and then I said to him—" Go :
you must either *jump or hang*."   He calculated the
height, and hesitating, determined rather to run the
chance of his sentence than to break his legs.   He was
preparing to return to his dungeon : at a moment when
he least expected it, we gave him a push over : he
shrieked out whilst I bid him be silent.   I then returned to my cell : when on my straw I tasted the repose which the consciousness of a good deed always
brings.   The next day, on the flight of my companion
being discovered, I was questioned, and dismissed on
saying that I knew nothing of the affair.   Some years
afterwards, I met this unfortunate fellow, who looked
on me as his liberator. Since his fall he had been lame,
but had become an honest man.

I could not remain eternally at Arras; war had been
declared against Austria, and I set out with the regiment, and soon after was present at the rout of Mar-
quain which ended at Lille by the massacre of the
brave and unfortunate general Dillon.   After this we
were ordered against the camp at Maulde, and then
in that de la Lune, when, with the *infernal army* under
the command of Kellerman, I was engaged in the
battle against the Prussians of the 30th of October.
The next day I was made corporal of grenadiers :
thereupon it became necessary to baptise my worsted
lace, and I acquitted myself with much credit at the

drinking booth, when I know not how or why, I quarrelled with the serjeant-major of the regiment which I had just left. An honourable meeting, which I proposed, was agreed upon, but when on the ground my adversary pretended that the difference from rank would not allow of his measuring weapons with me. I sought to compel him by violence, he went to make complaint of me, and the same evening I was, together with my second, placed under arrest. Two days afterwards we were informed that we were to be tried by court-martial, and thereupon determined to desert. My comrade in his waistcoat only, with a cap on his head, like a soldier about to undergo punishment, walked before me, who had on a hairy cap, my knapsack, and musket, at the end of which was a large packet sealed with red wax, and inscribed " To the citizen commandant of the quarters at Vitry-le-Français. " This was our passport, and we reached Vitry in safety, and procured citizens' habits from a Jew. At this period the walls of every city were covered with placards, in which all Frenchmen were invited to fly to the defence of their country. At such a juncture the first comers were enrolled : a quarter-master of the 11th chasseurs received us, gave us our route, and we immediately started for the depôt at Philippeville.

My companion and self had but little cash, when fortunately a lucky windfall was in waiting for us at Châlons. In the same inn with us was a soldier of Beaujolais, who invited us to drink. He was an open-hearted countryman of Picardy, and as I conversed with him in the provincial dialect of his country, whilst the glass was circulating we grew such great friends, that he shewed us a portfolio filled with assignats, which he said he had found near Chateau-l'Abbaye. " Comrades," said he, " I cannot read, but if you will tell me what these papers are worth, I will give you a share." The Picard could not have asked any one better able to inform him, and in bulk he had much the greater quantity ; but he had no suspicion that we had retained in value nine-tenths of the sum. This little supply was not useless during the remainder of our journey, which we finished with much glee. Arrived at our place of destination, we had still enough left to keep the pot boiling. A short time afterwards we were sufficiently skilled in horsemanship to be appointed to one of the squadrons on service, and we reached the army two days before the battle of Jemmappes. It was not the first time that I had smelt powder, and I was no coward; indeed I had reason to know that I had found favour in the eyes of my officers, when my captain informed me, that having been discovered to be a deserter, I should be most certainly arrested. The danger was imminent, and that same evening I saddled my horse, intending to go over to the Austrians. I soon reached their out-posts; and on asking to be admitted, was incorporated at once with the cuirassiers of Kinski. What I most feared was lest I should be compelled next day to cross swords with the French, and I hastened to avoid any such necessity. A pretended illness enabled me to be left at Louvain, where after passing some days in the hospital, I offered to give the officers of the garrison lessons in fencing. They were delighted with the proposal, and supplied me with masks, gloves, and foils; and an assault, in which 1 disarmed two or three pretended German masters was enough to give them the highest opinion of my skill. I soon had many pupils, and reaped a good harvest of florins.

I was too much elated with my success, when at the end of a brisk attack on a brigadier, I was condemned to undergo twenty stripes of the cat, which, according to custom, were given to me on parade. This transported me with rage, and I refused to give another lesson. I was ordered to continue, with a choice of giving lessons or a fresh flogging. I decided on the former; but the cat annoyed me, and I resolved to dare all to escape from it. Being informed that a lieutenant was about to join the army under general

Schroeder, I begged to accompany him as his servant; to which he agreed, under the idea that I should make a St George of him; but he was mistaken, for as we approached Quesnoi I took French leave, and directed my journey towards Landrecies, where I passed for a Belgian who had left the Austrian banner. They wished me to enter a cavalry regiment, but the fear of being recognised and shot, if ever I should be brigaded with my old regiment, made me give the preference to the 14th light regiment (the old chasseurs of the barriers.) The army of the Sambre and Meuse was then marching towards Aix-la-Chapelle; the company to which I belonged received orders to follow it. We set out, and on entering Rocroi I saw the chasseurs of the 11th. I gave myself up for lost, when my old captain, with whom I could not avoid an interview, gave me courage. This worthy man, who had taken an interest in me ever since he had seen me, cut away amongst the hussars of Saxe-Teschen, told me that as an amnesty would henceforward place me out of the reach of all pursuit, he should have much pleasure in again having me under his order. I told him how glad it would make me; and he, undertaking to arrange the affair, I was once more reinstated in the 11th. My old comrades received me with pleasure, and I was not less pleased to find myself once again amongst them; and nothing was wanting to complete my happiness, when love, who is always busy, determined on playing me one of his tricks. It will not be thought surprising that at seventeen I captivated the house-keeper of an old gentleman. Manon, for that was her name, was near twice my age, but then she loved me very tenderly, and proved it by making every sacrifice to me unhesitatingly. I was to her taste the handsomest of chasseurs, because I was hers, and she wished that I should also be the most dashing. She had already given me a watch, and I was proudly adorned with various jewels, proofs of the love with

which I had inspired her, when I learnt that Manon
was accused by her master of robbery. Manon confessed the fact, but at the same time, to assure herself
that after her sentence I should not pass into another's
arms, she pointed me out as her accomplice, and even
asserted that I had proposed the theft to her. It had
the appearance of probability, and I was consequently
implicated, and should have extricated myself with
difficulty if chance had not brought to light some
letters of hers, which established my innocence.
Manon, conscience-stricken, retracted. I had been
shut up in the house of confinement at Stenay,
whence I was set at liberty, and sent back as white
as snow. My captain, who had never thought me
guilty, was delighted at seeing me again; but the
chasseurs could not forgive my being even suspected;
and in consequence of various allusions and comments,
I had no less than six duels in as many days. In the
last I was badly wounded, and was conveyed to the
hospital, where I remained for a month before I recovered. On going out, my officer, convinced that
these quarrels would be renewed if I did not go away
for a time, gave me a furlough for six weeks. I went
to Arras, where I was much astonished to find my
father in a public employment. As an old baker, he
had been appointed to watch over the supplies of the
commissariat. He opposed the distribution of bread
at a time of scarcity; and this discharge of his duty,
although he performed it gratis, was so offensive, that
he would assuredly have been conducted to the guillotine had he not been protected by citizen (now
lieutenant-general) Souham, commandant of the 2d
battalion of Corrèze, into which I was temporarily
drafted.

My furlough being out, I rejoined my regiment at
Givet, whence we marched for the county of Namur.
We were quartered in the villages on the banks of
the Meuse; and as the Austrians were in sight, not a

day passed without some firing on both sides. At the termination of an engagement more serious than usual, we were driven back almost under the cannon of Givet; and in the retreat I received a ball in my leg, which compelled me to go again to the hospital, and afterwards to remain at the depôt; and I was there when the Germanic legion passed, principally composed of a party of deserters, fencing-masters, &c. One of the chief officers proposed that I should enter this corps, offering me the rank of quarter-master. "Once admitted," said he, "I will answer for you, you shall be safe from all pursuit." The certainty of not being asked for, joined to the remembrance of the disagreeables of my intimacy with Manon, decided me; I accepted the offer, and the next day was with the legion on the road to Flanders. No doubt, in continuing to serve in this corps, where promotion was very rapid, I should have been made an officer, but my wound opened afresh, with such bad symptoms, that I determined to ask for leave again, which on obtaining, I was six days afterwards once more at the gates of Arras.

CHAPTER II.

Joseph Lebon—The orchestra of the guillotine, and the reading
of the bulletin—The aristocrat parrot—Citizeness Lebon—Ad-
dress to the Sans Culottes—The apple-woman—New amours—
I am imprisoned—The jailor Beaupré—The verification of the
broth—M. de Bethune—I get my liberty—The sister of my
liberator—I am made an officer—The quarters of St Sylvester
Capelle—The revolutionary army—The retaking of a vessel—
My betrothed—A disguise—The pretended pregnancy—I marry
—I am content without being beaten—Another stay at the
Baudets—My emancipation.

On entering the city, I was struck with the air of
consternation which every countenance wore; some
persons whom I questioned looked at me with contempt, and left me without making any reply. What
extraordinary business was being transacted? Penetrating the crowd, which was thronging in the dark
and winding streets, I soon reached the fish-market.
Then the first object which struck my sight was the
guillotine, raising its blood-red boards above the silent
multitude. An old man, whom they had just tied to
the fatal plank, was the victim; suddenly I heard the
sound of trumpets. On a high place which overlooked
the orchestra, was seated a man, still young, clad in a
Carmagnole of black and blue stripes. This person, whose
appearance announced monastic rather than military
habits, was leaning carelessly on a cavalry sabre, the
large hilt of which represented the Cap of Liberty; a
row of pistols ornamented his girdle, and his hat,
turned up in the Spanish fashion, was surmounted by
a large tri-coloured cockade: I recognised Joseph
Lebon. At this moment his mean countenance was
animated with a horrid smile; he paused from beating
time with his left foot; the trumpets stopped; he made
a signal, and the old man was placed under the blade.
A sort of clerk, half drunk, then appeared at the side
of the " avenger of the people," and read with a hoarse

voice a bulletin of the army of the Rhine and Moselle.
At each paragraph the orchestra sounded a chord;
and when the reading was concluded, the head of the
wretched old man was stricken off amidst shouts of
" Vive la republique!" repeated by the satellites of the
ferocious Lebon. I shall never forget, nor can I
adequately depict the impression of this horrible sight.
I reached my father's house almost as lifeless as the
miserable being whose agony had been so cruelly prolonged; and then I learnt that he was M. de Mongon,
the old commandant of the citadel, condemned as an
aristocrat. A few days before, they had executed at
the same place, M. de Vieux-Pont, whose only crime
was that of having a parrot, in whose chatterings there
were some sounds like the cry of " Vive le roi!" The
parrot had escaped the fate of his master; and it was
said that it had been pardoned at the entreaty of the
citizeness Lebon, who had undertaken to convert it.
The citizeness Lebon had been a nun of the abbey of
Vivier: with this qualification added to many others,
she was the fitting consort of the ex-curate of Neu-
ville, and exercised a powerful influence over the
members of the commission at Arras, in which were
seated, as judges or jurymen, her brother-in-law and
three uncles. The ex-nun was no less greedy of gold
than blood. One evening at the theatre, she ventured
to make this address to the crowded auditory:—
" Ah, Sans Culottes, they say it is not for you that the
guillotine is at work! What the devil, must we not
denounce the enemies of the country? Do you know
any noble, any rich person, any aristocratical shopkeeper? Denounce him and you shall have his money-
bags." The atrocity of this monster was only equalled
by that of her husband, who abandoned himself to the
greatest excesses. Frequently after his orgies he was
seen running through the city making bestial propositions to one young person, brandishing a sabre over
another's head, and firing pistols in the ears of women
and children.

D

An old apple-woman, with a red cap and sleeves tucked up to the shoulders, carrying a long stick of hazel-wood, usually attended him in his walks, and they were frequently met arm-in-arm together. This woman, called mother Duchesne, in allusion to the famous father Duchesne, figured as the Goddess of Liberty in several democratic solemnities. She regularly assisted at the sittings of the commission, for which she prepared the arrests by her speeches and denunciations. She thus brought to the guillotine all the inhabitants of one street, which was left entirely desolated.

I have often asked myself how, in the midst of such deplorable scenes, the taste for pleasure and amusement lost none of its relish. The fact is, that Arras continued to offer to me the same dissipations as ever; the ladies were as accessible; and I was easily convinced of that, as in a very few days I rose gradually in my amours from the young and pretty Constance, only child of corporal Latulipe, canteen-keeper of the citadel, to the four daughters of a notary, who had an office at the corner of the Rue des Capucines. Lucky should I have been had I confined myself to that, but I began to pay my homage to a beauty of the Rue de la Justice; and one day I met my rival in my walks. He, who was the old musician of the regiment, was one of those men who, without boasting of the success which they have obtained, hint in plain terms that they have experienced refusals. I charged him with boasting in this way, and he became enraged; I provoked him the more, and the more angry he grew: I had forgotten my own cause of anger with him, when I remembered that I had good grounds of offence. I demanded an explanation, which was useless; and he only consented to meet me after I had inflicted on him the most degrading humiliation. The rendezvous was fixed for the next morning. I was punctual; but scarcely had I arrived when I was surrounded by a troop of gendarmes and police officers, who demanded

my sword and ordered me to follow them. I obeyed,
and was soon enclosed within the walls of the
Baudets, whose use had been changed since the terrorists had put the population of Arras in a state of
periodical decapitation. The jailor, Beaupré, covered
with an enormous red cap, and followed by two large
black dogs, who never quitted him, conducted me to a
vast garret, where he held in his keeping the principal
inhabitants of the country. There, deprived of all
communication from without, they scarcely received
nourishment, and not even that until it had literally
been overhauled by Beaupré, who carried his precaution so far as to plunge his filthy dirty hands in the
broth, to assure himself that there were no arms or
keys. If anybody complained, he said to him, " Umph!
you are very difficult to please for the time you have left
to live.   How do you know that it will not be your turn
tomorrow ?   Oh, by the way, what is your name ? "—
" So and so."—" Ah! by my faith it is your turn tomorrow!"   And the predictions of Beaupré were the less
likely to fail as he himself pointed out the individuals
to Joseph Lebon, who, after his dinner, consulted him
saying, " Who shall we bathe tomorrow ?"

Amongst the gentry shut up with us was the count
de Bethune. One morning they sent for him to the
tribunal.   Before leading him out to the fore court,
Beaupré said to him abruptly, " Citizen Bethune, since
you are going down there, am not I to have all you leave
behind you ?"—" Certainly, M. Beaupré," answered
the old man tranquilly.   " There are no misters now,"
said the grinning wretch of a jailor, " we are all citizens; " and at the gate he again cried out to him,
" Adieu, citizen Bethune!" M. de Bethune was however
acquitted. He was brought back to prison as a suspected person.   His return rejoiced us all; we thought
him saved, but the next day he was again called up.
Joseph Lebon, during whose absence the sentence of
acquittal had been passed, arrived from the country :
furious at being deprived of the blood of so worthy

a man, he had ordered the members of the commission to assemble immediately, and M. de Bethune, condemned at the next sitting, was executed by torchlight.

This event, which Beaupré announced to us with ferocious joy, gave me serious uneasiness: every day they condemned to death men who were ignorant even of the cause of their arrest, and whose fortune or situation in society never intended them for political commotion: and on the other hand, I knew that Beaupré, very scrupulous as to the number, thought not of the quality; and that frequently, not seeing immediately the number of individuals pointed out, sent the first who came to hand, that the service of the state might suffer nothing from delay. Every moment then might place me in the clutch of Beaupré, and you may believe that this idea was not the most satisfactory in the world.

I had been already detained sixteen days, when a visit from Joseph Lebon was announced; his wife accompanied him, and he had in his train the principal terrorists of the country, amongst whom I recognised my father's old barber, and an emptier of wells, called Delmotte, or Lantilette. I asked them to say a word for me to the representative, which they promised; and I augured the better of it as they were both in good estimation. However, Joseph Lebon went through the rooms, questioning the prisoners in a brutal manner, and pretending to address them with frightful harshness. When he came to me, he stared at me, and said in a tone half severe and half jesting, " Ah! ah! is it you, François? What, you an aristocrat,—you speak ill of the Sans Culottes,—you regret your old Bourbon regiment,—take care, for I can send you to be cooked (guillotined.) But send your mother to me." I told him, that being so strictly immured *(au secret)* I could not see her. " Beaupré," said he to the jailor, " let Vidocq's mother come in;" and went away, leaving me full of hope, as he had evidently

treated me with marked amenity. Two hours afterwards I saw my mother, who told me what I knew
not before, that the musician whom I had challenged
had denounced me. The denunciation was in the
hands of a furious jacobin, the terrorist Chevalier, who,
out of friendship to my rival, would certainly have
been much against me, if his sister, at the persuasion
of my mother, had not prevailed on him to exert
himself to procure my discharge. Having left prison,
I was conducted with great state to the patriotic
society, where they made me take the oath of fidelity
to the republic, and hatred to tyrants. I swore all they
desired. What sacrifices will not a man make to
procure his freedom!

These formalities concluded, I was replaced in the
depôt, where my comrades testified much pleasure at
seeing me again. After what had passed, I should
have been deficient in gratitude had I not looked on
Chevalier as my deliverer; I went to thank him, and
expressed to his sister how much I was touched at
the interest which she had so kindly testified to a poor
prisoner. This lady, who was the most amorous of
brunettes, but whose large black eyes did not compensate for their ugliness, thought that I was in love
because I was polite; she construed literally some
compliments which I paid her, and from the first
interview, she so greatly misinterpreted my sentiments
as to cast her regards upon me. Our union was talked
of, and my parents were questioned on the point, who
answered that eighteen was too young for marriage, and
so the matter went on. Meanwhile battalions were
formed at Arras, and being known as an excellent
driller, I was summoned with seven other subaltern
officers to instruct the 2d battalion of Pas-de-Calais,
to which belonged a corporal of grenadiers of the
regiment of Languedoc, named Cæsar, now *garde
champêtre* at Colombre or Pateux, near Paris. He
was our adjutant major. As for me, I was promoted
to the rank of sub-lieutenant on arriving at St Syl-

vestre-Capelle, near Bailleul, where we quartered.
Cæsar had been fencing-master in his own regiment,
and my prowess with the advanced guard of Kinski's
cuirassiers was well known. We resolved to teach
the practice as well as the theory of fencing to the
officers of the battalion, who were much pleased at
such an arrangement. Our lessons produced us some
money, but not enough for our wants, or if you please,
the desires of men of our abilities. It was particularly
in good living that we were found wanting. What
increased our regrets and appetites was, that the
mayor with whom we lodged (my comrade and I) kept
an excellent table. We sought in vain the means of
increasing our supplies; an old domineering servant,
named Sixca always defeated our intentions, and disturbed our gastronomic plans. We were disheartened
and starving.

At length Cæsar found out the secret of breaking
the charm which kept us from the table of the municipal functionary. At his suggestion, the drum-major
came one morning to beat the morning call under the
mayor's windows. Judge of the disturbance. It may
be surmised that the old Mægara did not fail to
request an intervention in putting a stop to this
uproar. Cæsar promised with a mild air to use all
his influence to put a stop to the noise, and then ran
to beg the drum-major to renew the cause of complaint ; and the next morning there was a row sufficient
to awaken the dead from the adjacent church-yard;
and at length, not to do things by halves, he sent the
drum-major to practice with his boys at the back of
the house ; a pupil of the abbé Sicard could not have
endured it. The old woman came to us, and invited
the cunning Cæsar and me very graciously; but that
was not enough. The drummers continued their
concert, which only concluded when their respectable
chief was admitted, as well as ourselves, to the municipal banquet. From that time no more drums were
heard at St Sylvestre-Capelle, except when detachments

were passing by, and everybody was at peace except myself, whom the old woman began to threaten with her obliging favours. This unfortunate passion brought on a scene which must still be remembered in that part of the country, where it made much noise at the time.

It was the village feast, dancing, singing, drinking went on; and I bore my part so ably that they were compelled to lead me to bed. The next day I awoke before daybreak: as after all similar orgies, I had a giddy head, my mouth parched, and my stomach disordered; I wanted something to drink; and on rising I felt a hand as cold as a well-rope encircling my neck; my head was still wandering and weak from the over-night's debauch, and I shrieked out lustily. The mayor, who slept in an adjoining chamber, ran with his brother and an old servant, both armed with cudgels. Cæsar had not returned, and reflection had convinced me that the nocturnal visitor could only be Sixca; and pretending to be greatly alarmed, I told them that some hobgoblin had come to my side, and had glided out at the foot of the bed. They then laid on several blows with their sticks; and Sixca, perceiving that she would soon be killed, cried out "Gentlemen, do not strike, it is I—it is Sixca. I walked in my sleep to the officer's bed." At the same time she showed her head, and did well; for although they recognised her voice, yet the superstitious Flemings were about to renew the application of the bastinado. As I have said, this adventure, which almost realizes certain scenes of "My Uncle Thomas," and "The Barons of Felsheim," made much noise throughout the place. It spread even to Cassel, and procured me many intrigues. I had, amongst others, one with a pretty bar-maid, whom I should not allude to if she had not first taught me, that at the counter of some coffee-houses a good-looking fellow may get change for cash which he has not paid.

We had been quartered for three months when the division was ordered to Stinward. The Austrians had given tokens of an intention to proceed to Poperingue, and the 2d battalion of the Pas-de-Calais was placed in the first rank. The night after our arrival the enemy surprised our outposts, and penetrated to the village of Belle, which we occupied, and we formed in battle array in the greatest haste. In this nocturnal manœuvre our young recruits evinced that intelligence and alacrity which are only to be found in Frenchmen. About six o'clock in the morning, a squadron of Wurmser hussars debouched on our left, and charged us without being able to break through our ranks. A column of infantry which followed them, attacked us at the same time with the bayonet; and it was only after a brisk encounter that our inferiority of numbers compelled us to fall back upon Stinward, our head-quarters.

On arriving there I received the congratulations of general Vandomme, and a billet for the hospital of St Omer, for I had had two sabre cuts in fighting with an Austrian hussar, who was killed whilst crying " *Ergib dich ! ergib dich !* (surrender, surrender.)"

My wounds were not very severe, since at the end of two months I was enabled to rejoin the battalion which was at Hazebrouek. I then saw the strange corps called the Revolutionary Army.

The men with pikes and red caps, who composed it, took with them everywhere the guillotine. The convention had not, they said, found any better way of securing the fidelity of the officers of the fourteen armies which it had on foot, than by placing before their eyes the instrument of punishment reserved for traitors. All that I can say is, that this mournful sight almost killed with fear the inhabitants of the country through which it passed. It did not much flatter the military, and we had many quarrels with the Sans-culottes, who were called the body guard of the guillotine. I beat one of the party, who took upon himself to censure my gold epaulettes, when the regulation only ordered those of worsted. My fine array would have

brought misfortune on me, and I should have paid
dearly for my disregard of the sumptuary law, if I had
not been allowed to start for Cassel, where I was joined
by my battalion, which was then arrayed like the other
regiments : these officers became plain soldiers, and it
was in that capacity that I was directed to enter the
28th battalion of volunteers, which formed part of the
army destined to drive the Austrians from Valenciennes and Condé.

The battalion was quartered at Fresnes. In the farm
house in which I was billeted, there arrived one day
the whole family of a pilot, consisting of the husband,
wife, and two children, one of whom was a girl of
eighteen, who was remarkably handsome. The Austrians had taken the boat, laden with grain, which was
their whole fortune; and these poor people, reduced to the
garments which covered them, had no resource left but
to take refuge with my host, their relation. This circumstance, their pitiable condition, and the beauty of
the young girl Delphine, touched my heart.

During a foraging party, I discovered their boat,
which the enemy were only gradually unlading and
measuring out. I proposed to a dozen of my comrades to carry off the spoils from the Austrians. They
acceeded to the proposition; our colonel gave his consent; and on a stormy night, we approached the vessel
without being observed by the officer in charge, whom
we despatched to feed the fish of the Escaut with five
strokes of the bayonet. The wife of the pilot, who
would follow us, instantly ran for a bag of florins
which she had concealed in the grain, and gave them
to my charge. We then loosened the boat, to let it
float to a point where we had an entrenched post, but
at the moment it got into the stream, we were surprised by the challenge of a guard, whom we had not
observed amongst the bulrushes which concealed him.
At the report of his gun which accompanied his second
call to us, the next piquet flew to arms, and in a moment the bank was covered with soldiers, who fired a

shower of balls at the boat, which we were compelled
to quit.   My comrades and I cast ourselves on a sort
of raft which we had, and the woman did the same;
but the pilot, forgotten in the confusion, or stopping
with a hope of escape, was taken by the Austrians,
who were not sparing of their blows and kicks.   This
experiment had besides lost us three men, and I had
two fingers broken by a musket ball.   Delphine loaded
me with caresses.   Her mother having set out for
Ghent, where she knew her husband had been sent as
prisoner of war, we betook ourselves to Lille.   I there
passed my time of convalescence.   As Delphine had a
portion of the money found in the grain, we led a very
pleasant life.   We talked of marriage, and the affair
was so far arranged that I started one morning for
Arras, whence I was to return with the licence and
my parents' consent.   Delphine had already procured that of her parents, who were still at Ghent.
A league from Lille, I remembered that I had forgotten my hospital billet, which it was indispensably
necessary to produce before the municipality of Arras,
and I returned for it.   Arrived at the hotel, I went to
the room we occupied and knocked; no one answered.
It was impossible that Delphine could be out so early,
it being scarcely six o'clock.   I knocked again, and
Delphine opened the door, stretching her arms and
rubbing her eyes like some one who has been suddenly
awakened.   To prove her, I proposed that she should
go with me to Arras, that I might present her to my
parents, and she very tranquilly agreed.   My suspicions
were disappearing, and yet something whispered to me
that she was deceiving me.   I at length perceived that
she frequently glanced towards the wardrobe.   I
pretended a desire to open it, which my chaste betrothed opposed, and gave me one of those excuses
which a woman always has ready.   But I was determined; and at length opened the closet, where I
found concealed, beneath a heap of dirty linen, the doctor who had attended me during my convalescence.

He was old, ugly, and misshapen. The first feeling was the humiliation of having such a rival; and yet I should have been more enraged at finding a good looking fellow, but this I leave for the decision of the numerous lovers who have been similarly circumstanced. As for me, I wished to begin by knocking out the brains of the intriguing Esculapius, but (which seldom happened to me) reflection restrained me. We were in a town of war, where they might play me some trick about my leave of absence. Besides Delphine was not my wife; I had no right over her. I determined on kicking her out; after which, I threw her from the window her clothes, and money enough to take her to Ghent. I allowed myself to retain the remainder of the money, which I thought I had lawfully acquired, since I had directed the splendid expedition which had rescued it from the clutch of the Austrians. I forgot to say that I allowed the doctor to return unmolested.

Having got rid of my faithless she, I determined on remaining at Lille, until the time of my furlough should expire; but it is as easy to conceal ourself in this city as at Paris, and my residence would have been undisturbed but for an affair of gallantry of which I shall spare the details. It will suffice to say, that being arrested in female attire, at the moment I was flying from the rage of a jealous husband, I was taken to the police office, where I at first obstinately refused to give any account of myself; for in fact, by speaking, I should either destroy the female who had been kind to me, or announce myself as a deserter. Some hours confinement changed my resolution; a superior officer to whom I had appealed to receive my declaration, and to whom I candidly stated the facts, seemed to take some interest for me. The commandant-general of the division wished to hear from my own lips this recital, which made him laugh to excess. He then gave orders that I should be set at liberty; and caused a line forthwith to be given to me to rejoin the 28th battalion at Brabant : but instead of following this destination, I went to Arras, determined only to enter the service again at the last extremity.

My first visit was to the patriot Chevalier. His influence with Joseph Lebon made me hope that I should obtain through his interest an extension of leave, which he procured for me, and I was again introduced to the family of my benefactor. His sister, whose kind intentions towards me are already known, redoubled her kindness; and on the other hand, the habit of seeing her daily familiarised me with her ugliness; in short, matters came to such a point that I was not at all surprised to hear her one day declare that she was pregnant. She made no mention of marriage, not even pronouncing the word; but I saw but too clearly that to this complexion it must come at last, lest I should incur the vengeance of her brother, who would not have hesitated to denounce me as an aristocrat, and moreover a deserter. My parents, struck with all these considerations, and conceiving the hope of keeping me near them, gave their consent to the marriage, which the Chevalier family were very anxious about. It was at last settled, and I became a husband at eighteen years of age. I thought myself also almost the father of a family, but scarcely had a few days elapsed, when my wife confessed that her pretended pregnancy was the result of a plan to induce me to marry her. The excessive satisfaction which such an avowal gave me may be conceived; but the same motives which had decided me on contracting the alliance compelled me to be silent; and I determined to keep my own counsel, enraged as I was. A mercer's shop which my wife had opened turned out very badly; I thought that I found the cause of it in the repeated absence of my wife, who was all day at her brother's. I made my observations; and received orders to rejoin my regiment at Tournai. I might have complained of this expeditious mode of getting rid of a troublesome husband; but I was so much tired of the yoke of Chevalier, that I resumed with joy my uniform, which I had cast off with so much pleasure.

At Tournay, a veteran officer of the Bourbon regiment, then adjutant-general, attached me to his office as a deputy, and particularly in the serving out of clothing. Business soon demanded that a man of trust should be dispatched to Arras. I set out post, and arrived in the city at eleven o'clock at night. As I was charged with orders, the gates were opened to me, and by an impulse for which I cannot account, I was induced to run to my wife's abode. I knocked for a long time, and no one answered. A neighbour, at length, opened the door, and I ran up stairs with all speed to my wife's chamber. On approaching, I heard the clank of a falling sabre, then a window opened, and a man leaped out into the street. It is needless to say that they had recognised my voice. I went down stairs with great haste, and soon overtook my Lovelace, in whom I recognised an adjutant-major of the 17th horse chasseurs, quartered at Arras. He was half naked; I led him back to my conjugal domicile, when he finished his toilette, and we then separated, on agreeing to fight the next day.

This scene had roused the whole neighbourhood. The greater part of the people, assembled at their windows, had seen me seize on the guilty adjutant, who had been found guilty of the fact in their presence. I had no lack of witnesses to prove and obtain the divorce, and that was what I intended to do; but the family of my chaste wife, who were desirous of keeping a protector for her, exerted themselves to check my measures, or at least to paralyze them. The next day, before I could meet the adjutant-major, I was arrested by the police and by gendarmes, who spoke of placing me in the Baudets. Fortunately for me, I plucked up courage, as I saw that there was nothing discouraging in my situation : I demanded to be carried before Joseph Lebon, which could not be denied

me. I appeared before the representative of the people, whom I found surrounded by an enormous pile of
letters and papers—" What, is it you," said he to me,
" who come here without permission—and for mal-
treating your wife too ?"   I saw what course I should
pursue, I produced my orders, I called for the testimony of my neighbours against my wife, and that of the
adjutant-major himself, who could not gainsay the
facts.   Indeed, I so clearly explained the affair, that
Joseph Lebon was forced to confess that the wrongs
were not of my committing; but out of regard, however, to his friend Chevalier, he made me promise
not to remain long at Arras; and as I feared the wind
might veer against me, as I had seen it with many
others, I undertook to comply with his request as
promptly as possible.   Having completed my mission,
I bade farewell to all my friends, and the next morning found me on the road to Tournay.

CHAPTER III.

Residence at Brussels—Coffee-houses—The gastronom'c gendarmes—A forger—The roving army—The baroness and the
baker boy—The disappointment—Arrival at Paris—A gay
lady—Mystification.

I DID not find the adjutant-general at Tournay, he
had set out for Brussels, and I set out on the following day by the diligence to join him there.   At the
first glance, I recognised amongst the travellers those
individuals whom I had known at Lille, as passing the
whole day at the public-houses, and living in a very
suspicious manner.   To my great astonishment, I
found them clothed in uniforms of different regiments,
one having the epaulettes of lieutenant-colonel, the
others those of captain or lieutenant.   How can they

have got them, thought I, for they have never seen
service. I was lost in conjecture. On their side,
they appeared at first much confused at the rencontre;
but soon recovering, they testified a mutual surprise
at finding me only a plain soldier. When I had explained to them how the regulation of the battalion
had deprived me of my rank, the lieutenant-colonel
promised me his protection, which I accepted, although
scarcely knowing what to think of my protector. I
saw clearly, however, that he had plenty of money,
and paid for all at the table d'hôte, where he testified
a violent republican feeling, at the same time affecting
to have sprung from an ancient family.

I was not more fortunate at Brussels than at Tournay; the adjutant-general, who seemed to fly from
me, had gone to Liege, for which place I set out, relying on not taking an useless journey this time; but
on arriving, I learnt that my man had taken the road
to Paris on the previous evening, having been summoned to appear at the bar of the convention. His
absence would not be longer than a fortnight. I
waited, but no one arrived. Another month passed,
and still no adjutant. My cash was sensibly diminish-
ing, and I resolved on returning to Brussels, where I
hoped to find some means of extricating myself from
my embarrassment. To speak with that candour on
which I pique myself in giving this history of my life,
I must confess that I had begun not to be over scrupulous in my choice of these means; my education
had not made me a very precise man in such matters,
and the injurious society of a garrison, which I had
been used to from my childhood, had corrupted a
naturally honorable mind.

It was then, without doing much violence to my
delicacy, that I saw myself installed, at Brussels, with
a gay lady of my acquaintance, who, after having been
patronised by general Van-der-Nott, had fallen a little
lower into public society. Idle, as are all who have
but a precarious mode of existence, I passed whole

days and nights at the Café Turc or the Café de la
Monnaie, the rendezvous of knights of the post, and
professed gamblers.   These fellows spent liberally, and
played the devil's games; and as they had no osten-
sible means of living, I could not divine how they
managed to carry on the war. A young fellow with
whom I had associated myself, and whom I questioned
on this subject, appeared struck at my inexperience,
and I had the greatest difficulty in persuading him that
I was really a novice. " The men whom you see
there every day, and all day," said he, " are sharpers;
those who only come once, and do not appear again,
are dupes, who lose their money."

Thus instructed, I made many remarks, which till
then had escaped me, I saw tricks of sleight of hand
almost incredible ; and what proved that there was still
something good within me, I was often tempted to tell
the pigeon whom they plucked. What happened to
me will prove that my intentions were guessed.

A party was one evening engaged at the Café Turc;
the dupe *(le gonse)* lost fifty louis, and demanding his
revenge on the next day, went away. Scarcely had
he gone out, when the winner, whom I now see daily in
the streets of Paris, approached me, and said with an
air of simplicity, " On my word, sir, we have played
with luck, and you were right to bet on me; I have
won ten games, which at four crowns a game, will
make your share ten louis—here they are." I told
him that he was mistaken, and that I had not interested myself in his play; he made me no answer, but
put the ten louis into my hand. " Take it," said the
young man who had initiated me into these mysteries,
and who was sitting next to me, " take it and follow
me." I obeyed mechanically, and when we reached
the street, my Mentor added, " They have discovered
that you watch the games, and fear lest you should
blow the concern; and as there are no means of in-
timidating you, because they know that you have a
strong arm and a mischievous hand, they have resolved

on giving you a slice of the cake, so you have a good means of existence before you, the two coffee-houses will be milch cows to you, whence you may draw your four or six crowns a day." In spite of the accommodating propensity of my conscience, I was desirous of replying, and making some observations—" You are a child," said my honourable friend ; " we do not talk of robbery here—it is fortune only ; and believe me, matters pass in the drawing-room as they do at the tavern—there they bubble, that is the word ; and the merchant, who in the morning whilst at his desk would think it a crime to rob you of an hour's interest, would very quietly cheat you at the gaming-table in the evening." How could I answer such unanswerable arguments ? I had nothing to reply but to keep the money, which I did.

These small dividends, joined to a remittance of a hundred crowns from my mother, enabled me to dash a little, and to show my gratitude to Emily, whose devotion to me I was not insensible of. Matters were in this agreeable train when I was one evening arrested at the Theatre du Parc, by several police-officers, and desired to produce my papers. This would have been a dangerous exhibition, and I said that I had none. They conducted me to the Madelonettes ; and the next morning, at my examination, I found that I was unknown, and they had mistaken me for another person. I said that my name was Rousseau, born at Lille, and added, that I had come to Brussels on pleasure, and had not thought it expedient to provide myself with papers. I then asked to be conducted to Lille, at my own expense, by two gendarmes, which was granted, and for a few crowns my escort agreed that poor Emily should accompany me.

Having left Brussels, I was so far safe ; but it was still more important that I should not reach Lille, where I should be certainly recognised as a deserter. Escape must be made at all risks, and this was Emily's opinion when I communicated my intention to her, and we executed our preconcerted plan on reaching Tournay. I told the gendarmes that before they left me at Lille the next day, where I should be at once set at liberty, I wished to treat them with a good supper. Already taken with my liberality and mirth, they accepted the invitation with much willingness, and in the evening, whilst they were sleeping on the table, stupified with rum and beer, thinking me in the same condition, I descended by the sheets from the second-floor window. Emily followed, and we struck into the cross-roads, where they would not think of pursuing us. We thus reached the suburbs of Notre-Dame at Lille, when I dressed myself in the cloak of the horse-chasseurs, taking the precaution to put a black patch on my left eye, which made it impossible to recognise me. But I did not judge it prudent to remain long in a city so near my birth-place, and we started for Ghent. There, by a rather romantic incident, Emily found her father, which determined her to return to her family. It is true, that she would not consent to part from me, but with an express stipulation that I should rejoin her as soon as matters, which I said called me to Brussels, should be arranged.

My business at Brussels was to begin again to levy rates on the Café Turc and the Café de la Monnaie. But to present myself at this city, I wanted papers which should prove that I was really Rousseau, born at Lille, as I had said at my examination before I made my escape. A captain of Belgian carabineers in the French service, named Labbre, undertook for fifteen louis to supply me with the necessary credentials. At the end of three weeks he brought me a copy of my register of birth, a passport, and a certificate of half-pay in the name of Rousseau, all done better than I ever saw them executed by any other forger. Thus protected, I went to Brussels; the commandant of the place, an old comrade of Labbre's, undertook to make all right.

Quieted in this particular, I hastened to the Café

Turc. The first persons whom I saw in the room were the pretended officers with whom I had travelled. They received me with acclamation; and judging from the recital of my adventures that my situation was not over splendid, proposed that I should take the rank of sub-lieutenant of horse chasseurs, doubtless because they saw the cloak I wore. So advantageous a promotion was not to be refused; and it was then conferred on me: and when I said Rousseau was only an assumed name, the worthy lieutenant-colonel told me to take any one which I preferred. It was impossible to be more obliging. I resolved on keeping the name of Rousseau, on which they gave me, not a brevet, but a line of route for a sub-lieutenant of the 6th chasseurs, travelling with his horse, and being entitled to lodgings and rations.

I thus found myself incorporated with the roving army (armée roulante) composed of officers without brevet, and without troops, and who, furnished with false certificates and false lines of march, imposed the more easily on the commissaries at war, as there was less method at this period in the military arrangements. It is certain, that during a tour which we made through the Netherlands, we got all our allowances without the least demur. Yet the roving army was not then composed of less than two thousand adventurers, who lived like fishes in water. What is still more curious is, that they promoted themselves as rapidly as circumstances would allow: an advancement was the more profitable, as increase of rank brought increase of allowances. I passed in this manner to be captain of hussars; one of my comrades became chief of a battalion; but what most astonished me was, the promotion of Auffray, our lieutenant-colonel, to the rank of brigadier-general. It is true, that if the importance of the rank and the notoriety of a promotion of this kind rendered it more difficult to keep up the deception, yet the very audacity of such a step bade defiance to suspicion.

Returned to Brussels, we showed our billets, and I was sent to a rich widow, the baroness d'I——. I was received in the manner in which all Frenchmen were welcomed at Brussels at this period—that is, with open arms. A very handsome bed-chamber was placed at my sole disposal, and my hostess, delighted at my reserved conduct, assured me in the most gracious manner, that if her hours suited me, a place at her table would always be prepared for me. It was impossible to resist such pressing politeness, and I was profuse in my thanks, and I took my seat at her board the same day with three other guests, who were ladies, older than the baroness, who was about fifty. They were all charmed with the prepossessing manners of the captain of hussars. At Paris I should have felt somewhat awkward in such society, but I did very well at Brussels for a young man whose premature introduction to the world had necessarily injured his education The baroness doubtlessly made some such reflections, for she paid me such little attentions as gave me much food for thought.

As I was sometimes absent to dine with the general, whose invitations I told her it was impossible to refuse, she desired me to present him and my other friends to her. At first I was not over desirous of introducing my associates to the society of this lady, who saw much company, and might have guests at her house who might guess our little speculations. But the baroness insisted on it, and I consented, at the same time stipulating that the general should only meet a small party, as he was desirous of keeping up a sort of incognito. He came; and the baronesss, who received him with marked attention, seated him near her, and talked to him for so long a time in an under tone that I was rather piqued. To disturb this tête-a-tête, I imagined that it would be a good plan to ask the general to sing us something, and accompany himself on the piano. I knew that he could not make out a note, but I relied that the usual persuasions which guests make on such occasions would at least occupy his attention for some minutes. My stratagem only half succeeded; the lieutenant-colonel, who was of the party, seeing that the general was so much pressed, kindly offered himself as his substitute, and accordingly seated himself at the piano, and sung some little ditties with sufficient taste to procure him universal approbation, whilst I all the time wished him at the devil.

At last this interminable evening concluded, and each person withdrew, I raging with anger and plotting revenge against the rival who I imagined was about to carry off from me, I will not say the love, but the kind attentions of the baroness. Full of this idea, I went to my general at his rising, who was much surprised to see me so early. "Do you know," said he, without giving me time to break in upon his conversation, "do you know, my friend, that the baroness is —" "Who spoke of the baroness?" interrupted I abruptly, "it is no matter what she is or what she is not."—"So much the worse," he replied, "if you are not speaking of her, I have nothing to understand." And, continuing thus to puzzle me for some time, he ended by telling me that his conversation with the baroness was concerning me only, and that he had so far pushed my interest, that he believed that she was quite disposed to—to marry me.

I at first thought that my poor comrade's head was turned. That one of the richest women of rank in the United Provinces would marry an adventurer, of whose family, fortune, and ancestors she knew nothing, was an idea that would have staggered the most credulous. Ought I, moreover, to engage in a deceit which must be discovered, sooner or later, and must ruin me? Besides, was I not really and actually married at Arras? These objections, and many others, which the remorse I must experience at deceiving the excellent woman who had treated me so kindly,

excited in my mind, did not for an instant stop my
comrade, who thus answered them :—

" All you say is very fine, and I am quite of your
opinion; and to follow my natural bias for virtuous
behaviour, I only want 10,000*l.* a-year. But I see no
reason for being scrupulous in your case. What does
the baroness want? A husband, and a husband to
her liking. Are you not that husband? Are you
not determined to pay her every attention and to
treat her as a person who is necessary to you, and of
whom you have had no cause to complain? You
talk of the inequality of your fortunes,—the baroness
thinks not of that. You only want, to complete the
matter, one single thing—a title of rank, which I will
give you,—yes, I will give it to you! Why do you
stare so? Listen, and do not interrupt me. You must
be acquainted with some young nobleman of your own
age and country; you are he, and your parents have
emigrated and are now at Hamburgh. You entered
France to endeavour to recover a third of the value
of your paternal property, and to carry off the plate
and a thousand double-louis concealed beneath the
flooring of the drawing-room at the breaking out
of the revolution: the presence of some strangers, the
haste of departure, which an arrest issued against
your father would not allow you to delay, has prevented you from getting this treasure. Arrived in
this country, disguised as a journeyman tanner, you
were denounced by the very person who had pledged
himself to aid your enterprise; outlawed by the sentence of the republican authorities, you were nearly
losing your head on the scaffold, when I fell in with
you, half dead from inquietude and necessity. An old
friend of the family, I procured for you the brevet of
an officer of hussars, under the name of Rousseau,
until an opportunity should offer of rejoining your
noble parents at Hamburgh. The baroness already
knows all this; yes, all, except your name, which, for

appearances' sake, I did not tell her; but in fact, because I did not know what appellation you might chuse to assume. That is a confidence which I left for yourself to communicate.

"Thus the affair is quite settled, and you are a gentleman, nothing can be said against that. Say nothing to me of your jade of a wife; you were divorced at Arras under the name of Vidocq, and you are married at Brussels under the name of count B——. Now listen to me. So far our business has gone on well, but that may be entirely marred at any moment. We have already met with some very inquisitive commissaries, and we may find others still less civil, who may cut off our supplies, and send us to the fleet at Toulon. You understand me, I know. The best that can happen to you will be to take up your knapsack and accoutrements in your old regiment, or else be shot for a deserter; but by marrying you acquire the means of a splendid life, and will be enabled to assist your friends. Since we have come to this point, let us understand each other; your wife has a hundred thousand florins a-year; there are three of us, and you shall give us each a pension of a thousand crowns, payable in advance, and I shall expect besides a premium of thirty thousand francs for having made a count of a baker's son."

I was quite stupified: but this harangue, in which the general had so skilfully stated all the difficulties of my situation, overcame all my opposition, which, to say the truth, was not very obstinate. I agreed to everything, and then returned to the baroness. The count de B—— fell at her feet; and the scene was so well played, and, though it may be scarcely believed, I entered so completely into the spirit of my part, that I even for a moment surprised myself—which I am told sometimes happens to impostors. The baroness was charmed at the sallies and sentiment with which my situation inspired me. The general was rejoiced with my success, as was every other

person.   Several expressions escaped me which
savoured a little of the canteen, but the general had
told the baroness that political events had caused my
education to be strangely neglected, and this explanation was satisfactory to her.   Subsequently, marshal Suchet was no less easily satisfied, when Coignard,
addressing him as " M. le *duque* d'Albufera," excused
himself by the plea, that having emigrated when very
young, he could consequently have but a very imper-
fect knowledge of the French language.

We sat down to table and dined in high spirits.
After the dessert the baroness whispered me thus :—
" I know, my dear sir, that your fortune is in the
hands of the jacobins, and your parents at Hamburgh
may be in some difficulty, oblige me by remitting to
them a bill for three thousand florins, which my
banker will send you to-morrow morning."   I was
about to express my thanks, when she rose from table
and went into the drawing-room.   I took the opportunity of telling the general what had just occurred.
" Well, simpleton," said he, " do you think you are
telling me any news ?   Was it not I who hinted to
the baroness that your parents must be in want of
money ?   We are at this moment your parents,—our
funds are low; and to run any risk in procuring more,
would be to hazard too foolishly the success of this
adventure; I will undertake to negociate the bill.   At
the same time I suggested to the baroness that a
supply of cash was needful for you to make some
figure before your marriage, and it is understood that
from now until the consummation of the marriage you
shall have five hundred florins a month."   I found
the next day this sum on my dressing-table, where
also was placed a handsome dressing-case and some
trinkets.

Yet the register of my birth, as count de B——
whose name I had assumed, and which the general
wished to procure, thinking that the other credentials
might be forged, did not arrive; but the baroness,

whose blindness must appear inconceivable, to those who
are not in a situation to know to what extent credulity
can go, and the audacity of some rogues, consented
to marry me under the name of Rousseau.   I had
all the necessary papers to justify my claim to that.
Nothing was wanting but my father's consent; that
was easily procured through the instrumentality of
Labbre, whom we had under our thumb; but although
the baroness had consented to marrying me under a
name which she knew was not my own, yet she felt
some repugnance at being as it were an accomplice in
a falsehood, for which the only excuse was, that it
saved my head from the block.   Whilst we were planning a means for avoiding this, we learnt that the
number of the armée roulante had become so considerable, that the eyes of government were opened,
and that the most severe orders had been issued to
check the abuse.   We divested ourselves of uniforms,
believing that we should then have nothing to fear,
but the enquiries were so active that the general was
compelled to set out suddenly for Namur, where he
thought he should be less liable to detection.   I explained his abrupt departure to the baroness, by
attributing it to the general's having been in fear of a
reprimand for having procured me a commission under
an assumed name.   This circumstance made her very
uneasy for me, and I could only calm her fears by
setting out for Breda, to which place she would accompany me.

I am not very well calculated to play the senti-
mental, and it would compromise the tact and
finesse, for which I have some credit, if I made a
parade and fuss, but I may be believed when I say
that so much attachment affected me.   The whispers
of remorse, to which we cannot be always deaf at
nineteen, were heard; I saw the abyss into which I
was leading an admirable woman who had been so
generous towards me; I pictured her as driving from
her with horror the deserter, the vagabond, the biga-

F

mist, the forger; and this idea determined me to tell her all. Away from those who had drawn me into this imposture, and who had just been arrested at Namur, I decided on the measures I would adopt; and one evening, after supper, I determined on breaking the ice. Without detailing my adventures, I told the baroness, that circumstances which I could not explain compelled me to appear at Brussels under the two names by which she knew me, but that neither was the real one. I added, that events forced me to quit the Netherlands without the power of contracting an union which would have ensured my happiness, but that I should for ever preserve the recollection of the kindness which she had so generously evinced f⌐r me.

I spoke long, and with an emotion which increased my utterance and warmth of manner—and I am now astonished at the facility of my own eloquence when I think of it—but I feared to hear the reply of the baroness. Motionless, pale, and with a glazed eye, she heard me without interruption; then looking at me with a glance of horror, she rose abruptly and ran to shut herself up in her room. I never saw her again. Enlightened by my confession, and by some words which without doubt fell from me in the embarrassment of the moment, she saw all the dangers from which she had escaped, and unjustly suspected me perhaps of being even more culpable than I was; she might think that she had escaped from some vile criminal, whose hands might have been embrued in blood! On the other hand, if this complication of disguises might render her more apprehensive, the spontaneous avowal that I had made was sufficient to have quelled her fears; and this idea probably took hold of her, for the next day when I arose, the land-lord gave me a casket, containing fifteen thousand francs in gold, which the baroness had left for me before her departure, at one o'clock in the morning, which I was glad to hear of, as her presence would have troubled me. Nothing now detaining me at

Breda, I packed my trunks, and some hours afterwards set out for Amsterdam.

I have already said, and now repeat, that certain portions of this adventure may appear unnatural, and some may call them altogether false, but nothing is more true. The initials I have given will suffice to explain it to any person who knew Brussels thirty years ago. Besides, there is nothing uncommon in the affair, nothing more than is read of in the commonest romance. If I have entered into minute details, it is not to ensure a melo-dramatic effect, but with the intention of putting too credulous persons on their guard against a species of deception more frequently employed, and with more success than may be generally thought, in all classes of society; and such is the aim of these Memoirs. Let them be reflected on in every particular, and who knows but that some fine morning the duties of attorney-general, judge, gendarme, and agent of police, may be discovered to have become sinecures.

My stay at Amsterdam was very short. Having converted into cash two bills of those left me by the baroness, I set out, and on the 2d of March 1796 made my entrance into the capital, where at a future day my name was destined to make some noise. I put up at the hotel du Gaillard-Bois in Rue de l'Echelle, and first employed myself in changing my ducats into French money, and in selling a quantity of small jewellery and trinkets, now superfluous to me, as I resolved on establishing myself in some village in the environs, and entering into some business ; but this project was not to be realized. One evening, one of those persons who are always to be found in hotels seeking acquaintance with travellers, proposed to present me at a house where there was a party. I unfortunately consented, confiding in my experience of the Café Turc and the Café de la Monnaie ; but I soon found that gamblers of Brussels were but bunglers in comparison with these gentlemen, of whose society I now

formed one. Now the games of chance are better
managed and more equal; but at that time, the police
tolerating those places called etouffoirs, they were
not contented with slipping a card or managing the
suits as they liked—sometimes at M. Lafitte's, Messrs
de S——, jun., and A. de la Rock's—the knowing
ones had conventional signs so combined that they
must succeed. Two sittings cleared me of a hundred
louis; I had enough to spare still, but it was decreed
that the money of the baroness should soon leave my
company. The destined agent of its dissipation was
a very pretty woman, whom I met at a table d'hote
which I sometimes frequented. Rosine, for that was
her name, at first showed an exemplary disinterested-
ness. A month afterwards I was her acknowledged
lover, without having spent anything but for dinners,
theatres, coach-hire, gowns, gloves, ribands, flowers,
&c., all which things *cost nothing* at Paris, when we
do not pay for them.

More and more enamoured of Rosine, I never left
her. One morning, whilst at breakfast, I found her
thoughtful; I pressed her with enquiries, which she
resisted, and finished by avowing to me that she was
troubled about a trifle due to her milliner and upholsterer. I offered my services instantly, which were
refused with remarkable magnanimity, and I could not
even learn the names of her two creditors. Many
very excellent people would have left the matter here,
but, like a true knight, I had not a moment's rest
until Divine, the waiting-maid, had given me the
desired addresses. From the Rue Vivienne, where
Rosine lived, who was called madame de Saint Michel,
I ran to the upholsterer, in the Rue de Clery. I told
him the purpose of my visit, and he immediately
overwhelmed me with politenesses, as is usually the
case under such circumstances. He handed me the
bill, which, to my consternation, amounted to twelve
hundred francs; but I was too far gone to recede now.
At the milliner's the same scene took place, with an

additional hundred francs; it was sufficient to have intimidated the boldest, and yet matters had not reached their climax. Some days after I had paid the creditors, they brought me jewels to purchase, to the amount of two thousand francs, and other similar expenses perpetually occurred. I saw my money fly away in this way, but fearing that it would not be so easily replenished, I parted with it less freely from day to day. However, I went on, and found that at the end of two months I had spent the moderate sum of fourteen thousand francs. This discovery made me serious, and Rosine immediately perceived it. She guessed that my finances were getting low. Women have great tact in this respect, and are but rarely deceived; and without being exactly cold towards me, she yet showed a kind of reserve, and on my manifesting astonishment, she answered me with singular abruptness, " that private matters put her out of temper." That was a trick, but I had been too deeply a sufferer already by my interference in these private matters to proffer again to arrange them, and I advised her with an air of coolness to have patience. She became only more contemptuous, passed some days in pouting, and then the storm burst.

At the conclusion of some trifling discussion, she said with a very flippant tone " that she did not choose to be crossed, and that those who could not put up with her ways had better remain at home." That was plain speaking; but I was weak enough to appear not to understand her. New presents brought back a temporary renewal of kindness, which however could no longer impose upon me. Then knowing all that she could get from my blind infatuation, Rosine soon returned to the charge for cash for a letter of credit for two thousand francs, which she had to pay or go to prison. Rosine in prison! The idea was insupportable, and I was about to discharge the debt at once, when chance placed in my way a letter which opened my eyes.

It was from the platonic friend of Rosine, who was staying at Versailles, and this interesting personage asked " when the pigeon would be quite plucked," that he might make his appearance. I intercepted this agreeable missive in the hands of Rosine's porter. I went to the perfidious woman, but she was absent: and enraged and humiliated at the same time, I could not restrain myself. I was in the bed-room, and at one kick I overthrew a stand covered with china, and a cheval glass was shivered to atoms. Divine, the waiting-maid, who had followed me, went down on her knees and begged me to pause from what would cost me so dear: I looked at her and hesitated, and a remnant of common sense induced me to think that she was right. I questioned her—and the poor girl, who had always been gentle and attentive, told me all about her mistress. It is the more in place to mention her statement, as the same things occur daily at Paris.

When Rosine met me she had not had anybody for two months: and thinking me fair game, from the expensive way I got rid of my money, conceived the plan of profiting by it; and her lover, whose letter I had intercepted, had consented, and went to Versailles to stay until my money should be exhausted. It was in the name of this lover that the proceedings had been carried on for the bill of exchange which I had formerly taken up, and the debts of the milliner and upholsterer were equally false.

Although cursing my egregious folly, I was yet astonished not to see the honourable lady, who had so well tricked me, return. Divine told me that most probably the porter had told her that I had got the letter, and that she would not very speedily appear. This conjecture was well founded. On learning the catastrophe which had prevented her from plucking the last feather from my wing, Rosine had set out in a hackney-coach for Versailles to rejoin her friend. The finery, which she left in her furnished apartments, was not sufficient to pay for the two months' lodging due to the landlord, who, when I was going out, compelled me to pay for the china and cheval glass which I had broken in my first transports of anger.

Such violent inroads had dreadfully reduced my finances. Fourteen hundred francs alone remained of the ducats of the baroness! I left the capital with horror, as it had been so unpropitious to me, and resolved to regain Lille, where, knowing the localities, I might at least find resources which I should in vain seek for at Paris.

CHAPTER IV.

The gypsies—A Flemish fair—Return to Lille—Another acquaintance—The Bull's-eye—The sentence of punishment—St Peter's tower—The prisoners—A forgery.

LILLE, as a fortified and frontier town, offered great advantages to all who, like myself, were likely to find there useful acquaintances, either amongst the military of the garrison, or that class of persons who, with one foot in France and the other in Belgium, have really no home in either; and I relied a little on this for recovering myself, and my hope was not groundless. In the 13th chasseurs I met several officers of the south, and amongst the rest a lieutenant named Villedieu, whom we shall presently hear more of. All these persons had only known me in the regiment under one of those *noms de guerre*, which it was the custom at this time to assume, and were therefore not astonished at seeing me bear the name of Rousseau. I spent the day with them at the café or fencing-rooms, but this was not very lucrative, and I actually began to be in want of money. At this juncture a visitor of the café, whom they called Rentier, from his regular life, and who had made me many compliments, of which he

was very prodigal to all the world, enquired with
some interest into my affairs, and asked me to travel
with him.

To travel was all very well; but in what quality? I
was no longer of an age to engage myself as Merry
Andrew or valet-de-chambre of monkies and bears,
and nobody would doubtless make me such a proposition; but yet it was necessary to know in what
capacity. I asked my new protector very modestly what duties I had to perform in his service.
" I am an itinerant doctor," said this man, whose
bushy eye-brows and sun-burnt skin gave him a singular physiognomy; " I cure secret diseases with an infallible recipe. I cure animals, and lately restored the
horses of a squadron of the 13th chasseurs, whom the
veterinary surgeon had given over."—" Well," said
I to myself, " once more a doctor." But there was
no receding : we agreed to start next morning and to
meet at five in the morning at the gate leading to the
Paris road.

I was punctual at the rendezvous, and my friend,
who was equally punctual, seeing my trunk strapped
at the back of a lad, said that it would be useless to
take it, as we should be only three days away, and must
go on foot. At this observation I sent my goods back
to the inn, and we walked on at a brisk rate, having,
as my guide said, to make five leagues before mid-day.
About this time we reached a solitary farm-house,
where he was received with open arms and saluted by
the name of Caron, which was strange to me who had
always heard him called Christian. After a few words
the master of the house went into his chamber and
returned with two or three bags of crowns, which he
spread on the table. My friend took them, and examining them singly with an attention which appeared
to me affected, put aside one hundred and fifty and
counted out a like sum for the farmer in different
money, with a premium of six crowns: I understood
nothing of this operation, which was carried on in a

Flemish dialect, of which I understood but very little.
I was then much astonished when on leaving the farm,
where Christian had said he would soon return, he
gave me three crowns, saying that I ought to have a
share of the profits. I could not learn what the profits were, and said so. " That is my secret," said he,
with a mysterious air; " you shall know it at a future
time, if I am satisfied with you." I told him that
he might rely on my discretion since I knew nothing,
only that he had changed crowns for another coin.
He told me that this was the only point on which I
ought to be silent, to avoid difficulties, and I therefore
took the money without knowing what was to result
from all this.

For four days we made similar excursions to various
farms, and every evening I touched two or three
crowns. Christian, whom they all called Caron, was
well known in this part of Brabant, but only as a doctor; for, although he everywhere carried on his change
of monies, the conversation was always about healing
man or beast. I found besides that he had a reputation for removing the charms cast on animals. A proposal, which he made me as we entered the village of
Wervique, initiated me into this species of magic—
" May I rely on you?" said he to me, stopping
suddenly.—" Certainly," said I; " but for what and
how?"—" Listen, and learn."

He took from a sort of game-bag four square
packets made up like those of chemists, and apparently containing some specifics; he then said, " You
see these four farms, situated at some distance from
each other, you can enter them the back way, taking
care that no one sees them; get into the stable, and
throw into the manger the powder of one of these
packets. Take great care that you are not discovered
—I will take care of the rest." I objected to this, as
I might be surprised at the moment I was climbing
the gate and they would seize me, and perhaps put
some awkward questions. I refused point blank, in

spite of the perspective of the crowns, and all Christian's eloquence failed in persuading me. I even said that I would quit him at once, unless he would disclose to me his real condition and the mystery of his exchange of money, which seemed to me extremely suspicious. This declaration seemed to embarrass him, and, as we may learn, he endeavoured to draw me off the scent, in making me a half confidence.

"My country?" said he, answering my latter question, "I have none. My mother, who was hanged last year at Témeswar, belonged to a gang of gypsies (Bohemiens) who were traversing the frontiers of Hungary and Bannat, where I was born in a village on the Carpathian mountains. I say Bohemiens that you may understand, for that is not our proper name, we call ourselves Romamichels in a language which we are forbidden to teach to any persons; we are also forbidden to travel alone, and that is the reason why we are generally in troops of fifteen or twenty. We have had a long run through France, curing charms and spells of cattle, but this business is pretty well destroyed at present. The countryman has grown too cunning, and we have been driven into Flanders, where they are not so cunning, and the difference of money gives us a finer opportunity for the exercise of our industry. As for me, I have been at Brussels on private business which I have just settled, and in three days I rejoin the troop at the fair of Malines. It is at your pleasure to accompany me : you may be useful to us. But we must have no more nonsense now ! "

Half embarrassed as to where I should shelter my head, and half curious to see the termination of this adventure, I agreed to go with Christian, without at all understanding how I could be useful to him. The third day we reached Malines, whence he told me we should return to Brussels. Having traversed the city, we stropped in the Faubourg de Louvain, before a wretched looking house with blackened walls, furrowed with wide crevices, and many bundles of straw as sub-

stitutes for window glasses. It was midnight, and I had
time to make my observations by the moonlight, for
more than half an hour elapsed before the door was
opened by one of the most hideous old hags I ever
saw in my life. We were then introduced to a long
room where thirty persons of both sexes were indiscriminately smoking and drinking, mingling in strange
and licentious positions. Under their blue loose frocks,
ornamented with red embroidery, the men wore blue
velvet waistcoats with silver buttons, like the Andalu-
sian muleteers; the clothing of the women was all of
one bright colour : there were some ferocious countenances amongst them, but yet they were all feasting.
The monotonous sound of a drum, mingled with the
howling of two dogs tied under the table, accompanied
the strange songs, which I mistook for a funeral
psalm. The smoke of tobacco and wood, which
filled this den, scarcely allowed me to perceive in the
midst of the room a woman who, adorned with a
scarlet turban, was performing a wild dance with the
most wanton postures.

On our entrance there was a pause in the festivity;
the men came to shake hands with Christian and the
women to embrace him, and then all eyes were turned
on me, who felt much embarrassed at my present situation. I had been told a thousand strange stories
of the Bohemiens, which did not encrease my comfortable feelings : they might take offence at any scruples I should make, and might get rid of me before it
was even known where I had gone to, since no one
could trace me to such a haunt. My disquietude became sufficiently apparent to attract the attention of
Christian, who thought to assure me by saying that
we were at the house of the duchess (a title which is
equivalent to that of mother amongst such comrades),
and that we were in perfect safety. My appetite decided me on taking my part at the banquet. The gin
bottle was often filled and emptied, when I felt an inclination to go to bed. At the first word that I said

Christian conducted me to a neighbouring closet, where were already on clean straw several Bohemiens. It did not suit me to be particular; but I could not prevent myself from asking my patron why he, who had always before selected such good quarters, had made choice of so bad a sleeping place? He told me that in all towns, where there was a house of the Romamichels they were constrained to lodge, under pain of being considered as a false brother, and as such punished by a council of the tribe. Women and children all slept in this military bed; and the sleep which soon overtook them, proved that it was a familiar couch.

At break of day everybody was on foot, and the general toilet was made. But for their prominent features, without their raven-black tresses and that oily and tanned skin, I should scarcely have recognised my companions of the preceding evening. The men, clad in rich jockey holland vests, with leathern sashes like those worn by the inhabitants of Poissy, and the women covered with ornaments of gold and silver, assumed the costume of Zealand peasants: even the children, whom I had seen covered with rags, were neatly clothed, and had an entirely different appearance. All soon left the house and took different directions, that they might not reach the market place all together where the country people were assembling in crowds. Christian, seeing that I was preparing to follow him, told me that he should not have need of me the whole day, and that I might go wherever I pleased until evening, when we were to meet at the house of the duchess. He then put some crowns in my hand and left me.

As in our conversation of the previous evening he had told me that I was not compelled to lodge with the troop, I began by ordering a bed at the inn. Then, not knowing how to kill time, I went to the fair, and had scarcely gone round it four or five times when I met face to face an old officer of the recruiting bat-

talions, named Malgaret, whom I had known as making
one of the gambling set at the Café Turc at Brussels.
After the first salutations, he asked me why I was
staying at Malines.   I told him a history, and he was
equally communicative about his travels; and we were
thus content, each thinking that he had imposed on
the other.   Having taken some refreshments we returned to the fair, and every part where there was a
crowd I met some of the lodgers of the duchess.
Having told my companion that I had no acquaintance
at Malines, I turned my head that they might not recognise me, for I did not much care to confess that I
had such friends; but I had too cunning a fox to deal
with.   " Look," said he to me, looking me full in the
face, " look at those people who are regarding you so
attentively.   Pray do you know them?"   Without
turning my head I replied that I had never seen them
before, and did not even know who they were.   " Who
they are!" replied my companion, " I will tell you—
supposing you to be ignorant—they are robbers! "—
" Robbers!" I replied.   " How do you know it?"
" In the same way that you shall soon know if you
will follow me, for it is a fair bet that we shall not have
far to go without finding them at work.   Come along
—here they are."
    Raising my eyes towards a crowd in front of a me-
nagerie, I perceived one of the false jockeys taking the
purse of a fat grazier, whom we saw the next moment
seeking for it in his pockets : the Bohemien then entered a jeweller's shop, where were already two of the
pretended Zealand peasants, and my companion assured me that he would not come out until he had
pilfered some of the jewels that were shown to him.
We then left our post of observation to go and dine together : and, at the end of the repast, seeing my companion disposed to talk, I pressed him to tell me precisely who the people were whom he had pointed out
to me, assuring him that, in spite of appearances, I

G

knew but very little of them.   He complied, and told
me as follows :

" It was in the prison (Rasphuys) of Ghent, where
I passed six months, some years since, at the end of a
game at which some *doctors* (loaded dice) were discovered, that I made acquaintance with two men of
the troop now at Malines.   We were in the same cell,
and as I passed myself off for an accomplished thief,
they told me, without distrust, all their light-fingered
tricks : and even gave me the minutest details of their
singular existence.   These people come from the
country about Moldavia, where a hundred and fifty
thousand of them vegetate, like the Jews in Poland,
without the power of fulfilling any office but that of
executioner.   Their name changes with their change
of country ; they are ziguiners in Germany, gypsies in
England, zingari in Italy, gitanos in Spain, and Bohemiens in France and Belgium.   They thus traverse all
Europe, exercising the lowest and most dangerous
trades.   They clip dogs, tell fortunes, mend crockery,
repair saucepans, play wretched music at the public-
house doors, speculate in rabbit-skins, and change foreign money which they find out of the usual circulation.

" They sell specifics against the illness of cattle, and
to promote the business, they dispatch trusty envoys,
who, under pretences of making purchases, get
into the stables, and throw drugs into the mangers,
which make the cattle sick.   They then present themselves, and are received with open arms, and knowing
the nature of the malady, they easily remove it, and
the farmer hardly knows how to be adequately grateful.   This is not all; for before they quit the farm,
they learn whether the husbandman has any crowns of
such and such a year, or such and such a stamp, promising to give a premium for them.   The interested
countryman, like all persons who but seldom find an
opportunity of getting money, spreads his coin before

them, of which they invariably contrive to pilfer a portion. What is almost incredible is, that they are seen to repeat with impunity the same trick frequently, at the same house. Indeed, what is most villanous of all in their transactions is, that they profit by these circumstances, and their knowledge of the localities of the country, to point out to burglars the detached farms in which there is money, and the means of getting at it, and it is needless to add, that they come in for their share of the spoil."

Malgaret gave further details concerning the Bohemiens, which determined me on quitting their dangerous society as speedily as possible.

He was speaking thus, looking into the street from time to time from the window near which we were seated, when suddenly I heard him exclaim, " Oh, the devil ! My friend of the Rasphuys at Ghent ! "— I looked out, and saw Christian walking very fast, and with an air of busy import. I could scarcely help exclaiming aloud. Malgaret, profiting by the trouble into which his explanation had thrown me, had not much difficulty in extracting from me how I was associated with the Bohemiens. Seeing me resolved on quitting their company, he proposed that I should accompany him to Courtrai, where, he said, he had some game in view. After having taken from the inn the few things I had brought from the house of the duchess, I set out with my new associate, but we did not find at Courtrai the friends whom Malgaret had relied on meeting there, and it was our cash, and not theirs, that was spent. Despairing of their appearance, we returned to Lille; I had still one hundred francs left, and Malgaret gambled with them on our mutual account, and lost them, together with what he had of his own, and I afterwards learnt that he had confederated with his antagonist to cheat me out of what I had left.

In this extremity, I had recourse to my abilities; and some fencing-masters, to whom I spoke of my situa-

tion, gave me a benefit at a fencing-match, which produced me a hundred crowns.   Set up with this sum,
which for a time secured me from want, I frequented
public places, balls, &c.   I then formed an intimacy, of
which the circumstances and consequences decided the
destiny of my whole life.   Nothing could be more
simple than the commencement of this important epi-
sode of my history.   I met at the Bal de la Montagne
with a young lady, with whom I was soon on good
terms.   Francine, for that was her name, appeared
much attached to me, and at every moment made me
protestations of fidelity, which did not, however, prevent her from giving private interviews to a captain of
engineers.

I one day surprised them supping at a tavern in the
place Riourt, and transported with rage, I heartily
thumped the astonished pair.   Francine, with her hair
hanging loose, fled; but her partner remained, and
making a charge against me, I was arrested and conducted to the prison of Petit Hôtel.   Whilst my trial
was preparing, I was visited by many females of my
acquaintance, who made it a duty to offer me their
consolations.   Francine learnt this, and her jealousy
aroused, she dismissed the unfortunate captain, withdrew the charge against me which she had made at
the same time with his, and beseeching me to receive
her, I weakly consented.   The judges heard of this
fact, which was tortured into a premeditated plan
between me and Francine, and I was sentenced to
three months imprisonment.   From the Petit Hôtel
I was transferred to St Peter's Tower, where I obtained a chamber called the Bull's-eye.   Francine
remained with me there for a part of the day, and the
remainder I passed with the other prisoners, amongst
whom were two old serjeant-majors, Grouard and
Herbaux, the latter, son of a boot-maker at Lille,
both condemned for forgeries; and a labourer, named
Boitel, condemned to six years' confinement for stealing garden-tools; this latter, who was the father of a

large family, was always bewailing his imprisonment, which, he said, deprived him of the means of working a small farm, which he only knew how to turn to advantage. In spite of the crime he had committed, much interest was evinced in his favour, or rather towards his children, and many inhabitants of his district had drawn up and presented petitions in his favour, which were as yet unanswered, and the unfortunate man was in despair, often repeating that he would give such and such a sum for his liberty. Grouard and Herbaux, who were in St Peter's Tower, waiting to be sent to the gallies, thought they could get him pardoned by means of a memorial, which they drew up, or rather plotted together; a plan which was ultimately so injurious to me.

Grouard began to complain that he could not work quietly in the midst of the uproar of the common room, in which were eighteen prisoners singing, swearing, and quarrelling all day. Boitel, who had done me some little kind offices, begged me to lend my chamber to the compilers of his memorial, and I consented, although very unwillingly, to give it up to them for four hours a day. From the next morning they were there installed, and the jailor frequently went there secretly. These comings and goings, and the mystery which pervaded them, would have awakened suspicions in a man accustomed to the intrigues of a prison, but ignorant of their plans, and occupied in drinking with the friends who visited me, I interested myself but too little with what was going on in the Bull's-eye.

At the end of eight days, they thanked me for my kindness, telling me that the memorial was concluded, and that they had every reason to hope for the pardon of the petitioner, without sending it to Paris, from the influence of the representations of the people at Lille. All this was not very clear to me, but I did not give it much attention, thinking it no business of mine; and there was no occasion for me to concern myself. But it took a turn which threw blame on my carelessness, for scarcely had forty-eight hours elapsed after the finishing of the memorial, when two brothers of Boitel arrived express. and came to dine with him at the jailor's table. At the end of the repast, an order arrived, which being opened by the jailor, he cried, " Goods news by my faith! it is an order for the liberation of Boitel;" at these words they all arose in confusion, embraced him, examined the order, and congratulated him; and Boitel, *who had sent away his clothes, &c. the previous evening*, immediately left the prison, without bidding adieu to any of the prisoners.

Next day, about ten o'clock in the morning, the inspector of the prisons came to visit us; and on the jailor's showing him the order for Boitel's liberation, he cast his eye over it, said that it was a forgery, and that he should not allow the prisoner to depart until he had referred to the authorities. The jailor then said that Boidel had left on the previous evening. The inspector testified his astonishment that he should have been deceived by an order signed by persons whose names were unknown to him, and at last placed him under a guard. He then took the order away with him, and soon made himself certain that, independently of the forgery of the signatures, there were omissions and errors in form which must have struck any person at all familiar with such papers.

It was soon known in the prison, that the inspector had placed the jailor under arrest, for having allowed Boitel to go out under a false order, aud I began to surmise the truth. I desired Grouard and Herbaux to tell me the whole, observing indistinctly, that the affair might compromise me; but they swore most solemnly that they had done nothing but draw up the memorial, and were themselves astonished at its prompt success. I did not believe a word of this, but having no opposing proofs, I was compelled to wait for the event. The next day I was summoned to the court, before the judge, and answered, that I knew nothing of the framing of the forged order, and that I had only lent my room, as the only quiet place in the prison, for the preparation of the justificatory memorial. I added, that all these facts could be corroborated by the gaoler, who frequently went into the room during their work, appearing to be much interested for Boitel. Grouard and Herbaux were also interrogated, and then placed in solitary confinement, whilst I returned to my chamber. Scarcely had I entered it, when Boitel's bedfellow came to me, and told me the whole plot, which I had only before suspected.

Grouard, hearing Boitel so often repeat that he would willingly give a hundred crowns to procure his liberty, had planned with Herbaux the means of getting him out, and they had devised no mode so simple as that of forging a false order. Boitel was let into the plot, as may be supposed: they only told him, that as there were many persons to gain over, he must give four hundred francs. It was then that they applied for my chamber, which was indispensable for the due concoction and forging of the order, without being perceived by the other prisoners; moreover, the gaoler was in their confidence, to judge by his frequent visits, and the circumstances which had preceded and followed the departure of Boitel. The order had been brought by a friend of Herbaux, named Stofflet. He appeared besides only to decide Boitel on giving four hundred francs, which the forgers had persuaded him was to be shared with me, although I had rendered him no other service than that of lending my room.

Thus instructed, I at first wished the person who had given me these particulars to make a declaration of the particulars, but he obstinately refused, saying that he would not reveal to justice a secret confided to his oath; and besides, he did not feel desirous of being knocked on the head by the prisoners for *turning nose (pour avoir mangé le morceau.)* He dissuaded me even from informing the judge, telling me that I was in no

danger. But on arresting Boitel in the country, and
bringing him to Lille, and putting him in solitary confinement, he named as the aiders and abettors in his
escape, Grouard, Herbaux, Stofflet, and Vidocq. On
this confession, we were questioned at the tower, and I
persisted in my first declaration, although I could
have extricated myself in a moment, by disclosing all
that Boitel's bedfellow had told me; but I was so
fully convinced that it was impossible to substantiate
any charge against me, that I was thunderstruck when,
at the expiration of my three months, I was prevented
from quitting the prison by an entry stating me as
arraigned as an " accomplice in the forgery of authentic and public documents."

CHAPTER V.

Three escapes—The *Chauffeurs*—The suicide—The interrogatory
—Vidocq accused of assassination—Sent back on a complaint—
Fresh escape—Departure for Ostend—The smugglers—Vidocq
retaken.

I THEN began to think that this affair might turn out
badly for me ; but any others tatement without proof
would be more dangerous to me than silence, which it
was now too late to think of breaking. All these
reflections affected me so much, that I had a severe
illness, during which time Francine attended me most
carefully. I was scarcely convalescent, when, unable
to support the state of incertitude in which I found my
affairs, I resolved on escaping, and to escape by the
door, although that may appear a difficult step. Some
particular observations made me choose this method in
preference to any other. The wicket-keeper at St
Peter's Tower was a galley-slave from the Bagne
(place of confinement) at Brest, sentenced for life.
After the revision of the penal laws and the code of

1791, he had obtained a commutation of six years
confinement in the prison at Lille, where he had made
himself useful to the jailor, who, persuaded that a man
who had passed four years at the Bagne must be as
watchful as an eagle, since he must know every method
of escape, promoted him to the office of gate-keeper,
which he thought he could not confide to more trustworthy hands.   It was, however, on the stupidity of
this prodigy of cunning that I relied for the success of
my project; and it appeared the more easy to deceive
him, as he was so confident in his own sagacity.   In a
word, I relied on passing by him under the disguise of
a superior officer, charged with visiting St Peter's
Tower, which was used as a military prison, twice a-
week.

Francine, whom I saw daily, got me the requisite
clothing, which she brought me in her muff.   I immediately tried them on, and they suited me exactly.
Some of the prisoners who saw me thus attired
assured me that it was impossible to detect me.   I was
the same height as the officer whose character I was
about to assume, and I made myself appear twenty-
five years of age.   At the end of a few days, he made
his usual round, and whilst one of my friends occupied
his attention, under pretext of examining his food, I
disguised myself hastily, and presented myself at the
door, which the gaol-keeper, taking off his cap, opened,
and I went out into the street.   I ran to a friend of
Francine's, as agreed on in case I should succeed, and
she soon joined me there.

I was there perfectly safe, if I could resolve on
keeping concealed; but how could I submit to a slavery almost as severe as that of St Peter's Tower.
As for three months I had been enclosed within four
walls, I was now desirous to exercise the activity so
long repressed.   I announced my intention of going
out; and, as with me an inflexible determination was
always the auxiliary of the most capricious fancy, I
did go.   My first excursion was safely performed, but

the next morning, as I was crossing the Rue Ecre-
moise, a serjeant named Louis, who had seen me during my imprisonment, met me, and asked if I was free.
He was a severe practical man, and by a motion of his
hand could summon twenty persons. I said that I
would follow him; and begging him to allow me to
bid adieu to my mistress, who was in a house of Rue
de l'Hopital, he consented, and we really met Francine, who was much surprised to see me in such company; and when I told her that having reflected that
my escape might injure me in the estimation of my
judges, I had decided on returning to St Peter's Tower,
to wait the result of the process.

Francine did not at first comprehend why I had
expended three hundred francs, to return at the end
of four months to prison. A sign put her on her
guard, and I found an opportunity of desiring her to
put some cinders in my pocket whilst Louis and I took
a glass of rum, and then set out for the prison. Having
reached a deserted street, I blinded my guide with a
handful of cinders, and regained my asylum with all
speed.

Louis having made his declaration, the gendarmes
and police-officers were on the full cry after me; and
there was one Jacquard amongst them who undertook
to secure me if I were in the city. I was not unac-
quainted with these particulars, and instead of being
more circumspect in my behaviour, I affected a ridiculous bravado. It might have been said that I ought
to have had a portion of the premium promised for my
apprehension. I was certainly hotly pursued, as may
be judged from the following incident.

Jacquard learnt one day that I was going to dine in
Rue Notre-Dame. He immediately went with four
assistants, whom he left on the ground-floor, and
ascended the staircase to the room where I was about
to sit down to table with two females. A recruiting
serjeant, who was to have made the fourth, had not
yet arrived. I recognised Jacquard, who never having
seen me, had not the same advantage, and besides my

disguise would have bid defiance to any description of
my person. Without being at all uneasy, I approached,
and with the most natural tone I begged him to pass
into a closet, the glass door of which looked on the
banquet-room. " It is Vidocq whom you are looking
for," said I; "if you will wait for ten minutes you
will see him. There is his cover, he cannot be long.
When he enters, I will make you a sign; but if you
are alone, I doubt if you can seize him, as he is armed,
and resolved to defend himself."—" I have my gendarmes on the staircase," answered he, " and if he
escapes——" " Take care how you place them then,"
said I with affected haste. " If Vidocq should see
them he would mistrust some plot, and then farewell
to the bird."—" But where shall I place them?"—
" Oh, why in this closet—mind, no noise, that would
spoil all; and I have more desire than yourself that he
should not suspect anything." My commissary was
now shut up in four walls with his agents. The door,
which was very strong, closed with a double lock.
Then, certain of time for escape, I cried to my prisoners, " You are looking for Vidocq—well, it is he
who has caged you; farewell." And away I went
like a dart, leaving the party shouting for help, and
making desperate efforts to escape from the unlucky
closet.

Two escapes of the same sort I effected, but at last
I was arrested and carried back to St Peter's Tower,
where, for greater security, I was placed in a dungeon
with a man named Calendrin, who was also thus
punished for two attempts at escape. Calendrin, who
had known me during my first confinement in the prison, imparted to me a fresh plan of escape, which he
had devised by means of a hole worked in the wall of
the dungeon of the galley-slaves with whom we could
communicate. The third night of my detention all
was managed for our escape, and eight of the prisoners
who first went out were so fortunate as to avoid

being detected by the sentinel, who was only a short distance off.

Seven of us still remained, and we drew straws, as is usual in such circumstances, to determine which of the seven should first pass. I drew the short straw, and undressed myself that I might get with greater ease through the hole, which was very narrow, but to the great disappointment of all, I stuck fast without the possibility of advancing or receding. In vain did my companions endeavour to pull me out by force, I was caught as if in a trap, and the pain of my situation was so extreme, that not expecting further help from within, I called to the sentry to render me assistance. He approached with the precaution of a man who fears a surprise, and presenting his bayonet to my breast, forbade me to make the slightest movement. At his summons the guard came out, the porters ran with torches, and I was dragged from my hole, not without leaving behind me a portion of my skin and flesh. Torn and wounded as I was, they immediately transferred me to the prison of Petit Hotel, when I was put into a dungeon, fettered hand and foot.

Ten days afterwards I was placed amongst the prisoners, through my intreaties and promises not to attempt again to escape. Up to this time I had lived with men who were sharpers, robbers, and forgers; but here I found myself in the midst of most hardened villains, and of this number was one of my fellow-townsman, named Desfosseux, a man of wonderful ingenuity, prodigious strength, and who, condemned to the gallies from the age of eighteen, had escaped from the Bagne three times, whence he was to be sent again with the next chain of convicts. He told all his exploits and hair-breadth 'scapes with much coolness, and said that no doubt " one day or other the guillotine would make sausage-meat of his flesh." In spite of the secret horror with which this man inspired me, I took a pleasure in conversing with him of the

wild life he had led, and what most induced me to make
so many enquiries of him, was that I hoped he would
be able to aid me with some means of escape. With the
same motive, I associated with many individuals imprisoned as part of a band of forty or fifty Chauffeurs,
who infested the adjacent districts, under the command of the famous Sallambier. They were named
Chopine (called the Nantzman), Louis (of Douay),
Duhamel (called Lilleman), Auguste Poissard (called
the Provençal), Caron the younger, Caron the Hump-
back, and Bruxellois (called the Daring), an appellation which he deserved for an act of courage which is
seldom heard of even in bulletins.

At the moment of entering a farm with six of his
comrades, he thrust his left hand through an opening
in the shutter to lift the latch, but when he was drawing it back, he found that his wrist had been caught in
a slip knot. Awakened by the noise, the inhabitants
of the farm had laid this snare, although too weak to
go out against a band of robbers which report had
magnified as to numbers. But the attempt being thus
defeated, day was fast approaching, and Bruxellois saw
his dismayed comrades looking at each other with
doubt, when the idea occurred to him that to avoid
discovery they would knock out his brains. With his
right hand he drew out his clasp knife with a sharp
point, which he always had about him, and cutting off
his wrist at the joint, fled with his comrades without
being stopped by the excessive pain of his horrid
wound. This remarkable deed, which has been attributed to a thousand different spots, really occurred in
the vicinity of Lille, and is well authenticated in the
northern districts, where many persons yet remember
to have seen the hero of this tale, who was thence
called Manchot (or one-armed), executed.

Introduced by so distinguished a worthy as my
townsman Desfosseux, I was received with open arms
in the circle of bandits, where from morning to night

the means of escape was our only theme. Under these circumstances, as in many others, I remarked that with prisoners, the thirst for liberty, becoming the engrossing idea, produced plots inconceivable by the man who discusses them at his ease. Liberty!— in this word all is centered, this thought pursues the prisoner throughout the tedious day, and during the wintry nights spent in utter darkness, when abandoned to all the tormenting impulses of impatience. Enter any prison, you will hear shouts of noisy mirth, you may almost imagine yourself at a place of entertainment; approach—mouths grin horribly a ghastly smile, but the eyes betray no pleasure, they are stern and haggard; this assumed gaiety is forced in its hideous yells, like that of the jackal, which dashes against its cage, striving to burst the bars.

Well knowing what men they had to guard, our jailors watched us with a care that marred all our plans, the only opportunity which gave a chance of success, however, at last offered itself, and I seized on it before my companions, cunning as they were, had even thought of it. We were about eighteen of us in the anti-room of the examining judge, where we had been conducted for the purpose of being interrogated, which was guarded by soldiers and two gendarmes, one of whom had laid down his hat and cloak near me, whilst he went to the bar, whither his companion was also summoned by the ringing of a bell. I put his hat on my head instantly, and wrapping myself in his cloak, took a prisoner under my arm as if I was taking him out for a pressing necessity; I went to the door, which the corporal of the guard immediately opened, and we got out once more. But what could we do without money or papers? My comrade went into the province, and I, at the risk of being retaken, returned to Francine, who, overjoyed at seeing me, determined on selling her furniture, and flying with me to Belgium. This was determined on, when a most unexpected event, attributable only to my incredible carelessness, completely overthrew our plan.

The night before our intended departure, I met in the dusk of the evening a woman of Brussels, named Eliza, with whom I had been on intimate terms. She embraced me, and begged me to go and sup with her, and, conquering my weak objections, kept me with her until the next day. I persuaded Francine, who had sought me everywhere, that, pursued by police-officers, I had been compelled to take refuge in a house which I could not quit till daybreak. She was at first satisfied; but having by accident discovered that I had passed the night with a female, her jealousy burst forth in overwhelming and tearful reproaches against my ingratitude, and in her rage she swore that she would have me arrested. To put me in prison was certainly the best mode of putting a stop to my infidelities; but Francine was a woman of her word, and I deemed it prudent to allow her anger to evaporate, intending to return after some time, and start with her as we had agreed on. However, as I needed my clothes, and did not wish to ask for them, for fear of a fresh burst of temper, I went alone to our chamber, of which she had the key, and forcing a shutter, I took out what I wanted, and left the house.

At the end of five days, clothed like a countryman, I left the place I had inhabited in the suburbs, and going into the city, I went to the house of a seamstress, a friend of Francine's, on whose mediation I relied for reconciling us. This woman seemed so greatly embarrassed, that fearing I should implicate her, I only begged her to go and seek my mistress. "Yes," said she, with a very remarkable air, and without looking at me. She went out, and I was left alone to reflect on my strange reception.

A knock at the door was heard, which I hastened to open, thinking that I should receive Francine in my arms, when, a crowd of gendarmes and police-

officers appeared, who seizing me, I was carried before
the magistrate, who began by asking me where I had
been during the last five days. My answer was brief,
as I never implicated those who sheltered me. The
magistrate observed, that my obstinacy in refusing him
any explanation would go much against me, and that
my head was in jeopardy, &c. &c. I only laughed, as
imagining this remark to be a trap to force me to confess through fear. I persisted in my silence, and was
remanded to the Petit Hotêl.

Scarcely had I set foot in the street, when all eyes
were fixed on me. People called to each other and
whispered, which I thought was caused by my disguise, and I scarcely heeded it. They made me enter
a cell, where I was left alone in the straw heavily
ironed. At the end of two hours the jailor came,
who, pretending to pity me, and take an interest in
me, told me that my resolution not to confess where
I had spent the last five days, would injure me in the
estimation of the judges; but I was immoveable, and
two more hours elapsed, when the jailor returned with
a turnkey, who took off my fetters, and desired me to
go down to the office, where two judges were in attendance. I was again questioned, and made a similar
reply, and they then stripped my clothes entirely off,
and stamped on my right shoulder a blow that
would have killed an ox, which was to mark me; my
clothes were taken away, after being described in the
procès-verbal; and I was sent back to my cell, covered
with a shirt of sail-cloth, in a surtout half black and
half grey, in rags, which had served at least two
generations of prisoners.

All this gave me food for reflection. It was evident
that the seamstress had denounced me, but for what?
She had no complaint to make of me. In spite of her
fury, Francine would have reflected twice, before she
denounced me; and if I had withdrawn for some days,
it was rather because I did not wish to irritate her by
my presence, than from any fear of consequences.

Why these reiterated inquiries, these mysterious words of the jailor, and this description of my attire? I was lost in a labyrinth of conjecture, and for twenty-five hours I was kept in the strictest solitary confinement; I then underwent an examination which informed me of all.

"What is your name?"

"Eugene François Vidocq."

"What is your profession?"

"Military."

"Do you know the girl Francine Longuet?"

"Yes; she is my mistress."

"Do you know where she is at this moment?"

"She should be at a friend's house, for she sold her own furniture."

"What is the name of this friend?"

"Madame Bourgeois."

"Where does she live?"

"At a baker's in the Rue St André."

"How long had you left the woman Longuet when you were arrested?"

"Five days."

"Why did you leave her?"

"To avoid her anger; she knew that I had passed the night with another female, and in a fit of jealousy threatened to have me arrested."

"Who was the woman with whom you passed the night?"

"A former mistress."

"What is her name?"

"Eliza—I only know her by that name."

"Where does she live?"

"At Brussels, whither, I believe, she has returned."

"Where are the things which you had in the house of the woman Longuet?"

"In a place that I can point out if need be."

"How could you get them, having quarrelled with her, and not wishing to see her?"

"After our quarrel in the café, where she found

H 2

me, she threatened to call for the guard to seize me:
knowing her perverseness, I ran down the bye streets,
and reached the house before her, which I had hoped
to do, and wanting some clothes, I forced a shutter
to effect my entrance, and then took out what I wanted.
You just now asked me where these things are, and
I will now tell you, they are in the Rue Saint-Sauveur,
at the house of Duboc, who will corroborate this."

"You do not speak truth—before you left Francine
at her house, you had a great quarrel; it is said that
you struck her."

"That is false; I did not see Francine at her own
home after the quarrel, and consequently I could not
have maltreated her.   She can corroborate this."

"Do you know this knife?"

"Yes; it is the one I generally use at my meals."

"You see the blade and haft are covered with blood.
Does not the sight of it make any impression on
you?   You are agitated!"

"Yes," I replied with emotion; "but what has
happened to Francine?   Tell me, and I will give every
possible explanation."

"Did nothing particular happen to you when you
carried off your clothes?"

"Nothing that I can at all call to mind."

"You persist in your declarations?"

"Yes."

"You are imposing on justice;—that you may have
time for reflection on your position, and the consequences of your obstinacy, I shall now delay the remainder of your examination until to-morrow.—Gen-
d'armes, watch this man most carefully—Go."

It was late when I returned to my cell, where they
brought me my allowance, which the trouble I experienced from the result of the interrogatory, would
not allow me to eat; I could not sleep, and passed
the whole night without closing an eye.   Some
crime had been committed, but on whom?   By
whom?   Why was I inculpated?   I had asked myself

that question a thousand times, without getting at any rational solution, when they came to fetch me on the following morning to renew my examination. After the usual questions, a door was opened, and two gendarmes entered, supporting a female. It was Francine—Francine pale, and altered so as to be scarcely recognizable. On seeing me, she fainted; and when I wished to approach her, I was withheld by the gendarmes. They took her away, and I alone remained with the examining judge, who asked me if the sight of the unfortunate woman did not prompt me to confess all? I protested my innocence, asserting that I did not know till that instant that Francine was ill. I was led back to prison, but not to solitary confinement, and I could then hope that I might be informed of all the events of which I was so singularly the victim. I questioned the jailor, but he would not answer me; I wrote to Francine, although I was told that the letters would be detained by the judge, and that she was dismissed. I was on thorns, and at last determined on sending for counsel, who, after having learnt the accusation, told me that I was charged with attempting to assassinate Francine. On the very day I left her, she had been found expiring, stabbed with a knife in five places, and bathed in blood. My precipitate flight—the secret carrying away of my clothes, which it was known that I had taken from one place to another, as if to elude the search of justice—the broken shutter in my room—the footmark which resembled mine,— all tended to confirm the suspicions of my guilt, and my disguise still more corroborated it.

It was thought that I only disguised myself and returned, to learn whether she had died without accusing me. One particular, which would have been in my favour under any other circumstances, now aggravaged the charge against me ; as soon as the physicians would allow Francine to speak, she declared that she had stabbed herself, in despair, at finding that she was abandoned by a man for whom she had sacrificed all. But her attachment to me rendered her testimony suspected, and it was believed that she only spoke thus to save me.

My counsel had terminated this narrative at least a quarter of an hour, and I was still listening like a man oppressed with the night-mare. At the age of twenty I was suffering under the weight of the two-fold accusation of forging and assassination, without having even dreamt of committing such crimes. I even reflected whether I would not hang myself at the bars of my cell with a straw rope. I was losing my senses, but at last collected myself sufficiently to detail all the facts requisite for my exculpation. In the after-examination they insisted strongly on the blood which the porter, who had carried my luggage, stated he had seen on my hands. This blood had flowed from a cut inflicted by the glass of a window which I had broken to remove the shutter, and I could produce two witnesses of this fact. My counsel, to whom I told all my grounds of defence, assured me, that united with the testimony of Francine, which alone had been of no avail, I should be acquitted, which was the case a few days afterwards. Francine, although still very weak, came immediately to see me, and confirmed all the particulars which the examination had first acquainted me with.

I was thus relieved of an enormous weight, without being yet entirely freed from uneasiness: my repeated escapes had delayed the decision of the accusation of forgery, in which I had been implicated, and nothing indicated its termination, for Grouard had also escaped. The result of the charge from which I had just been freed, had, however, given me a hope, and I thought nothing of attempting to escape, when an opportunity presented, which I seized, as it were, by instinct. In the chamber in which I was placed, were the temporary prisoners, and on fetching away two of them one morning, the jailor forgot to close the door, which I perceived, and descending to the ground-floor, found, on looking about me, that I had a chance. It was scarcely daybreak, and the prisoners were all asleep ; I had met no one on the staircase, and there was no one at the gate which I cleared; but the jailor, who was drinking a dram at a public-house opposite the prison, pursued me, crying loudly, " Stop him ! Stop him ! " He cried in vain, for the streets were empty, and the desire of liberty gave me wings. In a few minutes, I got out of sight of the jailor, and soon reached a house in Rue Saint Sauveur, where I was very certain they would not come to seek for me. I was now compelled to quit Lille as quickly as possible, as I was too well known there to be long in safety.

At nightfall, all were on the look out, and I learnt that all the gates were closed, and no one was let out but through the wicket, where police-officers and disguised gendarmes were stationed to examine all comers. The gates thus closed on me, I resolved on descending the ramparts, and knowing the spot well,. I went at ten o'clock at night to the bastion of Notre-Dame, which I judged the most propitious place for the execution of my project. Having tied to a tree a cord, which I had procured for the purpose, I began to slide down, but the weight of my body impelling me more rapidly than I anticipated, the friction of the cord made my hands so hot that I was compelled to let go about fifteen feet from the ground, and fell so heavily on my right foot, that I sprained it, and in endeavouring to get out of the ditch I thought I should never be able to effect it. Unheard-of efforts at length extricated me, but on reaching the plain I could move no farther.

There I was, swearing most emphatically against all ditches, ropes, and sprains, but this did not relieve my embarrassment, when a man passed me with one of those cars so common in Flanders. A crown-piece, my only one, prevailed on him to place me on his car, and convey me to the next village. On reaching his house he laid me on a bed, and rubbed my foot with brandy and soap, whilst his wife assisted him very efficiently, although staring with wonder at my clothes, stained with the mud of the ditch. They did not ask for any explanation, but I thought it expedient to give one; and to prepare myself for it, I pretended that I was greatly in want of sleep, and my host left me. At the end of two hours I called them, like a man just awaking, and told them in a few words, that in conveying smuggled tobacco up the ramparts, I had fallen, and my comrades, pursued by the custom-house officers, had been compelled to leave me in the ditch; and I added, that I left myself in their hands to do as they pleased with me. These good creatures, who hated the custom-house officers as cordially as the inhabitant of any frontier town ever does, assured me that they would not for the world betray me. To try them, I asked if there was no means of conveyance to my father's house, who lived at the other side, and they said that such a step would expose me, and that it would be better to wait a few days, until I was well. I consented, and to remove all suspicions, it was agreed that I should pass for a relation on a visit. No one, however, made the least observation.

Quieted on this head, I began to reflect on my next step, and what I must do. I determined on leaving these parts, and going into Holland. But to execute this plan money was indispensable, and except my watch, which I had offered to my host, I possessed only four shillings and tenpence. I might go to Francine, but then, of course, she was closely watched; and to send her any message would infallibly hazard her safety. At least, I must wait until the heat of the first pursuit was over. I did wait, and at the end of a fortnight I determined to write to Francine, which I entrusted to my host, telling him that, as this female was the go-between of the smugglers, he must use much

caution in visiting her. He fulfilled his commission
with much care, and brought me next day one hundred
and twenty francs in gold. The next day I bade
farewell to my friends, whose charges were extremely
moderate, and at the end of six days reached Ostend.

My intention, as at my first visit to this city, was to
go to America or India, but I only met with Danish
and Dutch skippers, who refused to take me without
credentials. The little cash which I had brought from
Lille diminished rapidly, and I was approaching that
situation with which we become more or. less fami-
liarized, but which is not the less disagreeable on that
account. Money certainly does not produce wit, nor
talents, nor understanding; but the quiet of mind
which it superinduces, the equanimity which it affords,
amply supply the place of these qualities; whilst in
the absence of this equanimity these gifts are of no
avail with many who possess them. The result is,
that at the moment when we have most need of all
the resources of the invention to procure money, we
are deprived of these resources by the very want of
the money itself. I was assuredly placed in the latter
of these conditions, and yet I must dine—an operation frequently more difficult than may be imagined
by those happy mortals who think that appetite can
be the only thing lacking.

I had heard much of the adventurous and lucrative
life of the coasting smugglers, of whom the prisoners
had boasted with enthusiasm; for this profession was
often followed through inclination, by individuals
whose fortune and situation did not compel them to
adopt so perilous a life. I confess, for my part, that
I was not seduced by the prospect of passing whole
nights under cliffs, in the midst of rocks, exposed to
all winds, and above all, to the shots of the custom-
house officers.

It was with real repugnance that I went to the
house of a man named Peters, to whom I was directed,

as one deeply engaged in the pursuit, and able to introduce me to it. A sea-gull nailed on his door with extended wings, like the owls and weasels that we see on barns, guided me. I found the worthy in a sort of cellar, which by the ropes, sails, oars, hammocks, and barrels, which filled it, might have been taken for a naval depôt. From the midst of a thick atmosphere of smoke which surrounded him, he viewed me at first with a contempt which had not a good appearance, and my conjectures were soon realized, for I had scarcely offered my services than he fell upon me with a shower of blows. I could certainly have resisted him effectually, but astonishment had in a measure deprived me of the power of defence; and I saw besides, in the court-yard, half a dozen sailors and an enormous Newfoundland dog, which would have been powerful odds. Turned into the street, I endeavoured to account for this singular reception, when it occurred to me that Peters had mistaken me for a spy, and treated me accordingly.

This idea determined me on returning to a dealer in hollands, who had told me of him, and he, laughing at the result of my visit, gave me a pass-word that would procure me free access to Peters. Thus empowered, I again went to his formidable abode, having first filled my pockets with large stones, which, in case of a second attack, might protect my retreat. Fortunately I had no need of them. At the words " Beware of the sharks " (custom-house officers), I was received in a most amicable manner, for my strength and activity made me a valuable acquisition to the fraternity, who are often compelled to carry with speed from one spot to another the most oppressive loads. A Bourdeaux man, who was one of the gang, undertook to initiate me, and teach me the stratagems of the profession, which, however, I was called on to put in practice before my tuition had progressed very far.

I slept at Peters's house with a dozen or fifteen smugglers, Dutch, Danish, Swedish, Portuguese, and

Russian; there were no Englishmen, and only two Frenchmen. The day after my installation, as we were all getting into our hammocks, or flock beds, Peters entered suddenly into our chamber, which was only a cellar contiguous to his own, and so filled with barrels and kegs that we could scarcely find room to sling our hammocks. Peters had put off his usual attire, which was that of ship-caulker, or sail-maker, and had on a hairy cap, and a long red shirt, closed at the breast with a silver pin, fire-arms in his belt, and a pair of thick large fishermen's boots, which reach the top of the thigh, or may be folded down beneath the knee.

"A-hoy! a-hoy!" cried he, at the door, striking the ground with the butt end of his carbine, "Down with the hammocks, down with the hammocks! We will sleep some other day. The Squirrel has made signals for a landing this evening, and we must see what she has in her, muslin or tobacco. Come, come, turn out my sea-boys."

In a twinkling everybody was ready. They opened an arm-chest, and every man took out a carbine or blunderbuss, a brace of pistols, and a cutlass or boarding pike, and we set out, after having drank so many glasses of brandy and arrack that the bottles were empty. At this time there were not more than twenty of us, but we were joined or met, at one place or another, by so many individuals, that on reaching the sea-side we were forty-seven in number, exclusive of two females and some countrymen from the adjacent villages, who brought hired horses, which they concealed in a hollow behind some rocks.

It was night, and the wind was shifting, whilst the sea dashed with so much force that I did not understand how any vessel could approach without being cast on shore. What confirmed this idea was, that by the starlight I saw a small boat rowing backwards and forwards, as if it feared to land. They told me afterwards that this was only a manœuvre to ascertain

I

if all was ready for the unloading, and no danger to
be apprehended.   Peters now lighted a reflecting
lanthorn, which one of the men had brought, and
immediately extinguished it, the Squirrel raised a
lanthorn at her mizen, which only shone for a moment
and then disappeared like a glow-worm on a summer's
night.   We then saw it approach, and anchor about
a gun shot off from the spot where we were.   Our
troop then divided into three companies, two of which
were placed five hundred paces in front, to resist the
revenue officers if they should present themselves.
The men of these companies were then placed at
intervals along the ground, having at the left arm a
packthread which ran from one to the other: in case
of alarm, it was announced by a slight pull, and each
being ordered to answer this signal by firing his gun,
a line of firing was thus kept up, which perplexed the
revenue officers.   The third company, of which I was
one, remained by the sea-side, to cover the landing
and the transport of the cargo.

All being thus arranged, the Newfoundland dog already
mentioned, and who was with us, dashed at a word into
the midst of the waves and swam powerfully in the
direction of the Squirrel, and in an instant afterwards
returned with the end of a rope in his mouth.   Peters
instantly seized it, and began to draw it towards him,
making us signs to assist him, which I obeyed mechanically.   After a few tugs, I saw that at the end
of the cable were a dozen small casks, which floated
towards us.   I then perceived that the vessel thus
contrived to keep sufficiently far from the shore, not
to run a risk of being stranded.

In an instant the casks, smeared over with something that made them water-proof, were unfastened
and placed on horses, which immediately dashed off
for the interior of the country.   A second cargo arrived with the same success; but as we were landing
the third, some reports of fire-arms announced that
our out-posts were attacked.   " There is the beginning

of the ball," said Peters, calmly; " I must go and see who will dance;" and taking up his carbine, he joined the out-posts, which had by this time joined each other. The firing became rapid, and we had two men killed, and others slightly wounded. At the fire of the revenue officers, we soon found that they exceeded us in number, but alarmed, and fearing an ambuscade, they dared not to approach, and we effected our retreat without any attempt on their part to prevent it. From the beginning of the fight the Squirrel had weighed anchor and stood out to sea, for fear that the noise of the firing should bring down on her the government cruiser. I was told that most probably she would unload her cargo in some other part of the coast, where the owners had numerous agents.

On the return to Peter's house, at break of day, I threw myself into my hammock, and did not leave it for eight and forty hours : the fatigue of the night, the moisture which penetrated my clothes, whilst exercise had made me perspire profusely, and the uneasiness of my new situation, all combined to make me ill, and a fever seized me. When it left me, I told Peters that I found the employment too hard, and that I should be glad if he would allow me to go. He agreed more quietly than I expected, and gave me a hundred francs. I have since learnt that he had me followed for several days, to be assured whether or no I took the road to Lille, which I had told him was my intention.

I did go to that city, led by a childish wish to see Francine, and take her with me to Holland, where I had formed a plan of a small establishment. But my imprudence was soon punished; for two gendarmes, who were drinking in a pot-house, saw me crossing the street, and they resolved on following me to ask for my papers. They overtook me at a turning, and the trouble which their appearance caused me, determined them on apprehending me. They took me to the brigade prison, where I was already looking out for means of escape, when I heard some one say to

the gendarmes, " Here is the guard of Lille; is there
any one for the prison?" Two men of the Lille
brigade came to the prison and asked if there was any
game in the trap ? " Yes," said the fellows who took
me, " we have one named Leger (my assumed name)
whom we found without a passport." They opened the
door, and the brigadier of Lille, who had often seen
me at the Petit Hôtel, cried " By Jove, 'tis Vidocq!"
I was compelled to confess it, and setting out, I
entered Lille a few hours afterwards, between my two
body guards.

<hr />

CHAPTER VI.

The pewter keys—The quacks—Vidocq an hussar—He is retaken
—The siege of the dungeon—Sentence—Condemnation.

I FOUND at the Petit Hôtel the greater number of the
prisoners who had been emancipated before my escape.
Some of them had made but a very short absence, and
were speedily apprehended, charged with fresh crimes,
or fresh offences. Amongst them was Calandrin, of
whom I have spoken about: enlarged on the 11th,
he was retaken on the 13th, charged with burglary,
and being an accomplice of the Chauffeurs, whose
name alone inspired universal dread. On the strength
of the reputation which my various escapes had procured for me, these men looked on me as one on
whom they might rely. On my side, I could scarcely
separate myself from them. Accused of capital
offences, they had a powerful motive for being secret
concerning our attempts, whilst the unfortunate
" petty larceny rascal " might denounce us, in the dread
of being accused of being privy to our designs. This
is the logic of the prison. This escape, however, was

not so very easy a matter as may be surmised, when I say that our dungeons, seven feet square, had walls six feet thick, strengthened with planking crossed and rivetted with iron ; a window, two feet by one, closed with three iron gratings placed one after the other, and the door cased with wrought iron. With such precautions, a jailor might depend on the safe keeping of his charge, but yet we overcame it all.

I was in a cell on the second floor with Duhamel. For six francs, a prisoner, who was also a turnkey, procured us two files, a ripping chisel, and two turnscrews. We had pewter spoons, and our jailor was probably ignorant of the use which prisoners could make of them. I knew the dungeon key; it was the counterpart of all the others on the same story; and I cut a model of it from a large carrot; then I made a mould with crumb of bread and potatoes. We wanted fire, and we procured it by making a lamp with a piece of fat and the rags of a cotton cap. The key was at last made of pewter, but it was not yet perfect; and it was only after many trials and various alterations that it fitted at last. Thus masters of the doors, we were compelled to work a hole in the wall, near the barns of the town-hall. Sallambier, who was in the dungeons below, found a way to cut the hole, by working through the planking. All was ready for our escape, and it was fixed for the evening, when the jailor told me that my term of dungeon imprisonment had expired, and I should be placed again with the other prisoners.

A favour was never less welcome; I saw all my preparations useless, and I might wait for a long time for circumstances as favourable. I was however compelled to follow the jailor, whom I wished at the devil with his congratulations. This disappointment affected me so greatly that all the prisoners saw it. One of them having learnt my secret from me, made some very just observations on the danger I ran in escaping with such men as Sallambier and Duhamel, who would perhaps not be out of prison twenty-four hours without committing a murder. He even made me promise to let them go, and wait myself for some other opportunity. I followed his advice, and it was well that I did so; I even took the precaution of telling Duhamel and Sallambier that they were suspected, and that they had not a moment to spare in saving themselves. They followed my advice literally, and two hours afterwards they had joined a band of forty-seven Chauffeurs, of whom twenty-eight were executed the following month at Bruges.

The escape of Duhamel and Sallambier made a great noise in the prison, and throughout the city. They found some extraordinary circumstances belonging to it, but the jailor was the more astonished that I had not made one of the party. It was necessary to repair the breach they had made, and workmen came; and they stationed at the bottom of the staircase a guard with orders not to let any one pass. The thought came to me of deceiving the sentinel, and getting out by the breach which was to have aided my escape before.

Francine, who came every day to see me, brought me three ells of tri-coloured ribbon, which I had requested her to procure. With one piece I made a belt, and ornamenting my hat with the rest, I passed, muffled up, by the soldier: who, taking me for a municipal officer, presented his arms. I ascended the staircase quickly—reached the opening, which I found guarded by two centinels, one in the granary of the town-hall, and the other in the passage of the prison. I told the latter that it was impossible for a man to pass through this opening: he insisted on the contrary; and his comrade, as if plotting with me, said that I could get through with my clothes on. I said I would try: and creeping through the hole I got into the barn. Pretending that I had hurt myself in passing, I told my two men that as I was on that side I should go round by another way. " In this case," said he, who was in the granary, "wait whilst I open the door;" and putting the key in the lock, I jumped at two bounds down the stair-case of the town-hall and got into the street with my ribbon still on, and which would again have caused my arrest had not the day been drawing to a close.

I was scarcely out, when the jailor, who rarely lost sight of me said, "Where is Vidocq?" They told him that I was taking a turn in the yard; but when he went there to convince himself, he sought me every where in vain, calling loudly over all parts of the prison (an official search would not have been more successful), no prisoner had seen me go out. It was soon known that I was no longer in the prison; but how then could I have escaped? Of this no one knew anything—not even Francine, who most ingenuously declared that she knew nothing of how I had liberated myself, for she had brought me the ribbon without knowing the purpose for which I intended it. She was however confined; but this revealed nothing, the soldiers, who had allowed me to pass, taking good care not to implicate themselves.

Whilst they were thus punishing the pretended authors of my escape, I left the city and reached Courtrai, where the juggler Olivier and the quack Devoye enrolled me in their troop to play pantomime. I saw there many prisoners who had escaped, whose acting costume, which they always wore (because they had no other) served greatly to mystify the police. From Courtrai we returned to Ghent, whence we were soon to depart for the fair of Enghien. We were in this latter city for five days: and the receipt, of which I had a share, was very good; when one evening, as I was about to go on the stage, I was arrested by the police officers, to whom I had been betrayed by the Merry Andrew, out of malice at seeing me fill the chief characters. I was again taken back to Lille, where I learnt, to my great grief, that my poor Francine had been sentenced to six months' confinement for having aided my escape. The turnkey Baptiste—whose only crime was that of having taken me for a superior officer, and having allowed me in this capacity to quit St Peter's Tower—the unlucky Baptiste was also imprisoned for the same fault. The terrible charge against him was, that the prisoners (overjoyed at an opportunity of revenging themselves) declared that a hundred crowns had made him take a young man of nineteen for an old soldier on the shady side of fifty.

As for me, I was sent to the prison of the department of Douai, where I was treated as a dangerous man; that is to say, I was thrust into a dungeon with my hands and legs in fetters. I found there my townsman Desfosseux and a young man named Doyenette, condemned to chains for sixteen years for a burglary effected with his father, mother, and two brothers under fifteen years of age. They had been four months in the dungeon where I was put, lying on straw, eaten up with vermin, and living on bean-bread and water. I ordered my provisions, which were soon consumed; we then talked over our business, and my fellow prisoners told me that for the last fortnight they were making a hole under the pavement of the dungeon which would open at the level of the Scarpe which washed the prison walls. I at first regarded the enterprise as difficult, as it was necessary to pierce a wall five feet thick and yet avoid the observation of the jailor, whose frequent visits would not allow of our suffering a morsel of rubbish to be seen.

We eluded detection from this by throwing out of the window, which overlooked the Scarpe, every handful of rubbish that we got from our mine. Desfosseux had besides found means of ridding us of our fetters, and we worked with less fatigue and difficulty. One of us was always in the hole, which was already large enough to admit a man. We thought that we had at length terminated our labours and our captivity, when we discovered that the foundations, which we had imagined to be composed of common stone, were formed of masses of sand-stone of large size. This compelled us to enlarge our subterranean gallery, and for a week we worked at it unremittingly. To conceal the disappearance of that one of us who might be at work when the guard went round, we had filled a vest and shirt with straw and placed the figure in the posture of a sleeping man.

After fifty-five days and nights of unrelaxing toil, we at last so far completed our work that we had but one stone to remove and then should reach the river's banks. One night we determined on making an essay, and all appeared favourable to our design; the jailor had locked up earlier than usual, and a dense fog gave us a confident hope of avoiding the sentinel of the bridge. The shaken stone yielded to our efforts, and fell inside the aperture we had made; but the water followed it at the same time as if impelled by the sluice of a mill. We had calculated our distance incorrectly, and the hole being made some feet beneath the level of the river, we were soon deluged. At first we endeavoured to plunge through the opening; but the rapidity of the current precluded all attempts, and we were compelled to call for help, or remain immersed in water for the whole night. At our cries the jailor and turnkeys ran to our assistance, and were greatly astonished at finding themselves mid-leg deep in water. All was soon discovered and the mischief repaired, whilst we were shut up singly in dungeons in the same gallery.

This catastrophe filled me with very sad reflections, from which I was very soon aroused by the voice of Desfosseux, who told me, in slang terms, not to despair, but to take courage by his example. Desfosseux was certainly endowed with a strength of mind which nothing could depress : cast half naked on the straw in a dungeon, where he could scarcely lie at length, loaded with thirty pounds weight of fetters, he yet sang with great vociferation, and was only devising means of escape, that he might again do some evil deed; and opportunity was not long wanting.

In the same prison with us were confined the jailor of the Petit Hôtel of Lille, and the turnkey Baptiste, both accused of having aided my escape for a bribe. The day of their trial having arrived, the jailor was acquitted, but Baptiste's sentence was deferred, the tribunal having decreed a fresh process, in which I was to be heard. Poor Baptiste then came to me, begging me to tell the truth. At first I only gave him evasive answers; but Desfosseux having told me that the man might serve us, and that we must arrange terms with him, I promised to do what he wished: on which he made me vast professions of gratitude and offers of service. I took him at his word, and desired him to bring me a knife and two large nails, of which Desfosseux had told me that he had need, and in an hour I had them brought to me. On learning that I had procured them, Desfosseux made as many jumps as his fetters and his bounded space would allow: Doyenette equally gave himself up to the most excessive joy; and, as gaiety is in general catching, I felt myself too in a mirthful mood, without exactly knowing why.

When these transports had a little subsided, Desfosseux desired me to look at the roof of my dungeon and observe if there were not five stones whiter than the rest: and on my replying in the affirmative, he desired me to try the divisions with the point of my knife, which I did, and found that the cement had been replaced by crumb of bread, whitened with scraping: and Desfosseux told me that the prisoner, who had been there before me, had done this to remove the stones and save himself, when he had been taken to another part of the prison. I thus transferred the knife to Desfosseux, who employed himself with activity in opening a passage to my dungeon, when we were served similarly to my predecessor. The jailor having got wind of something, changed our dungeons, and placed us all three in a dungeon next to the Scarpe, where we were chained together: so that the least movement of one of us was communicated to the others, a horrid punishment when prolonged, and which ends in a total deprivation of sleep. At the end of two days Desfosseux, seeing us dejected, resolved on using a means which he only resorted to on desperate occasions, and which he reserved as the preparatory steps towards escape.

Like many of the galley-slaves he carried secretly about him a case full of files with which he set to work, and in less than three hours our fetters fell off, we cast them through the grating into the river. The jailor coming to visit us the moment after to see if we were quiet, almost fell backwards at finding us freed from our irons, and asked us what we had done with them: to which we only replied with jokes. The inspector of the prison arriving, together with an attendant bailiff named Hurtrel, we were compelled to undergo a fresh examinatiou: and Desfosseux, who was much irritated, said, "You ask for our fetters? Well, the worms have eaten them, and will eat as many as you may load us with."—The inspector then suspecting that we had the famous herb which cuts iron, which no botanist has ever yet discovered, ordered us to strip and be examined from head to foot, and then again loaded us with irons, which were again cut off the following night; for the precious case was not discovered. This time we reserved to ourselves the pleasure of throwing them on the ground in the presence of the inspector and Hurtrel the bailiff, who did not know what to think of it. The report spread through the city that there was in the prison a conjuror who took fetters off by only touching them. To cut short all these accounts, and particularly to avoid drawing the attention of the other prisoners to means of getting rid of their chains, the public accuser gave an order to shut us up and watch us with particular care—a recommendation which did not prevent us from quitting Douai sooner than they expected, or than we ourselves had the least idea of.

Twice a week we had leave to consult our counsel in the gallery, of which one door led to the court of justice, and I contrived to get an impression of the lock ; Desfosseux made a key, and one fine day, whilst my counsel was engaged with another client, accused of two murders, we all three got out without being seen. Two other gates, which opposed us, were broken open in a twinkling, and the prison was soon left behind us. But yet I was uneasy : six francs was our whole stock, and we could not get far with such a sum ; which I told my companions, who looked at each other with a sinister smile : and on my repeating my observation, they told me that on the next night they intended to enter a house in the neighbourhood with which they were well acquainted.

I had no intention of turning housebreaker, any more than when I was amongst the Bohemiens. I had profitted by the experience of Desfosseux in escaping, but never contemplated uniting myself with such a villain : and yet I was not desirous of entering into any explanation. By evening we had reached a village on the road to Cambrai ; we had not eaten since our escape from prison, and were sorely pressed by hunger. It was absolutely necessary to get provisions in the village. The half-naked appearance of my companions might give rise to suspicion, and it was agreed that I should go for the food. I went to a public-house, where, after having taken some bread and brandy, I went out by a different door from that at which I had entered, directing my steps in the opposite direction to that in which I had left the two men whose company I was so greatly desirous of getting rid of. I walked all night, and only stopped at break of day to sleep a few hours on a hay-stack.

Four days afterwards I reached Compeigne, on my way to Paris, where I trusted to find some means of existence until my mother could send me some succour. At Louvres, meeting a regiment of black hussars, I asked the quarter-master if I could enter, but he told me that they did not enlist; and the lieutenant, to whom I afterwards applied, gave me the same reply, but touched by the embarrassment of my situation, he agreed to keep me to clean the extra horses which he was going to procure at Paris. A cap of a police officer and an old cloak which was given to me, enabled me to clear the barrier unquestioned, and I went to the military school with the detachment, which I afterwards accompanied to the depôt, at Guise. On arriving in this city I was presented to the colonel, who, although suspecting me to be a deserter, engaged me under the name of Lannoy, which I assumed without being able to justify by any credentials. Concealed by my new uniform, and mingling with the rank of a numerous regiment, I thought myself secure, and begun to think of making my way as a soldier, when an unfortunate accident again befel me.

On entering the barrack one morning I met a gendarme who had left Douai for Guise. He had so frequently seen me, that he knew me at first sight and called to me. We were in the midst of the street, and thoughts of escape were useless, I therefore went up to him and boldly feigned to be glad to see him. He replied to me, but with an air that seemed to augur me no good. Whilst thus together, a hussar of my squadron, seeing me with the gendarme, approached, and said to me, "Well, Lannoy, what are you doing with the round hats?" "Lannoy," said the gendarme with astonishment. "Yes, it is a *nom de guerre*." "Oh, we will see about that," said he, seizing my collar. I was compelled to follow him to prison, and my identity being confirmed, in opposition to my statements at the regiment, I was by a cursed chance again sent to Douai.

This sentence completely overpowered me, and the intelligence that reached me at Douai was not calculated to set me at rest. I heard that Grouard, Herbaux, Stofflet, and Boitel, had decided by lot, that one of them should confess the execution of the forgery, but

K

as this forgery could only be the work of one person,
they determined on accusing me, thus punishing me
for what I had said of them at my last examination;
and I learnt besides that the prisoner who could have
corroborated my statement, was dead.   If anything
could console me, it was that I had escaped in time
from Desfosseux and Doyennette, who had been taken
four days after our escape with their booty about them,
in a mercer's shop in Ponte-a-Marcq. I soon saw them,
and as they were astonished at my abrupt departure, I
told them that the arrival of a gendarme at the public-
house where I was purchasing provisions, had compelled me to fly with speed.   Again united, we formed
new plans of escape, which the approach of our trials
rendered of great importance to us.

One evening a convoy of prisoners arrived, four of
whom, ironed, were placed with us.   They were the
brothers Duhesme, rich farmers of Bailleul, where they
had enjoyed the best reputation, until an unexpected
accident unfolded their real characters.   These four
persons, men of powerful strength, were at the head of
a band of Chauffeurs, who had struck terror into the vicinity, without any person being able to identify them.
The prattling of a little girl of one of the Duhesme's
at last exposed the affair.   This child, chatting at a
neighbour's house, said that she had been very much
frightened the night before. "And with what ? " said the
curious neighbour.   " Oh, papa came home again with
the black men."   " The black men ? "   " Yes, the men
who go out with papa every night and come home in
the day time and count out money; my mother lights
the candle, and my aunt Genevieve also, because my
uncles are amongst the black men. I asked my mother
one day what it was all about, and she said, Be discreet
my child, your father has a black hen who finds him
in money, but.it is only at night, and that he should not
scare it, he makes his face as black as her feathers. Be
silent, for if you tell anybody what you have seen, the

black hen will never come again." We may easily divine that it was not to visit the mysterious hen that the Duhesmes blackened their faces with smoke. The neighbour, who guessed as much, communicated her suspicion to her husband, who, in his turn, questioned the little girl, and convinced that the favourites of the black hen were Chauffeurs, he made a deposition, and on measures being taken, the band was apprehended, all disguised, as they were about to sally out on an expedition.

The youngest Duhesme had, in the sole of his shoe, a knife-blade, which he had contrived to conceal on the road from Bailleul to Douai. Being told that I knew the way of the prison, he communicated this to me, asking me if it were not possible to effect an escape with its assistance. I was reflecting about it, when a justice of the peace, attended by gendarmes, came to make a strict search throughout our room, and about our persons. No one amongst us knowing the reason of this, I thought it prudent to hide in my mouth a small file which I had always about me, but one of the gendarmes having watched me, cried "He is going to swallow it!" "Swallow what?" Everybody looked, and we then learnt that they wanted to find the seal which had served to stamp the forged order for Boitel's liberation. Suspected, as we have just learnt, of having got it, I was transferred to the prison of the Town Hall, and thrust in a dungeon so chained that my right hand was confined to my left leg, and my left hand to my right leg. The dungeon was moreover so damp, that in twenty minutes the straw which they had thrown me was as wet as if it had been dipped in water.

I remained eight days in this frightful state, and when they found that it was impossible I could have got rid of the seal in the way suspected, I was ordered to the usual prison. On learning this intelligence, I pretended, as is often done under such circumstances, to be exceedingly weak and scarcely able to bear the

light of day. The unwholesome state of the dungeon
made this very probable, and the gendarmes fell completely into the snare and carried their complaisance so
far as to cover my eyes with a handkerchief, and then
deposited me in a hackney-coach.   On the road I
took off the handkerchief and opening the door, with a
dexterity never yet surpassed, and jumped out into the
street, the gendarmes sought to follow, but impeded by
their sabres and jack boots, they had scarcely got out of
the carriage when I was at a considerable distance.   I
quitted the city instantly, and resolved on embarking, I
reached Dunkirk with some money which my mother
had transmitted to me.   I there made friends with the
supercargo of a Swedish brig, who promised to get me
a berth on board.

Whilst waiting for orders to sail, my new friend proposed that I should accompany him to Saint Omer,
where he was going to get a large quantity of biscuit.
I did not fear recognition in my sailor's clothes, and
agreed, as it was impossible to refuse a man to whom I
was under such great obligations.   I went with him,
but my turbulent character would not allow me to remain quiet in a pot-house row, and I was arrested as a
riotous fellow and taken to the watch-house.   There
they asked for my papers, of which I had none, and my
answers inducing a belief that I might be an escaped
prisoner, they sent me the next day to the central prison of Douai, without allowing me to bid adieu to the
supercargo, who was doubtlessly much surprised at this
occurrence.   At Douai they put me once more in the
prison of the Town Hall, where at first the jailor evinced
much kindness towards me, which did not however last.
At the termination of a quarrel with the turnkeys, in
which I took too active a part, I was thrown into a
dark cell under the tower.   There were five of us, one
of whom, a deserter sentenced to death, was talking of
nothing but suicide, until I desired him not to think
of that, but rather devise means of escape from this
dismal hole, where the rats, which ran about like rab-

bits in a corn field, eat our bread and bit our faces whilst we slept. With a bayonet, stolen from one of the soldiers of the national guard who did duty at the prison, we commenced working a hole in the wall, in a direction in which we heard a cobbler hammering his leather. In ten days, and as many nights, we penetrated six feet in depth and seemed to get nearer the cobbler's hammer. On the eleventh day, in the morning, on drawing out a brick, I saw daylight from a window which looked into the street, and gave light to a place where the jailor kept some rabbits.

This discovery inspired us with fresh courage, and the evening visit being concluded, we took from the hole all the loosened bricks, of which there were two courses, and placed them behind the dungeon door, which opened inwards, so as to barricade it, and then set to work with so much industry, that daylight surprised us, when the hole, six feet large at the opening, was only two feet at the end. The jailor came with our allowances, and finding some resistance, opened the wicket, and saw the high pile of bricks, to his great astonishment. He desired us to open the door, and on our refusal the guard came, then the commissary of the prison, then the public accuser, then the municipal officers clothed with the tri-colored scarves. We held a parley, and during this time one of us continued working at the hole, which the darkness did not disclose. We might perhaps escape before the door was forced, when an unexpected event deprived us of our last hope.

The jailor's wife, in going to feed the rabbits, had observed rubbish scattered on the floor. In a prison, nothing is indifferent, and she carefully examined the wall, and although the bricks had been so replaced as to conceal the hole, she yet saw that they had been separated; and on calling for the guard, with a blow from the butt end of a musket, our bricks were knocked out and we were discovered. On both sides they called to us to clear the door-way, or they would fire on us.

Entrenched behind the materials, we answered that
the first who entered should be knocked on the head
with bricks and irons. So much determination alarmed
the authorities, and they left us for a few hours to calm
ourselves. At noon, a municipal officer appeared at
the wicket, which as well as the hole had been sedulously guarded, and offered us an amnesty, which we
accepted, but scarcely had we removed our *chevaux-de-
frise*, when they attacked us with the butt end of muskets, flat side of sabres, and bunches of keys, even the
jailor's mastiff joined the party : he jumped at me
and bit me most severely all over. They then led us
into the court yard, where a body of fifteen men held
us, lying on our faces, whilst they rivetted our fetters.
This job done, they cast me into a dungeon yet more
horrible than that I had left, and it was not till the
next day that the surgeon Dutilleul, (now keeper at
the hospital of St Maûdé) came to dress the bites and
bruises which covered me.

I had scarcely recovered from this when the day of
trial came, which my repeated escapes and those of
Grouard, who fled just as I was retaken, had deferred
for eight months. The trial began, and I saw that I
was lost; my companions accused me with an animosity, explained by my retarded confessions, which were
useless to myself, and had not at all injured them.
Boitel declared that I had asked him how much I would
give to get out of prison. Herbaux confessed that he
had forged the order, but not added the signatures, and
said besides that I had persuaded him to forge it, and
then taken it from him without his thinking it of the
least importance. The jury thought that nothing indicated that I had materially aided the crime; all the
charge against me was confined to allegations without
proof, that I had furnished the seal. However, Boitel,
who remembered having begged for the forged order;
Stofflet, who had brought it to the jailor; Grouard,
who had at least assisted at the whole operation, were
acquitted ; whilst Herbaux and I were condemned to

eight years' imprisonment. This was the termination
of the sentence, which I subjoin accurately, in reply to
the tales which malevolence and stupidity have circulated. Some say that I was sentenced to death for numerous murders; others state that I had long been
chief of a band which robbed the diligences; the most
moderate state that I was condemned to perpetual
labour at the gallies for robbery and housebreaking; and
it has been asserted that I (at a later period) incited
wretches to crime that I might show my vigilance in
pouncing upon them; as if there were not a sufficient
number of the really guilty. Certainly false comrades,
as are everywhere found, even amongst robbers, sometimes instructed me in the plans of their accomplices:
certainly to confirm the intent whilst we prevented
the crime, it was sometimes necessary to allow of a
partial commission of the deed, for experienced rogues
are never caught but in the very act: and I ask, is there
anything in this which has the appearance of an inducement to do ill. This imputation emanated from
the police, amongst whom I have some enemies; but
the imputation fails before the publicity of judicial facts,
which would not have failed in revealing the infamies
with which I am charged; and it also fails before the
operations of the brigade of safety, which I directed. It
is not when proof is given that we have recourse to deception, and the confidence of the clever men who have
preceded M. Delavau, in the office of chief magistrate,
will acquit me of such wretched expedients. " He is
a lucky fellow," said, one day, the police officers who
had failed in an enterprise in which I succeeded, to
M. Angles. " Well," said he, turning his back on
them, " Do you be lucky fellows too."
    Parricide is the only crime of which I have not been
charged, and yet I declare that I never was sentenced
to, nor underwent, but the sentence which I here subjoin. My pardon will prove this; and when I assert that
I never aided in this miserable forgery, I should be
believed, for it was at last but a prison joke, which, if

proved, would at present only subject the offender to
a sentence of corporal punishment. But it was not the
suspected accomplice in a foolish forgery that was to be
punished; it was the disorderly, rebellious and impudent
prisoner, the chief of so many plans of escape, of whom
an example must be made, and I was sacrificed.

" SENTENCE.

" *In the name of the* FRENCH REPUBLIC, *one and
indivisible.*

" It appears, by the criminal tribunal of the department of the north, that the act of accusation made the
twenty-eighth Vendemaire, in the 5th year, against certain men; namely, Sebastien Boitel, aged about forty, a
labourer, living at Annoulin; César Herbaux, aged
twenty, ci-devant serjeant-major in the chasseurs of
Vandamme, living at Lille; Jean François Grouard,
aged nineteen years and a half, second conductor
of the military transports, living at Lille; Eugène
Stofflet, aged twenty-three years, a broker, living at
Lille; and François Vidocq, a native of Arras, aged
twenty-two years, living at Lille; charged with forgery of a public and authentic document, by the director of the jury of the division of Cambrai, in manner following:

" The undersigned, judge of the civil tribunal of the
department of the north, exercising the functions of
director of the jury of the division of Cambrai, for
formal indictments, states, that by virtue of a judgment
given the seventh Fructidor last, by the criminal tribunal of the department of the north, superseding and
annulling the acts of accusation, drawn up the twentieth and twenty-sixth of last Germinal, by the director
of the jury of the division of Lille, charged the herein-
named César Herbaux, François Vidocq, Sebastien
Boitel, Eugène Stofflet, and Brice Coquelle, prisoners
now present, and André Bordereau, prisoner, absent,
with the crime of forging a public and authentic docu-

ment, to procure the escape of the said Sebastien Boitel, from the house of confinement, called St Peter's Tower, at Lille, where he was confined ; and particularly the said Brice Coquelle, with having, by means of this forgery, allowed the escape of the prisoner entrusted to his care, as jailor of the said house of confinement. All the charges, together with the necessary papers, would have been sent to the undersigned to be submitted to a new indictment, but on the examination of the said papers it was discovered that the said Jean François Grouard, detained in the house of confinement, called St Peter's Tower, implicated in the charge, had been omitted by the director of the beforementioned jury, whereupon, on the orders of the commissioner of the executive power, and by virtue of an order of the twenty-fourth Fructidor, a decree was issued against the said Grouard, and thereupon, after having heard a decree of sentence, as being concerned in the said forging; that no plaintiff appearing in the two days of the remand of the accused to the house of confinement in this division, the undersigned proceeded with the examination of the papers relative to the causes of the detention and arrest of all the accused. That having corroborated the charges of the crimes of which they were respectively accused, it was found that the offences were of a nature to deserve severe and notorious punishment, and consequently, having consulted the commissioner of the executive power, he has this day passed a decree, by which he has ordered all the said defendants before a special jury of accusation, and by virtue of the decree, the undersigned has drawn up the present act of accusation to be, after the formalities required by law, presented to the said jury :

" The undersigned declares, that in consequence, there resulted from the examination of the papers, and particularly the indictment drawn up by the clerk of the tribunal of peace of the fourth section of the commune of Lille, the nineteenth of Nivose last, and the ninth and twenty-fourth Prairial following, by the justice of the peace for the south, of the commune of Douai (which indictment is hereunto annexed.)

" That the said Sebastian Boitel, a prisoner in the house of confinement, called St Peter's Tower, at Lille, had been set at liberty by virtue of a forged order from the committee of legislation, and the tribunal of Cassation, dated at Paris, the twentieth Brumaire, in the fourth year of the republic, signed Carnot, Lesage-Cenault, and Le Coindre, at the back of which was the seal of the representative of the people Talot, addressed to the said Brice Coquelle; that this order and seal, which the latter used for his own purpose, were not those of the committee of legislation and the said representative Talot; and thence it is proved that this order and seal are a forgery of a public and authentic document, and that the forgery was evident on the slightest inspection, inasmuch as it was intituled ' Order of the Committee of Legislation, Tribunal of Cassation ;' a ridiculous title, confounding, in one and the same authority, two distinct authorities.

" That the ninth Prairial last, there was found in one of the dungeons of the house of confinement at Douai, a brass seal without a top, hid at the foot of a bed ; that the said Vidocq had slept there previously ; that the seal is the same as that which was found attached to the forged order, and presents a precisely similar impression ; that, after the visit of the said judge of the south of Douai, made on the day before, from the dungeon in which the said Vidocq then was, they heard, on turning over the straw bed, something fall, sounding like brass or silver ; that Vidocq threw himself on it, and managed to withdraw what had fallen, and to substitute in its place a piece of a file which he produced ; that he had been seen previously with the seal by the said Herbaux and Stofflet, to whom he had confessed having been lieutenant of the battalion of which the seal bore the name.

" That the said Herbaux, François Vidocq, Sebas-

tien Boitel, Eugène Stofflet, Brice Coquelle, André
Bordereau, and Jean François Grouard, are charged
with being the authors and contrivers of the said forgery, and having thereby effected the escape of the
said Sebastien Boitel, from the house of confinement
where he had been confined, by virtue of a sentence of
condemnation to imprisonment.

" That the said Brice Coquelle is, besides, charged
with having, by means of this false order, allowed to
escape from the said house of confinement the said
Sebastien Boitel, committed to his custody, as jailor
of the said prison ; that the said Brice Coquelle was
convicted before the jury at Lille, of having set at
liberty the said Sebastien Boitel, the third Frimaire
last, by virtue of the forged order.

" That this paper was conveyed to him by Stofflet,
who carried it to him, and who was recognised before
the judge as having been the bearer of it ; that the said
Stofflet had been at the prison five or six times in the
space of ten days, and always enquired for Herbaux,
with whom he remained for two or three hours ; that
Herbaux and Boitel were together in the same prison,
and that the said Stofflet spoke equally to one as to
the other ; that the pretended order was addressed to
him, and that he could not suspect the forgery, not
knowing the signature ; that the said Stofflet confessed that he was suspected of having carried a letter
to St Peter's Tower, but that it was a forgery ; that
he had been many times at the house of confinement
to speak to the said Herbaux, but had never taken
any letters to him, and that Brice Coquelle had
asserted falsely in saying that he had recognized him
before the judge, as having brought him the forged
order, by virtue of which he had set Sebastien Boitel
at liberty.

" That François Vidocq had declared that he only
knew Boitel in prison ; that he knew he had left by
virtue of an order brought to Coquelle, who was
drinking with the brothers of Coquelle and Prevôt,

another prisoner, that he had been to sup with them at the cabaret of Dordreck, and that Coquelle and Prévôt had not returned till midnight; that he declared to the judge at Douai, that the seal found at the foot of the bed did not come from him; that he had not served in the battalion of which the seal bore the name, and did not know whether this battalion had been incorporated into one of those in which he had served; that if he made any resistance at the visit to his dungeon, it was in consequence of the piece of file which he had, fearing that it might create a suspicion that he would use it to loosen his fetters.

" That the said Boitel had stated that he had been sentenced to St Peter's Tower in consequence of a sentence to six years' imprisonment; that he well remembered that one day Herbaux and Vidocq had asked him how much he would give to be set at liberty; that he promised them twelve louis, and gave them seven, promising the remainder when he was at home; that he went out of prison with his two brothers and Brice Coquelle; that he had been with them to the Dordreck, to drink some wine, until ten o'clock in the evening: that he well knew that he had got out of prison through a false order, forged by Vidocq and Herbaux, but that he did not know by whom it had been brought.

" That the said Grouard had declared, in presence of the undersigned, that he knew of the liberation of the said Boitel, by virtue of a superior order; that after his going away he had seen the said order; that he had suspected it to be a forgery, and thought he recognized the writing of Herbaux; and that as for himself, he did not at all assist, either in the sending away Boitel or in the fabrication of the forgery.

" That the said Herbaux declared to the undersigned, that being with Vidocq and the other prisoners, they were conversing about Boitel; that the said Vidocq defied him to draw up an order by which the liberation of Boitel could be effected; that he ac-

cepted the challenge, and took the first paper
that came to hand and made the order in question,
without putting any signature to it; that he left it
on the table; that Vidocq obtained it, and that it
is the same order through which Boitel's escape was
effected.

" That as to André Bordereau, not apprehended,
it appears that he must have known of the forgery,
because the day Boitel got out of prision he went to
deliver a letter to Stofflet from Herbaux, and the day
after Bortel's escape he visited him at Annoulin,
whither Boitel had fled.

" It results from all these details, attested by the
said documents and indictments, that a forgery of a
public and authentic paper has been committed; and
that by virtue of this forgery the said Sebastien Boitel
escaped from the house of confinement called St
Peter's Tower, at Lille, where he was confined under
custody of the jailor; that this escape took place the
third Frimare last; a double crime, on which, according
to the penal code, the jury will have to decide, if
there be any accusation against the said Boitel,
Stofflet, Vidocq, Coquelle, Grouard, Herbaux, and
Bordereau, by reason of the offences committed, mentioned in this indictment.

" Given at Cambrai, the twenty-eighth Vendemiaire,
in the fifth of the Republic, one and indivisible."

(Signed) " NOLEKERICK."

" The declaration of the jury of the criminal court
of the division of Cambrai from the sixth Brumaire to
the fifteenth, written below the indictment, and stating
that there is a criminal charge made out as mentioned
in the said indictment.

" The order of seizure, made by the director of
the jury of the said division the same day, against the
said Sebastien Boitel, César Herbaux, Eugène Stofflet,
François Grouard, and François Vidocq.

" The procès-verbal of the return of these persons

to the court of justice of the department, the twenty-first of last Brumaire.

" And the declaration of the special jury of judgment, the same date, stating :—

" 1st, That the forgery mentioned by the indictment is made out.

" 2d, That César Herbaux, accused, is convicted of having committed this forgery.

" 3d, That he is convicted of having committed it designedly, and with an intent to do wrong.

" 4th, That François Vidocq is convicted of having committed this forgery.

" 5th, That he is convicted of having committed it designedly, and with an intent to do wrong.

" 6th, That it is proved that the said forgery has been committed on a public and authentic paper.

" 7th, That Sebastien Boitel, accused, is not convicted of having by gifts and presents incited the guilty person or persons to commit the said forgery.

" 8th, That Eugène Stofflet is not convicted of having aided and assisted the guilty person or persons, either with the means which prepared, or the facilities which aided the execution of the said forgery, or in the act itself which consummated the deed.

" 9th, That Jean François Grouard is not convicted of having aided and assisted the guilty person or persons, either with the means which prepared, or the facilities which aided the execution of the said forgery, or in the act itself which consummated the deed.

" In consequence of the said declaration, the president pronounced, in conformity with the four hundred and twenty-fourth article of the law, from the third of Brumaire to the fourth, code of crimes and punishment, that the said Sebastien Boitel, Eugène Stofflet, and Jean François Grouard, are and remain acquitted of the charge laid to them; and the guardian of the house of justice of the department is ordered to set them free immediately, unless they be detained for any other reason.

" The tribunal having heard the commissioner of the executive power, and the citizen Despres, counsel for the prisoners, sentences François Vidocq and César Herbaux to the punishment of the galleys for eight years, conformably to the forty-fourth article of the second section of the second chapter of the second part of the penal code, which has been read, and which runs thus :—

" If the said crime of forgery is committed on a public and authentic paper, the punishment shall be eight years at the galleys.

" Ordered, conformably with the twenty-eighth article of the first chapter of the penal code, which has also been read, and runs thus :—

" ' Whoever shall have been condemned to the punishment of irons, imprisonment in the house of correction, to the rack, to confinement, before undergoing the sentence shall be first led to the public square of the city, where the criminal jury have been summoned, and shall then be tied to a post, placed on a scaffold, and shall remain there exposed to the gaze of the populace for six hours, if he be condemned to irons or solitary confinement; for four hours if he be condemned to the rack; for two hours if he be condemned to imprisonment; over his head, on a board shall be inscribed in large characters, his name, profession, residence, cause of his sentence, and judgment passed on him.'

" And by the four hundred and forty-fifth article of the law of the third and fourth Brumaire, code of crimes and punishments, which has been read and runs thus :—' The exposure shall be made in one of the public places of the commune, where the criminal tribunal holds its sittings.'

" That the said François Vidocq and César Herbaux shall be exposed for six hours on a scaffold, which shall be for that purpose erected on the public square of this commune.

" Ordered, that with all speed of the commissaries

of the executive power, this sentence be carried into effect.

"Given and pronounced at Douai, at the sitting of the criminal tribunal of the department of the North, the seventh Nivose, fifth year of the French Republic, one and indivisible; present, the citizens Delaetre, president; Havyn, Ricquet, Reat, and Legrand, judges, who signed the minutes of this said sentence.

"We command and order all officers on this our requisition, to carry the said sentence into effect; to our attorney-general and our officers at the inferior tribunals to give all requisite aid; to all commandants and their officers of the public departments to render all necessary assistance when they shall be legally called upon for the same.

"By virtue of which, the present judgment has been signed by the president of the court, and by the clerk.   With all speed,

　　　(Signed)   "LEPOINE, clerk."

On the margin is written: "Registered at Douai, the sixteenth Prairal, thirteenth year, folio 67 (back of the leaf) second case, received five francs, namely, two francs for as many sentences, three francs for as many discharges, and fifty centimes for charge on all.

　　　(Signed)   "DEMAG."

On the margin of the first part is written: "By a judge of the superior tribunal of the division of Bethune, conformably with the two hundred and thirty-seventh article of the civil code, and by the procès-verbal of this day, thirtieth Prairal, year thirteen, supplying the place of the absent president, reference approved.

　　　(Signed)   "DELDICQUE."

CHAPTER VII.

Departure from Douai—The prisoners revolt in the forest of Compeigne—Residence at the Bicêtre—Prison customs—The madhouse.

WORN out by the bad treatment of every species which I experienced in the prison of Douai, tormented by a watchfulness redoubled after my sentence, I took care not to make an appeal, which would keep me there some months. What confirmed me in my resolution was, the information that the prisoners were to be sent forthwith to the Bicêtre, and there, making one chain, to be sent on to the Bagne at Brest. It is unnecessary to say, that I relied on escaping on our route. As to the appeal, I was told that I could present a petition for pardon from the Bagne, which would have the same effect. We remained however some months at Douai, which made me regret bitterly that I had not made my petition for annulling the sentence.

At length the order of removal arrived, and, what would scarcely be credited from men doomed to the galleys, it was hailed with enthusiasm, so much were we tired of the torments of Marin, the jailor. Our new situation was not however much more satisfactory; the officer, Hurtrel, who accompanied us, I know not why, had ordered irons of a new construction, which fastened to each of our legs a ball of fifteen pounds weight, whilst we were secured two and two by a massive wrist-cuff of iron. Besides, the vigilance was extreme, and it was impossible to think of doing anything by address. An attack by main force could alone save us, and I proposed it to fourteen of my companions, who agreed on it, and it was settled that the project should be put in excution on our way through the forest of Compeigne. Desfosseux was

L 2

of the party, and by means of fine saws which he had always securely secreted about him, out fetters were cut in three days; the plaister of a particular sort of gum prevented our keepers from perceiving the trace of the instruments.

On reaching the forest and gaining the appointed spot, the signal was given, the fetters fell from us, and we leaped from the carriages which enclosed us to try and gain the thicket; but the five gendarmes and the eight dragoons who escorted us, charged sword in hand. We entrenched ourselves behind the trees, armed with the stones which are piled up to mend the roads, and with some weapons we had got hold of at the first moment of confusion. The soldiers hesitated for an instant, but, well armed and well mounted, they soon made up their minds, and at the first charge two of our party fell dead, five more terribly wounded, and the others falling on their knees cried for mercy. Surrender was now imperative; and Desfosseux, myself, and some others who had escaped, got into the carriage, when Hurtrel, who had kept at a very respectful distance from the affray, came up to a poor wretch, who certainly did not hurry himself very much, and thrust his sabre through him. Such baseness enraged us; the prisoners who had not yet ascended the carriages took up stones, and but for the aid of the dragoons, Hurtrel would have been knocked on the head. The soldiers bid us desist before we brought down destruction on ourselves; and the thing was so evident, that we were compelled to lay down our arms, that is the stones. This circumstance, however, put a termination to the annoyances of Hurtrel, who never approached us but with fear and trembling.

At Senlis we were placed in the temporary prison, one of the most horrible I ever tenanted. The jailor exercising the office of street-keeper, the prison was guarded by his wife; and what a creature was she! As we had made ourselves notorious, she thrust us into the most secret dungeons, convincing herself by previous personal examination that we had nothing about us that could aid escape. We were however trying the walls, when we heard her roar out, " Rascals, I am coming to you with my bastinado; I will teach you how to play music." We took her at her word, and all desisted. The next day we reached Paris, and were lodged in the outer boulevards, and at four in the afternoon we got in sight of Bicêtre.

On reaching the end of the avenue which looks on the road to Fontainebleau, the carriages turned to the right, and entered an iron gate, above which I read mechanically this inscription—" Hospice de la viellesse " (Hospital for the aged.) In the fore court many old men were walking, clothed in grey garments. They were paupers; and stared at us with that stupid curiosity which results from a monotonous and purely animal existence; for it often happens that a person admitted into a hospital, having no longer his own subsistence to provide for, renounces the exercise of his narrow faculties, and ends by falling into a state of perfect idiotcy. On reaching the second court, in which was the chapel, I remarked that the majority of my companions hid their faces with their hands or pocket-handkerchiefs. It may be supposed that they experienced some feeling of shame. No ; they were only thinking of allowing their faces to be seen as little as possible, so that if opportunity presented they might the more easily escape.

" Here we are," said Desfosseux to me: " you see that square building—that is the prison." We alighted at an iron door, guarded inside by a sentry. Having entered the office, we were only registered, our description being deferred until the next day. I perceived, however, that the jailor looked at us, Desfosseux and me, with a sort of curiosity, and I thence concluded that we had been recommended by the officer Hurtrel, who had preceded us a quarter of an hour from the time of the business of the forest of

Compiègne. Having opened many low doors, guarded
with iron plates, and the Bird-cage Wicket, we were
introduced to a large square yard, where about sixty
prisoners were playing at fives, and shouting so loudly
as to sound all over the place. At our appearance
their game ceased, and surrounding us, they examined
with much surprise the irons which loaded us. It
was, besides, to enter Bicêtre in the most favourable
manner, to be decked with such caparisons, for they
estimated the deserts of the prisoner, that is to say,
his boldness and talent for escape, by the precautions
taken to secure him. Desfosseux, who found himself
amongst friends, had no difficulty in introducing us
as the most distinguished personages of the north;
he did more, he particularly expatiated on my merits,
and I was accordingly surrounded and made much of
by all the worthies of the prison: Beaumont, Guil-
laume, Mauger, Jossat, Maltaisé, Corun, Blondy,
Troaflat, and Richard, one of the party concerned in
the murder of a Lyons courier, never left me. As
soon as my fetters were taken off, they took me to
the drinking-shop, where for two hours I did justice
to a thousand invitations, when a tall man, with a
police-officer's cap, who they told me was the room-
inspector, took us to a large place called Le Fort
Mahon, when we were clothed in the prison garb,
consisting of a frock half grey and half black. The
inspector told me, I should be brigadier, that is,
that I should preside at the giving out of the provisions amongst my table-companions, and I had, in
consequence, a good bed, whilst others slept on camp
couches. In four days I was known to all the prisoners; but although they had the highest opinion of
my courage, Beaumont wishing to try me, picked a
quarrel with me; we fought, and as he was an expert
boxer, I was completely conquered. I, however, had
my revenge in a room, where Beaumont, unable to
display the resources of his art, had the worst of it.
My first defeat, however, gave me a desire to be

instructed in the mysteries of this art, and the celebrated Jean Goupel, the Saint George of boxing, who
was at the Bicêtre with us, soon counted me amongst
those of his pupils who were destined to do him the
most honour.

The prison of Bicêtre is a neat quadrangular building, inclosing many other structures and many courts,
which have each a different name; there is the
grande cour (great court) where the prisoners walk;
the cour de cuisine (or kitchen court); the cour des
chiens (or dog's court); the cour de correction (or
court of punishment); and the cour des fers (or iron
court). In this last is a new building five stories
high; each story contains forty cells, capable of holding four prisoners. On the platform, which supplies
the place of a roof, was night and day a dog named
Dragon, who passed in the prison for the most watchful and incorruptible of his kind; but some prisoners
managed at a subsequent period to corrupt him
through the medium of a roasted leg of mutton, which
he had the culpable weakness to accept; so true is
it, that there are no seductions more potent than those
of gluttony, since they operate indifferently on all
organised beings. To ambition, to gaming, and to gallantry, there are bounds fixed by nature; but gluttony
knows nothing of age, and if the appetite sometimes
opposes its inert power, we are quits with it by a
good fit of indigestion. However, the Amphytrions
escaped whilst Dragon was swallowing the mutton;
he was beaten and taken into the cour des chiens,
where, chained up and deprived of the free air which
he breathed on the platform, he was inconsolable for
his fault, and perished piecemeal, a victim of remorse
at his weakness in yielding to a moment of gluttony
and error.

Near the erection I speak of is the old building,
nearly arranged in the same way, and under which
were dungeons of safety, in which were inclosed the
troublesome and condemned prisoners. It was in one

of these dungeons that for forty-three years lived the accomplice of Cartouche, who betrayed him to procure this commutation! To obtain a moment's sunshine, he frequently counterfeited death so well, that when he had actually breathed his last sigh, two days passed before they took off his iron collar. A third part of the building, called La Force, comprised various rooms, in which the prisoners were placed who arrived from the provinces, and are destined, like ourselves, to the chain.

At this period, the prison of Bicêtre, which is only strong from the strict guard kept up there, could contain twelve hundred prisoners; but they were piled on each other, and the conduct of the jailors in no way assuaged the inconvenience of the place : a sullen air, a rough tone, and brutal manners, were exercised towards the prisoners, and they were in no way to be softened, but through the medium of a bottle of wine, or a pecuniary bribe. Besides, they never attempted to repress any excess or any crime, and provided that no one sought to escape, they might do whatever they pleased in the prison, without being restrained or prevented. Whilst men condemned for those attempts which modesty shrinks from naming, openly practised their detestable libertinism, and robbers exercised their industry inside the prison without any person attempting to check the crime or prevent the bestiality.

If any man arrived from the country well clad, who, condemned for a first offence, was not as yet initiated into the customs and usages of prisons, in a twinkling he was stripped of his clothes, which were sold in his presence to the highest bidder. If he had jewels or money, they were alike confiscated to the profit of the society, and if he were too long in taking out his earrings, they snatched them out without the sufferer daring to complain. He was previously warned, that if he spoke of it, they would hang him in the night to the bars of his cell, and afterwards say that he had

committed suicide. If a prisoner; out of precaution,
when going to sleep, placed his clothes under his head,
they waited until he was in his first sleep, and then
they tied to his foot a stone, which they balanced at
the side of his bed; at the least motion the stone fell,
and aroused by the noise, the sleeper jumped up, and
before he could discover what had occurred, his packet
hoisted by a cord, went through the iron bars to the
floor above. I have seen, in the depth of winter, these
poor devils, having been deprived of their property in
this way, remain in the court in their shirts until some
one threw them some rags to cover their nakedness.
As long as they remained at Bicêtre, by burying themselves, as we may say, in their straw, they could defy
the rigour of the weather; but at the departure of the
chain, when they had no other covering than the frock
and trousers made of packing cloth, they often sunk exhausted and frozen before they reached the first resting place.

It is necessary, by facts of this nature, to explain
the rapid depravity of men whom it was easy to excite
to honest feelings ; but who unable to escape the
height of misery but by excess of wickedness, sought
an alleviation of their lot in the real or apparent ex-
aggeration of all species of crime.   In society, we
dread infamy; in the society of prisoners, there is no
shame but in not being sufficiently infamous.   The
condemned prisoners are a dictinct people; whoever
is cast amongst them must expect to be treated as an
enemy as long as he will not speak their language and
will not identify himself with their way of thinking.

The abuses I have mentioned are not the only ones;
there are others even more terrible. If a prisoner
were marked out as a false brother or as a sneak, he
was pitilessly knocked on the head, without any jailor
interfering to prevent it.   Matters came to such a
pitch, that it was necessary to assign a particular division to those individuals, who, giving an account of
their own doings had made any mention of their com-

rades which they thought could in any way compromise them. On the other hand the impudence of the
robbers, and the immorality of their keepers, were carried to such an extent, that they prepared openly in
the prison tricks of swindling and theft, which were
to be perpetrated on quitting the walls of the prison.
I will mention only one of these plans, which will suffice to evince the measure of credulity of the dupes
and the audacity of the plotters. These latter obtained
the address of certain rich persons living in the province, which was easy from the number of prisoners
who were constantly arriving. They then wrote
letters to them, called, in the slang language, ' letters
of Jerusalem,' and which contained in substance what
follows. It is useless to observe that the names
of places and persons change according to circumstances.

" Sir,—You will doubtlessly be astonished at receiving a letter from a person unknown to you, who is
about to ask a favour from you; but from the sad
condition in which I am placed, I am lost if some honourable person will not lend me succour: that is the
reason of my addressing you, of whom I have heard so
much that I cannot for a moment hesitate to confide
all my affairs to your kindness. As valet-de-chambre
to the marquis de ———— I emigrated with my master,
and that we might avoid suspicion we travelled on
foot and I carried the luggage, consisting of a casket
containing 16,000 francs in gold and the diamonds of
the late marchioness. We were on the point of joining the army at ————, when we were marked out
and pursued by a detachment of volunteers. The marquis, seeing how closely we were pressed, desired me
to throw the casket into a deep ditch near us, so that
it might not implicate us in case we were apprehended.
I relied on recovering it the following night; but the
country people, aroused by the tocsin which the commandant of the detachment ordered to be rung, began
to beat the wood in which we were concealed, with

so much vigour, that it was necessary to think only of escape. On reaching a foreign province, the marquis received some advances from the prince of ———; but these resources soon failing, he resolved on sending me back for the casket thrown into the ditch. I was the more certain of finding it, as on the day after I had thrown it from me, we had made a written memorandum of the localities, in case we should be for any length of time without being able to return for it. I set out, and entering France, reached the village of ——— without accident, near the spot where we had been pursued. You must know the village perfectly, as it is not three quarters of a league from your residence. I prepared to fulfil my mission, when the landlord of the auberge where I had lodged, a bitter jacobin and collector of national property, remarking my embarrassment when he proposed to drink to the health of the republic, had me apprehended as a suspected person : and as I had no passport, and unfortunately resembled an individual pursued for stopping the diligences, I was taken from prison to prison to be confronted with my pretended accomplices, until on reaching Bicêtre I was obliged to go to the infirmary, where I have been for two months.

" In this cruel situation, having heard mention of you by a relation of my master's, who had property in your district, I beg to know if I cannot, through your aid, obtain the casket in question and get a portion of the money which it contains. I could then supply my immediate necessities and pay my counsel, who dictates this, and assures me that by some presents, I could extricate myself from this affair.

" Receive, sir, &c.
(Signed) " N———."

Out of one hundred such letters, twenty were always answered : and astonishment will cease when we consider that they were only addressed to men known by their attachment to the old order of things, and that no-

M

thing reasons less than the spirit of party. It testified besides, to the person addressed, that unlimited confidence which never fails to produce its effect on self-love or interest; the person answered that he would agree to undertake to get the casket from its place of concealment. Another letter from the pretended valet-de-chambre stating, that being entirely stripped, he had agreed with the keeper of the infirmary for a very small sum to sell the trunk, in which was, in the false bottom, the plan already alluded to. Then the money arrived, and they received sums sometimes amounting to twelve or fifteen hundred francs. Some individuals, thinking to give a profound proof of sagacity, came even from the remotest parts of their province to Bicêtre, where they received the destined plan which was to conduct them to this mysterious forest, which, like the fantastic forests of the romances of chivalry, fled eternally before them. The Parisians themselves sometimes fell into the snare: and some persons may still remember the adventure of the clothseller of the Rue des Prouvaires, who was caught undermining an arch of the Pont Neuf, where he expected to find the diamonds of the duchess de Bouillon.

We may imagine that such manœuvres could not be effected but by the consent and with the participation of the keepers, since they received the correspondence of the treasure-seekers. But the jailor thought, that independently of the direct benefit he thence drew from it, by the increase of the money spent by the prisoners in viands and spirits, they being thus occupied would not think of escaping. On the same principle he tolerated the making varieties of things in straw, wood, and bone, and even false pieces of two sous, with which Paris was at one time inundated. There were also other crafts exercised; but these were done clandestinely: they made privately false passports with the pen, so well done as to pass currently, saws for cutting iron, and false hair, which were of great service in escaping from the Bagne—the galley-slaves being particularly recognizable by their shorn heads.   These various articles were concealed in tin-cases, which could be hid in the intestines.

As for me, always occupied with the idea of escaping from the Bagne and reaching a sea-port whence I could embark, I was night and day plotting the means of getting away from Bicêtre.   I at length imagined that by breaking through the quadrangle of Fort-Mahon and reaching the water-courses made under it, we might, by means of a short mine get into the court of the ideots I have before alluded to, whence there would be no difficulty in reaching the outside.   This project was executed in ten days and as many nights. During the whole time the prisoners, of whom we had any distrust, were always accompanied by a trusty man ; but we were obliged to wait until the moon should be on the wane.   At length, on the 3rd of October 1797, at two o'clock in the morning, we descended the water-course, thirty-three in number, provided with dark lanthorns, and we soon opened the subterranean passage and reached the court of the ideots. We wanted a ladder, or something instead of it, to climb the walls : and at last got hold of a long pole, and we were going to draw lots to decide who should first climb up, when a noise of chains suddenly broke the silence of night.

A dog came out from a kennel placed in an angle of the court; we stood motionless and held our breath, for it was an important moment.   After having stretched himself out and yawned, as if he had only wanted to change place, the animal put one foot into his kennel as if about to return, and we then thought ourselves saved.   Suddenly he turned his head to the place in which we were huddled together, and fixed on us two eyes which looked like burning coals.   A low growling was then followed with barkings which sounded all over the place.   Desfosseux wished to try and cut his throat, but he was of a size to render the issue of a contest doubtful.   It appeared best to us to lie down in a large open space, which served as a walking ground for the ideots; but the dog still kept up the concert, and his colleagues having joined him the din became so excessive that the inspector Giroux, fancying something particular was passing amongst his lodgers, and knowing his customers, began his round by Fort-Mahon, and almost fell backwards at finding no one. At his cries the jailor, turnkeys, and guard, all assembled. They soon discovered the road we had taken, and taking the same to get into the court of the ideots, they loosened the dog, who ran straight at us. The guards then entered the place where we were with fixed bayonets, as if about to carry a redoubt. They put handcuffs on us, the usual prelude of any important matter to be done in a prison; and we then returned, not to Fort-Mahon, but to the dungeon without however experiencing any bad treatment.

This attempt, the boldest of which the prison had for a long time been the theatre, threw the keepers into so much confusion that it was two days before they perceived that one of the prisoners of Fort-Mahon was missing: it was Desfosseux. Knowing all his address I thought him at a distance, when, on the morning of the third day, I saw him enter my dungeon pale, exhausted, and bleeding. When the door was closed on him he told me all his adventure.

At the moment when the guard had seized us, he had squatted down in a sort of tub, probably used for baths, and hearing no noise, he had left his retreat: and the pole had aided him in climbing several walls: but yet he always got back to the ideot's court. Day was just breaking, 'and he heard footsteps going and coming in the buildings, for they are nowhere earlier than in hospitals. It was necessary to avoid the gaze of the turnkey, who would soon be in the courts: the wicket of a room was half open—he glided in, and was about with much precaution to roll himself in a large heap of straw; but what was his astonishment to see it occupied by a man naked, his hair dishevelled, beard long, and eye haggard and bloodshot. The madman, for such he was, looked at Desfosseux with a fierce air, then made him a quick sign : and as he stood still, darted at him as if to attack him. A few caresses seemed to appease him : he took Desfosseux by the hand and made him sit down beside him, heaping all the straw round him in the manner and with the gestures of a monkey. At eight o'clock a morsel of black bread fell in at the door, which he took up, looked at, threw into a heap of dirt, and then picked it up and began to eat. During the day more bread was brought ; but as the madman was asleep Desfosseux seized and devoured it, at the risk of being himself devoured by his terrible companion, who might have been enraged at the abstraction of his pittance. At twilight the madman awoke, and talked for some time with inconceivable volubility ; night came on and his excitement sensibly increased, and he began to leap about and make hideous contortions, shaking his chains with a kind of pleasure.

In this appalling situation Desfosseux waited with impatience until the madman fell asleep to go out at the wicket. About midnight, hearing him move no longer, he advanced first one leg and then the other, when he was seized by the madman with a powerful grasp, who threw him on the straw and placed himself before the wicket, where he remained till daylight motionless as a statue. The next night another attempt, and another obstacle. Desfosseux, who grew distracted, employed his strength, and a tremendous struggle ensued: Desfosseux, being struck by his chains, and covered with bites and blows, was compelled to call for the keepers. They mistaking him at first for one of the madmen who had got loose, were also about to put him in a cell; but he managed to make himself known, and at length obtained the favour of being brought back to us.

We remained eight days in the dungeon, after which

I was put in the Chaussée, where I found a party of prisoners who had received me so well on my arrival. They were making good cheer and denied themselves nothing : for, independently of the money procured by the ' letters of Jerusalem,' they had got a supply from some females whom they knew, and who constantly visited them. Having become, as at Douai, the object of special vigilance, I still sought to escape : when at length the day arrived for the departure of the chain.

CHAPTER VIII.

The departure of the chain—Captain Viez and his lieutenant Thierry—The complaint of the galley-slaves—The visit from Paris—Humanity of the galley-serjeants—They encourage|plundering—The loaf converted into a portmanteau—Useless attempt to escape—The Bagne at Brest—The benedictions.

IT was the 20th of November 1797: all the morning we remarked a more than usual commotion in the prison. The prisoners had not left their cells, and the gates were every moment opened and shut with much noise : the jailors went to and fro with a busy air, and they were knocking off irons, in the great court, of which the sound reached our ears. About eleven o'clock two men clothed in blue uniforms entered Fort-Mahon, where for eight days I had been replaced with the companions of my essay to escape : it was the captain of the chain and his lieutenant. " Well," said the captain, smiling in a kind of familiar way, " have we any return horses (fugitive galley-slaves) ?" And whilst he spoke all pressed about, trying who should testify most respect to him. " Good day, M. Viez; good day, M. Thierry," resounded from all sides. These salutations were even repeated by the

prisoners who had never seen either Viez or Thierry,
but who assuming an air of acquaintance, hoped to
get some favour. It was no wonder if Viez was a
little giddy with so much applause; but as he was accustomed to these homages, it did not quite turn his
brain, and he knew very well what he was about. He
perceived Desfosseux. "Ah! ah!" said he, "here
is a darby cutter (one skilled in cutting off his chains),
who has travelled before with us. I heard that you
had a narrow escape of being a head shorter (guillotined) at Douai, my boy. You escaped well by
Jove; for, look you, it is better to go back to the
meadow (Bagne) than let the executioner play at
pitch and toss with your knowledge-box (head). Besides, my lads, let the world be quiet, and we shall get
beef and celery." The captain had only begun his
inspection and continued it, addressing similar jokes to
all his "merchandize," for by that name he called the
condemned prisoners.

The critical moment arrived, and we went into the
Cours des Fers, where the house-surgeon came to us
to examine if we were all in a state to bear the fatigues
of the journey. We were all pronounced adequate,
although some were in a most woful plight. Each
prisoner then puts off the prison livery and assumes
his own clothes; those who have none have a frock
and trousers of packing-cloth, insufficient to protect
them from the cold and damp. Hats and clothes, if at
all decent belonging to the prisoners, are torn in a
particular way to prevent escape; they take for instance the border off the hat and the collar from the
coat. No prisoner is allowed to retain more than six
francs; the overplus is given to the captain, who gives
it on the route in proportion as it is needed. This precaution is easily eluded by placing louis in large sous
hollowed out.

These preliminaries adjusted, we went into the great
court where were the guards of the chain, better
known as argousins, or galley serjeants, who were for

the most part men of Auvergne, water-carriers, messengers, or coalmen, who carried on their trade in the
intervals between the journeys. In the midst of them
was a large wooden chest containing the fetters which
are used in all similar expeditions. We were made to
approach two and two, taking care to match us in
height, by means of a chain of six feet in length, united
to the cordon of twenty-six prisoners, who could thus
only move in a body; each was confined to the chain by
a sort of iron triangle, called the cravat, which, opening
on one side by a turning screw, is closed on the other
with a nail firmly rivetted. This is the most perilous
part of the operation; the most turbulent and riotous
then keep quiet; for, at the least movement, instead of
falling on the anvil, the blows would break their skull,
which every stroke of the hammer grazes. Then a
prisoner comes with long scissars and cuts off the hair
and whiskers of the prisoners, pretending to leave
them irregular.

At five in the evening, the fettering was finished;
the argousins retired, and the prisoners alone remained.
Left to themselves, far from despairing, these men gave
themselves up to all the tumults of riotous gaiety. Some
vociferated horrible jokes, echoed from all sides with
the most disgusting shouts; others amused themselves
by provoking the stupid laughter of their companions
by beastly gestures. Neither the ears, nor the modesty
were even spared, all that was heard or seen was im-
moral and discordant. It is too true that once loaded
with fetters, the condemned thinks himself obliged to
trample under foot all that is honoured and respected
by the society which has cast him off; there are for
him no longer any restraints, but from material obstacles; his charter is the length of his chain, and he
knows no law but the stick to which his jailor accus-
toms him. Thrown amidst beings, to whom nothing is
sacred, he takes care how he testifies that steady resignation which betokens repentance; for then he
would be the butt of a thousand jokes, and his keepers,

troubled at his serious mood, would accuse him of meditating some plot. It is best, if he would keep them unsuspicious of his intentions, that he should always appear reckless and abandoned. A prisoner who sports with his destiny is never an object of mistrust; the experience of the greater part of the wretched beings who have escaped from the Bagnes prove this. What is certain is, that with us, those who had the greatest interest in escaping were the least dejected; they were the leaders. When night came on, they began to sing. Imagine fifty scoundrels, the greater part drunk, all screeching different airs. In the midst of this din a " return horse" thundered out with the lungs of a Stentor, some couplets of " The Galley Slave's Complaint."

> " The chain, the chain,
>   Makes us complain;
>   But never mind,
>   We may leave it behind.

> " Our coats are of a scarlet hue,
>   We wear no hats on our head
>   But caps, and they've taken our cravats too,
>   And left us queer ties instead.
>   'Tis true we are spoil'd children,
>   And have no right to complain;
>   And for fear of losing us, now and then,
>   They fasten us with a chain.

> " Oh, we will make articles fine and nice,
>   In wood, in straw, in wax,
>   And sell them below the market price,
>   For our shops will pay no tax.
>   And those who come to see our toys
>   Will purchase every day,
>   And the produce of our hands, my boys,
>   Will moisten well our clay.

*   *   *   *   *   *

"Then comes the time to fill the paunch,
    Bring in the beans so white !
They're not so good as a fine plump haunch,
    But we lack not appetite.
How much more wretched had been our lot,
    If, like many a jolly cadet,
Instead of the galleys, we'd chanc'd to 've got,
    To the abbey of Mont-a-r'gret."

All our companions were not so happy ; in the third cordon, composed of the least disorderly, we heard sobs, saw tears flowing; but these symptoms of grief, or of repentance, were hailed by the shouts and threats of the two other cordons, where I figured in the first rank as a dangerous fellow, from my address and influence.   I had near me two men, one a schoolmaster condemned for rape; and the other, an ex-officer of health, sentenced for forging, who, without mirth or melancholy talked together with a very calm and natural tone.

"We are going to Brest," said the schoolmaster.

"Yes," answered the officer of health, "we are going to Brest ; I know the country, I passed through it when I was sub aide-de-camp in the 16th brigade—a good country, upon my word—I shall not be sorry to see it again.

"Is there much amusement?" asked the pedagogue.

"Amusement!" said his companion, with an air of astonishment.

"Yes, amusement—I ask you, if we can procure any little pleasure if we are well treated,—if provisions are cheap."

"In the first place, you will be taken care of," replied the officer, "and well taken care of, for at the Bagne at Brest, only two hours are needed to find all the beans in the soup, while at Toulon the search would take eight days."

Here the conversation was interrupted by loud cries, proceeding from the second division.   They were

knocking on the head three prisoners, the ex-commis-
sary of war, Lemière, the staff-major, Simon, and a
robber named the Petit Matelot (little sailor), who were
accused of having betrayed their comrades by information, or of having defeated some plot in prison. The
person who had pointed them out to the vengeance of
the galley-slaves, was a young man, who would have
been a good study for a painter, or an actor. With
dilapidated green slippers, a hunting waistcoat, destitute of buttons, and nankeen pantaloons, which seemed
to defy the inclemency of the weather; his head dress
was a helmet without a peak, through the holes of
which a tattered night-cap was visible. In the Bicêtre,
he was only known by the name of 'mademoiselle,' and
I learnt that he was one of those degraded wretches,
who abandoned, in Paris, to a course of the most infamous prostitution, find at the Bagne a theatre
worthy of the most disgusting debaucheries. The argousins, who ran at the first noise, did not give themselves the least trouble to get the Petit Matelot from
the hands of the galley slaves, and he died four days
afterwards of the blows he had received. Lemière and
Simon would also have perished but for my interference; I had known the former when in the roving
army, where he had rendered me some service. I declared that it was he who had supplied me with the
tools necessary for undermining the walls at Fort-
Mahon, and thenceforward they left him and his companion unmolested.

We passed the night on the stones in a church, then
converted into a magazine. The argousins made regular rounds, to assure themselves that no one was
engaged in fiddling (sawing their fetters). At daybreak
we were all on foot; the lists were read over, and the
fetters examined. At six o'clock we were placed in
long cars, back to back, the legs hanging down outside,
covered with hoar frost and motionless from cold. On
reaching St Cyr, we were entirely stripped, to undergo
a scrutiny which extended to our stockings, shoes,

shirt, mouth, ears, nostrils, &c. &c. It was not only the files in cases which they sought, but also for watch springs, which enable a prisoner to cut his fetters in less than three hours. This examination lasted for upwards of an hour, and it is really a miracle that one half of us had not our noses or feet frozen off with cold. At bed-time, we were heaped together in a cattle stall, where we laid so close that the body of one served for the pillow of the person who laid nearest to him, and if any individual got entangled in his own, or any other man's chain, a heavy cudgel rained down a torrent of blows on the hapless offender. As soon as we had laid down on a few handfulls of straw, which had already been used for the litter of the stable, a whistle blew to command us to the most absolute silence, which was not allowed to be disturbed by the least complaint, even when, to relieve the guard placed at the extremity of the stable, the argousins actually walked over our bodies.

The supper consisted of a pretended bean soup, and a few morsels of half mouldy bread. The distribution was made from large wooden troughs, containing thirty rations; and the cook, armed with a large pot ladle, did not fail to repeat to each prisoner, as he served him, " One, two, three, four, hold out your porringer, you thief;" the wine was put into the same trough from which the soup and meat were served out, and then an argousin, taking a whistle, hanging to his button-hole, blew it thrice; saying, " Attention, robbers, and only answer by a yes or a no. Have you had bread?"—" Yes." " Soup?"—"Yes." "Meat?" —" Yes." Wine?"—"Yes." " Then go to sleep, or pretend to do so."

A table was laid out at the door, at which the captain, lieutenant, and chief argousins, seated themselves to take a repast superior to ours; for these men, who profitted by all occasions to extort money from the prisoners, took excellent care of themselves, and eat and drank abundantly. At this moment the stable offered one of the most hideous spectacles that can be imagined; on one side were a hundred and twenty men herded together like foul beasts, rolling about their haggard eyes, whence fatigue or misery banished sleep; on the other side, eight ill-looking fellows were eating greedily without, not for one moment, losing sight of their carbines or their clubs. A few miserables candles affixed to the blackened walls of the stable, cast a murky glare over this scene of horror, the silence of which was only broken by stifled groans, or the clank of fetters. Not content with striking us indiscriminately, the argousins made their detestable and brutal witticisms about the prisoners; and if a man, fevered with thirst, asked for water, they said to him, " Let him who wants water put out his hand." The wretch obeyed, mistrusting nothing, and was instantly overwhelmed with blows. Those who had any money were necessarily careful; they were but very few, the long residence of the majority in prison having for the most part exhausted their feeble resources.

These were not the only abuses which mark the progress of the galley chain. To economize to his own profit the expenses of the journey, the captain generally made one of the cordons to go on foot. But this cordon was always that of the strongest men, that is, the most turbulent of the condemned. Wo to the females whom they met, or the shops which they came near. The women were assaulted in the grossest manner, and the shops stripped in a twinkling, as I saw, at Morlaix, at a grocer's, who did not save even a loaf of sugar, or a pound of soap. It may be asked, what the guards were about during the commission of this offence ? The guards were pretending to be very busily preventing it, but without opposing any real obstacle to it, knowing that they would ultimately profit by the plunder, since the prisoners must sell their booty through their medium, or exchange with them for strong liquors. It was the same with the thefts made on the prisoners who were added to the chain in its passage; scarcely were they ironed, when their neighbours hustled them, and took from them all the little sums they might have.

Far from preventing or checking these spoliations, the argousins even suggested them, as I saw them do with an ex-gendarme who had sewed up a few louis in his leather breeches. "Here is some fat!" said they, and in less than three minutes, the poor devil was pennyless. At such times the party attacked call out loudly for the argousins, who take good care not to approach until the robbery be perfected, and they thump, with heavy cudgels, the poor wretch who has been plundered. At Rennes, the bandits I am speaking of carried their infamy to such an extent, as to despoil a sister of charity, who had brought us some tobacco and money, in a stall where we were to pass the night. The most crying of these abuses have disappeared, but many yet exist, which it will be difficult to root out, if we consider to what sort of men the conducting of the chain must be entrusted, and the materials they have to work upon.

Our toilsome journey endured for twenty-four days, and on reaching Pont-a-Lezen, we were placed in the depôt of the Bagne, when the prisoners perform a kind of quarantine, until they have recovered from their fatigue and it has been ascertained whether they have any contagious disease. On our arrival we were washed in pairs, in large tubs filled with warm water, and on quitting the bath our clothes were allotted to us. I received like the others, a red frock or cassock, two pair of trowsers, two sail cloth shirts, two pair of shoes, and a green cap; each garment and article was marked with the initials GAL, and the cap had besides a tin plate, on which was the number of the entry in the register. When they had given us our clothing, they rivetted an iron ring round the leg, but did not couple us.

The depôt of Pont-a-Lezen, being a sort of lazaretto, there was not a very rigorous vigilance kept up. I

was even told that it was easy to get out of the rooms
and climb the outside walls.   I learnt this from a man
named Blondy, who had once escaped this way from the
Bagne at Brest, and hoping to profit by this information,
I made arrangements to avail myself of the first opportunity. We sometimes had loaves given to us, weighing
eighteen pounds each, and on quitting Morlaix, I had
hollowed out one of these and filled it with a shirt, a
pair of trowsers, and some handkerchiefs.   It was a
new kind of portmanteau, and passed unsuspected.
Lieutenant Thierry had not given me to a special
watch, on the contrary, having learnt the grounds of
my condemnation, he had told the commissary, when
speaking of me, that with men as orderly as I was,
he could manage the chain as easily as a girls' school.
I had then inspired no mistrust, and looked about me
to execute my project.   I, at first, contemplated cutting through the wall of the room in which I was
placed.   A steel chisel left by accident on the foot of
my bed by a turnkey prisoner, who rivetted the ancle
cuffs, served me to make the opening, whilst Blondy
cut my irons.   This completed, my comrades made a
figure of straw, which they put in my place, to deceive the vigilance of the argousins on guard, and
soon, clothed in the garments I had concealed, I got
into the court-yard of the depôt.   The walls which
environed it were at least fifteen feet high, and to
climb them I found I must get something like a ladder,
a pole served as a proxy, but it was so heavy and so
long that it was impossible for me to drag it over the
wall, to aid my descent on the other side.   After many
trials, as vain as they were painful, I was compelled
to risk the leap, in which I succeeded so badly and
came down with so much violence on my legs that I
could scarcely drag myself into a bush that was near.
I hoped, that when the pain had somewhat abated, I
could escape before daybreak, but it became more excessive, and my feet swelled so prodigiously, that I
was compelled to give up all hopes of escape.   I

dragged myself along, as well as I was able, to the door
of the depôt, to return to my cell, thinking thereby
to diminish the number of blows which would be
assuredly bestowed upon me.   A sister whom I asked
for, and to whom I told all, had me conveyed into a
room where my feet were dressed.   This excellent
woman, who compassionated my lot, went to the commandant of the depôt, and obtained my pardon by her
solicitations, and at the end of three weeks, being
completely recovered, I was conveyed to Brest.

The Bagne is situated in the bosom of the bay;
piles of guns, and two pieces of cannon, mounted at
the gates, pointed out to me the entrance, into which
I was introduced, after having been examined by the
two guards of the establishment.   The boldest of the
condemned, however hardened, have confessed that
it is impossible to express the emotions of horror excited by the first appearance of this abode of wretchedness.   Each room containing twenty night camp
couches, called bancs (benches), on which lie six
hundred fettered convicts, in long rows, with red garbs,
heads shorn, eyes haggard, dejected countenances,
whilst the perpetual clank of fetters conspires to fill
the soul with horror.   But this impression on the convict soon passes away, who feeling that here he has
no cause to blush at the presence of any one, soon
identifies himself with his situation.   That he may not
be the butt of the gross jests and filthy buffoonery of
his fellows, he affects to participate in them; he even
exceeds them; and soon in tone and gesture this conventional depravity gets hold of his heart.   Thus, at
Anvers, an ex-bishop experienced, at first, all the out-
pourings of the riotous jokes of his companions; they
always addressed him as monseigneur, and asked his
blessing in all their obscenities; at every moment
they constrained him to profane his former character
by blasphemous words, and by dint of reiterating these
impieties, he contrived to shake of their attacks; at a
subsequent period he became the public-house keeper,

at the Bagne, and was always styled monseigneur, but he was no longer asked for absolution, for he would have answered with the grossest blasphemies.

It is on days of rest, particularly, that the recital of crimes often imaginary, of close connexions, and infamous compliances, complete the corruption of a man, whose punishment for a first fault exposes him to this pernicious contact. To prevent this, it has been in contemplation to do away with the system of Bagnes altogether. At first, opinion was unanimous on this point, but when a substitution of punishment became the matter in question, plans were very variously sketched out; some proposed penitentiaries, like those of Switzerland and the United States; others, and these are the majority, have advocated colonization, adducing the happy results, and prosperity of the English establishments in New South Wales, better known as Botany Bay.

Let us see if France is in a condition to enjoy these happy results and this prosperity.

CHAPTER IX.

Of the colonization of the convicts.

" SEE, say the partisans of colonization, see the flourishing report of New South Wales, it is only forty years since the English began to send convicts there, and already the country contains five cities; arts and luxury are cultivated, and printing is established. At Sydney Cove, the capital of the colony, there are philosophical and agricultural societies; a catholic and two methodist chapels. Although the greater part of the planters and under-magistrates are freed convicts, or those who have undergone

their sentence, yet all conduct themselves well and become excellent citizens. Women, the disgrace and
refuse of their sex in the metropolis, women already
mothers, but covering with opprobrium all that
pertained to them, are now, with new connexions,
models of sobriety and chastity. There is another
argument to be adduced in support of this system,
which has importance. The labour of the convicts
in England, competing with that of a number of regular and free workmen, has a mischievous tendency
in leaving the latter without work, and consequently
increase the numbers thrown on the parish for support; thus, instead of being productive, their labour is
injurious. In New South Wales, on the contrary, far
from rivalling the English workman, the transport
consumes his productions, since only English manu-
factures are admitted there. The importation amounts
to three hundred and fifty thousand pounds sterling,
and the exportation of indigenous productions is calculated at a third of this sum; a decided argument in
favour of colonization, and we may ask what prevents France from participating in so advantageous a
system?"

This is doubtlessly very grand, but will it be per-
manent? Can we draw the inference that it will be
equally applicable to France? To the first question, I
will say that, in England, they are scarcely more unanimous on the subject than we are as to the advantages of colonizing convicts in general, and as to
the results of the colonies of New South Wales, in
particular. Independently of every other consideration, however, they afford to British commerce most
valuable stations between India, China, the isles of
Junda, and all the oriental Archipelago. Such advantages, which might perhaps have been obtained
without having recourse to colonization, do not appear
however to compensate for the enormous expenses
which have at first occurred, and which continue still,
to the detriment of the nation; the government having,

for some years, had to support a number, varying from eight to ten thousand convicts, whom they are unable to employ usefully. This fact perfectly accounts for the proposition submitted to the House of Commons, to send out to New South Wales, and its auxiliary establishments, Irish emigrants; the poor's rates would proportionally decrease, and the emigrant planters would employ the transports, who by clearing away and preparations, would have paved the way for establishing themselves.

In the meantime, until the determination of government, the unemployed convicts lead, according to their own statements, a very agreeable life, since on a recent enquiry it has been found that many individuals have purposely committed an offence punishable by transportation, that they might be sent out to the colony. Humanity will certainly approve such results, if mildness soothes the manners of the convicts, but we know that idleness only increases bad inclinations, and this is proved from the return to vicious courses of those who return to England on the expiration of their sentence. Their amendment is scarcely more perceptible at the colony, for it is well known that of the three chapels, built at Sidney Cove, they have burnt two, with the intention of frustrating the order which constrains them to attend divine service.

The women, who are represented as purified by the change of hemisphere, testify for the greater part a sort of libertinism, incited in some measure by the vast numerical disproportion of the two sexes, which is as fourteen males for one female. Marriage with a convict, pardoned or freed, procuring them immediate liberty, the first thing sought by the women on their arrival at the depôt of Paramatta, is to get married to a man in these circumstances. They thus often get hold of an old man; a wretch, whom they leave after a few days, and return to Sydney, where they can freely abandon themselves to any species of excess. The result is, that surrounded by corrupt examples,

the females who are born from this promiscuous connexion prostitute themselves at a very tender age.

From these facts, accidentally elicited by inquiries
into the state of the country by parliamentary dis-
cussions, it results, that colonization is far from
influencing, as has been unfoundedly believed, the
morals of the convicts ; and it is besides now decided
that it would be almost impracticable for France.
The first and most potent objection is, the entire want
of a fitting place for transportation ; for to form an
establishment at Sainte-Marie de Madagascar, the only
one of the French possessions at all suitable for such
an object, would be sending to almost certain death, not
only the convicts, but the governors and guards.   The
small number of those whom the climate would not
have destroyed, would not fail to seize on the sta-
tionary vessels, turn pirates, as has been frequently
the case at New South Wales; and, instead of a peni-
tentiary establishment, we should find that we had
only formed a new horde of buccaniers.   Again, it is
impossible to think of sending the convicts to any of
our colonies, not even to Guyana, where the vast
savannahs would not be sufficient to secure an
indispensable isolation; and escapes would be soon
multiplied, and the colonists would call to mind the
lesson given, it is said, by Franklin to the English
government, who at that period were sending the
convicts to the United States.   It is asserted that
immediately on the arrival of a transport at Boston,
he sent to the minister, Walpole, four boxes of rattle-
snakes, begging him to set them free in Windsor park,
" so that," he said, " the species might be propagated
and become as advantageous to England as the convicts had been to North America."

Even at the present day, escapes at New South
Wales are more general than may be thought; and
this is proved by a passage from a narrative published
in London by a liberated convict, who, without heed-
ing how much he might compromise the reputation of

the establishment, was soon apprehended for committing fresh offences.

" When the termination of my exile had arrived, I had determined on quitting the colony; I embarked as servant to a gentleman and lady, formerly convicts, who had amassed sufficient to pay their expenses to England and settle there. It may be thought that my mind was quite satisfied and at ease, but this was not the case. I was never more disturbed nor more uneasy than at the moment when I embarked on board this vessel, and for this reason : I had clandestinely brought away with me six convicts, old companions of mine, and concealed them in the hold of the ship. They were men for whom I had a particular esteem; and it is the duty of a convict who leaves the land of exile never to leave a friend behind him if he can contrive the means of aiding his escape. What incessantly disturbed me was the necessity of providing for the wants of these men; and to do this I was obliged to turn thief again; so that from one moment to another I rendered myself and them liable to detection. Every evening I was obliged to visit the provisions of each person, and carry the produce of my thefts to them.

" There were a great many passengers on board, and I made each contribute in his turn, that it might be the less sensibly felt, and be the longer time of service to me. In spite of my precautions, I often heard them say one to the other, that their provisions went fast and they could not discover how. What most embarrassed me was the raw meat, which however my comrades were compelled to devour; and sometimes I could not get any, particularly when the moon shone brightly, and then I was compelled to steal a double allowance of bread. My master having desired me to cook for him and his wife, the opportunity was of course made profitable. If I made broth or a hash I took care to retain half, which took the road to the hold. All that I could get besides

went there too; for I frequented the cook's kitchen,
on whom I also constantly levied contributions.

" There was on board a friend of mine, a cooper,
who, having staid the time of his sentence, was returning like me to England. I had let him into my
confidence, and he served me greatly in my thefts on
the cook; for instance, he drew him on one side and
occupied him whilst I was carrying off something of
everything that came to hand. Besides the cooper,
there was a sailor on board who was also in the secret,
but who, as it will appear in the sequel, was a confidant too many.

" One Sunday, after we had been a month at sea,
the cooper and the sailor were talking together in the
forecastle, when a dispute arose about some trifle. I
was at the moment trying to open a chest to get some
provisions from it. when the sailor, who had left the
cooper, came up to me. Deceived by the darkness of
the night, for it was about nightfall, and taking me for
some other person, he struck me on the shoulder,
saying, ' Where is the captain?' I answered him,
and on recognizing me, he ran into the captain's cabin
crying with all his might, ' Murder! murder! we are
all lost! The ship will be taken; there are ten men
concealed in the hold, and so and so (meaning me and
the cooper) are in the plot; they want to murder us
and make off with the ship!'

" The captain, immediately calling his mate, went
with him on deck, and ordered all hands to assemble
there. When we had all met, the sailor again pointed
out me and the cooper as the principals in the plot,
asserting that there were ten men in the hold. They
went down with lights, but returned without discovering anything, so well had my men concealed themselves. At length, the captain not liking to be defeated,
determined on filling the hold with smoke, and the
poor devils were compelled to come out for fear of
being choked. On getting on deck they cut a most
miserable figure, for since their departure from Sydney

Cove they had neither been shaved nor washed, and their clothes were in rags. What made the sight still more wretched was, that the night was dark, and the deck was illuminated by a solitary lanthorn.

" The captain began by putting fetters on the new comers; then, after having questioned them, and being assured that there were only six of them, he made them lie down without food on the deck. The second act of the piece consisted in treating the cooper and myself in a similar manner. When we were all together, they threw a large sail over us, like a net, and thus we passed the night. The next day, early, we went below, one after the other, with a rope round our waists, to the bottom of the hold, and were put in a hole so dark that we could not see each other. We were left there on the bare plank, and for food we had a pint of water and a pound of biscuit daily. We received this distribution without seeing it; for the sailor who brought it to us announced his arrival by a cry to us to extend our hands; and on receiving this pittance we divided it amongst us entirely in the dark.

" We were kept in this situation for forty mortal days, that is, until the ship reached the Cape of Good Hope, where she was to touch. The captain went to the governor to announce to him that he had some fugitive convicts on board, and to ask whether he could not disembark them, and have them confined in the prison of Cape Town; but the governor said he would have nothing to do with such people, and would not allow them to be landed. However, the captain soon consoled himself for this, on learning that there was an Irish ship in the harbour laden with convicts for Botany Bay. He made an arrangement with the captain of this ship, and induced him to take my poor comrades with him. They were taken from their dungeon for this purpose, and I never saw them again."

The obstacles which I have mentioned are so serious that I shall not touch on the consequences of a naval war on the spot, intercepting all communication and all conveyances. In aid of the pursuits of science, we have seen belligerent powers afford a free passage to naturalists and mathematicians, but it may be doubted whether, for the sake of morals, the same favour would be shown to convicts, who might, after all, be only soldiers disguised.

Let us however for a moment admit that these obstacles are removed, and that transportation is possible, should it be perpetual for all convicts indifferently? Or should we go on the plan observed with the galley-slaves, by graduating the term of labour? In the first case, you would destroy all proportion between punishments and crimes; since the man who, according to this code would only have to serve a certain time at the galleys, would not see his country again any more than the man sentenced to transportation for life. In England, where the least period of sentence (seven years) is assigned as well to a robbery of twenty-four sous as for severe violence exercised against a magistrate, this disproportion exists; but it often palliates the severities of a legislation which punishes with death offences sentenced by us only to imprisonment. So, at the English assizes it is no uncommon thing to hear a prisoner, after sentence of transportation has been passed upon him, say, " Thank'ye, my lord."

If the transportation be not for life, we should fall into the delusion which the Counsels generally point out every year, by exclaiming against the mixing of the liberated convicts with the people. Our freed transports would return to society with nearly the same vices that they had contracted at the Bagne. All tends to confirm the idea that they would be more incorrigible than the transported Englishman, whom a national spirit for travelling and colonization frequently attaches to the soil where he has been transplanted.

Considering, then, colonization as nearly impossible,

it only remains to ameliorate, as much as possible, the
morals of the convicts; to introduce to the Bagnes
reforms pointed out by experience. The first would
consist in classing the convicts according to their
dispositions; and for that it would be necessary to
consult not only their present behaviour, but also
their previous conduct and acquaintance; a point not
at all considered at the Bagnes, where the only thought
is how to prevent escape. Men disposed to amend
might obtain those little indulgences now bestowed on
the most daring thieves—on convicts sentenced for
life, whom they favour that they may not think of
means of escape. It would, in fact, be proper to
abridge the punishments, to effect the improvement of
the prisoners; for the man whom a stay of six months
at the Bagne would correct, would leave it at the end
of five years entirely depraved.

Another precaution taken with those convicts who
have many years to labour is, that of coupling them
with those who have only a short sentence to undergo.
They think thus to give them watchmen, who, unaccustomed to blows of the stick, and fearing to prolong
their detention by being suspected as accomplices,
would tell of the least attempt at escape. It follows,
that the novice, yoked with the perfect villain, would
be soon corrupted. On the days of rest, when the
prisoners are not chained to the benches till evening,
he necessarily follows his companion into the society
of other bandits, who complete his degradation by
testifying whatever the passions can produce that is
most atrocious and appalling. I am understood. But
is it not disgraceful, to see publicly organised a prostitution which, even in the midst of great cities, shrinks
from the general eye into the shades of mystery?
Why are not these disgusting excesses prevented, by
shutting up in solitary confinement the young men
who are usually the victims reserved to figure in these
horrible Saturnalia.

It is also indispensably necessary to prevent the

abuses of ardent spirits, which excite the convicts to a state contrary to the calm so necessary for them to be kept in, if we would have reflection bring on repentance. We do not mean to say that they should be entirely separated, as is the case in the United States in some instances, but this can scarcely be put in force without inconvenience with men sentenced to hard labour; we must watch that the orders and regulations of the prison be properly carried into effect by the prisoners who receive them. At the same time that we should preserve the health of those unfortunates, we should prevent serious disorders. On the days of relaxation it often happens, that a convict, desirous of a debauch, pledges his allowance for a fortnight for the present advances of some comrades. He gets drunk and disorderly, and is accordingly beaten, and then reduced to water and bean soup, when he needs more nourishing provisions to support him. There are, besides, other modes of providing for these orgies, they rob the workshops, the magazines, and in the wood-yards. Some pilfer the copper-sheathing, of which they make six liard pieces, which they sell at a much lower price to the country people; others steal the tools with which the little toys are formed which are sold to visitors; others take logs of wood, which chopped into small pieces, go to the fires of the argousins, who are thus in a measure conciliated. I am told, that at the present day, this system has been reformed, and I am happy to hear it: all that I can say is, that when I was at Brest it was as " notorious as the sun at noon day," that no argousin ever bought fire-wood.

It is in the blacksmiths' workshops that the prisoners instruct each other in the art of forging false keys and other instruments for opening doors, such as ripping-chisels (cadets), pincers (monseigneurs), picklocks (rossignols), &c. &c. This objection is perhaps irremediable, in a port where ships are to be fitted out; but why should such workshops be allowed in prisons in the interior of the country? I will add, that the labour of the convicts, of whatever kind, is far from being as productive as that of free mechanics; but it is an abuse which it is nearly hopeless to think of eradicating or reforming. The cudgel may certainly compel the convict to work, because there is a decided difference between activity and rest; but no chastisement can awaken in the breast of the convict that instinctive ardour which alone accelerates labour, and directs it to perfection. Besides, government must consider as very insignificant the produce of a convict's daily work, since it is never alluded to in the budget or receipts of the state. The total expense of the galley-slaves (chiourmes), classed under its different heads, amounts to the sum of 2,718,900 francs (113,281*l.*); these are some of the expenses—

Dress of the prisoners .... 220,500 francs
Ditto freed convicts 23,012
Expenses for shoes and stockings... 72,900
Ditto for making fetters 11,250
Ditto of capture 7,000
Ditto of conveyance of chain 130,000

Then came the salaries of the clerks and officers, pay, clothing, allowance of the guard, &c.

To render these expenses really useful, and to pursue measures of amelioration, so long and loudly called for, and which can only be attained gradually, we cannot too strongly recommend to the guardians, that moderation of conduct which should not be departed from even in inflicting the severest punishment. I have seen the galley-guards goad the wretched convicts to desperation, by ill-treating them, as their humours might dictate; and as if to sport with their misery, one of these brutes would say to a new comer, " What is your name? I will wager that your name is Dust.—Well, my name is Wind, and I make the Dust fly;" and then bastinado him in a most severe manner. Many galley-guards have been assassinated for thus provoking the convict, and rous-

ing him to revenge that nothing will make him lose
sight of.

In the sequel of these Memoirs, I shall have occasion to return to this subject, when I touch on the
system of surveillance, which is a new punishment for
freed men.

The inconveniences and abuses that I have just
adverted to existed at the prison of Brest when I was
conducted thither, and were additional inducements to
make my sojourn as brief as possible. In such a situation, the first thing is to assure oneself of the discretion
of the comrade with whom we may be coupled. Mine
was a vine-cutter from Dijon, about thirty years old,
condemned to twenty-four years' labour for forcible
burglary; already half an ideot, misery and brutal
treatment had completely stupified him. Bowed beneath the stick, he seemed to have just preserved
the instinct of a monkey or a dog, and thus answered
the whistle of the galley-serjeants. He was of no use
to me, and I was compelled to look out for a mate who
would not fear or shrink from the perspective beatings
which are always liberally bestowed on convicts suspected of favouring, or even conniving at the escape of
a prisoner. To get rid of Bourguignon, I feigned
indisposition, and he was yoked to another, and when
I recovered, I was placed with a poor devil sentenced
to eight years labour for stealing chickens from a
church.

He had not entirely parted with his senses, and the
first time we were alone together, said to me—" Listen,
comrade; I can see you do not mean to live long at
the public expense—be frank with me, and you will
not lose by it." I told him that I intended to escape
at the first opportunity. " Well," said he, " I advise
you to bolt before the beasts of serjeants are quite
acquainted with your phiz;—but have you any cash?"
I told him that I had, and he then informed me that
he could procure me other habiliments, but that I must
buy a few utensils like one who meant to work out his

time quietly. These utensils were two wooden bowls, a wine keg, straps to support my fetters, and a small mattress stuffed with oakum. It was Thursday, the sixteenth day of my confinement at the Bagne, and on the Saturday evening I obtained sailor's clothes, which I immediately put on under my convict's frock. On paying the seller of them, I saw that he had about his wrists round cicatrices of deep burns, and I learnt, that being condemned to the gallies for life in 1776, he had been put to the torture at Rennes, without confessing the robbery of which he was accused. On the promulgation of the code of 1791, his sentence was commuted to twenty-four years' labour at the gallies.

The next day, my division went out, at the cannon's signal, to work at the pump, which was always in motion. At the wicket they examined, as usual, our manacles and clothing; knowing this practice, I had pasted over my sailor's garb a bladder painted flesh-colour. As I purposely left my frock and shirt open, none of the guards thought of examining me more closely, and I got out unsuspected. Arrived at this basin, I retired with my comrade behind a pile of planks, and my fetters having been cut the previous evening, soon yielded. Having got rid of these, I soon threw off my galley-frock and trowsers, and putting on under my leathern cap a wig which I had brought from Bicêtre, and having given my comrade the trifling recompense which I had promised him, I disappeared, cautiously gliding behind the piles of timber.

CHAPTER X.

The pursuit after the galley-slave—The village mayor—The
voice of blood—The hospital—Sister Françoise—Faublas the
second—The mother of robbers.

I PASSED through the wicket without difficulty, and
found myself in Brest, a place entirely unknown to
me; and the fear that my doubt as to what road I
should take might induce suspicion, increased my uneasiness.   At length, after a thousand ins and outs,
turnings and twistings, I reached the only gate of the
city, where was always stationed an old galley-guard,
named Lachique, who detected a convict by a look, a
motion, or turn; and what rendered his observations
more easy is, that whoever passes any time at the
Bagne, drags habitually and involuntarily that leg to
which the fetter has been fastened.   However, it was
necessary to pass this dreaded personage, who was
smoking very sedately, fixing his hawk's eye on all
who went in and came out.   I had been warned, and
determining to exercise all my effrontery, on getting
up to Lachique, I put down a pitcher of buttermilk,
which I had purchased to render my disguise the more
complete, and filling my pipe, I asked him for a light.
He gave it readily, and with all the courtesy he was
capable of, and after we had blown a few whiffs in each
others' faces, I left him and went on my way.
I went straight forward for three quarters of an
hour, when I heard the cannon shots which were fired
to announce the escape of a convict, so that the pea-
santry of the neighbourhood may be informed that
there is a reward of one hundred francs to be obtained
by the lucky individual who may apprehend the fugitive.
I saw many persons armed with guns and scythes scour
about the country, and beat every bush, and even the
smallest tufts of heath.   Some labourers appeared to
take their arms out with them as a precaution, for I

saw several quit their work with a gun which they took
out of a furrow. One of these latter passed near me
in a cross-road which I had taken on hearing the report
of the cannon, but they had no suspicion of me, for I
was clad very well, and my hat being off by reason of
the heat, they saw my hair curled, which could not
be the case with a convict.

I continued striking into all the bye-ways, and avoiding towns and detached houses. At twilight I met
two women whom I asked about the road, but they
answered me in a dialect which I did not comprehend,
but on showing them some money, and making signs
that I was hungry, they conducted me to a small village
to a cabaret, kept by the garde-champêtre (patrole),
whom I saw in the chimney nook, decorated with his
insignia of office. I was for a moment disturbed, but
soon recovering myself, I said I wished to speak to
the mayor. " I am he," said an old countryman with
a woollen cap and wooden shoes, seated at a small
table and eating an oaten cake. This was a fresh disappointment to me, who relied on escaping in my way
from the cabaret to the mayor's house. However, I
had the difficulty to contend with, and surpass in some
way or other. I told the wooden-shoed functionary,
that having lost myself on leaving Morlaix for Brest,
I had wandered about, and asking him at the same
time how far it was from this latter city, and expressing a desire to sleep there that evening.—" You are
five leagues from Brest," said he, " and it is impossible to reach it this evening; if you will sleep here, I
will give you a bed in my barn, and tomorrow you can
start with the garde-champêtre, who is going to carry
back a fugitive convict whom we apprehended yesterday."

These last words renewed all my terrors, for by
the tone in which they were uttered, I saw that the
mayor had not credited the whole of my story. I,
however, accepted his obliging offer; but after supper,
at the instant we reached the barn, putting my hands

in my pockets, I cried out with all the energy of a man in despair—" Oh, heavens! I have left at Morlaix my pocket-book, with my, passport and eight double louis. I must return this moment, yes, this very moment, but how shall I find my way? If the patrole, who knows the road, would go with me, we should be back in time in the morning to set out early with the galley-slave." This proposal routed all suspicions, for a man who wishes to escape seldom solicits the company he would fain avoid; on the other hand, the garde-champêtre, smelling a reward, had buttoned on his gaiters at the first word. We set out accordingly, and at break of day reached Morlaix. My companion, whom I had taken care to ply well with liquor on the road, was already pretty well in for it, and I completed him with some rum at the first pot-house we reached in the city. He staid there to wait for me at the table, or rather under the table, and he might have waited long enough.

I asked the first person I met to direct me on the road to Vannes, and on being told, I set out, as the Dutch proverb has it, " with my feet shod by fear." Two days passed without accident, but on the third, some leagues from Guemené, at a turning of the road, I met two gendarmes, who were returning from duty. The unexpected vision of yellow breeches and laced hats gave me uneasiness, and I made an effort to escape, when my two gentlemen desired me to halt, making at the same time a very significant gesture with their carbines. They came up to me, and having no credentials to show them, I invented a reply on the spur of the moment. " My name is Duval, born at l'Orient, deserter from the Cocarde frigate, now in the roadstead at St Malo." It is useless to say, that I had learnt all this during my stay at the Bagne, where we had daily accounts from all parts. " What!" cried the chief, " you must be Auguste—son of father Duval, who lives at l'Orient, on the terrace near the Boule d'or." I did not deny this, for it would have

been worse to have been detected as a fugitive convict.
" Parbleu !" added the brigadier, " I am sorry you are
caught, but that cannot now be helped; I must send
you to l'Orient or to St Malo." I begged him not to
send me to the former of these towns, not caring to be
confronted with my new relation, in case they should
desire to confirm the identity of my person. However, the quarter-master gave orders that I should be
conducted thither, and the next day I reached l'Orient,
when I was entered in the jailor's book, at Pontainau,
the naval prison, near the new Bagne, which was to be
peopled by convicts brought hither from Brest.

Being next day questioned by the commissary of the
marine, I again declared that I was Auguste Duval;
and that I had left my ship without permission, to go
and see my parents. I was then led back to prison,
where I found, amongst other sailors, a young man of
l'Orient, accused of striking a lieuteuant. Having
talked sometime with him, he said to me one morning,
" My boy, if you will pay for breakfast, I will tell you
a secret worth knowing." His mysterious air disturbed me, and made me anxious to know all; and
after breakfast he said to me, " Trust to me and
then I can extricate you. I do not know who you
are, but I am sure you are not young Duval, for he
has been dead these two years, at Saint Pierre, at
Martinique. (I started.) Yes, he has been dead
these two years, but no one knows it, so well are our
colonial hospitals regulated. Now I can give you
such statements about his family, that you may pass
for him even with his parents, for he left home when
he was very young. To make quite sure, you can
feign a weakness of intellect, produced by sea toil and
sickness. Besides, before Auguste Duval went to sea,
he had a mark tatooed on his left arm, as most sailors
have; I know it well; it was an altar with a garland
on it. If you will remain a fortnight in the cell with
me, I will mark you in a similar manner, so that all the
world could not detect the imposture."

My friend appeared frank and open-hearted, and I may account for the interest he took in me, by his desire to trick justice, a feeling that pervades the minds of all prisoners; for them to deceive it, mislead it, or delay it, is a pleasurable vengeance, which they willingly purchase at the expense of a few weeks' confinement. Here was such an opportunity, and the means were soon put in action. Under the windows of our room was a sentinel, and we began by pelting him with pieces of bread; and as he threatened to tell the jailor of us, we dared him to put his menaces into execution. On this, when he was relieved, the corporal, who was a meddling fellow, went to the office; and the next moment the jailor came to take us, without even telling us the reason of our removal. But we soon found it out, on entering a sort of hole in the sunken ditch, very damp, but tolerably light. Scarcely were we shut in, than my comrade commenced operations, in which he perfectly succeeded. It consisted only in pricking my arm with several needles tied together, and dipped in Indian ink and carmine. At the end of twelve days the wounds closed, so that it was impossible to tell how long they had been made. My companion also took advantage of this " leisure undisturbed," to give me additional details concerning the Duval family, whom he had known from childhood, and was in fact related to them, and instructed even in the minutest habitual trick of my Sosià.

These instructions were of unspeakable advantage to me, when, on the sixteenth day after of our detention in the dungeon, I was taken out to be confronted with my father, whom the commissary of marine had sent for. My comrade had so well described him, that I could not be mistaken on perceiving him. I threw my arms about his neck; he recognized me; his wife, who came soon after, recognized me; a female cousin and an uncle recognized me; and I was so undoubtedly Auguste Duval, that the commissary himself was convinced of it! But this was not sufficient to procure

my liberation; as a deserter from the Cocarde, I was
to be sent to Saint Malo, where she had left several
men at the hospital, and then be tried before the maritime court. To tell the truth, I felt no alarm at all
this; certain that I should find means of escape on my
journey, I set out at length, bathed with my parents'
tears, and the richer by several louis, which I added
to the stock already concealed about me.

Until we reached Quimper, where I was to be
handed over to another guard, no opportunity presented of bidding adieu to the company of gendarmes
who guarded me, as well as many other individuals,
robbers, smugglers, or deserters. We were placed in
the town jail, and on entering the chamber where I
was to pass the night, I saw at the foot of the bed a
red frock, marked on the back GAL., initials but too
well known to me. There, covered with a tattered
quilt, slept a man, whom, by his green cap decked with
the tin plate numbered, I recognized as a galley-slave.
Would he know, would he betray me? I was in a
spasm of fear, when the individual, awakened by the
noise of bolts and bars, sat up in his bed, and I knew
him to be a young fellow named Goupy, who went to
Brest at the same time as myself. He was condemned
to chains for life, for a forcible burglary in the environs
of Bernai, in Normandy; his father was a galley serjeant at Brest, where, most probably, he did not come
first purely for change of air. Not wishing to have
him continually before his sight, he had procured an
order for his removal to the Bagne at Rochfort, and
he was then on his road thither. I told him all my
affairs, and he promised secresy, and kept his promise
the more faithfully, as it would have profited him
nothing to betray me.

However, the guard did not stir immediately, and
fifteen days elapsed after my arrival at Quimper, without any mention of departure. This delay gave me
the idea of penetrating the wall and escaping; but
having found the impossibility of success, I managed

so as to obtain the confidence of the jailor, and got
an opportunity of executing my project by inspiring
him with an idea of false security. After having told
him that I had heard the prisoners plotting something,
I pointed out to him the place in the prison where they
had been at work. He made most minute search, and
naturally enough found the hole I had made; and this
discovery procured for me all his kindness. I sometimes found it overpowering, for the watch was kept
so regularly that all my schemes were routed. I began to think of going to the hospital, where I hoped to
be more fortunate in the execution of my projects.
To give myself a high fever, it was only necessary to
swallow tobacco juice for a couple of days, and then
the doctors ordered my removal. On getting to the
house, I got in exchange for my clothes a grey cap and
cloak, and was then put along with the rest.

It was a part of my plan to remain for some time
at the hospital, that I might know the ways in and out,
but the illness caused by the tobacco juice would only
last for three or four days, and it was necessary to
find some recipe which would bring on another complaint; for, knowing no one in the place, it was impossible for me to get a supply of tobacco juice. At
Bicetre, I had been taught how to produce those
wounds and sores, by means of which so many beggars
excite public pity, and get those alms which cannot be
worse bestowed. Of all these expedients, I adopted
that which consisted in making the head swell like a
bushel; first, because the doctors would be certainly
mistaken; and then because it gave no pain, and all
traces of it could be removed by the day following.
My head became suddenly of a prodigious size, and
great was the talk thereof amongst the doctors of the
establishment, who, not being as it appeared blessed
with a superabundance of skill, knew not what to
think of it. I believe some of them spoke of ele-
phantiasis, or of dropsy in the brain. But, be that as
it may, their brilliant consultation ended in the pre-

scription most common in hospitals, of putting me on the most strict regimen.

With money, such orders did not fret me; but yet I had only gold, and changing that might awaken suspicion. However, I determined to try a liberated convict, who acted as infirmary helper; and this fellow, who would do anything for money, soon procured for me what I desired. On my telling him that I was desirous of getting out into the town for a few hours, he said, that if I disguised myself, it would not be difficult, as the walls were not very high. It was, he said, the way he and his companions got out when they wanted anything. We agreed that he should provide me with clothes, and that he should accompany me in my nocturnal excursion, which was to be a visit to sup with some girls. But the only clothes he could procure for me inside the hospital were much too small, and we were compelled to suspend operations for a time.

Just at this time, one of the sisters of charity passed by my bed, whom I had already watched in performing very mundane duties; not that sister Françoise was one of those dandified nuns who were ridiculed on the stage, before the young nuns were transformed into boarders, and the white handkerchief was replaced by the green apron. Sister Françoise was about thirty-four, a brunette, with a deep colour, and her powerful charms created more than one unhappy passion, as well amongst the soldiers as the infirmary overseers. On seeing this seducing creature, who weighed perhaps nearly fifteen stone, the idea occurred to me that I would borrow for a short time her cloister garb. I spoke of it jestingly to my overseer, but he took it as if meant seriously, and promised on the ensuing night to get a part of sister Françoise's wardrobe. About two in the morning, I saw him come with a parcel, containing a gown, handkerchief, stockings, &c. which he had carried off from the sister's cell whilst she was at matins. All my bed-room companions, nine in

P

number, were soundly asleep, but I went out to put
on my attire. What gave me the most trouble was
the head-dress. I had no idea of the mode of arranging it, and yet the appearance of disorder in these
garments, always arranged with a scrupulous nicety,
would have infallibly betrayed me.

At length, sister Vidocq finished her toilet, and we
crossed the courts and gardens, ·and reached a place
where the wall could be easily scaled. I then gave
the overseer fifty francs, nearly all my store; he lent
me a hand, and I was soon in a lonely spot, whence I
reached the country, guided by my indefinite directions. Although much encumbered with my petti-
coats, I yet walked so fast as to get on at least two
leagues before sun-rise. A countryman whom I met,
going to sell his vegetables at Quimper, and whom I
questioned as to my road, told me that I was jour-
neying towards Brest. This was nót the way for me,
and I made the fellow comprehend that I wished to
go towards Rennes, and he pointed out to me a cross
road leading to the high route to this city, which I
immediately took, trembling at every moment, lest I
should meet any of the soldiers of the English army
then lying in the villages between Nantes and Brest.
About ten in the morning, on reaching a small hamlet,
I enquired if there were any soldiers near, evincing
much fear, which was real however, lest they should
examine me, which would have led to a detection.
The person whom I asked was a sacristan, full of
chatter and inquisitiveness, who compelled me to enter
the curate's house near at hand, to take some refreshment.

The curate, an elderly man, whose face betrayed
that benevolence so rare amongst the ecclesiastics who
come into towns to blazon forth their pretensions and
conceal their immorality, received me very kindly.
" My dear sister," said he, " I was about to celebrate
mass; as soon as that is over, you shall breakfast with
us." I was then compelled to go to church, and it

was no trifling embarrassment for me to make the signs and genuflexions prescribed to a nun. Fortunately, the curate's old female servant was at my side, and I got through very well by imitating her in every particular. Mass concluded, we sat down to table, and interrogatories commenced. I told the good people, that I was going to Rennes to perform penance. The curate asked nothing more; but the sacristan, pressing me rather importunately to know why I was thus punished, I told him, " Alas! it was for curiosity!" This closed the little man's mouth. My situation was, however, one of difficulty; I was afraid to eat, lest I should betray too manly an appetite; and again, I more frequently said ' M. le cure' than ' my dear brother;' so that my blunders would have betrayed all, had I not terminated the breakfast. I found means, however, to learn the names of the villages of the district, and, strengthened by the blessings of the curate, who promised not to forget me in his prayers, I went on my way somewhat more accustomed to my new attire.

I met few people on my way, the wars of the revolution had depopulated the wretched country, and I traversed the villages whilst the inhabitants were all in bed. Arriving one night at a hamlet, composed of a few houses, I knocked at the door of a farm-house. An old woman came to open it to me, and conducted me to a good-sized parlour, but which might have disputed the pre-eminence in dirt with the filthiest hovels of Galicia or the Asturias. The family consisted of father, mother, a young lad, and two girls, from fifteen to seventeen years of age. When I went in, they were making a kind of cake of buck-wheat flour, and were all around the fryingpan; and the group, reflected on à la Rembrandt, by the light of the fire only, formed a picture which a painter would have admired : but as for me, who had scarcely time to pay attention to the effects of the light, I expressed my desire for some refreshment. Out of respect to my sacred office, they gave me the first cakes, which I devoured without even feeling that they were so burning hot as to scorch my palate. I have often since sat down at sumptuous tables, where I have had abundance of most exquisite wines, and meats of the most delicate and delicious flavour, but I can never forget the cakes of the peasant of Lower Brittany.

On the termination of supper we had prayers, and then the father and mother lighted their pipes. Suffering greatly from agitation and fatigue, I expressed a wish to retire. "We have no bed to give you," said the master of the house, who, having been a sailor, spoke very good French: "you shall sleep with my two girls." I observed to him that going on a vow I must sleep on straw, adding that I should be contented with a corner in the stable. "Oh;" replied he, " in sleeping with Jeanne and Madelon you will not break your vow, for the bed is only made of straw. Besides, you cannot be in the stable, for that is already occupied by a tinker and two soldiers, who asked my leave to pass the night there." I could say nothing more; and but too glad to escape the soldiery, I reached the boudoir of the young ladies. It was a loft filled with cider apples, cheese, and smoked bacon : in one corner a dozen fowls were roosting, and lower down were hutched eight rabbits. The furniture consisted of a dilapidated pitcher, worm-eaten joint-stool, and the fragment of a looking-glass; the bed, like all in that country, was only a chest shaped like a coffin, half-filled with straw, and scarcely three feet wide.

Here was a fresh embarrassment for me; the two young girls undressed very deliberately before me, who had many and good reasons for seeming very shy. Independently of circumstances that may be guessed, I had under my female attire a man's shirt, which would betray my sex and my incognito. Not to be detected I took out a few pins very slowly, and when I saw the two sisters had got into bed I overturned, as if by accident, the iron lamp which lighted

us, and then took off my feminine habits without fear.
On getting between the sail-cloth sheets I laid down
so as to avoid all unlucky detection. It was a tormenting night : for without being pretty, mademoiselle
Jeanne, who could not stir without touching me, had
a freshness and plumpness but too attractive for a man
condemned for so long a period to the rigours of absolute celibacy. Those, who have ever been in a similar situation, will believe without difficulty that I could
not sleep for a single instant.

I was motionless, with my eyes open like a hare in
its form, when long before daylight I heard a knocking
with the butt end of a musket against the door. My
first idea, like every man in similar circumstances, was
that they had traced me, and were coming to apprehend me ; but I did not know where to conceal myself. The blows were redoubled : and I then bethought me of the soldiers sleeping in the stable, which
dissipated my fears. " Who is there ? " said the master
of the house, leaping up.—" Your soldiers."—" Well,
what do you want ?"—" Fire to light our pipes before
we set off." Our host then arose, and blowing up
the fire left in the ashes, he opened the door to
the soldiers. One of these, looking at his watch by the
lamp-light, said, " It is half-past four o'clock. Come,
let us go ; the rations are in good order. Come, to
the march, my lads." They went away, and our host,
putting out the lamp, went to bed again. As for me,
not wishing to dress myself in presence of my bed-
fellows any more than undress myself, I immediately rose, and lighting the lamp, put on my woollen
gown, and then going down on my knees in a corner,
pretended to pray until the family should awake. I
did not remain long in waiting. At five o'clock in the
morning the mother cried from her bed, " Jeanne, get
up, and get some soup ready for the sister, who wishes
to depart early." Jeanne got up, and the butter-milk
soup having been made and eaten with good appetite,

I left the good persons who had so kindly welcomed me.

Having walked all day without flagging, I found
myself at the close of the day in a village near the
environs of Vannes, when I remembered I had been
deceived by false or mistaken directions. I slept at
this village, and the next day I went through Vannes
at a very early hour. My intention was to get to
Rennes; but on leaving Vannes I met a person who
induced me to change my intention. On the same
route was a woman walking slowly, followed by a
young child, and carrying on her back a box of relics,
which she showed in the villages, whilst singing doleful
ditties, selling rings of St Hubert, or holy chaplets.
This woman told me that she was going to Nantes by
cross roads. I was desirous of avoiding the high
road, and did not hesitate to follow my new guide.
Besides, at Nantes I had resources which would be
lacking to me at Rennes, as we shall see.

At the end of eight days' walk, we reached Nantes,
when I left the woman and her relics at her lodgings
in the suburbs. As for me, I enquired for the Ile
Feydeau. When at the Bicêtre I had learnt from a
man named Grenier, called the Nantais, that there was
in this quarter a kind of auberge, where robbers met
without fear of disturbance. I knew that by using a
well-known name I should be admitted without difficulty; but I only remembered the address very vaguely,
and scarcely knew how and where to find out the
place. I adopted an expedient which succeeded. I
went into many houses and asked for M. Grenier; at
the fourth where I sought for this name, the hostess,
leaving two persons with whom she was conversing,
took me into a small room and said to me, " Have
you seen Grenier? Is he still sick (in prison)?"—
" No," answered I, " he is well (free)." And perceiving that I was all right with the mother of robbers,
I told her unhesitatingly who I was, and how I was

situated. Without replying, she took my arm, and opening a door let into the pannel, made me enter a low room where eight men and women were playing at cards and drinking brandy, &c. " Here," said my guide, presenting me to the goodly party, much astonished at the appearance of a nun, " here is a sister come to convert you all." At the same time I tore off my handkerchief, and three of the party, whom I had met at the Bagne, recognized me; they were Berry, Bidaut Mauger, and the young Goupy, whom I had met at Quimper; the others were fugitives from the Bagne of Rochfort. They were much amused at my disguise; and when supper had made us all very jolly, one of the females put on my nun's habits, and her gestures and attitudes, contrasted so strangely with this costume, that we all laughed till we cried, until the moment when we went to bed.

On waking, I found on my bed new clothes, linen, and in fact everything necessary for my toilet. Whence did they come? But this was of no consequence. The little money which I had not expended at the hospital of Quimper, where I paid dearly for everything, had been used on my journey; and without clothes, resources, or acquaintances, I was compelled to wait until I could write to my mother; and in the mean time accepted all that was offered me. But one circumstance of a particular nature abridged my stay at the Ile Feydeau. At the end of a week, my companions seeing me perfectly recovered from my fatigues, told me one evening that they intended on the next day to break into a house on the Place Graslin, and relied on my going with them; I was even to have the post of honour, that of working inside with Maguer.

But I did not intend to do this, and thought how I could make use of the circumstance to get away and go to Paris, where, near my family, my resources would not fail me; but it never entered into my calculations to enrol myself in a band of thieves; for although I had associated with robbers, and lived by my wits, I felt an invincible repugnance to entering on a career of crimes, of which early experience had taught me the perils and risks. A refusal would, on the other hand, render me suspected by my new companions, who, in this retreat, secure from sight or hearing, could knock me on the head with impunity, and send me to keep company with the salmons and smelts of the Loire; and I had only one course to take, which was to set out as quickly as possible, and this I resolved on doing.

Having exchanged my new clothes for a countryman's frock and eighteen francs to boot, I left Nantes, carrying at the end of a stick a basket of provisions, which gave me at once the appearance of an inhabitant of the environs. It is useless to observe, that I struck into the cross roads, where, by the bye, the gendarmes would be better stationed than on the high road, where persons who have any motives for avoiding justice rarely show themselves. This observation is applicable besides to the system of municipal police, whence, as I think, immense advantages could be drawn. Confined only to security, properly so called, it would then follow from one place to another the traces of malefactors who, now once striking out from the radius of large towns, defy all researches. At different periods, and always at seasons of great calamities, when the Chauffeurs were infesting the north; when famine desolated the districts of Calvados and Eure; when the Oise saw conflagrations nightly blazing; partial applications of this system were made, and the results proved the efficacy of the arrangement.

CHAPTER XI.

The market-place at Cholet—Arrival at Paris—History of captain
Villedieu.

On quitting Nantes, I walked for a day and two nights
without stopping at any village, and my provisions
were exhausted; still I went on hap-hazard, although
decided on reaching Paris or the sea shore, hoping to
get to sea in some ship, when I reached the first habi-
tations of a town which appeared to have been lately
the scene of a combat. The greater part of the houses
were nothing but a heap of rubbish, blackened by fire,
and all that surrounded the place had been entirely
destroyed. Nothing was standing but the church
tower, whence the clock was striking the hour for
inhabitants who no longer existed. This scene of
desolation presented at the same time the most whimsical occurrences. On the only piece of wall which
remained belonging to an auberge, were still the words
" Good entertainment for man and horse ; "—there the
soldiers were watering their horses in the holy-water
vessels ;—farther on, their companions were dancing to
the tune of an organ with the countrywomen, who,
ruined and wretched, had prostituted themselves to
the Blues (republicans) for bread. By the traces of
this war of extermination we might have thought ourselves in the midst of the wilds of America, or the
oases of the desert, where barbarous tribes were
cutting each others' throats with blind fury. Yet
there had only been there, on both sides, Frenchmen :
but every species of fanaticism made rendezvous there.
I was in La Vendée, at Cholet.

The master of a wretched cabaret, thatched with
broom, where I halted, gave me my cue, by asking me
if I had come to Cholet for the next day's market. I
answered in the affirmative, much astonished that one

should be held in the midst of these ruins, and even that the farmers of the environs had anything to sell; but my host told me that scarcely anything was brought to this market but cattle from distant districts; on the other hand, although no one had yet done anything to repair the disasters of the war, the amnesty was nearly terminated by general Hoche, and if republican soldiers were still found in the country it was that they might keep down the chouans,* who were becoming formidable.

I went to the market early the next day, and thinking to take advantage of it, I accosted a cattle-dealer, whose face was familiar to me, asking him to listen to me for a moment. He looked at me with distrust, taking me probably for a spy, but I hastened to relieve his suspicions, telling him that it was only a personal affair. We then entered a hovel where they sold brandy, and I then told him, that having deserted from the 36th demi-brigade to see my parents, who lived at Paris, I was desirous of getting some situation which would allow me to reach my destination without fear of arrest. This good fellow told me that he had no situation to offer me, but that if I would drive a drove of oxen as far as Sceaux, I might go with him. No proposal was ever accepted with more readiness, and I entered on my duties instantly, anxious to show my new master all the return I could testify for his kindness.

In the afternoon he sent me to carry a letter to a person in the town, who asked me if my master had desired me to take anything back with me; I said no, " Never mind," said the person, who was, I believe,

---

* Chouans, a contraction of the word chat-huant, a screech-owl; a title given to parties of Vendéeans, and afterwards to bands formed for plunder, who ravaged the western part of France subsequently to 1793, and were called by this name because, like owls, they came out only at night.— *Translator.*

a notary, "take him this bag with three hundred francs." I delivered this sum to the cattle dealer, to whom my punctuality gave confidence. We set out next day, and on the third morning my master calling to me, said, "Louis, can you write?"—"Yes, sir." "Reckon?"—"Yes, sir." "Keep an account?"—"Yes, sir."—"Ah, well; as I must go out of the road to see some lean beasts, at St Gauburge, you will drive the oxen on to Paris, with Jacques and Saturnin: you will be head man." He then gave me his instructions and left us.

By reason of my advancement, I no longer travelled on foot, which was a great relief to me; for the drivers of cattle are always stifled with dust, or up to their knees in mud, which increases as they proceed. I was besides, better paid and better fed, but I did not abuse these advantages, as I saw many other head drovers do on the journey. Whilst the food of the animals was converted by them into pullets, or legs of mutton, or exchanged with the innkeepers, the poor brutes grew visibly thinner.

I behaved myself most faithfully, so that on joining us at Verneuil, my master, who had preceded us, complimented me on the state of the drove. On reaching Sceaux, my beasts were worth twenty francs a-head more than any others, and I had spent ninety francs less than my companions for my travelling expenses. My master, enchanted, made me a present of forty francs, and cited me as the Aristides of cattle drovers, and I was in some sort quite an object of admiration at the market of Sceaux, and, in return, my colleagues would willingly have knocked me on the head. One of them, a chap of Lower Normandy, famed for strength and skill, endeavoured to disgust me with my avocation, by taking upon himself to inflict the popular vengeance upon me; but what could such a clumsy yokel do against the pupil of the renowned Goupy! The Low Norman cried craven, after one of the most

memorable boxing matches of which the inhabitants of
a fat cattle market ever preserved a remembrance.

My conquest was the more glorious, as I had testified much forbearance, and had only consented to
fight when it would have been impossible to avoid
it.   My master, more and more satisfied with me,
wished absolutely to engage me for a year, as foreman,
promising me a small share of the profits.   I had received no news of my mother; and here I found resources which I was about to seek at Paris;   and,
besides, my new dress disguised me so much that I
felt no fear of detection in my frequent excursions to
Paris.   I passed, in fact, many persons of my acquaintance, who paid no attention to me.   But one evening
as I was passing along the Rue Dauphine, to get to
the Barrière d'Enfer, some one tapped me on the
shoulder.   My first thought was to run for it, without
turning round, being aware that, whoever thus stops
you, relies on your looking back to seize you; but a
stoppage of carriages choked up the passage.   I therefore waited the result, and in a twinkling discovered
that it was a false alarm.

The person who had so much alarmed me, was no
other than Villedieu, the captain of the 13th chasseurs,
with whom I had been intimately acquainted at Lille.
Although surprised to see me with a hat covered with
waxed cloth, a smock frock, and leathern gaiters, he
testified much pleasure at the meeting, and invited
me to supper, saying that he had some marvellous
narratives to tell me.   He was not in his uniform, but
this did not astonish me, as the officers commonly
wore common clothes when staying in Paris.   What
struck me most was his uneasy air and excessive paleness.   As he expressed a wish to sup out of the barriers, we took a coach which conveyed us to Sceaux.

On reaching the Grand Cerf, we asked for a private
room.   We were scarcely served with what we asked
for, when Villedieu, double-locking the door and

putting the key in his pocket, said to me, with tears in his eyes, and with a wild air, "My friend, I am a lost man! Lost! undone! I am pursued, and you must get me a habit similar to your own. If you want it, I have money, plenty of money, and we will start for Switzerland together. I know your skill at escapes, and you, and you only can extricate me."

This commencement did not place me upon a seat of velvet; already much embarrassed myself, I did not much care to place myself again in the way of being apprehended, and to unite my fortunes with those of a man hotly pursued might lead to my detection. This reasoning, which I made to myself, decided me on being wary with Villedieu; and besides, as yet I did not know exactly what he wished to do. At Lille, I had seen him spending much more than his pay; but a young and handsome officer has so many ways of procuring money, that no one thinks any harm of that. I was then greatly astonished at the following details.

" I will not speak to you of those circumstances in my life which preceded your acquaintance with me ; it will suffice to say, that as brave and intelligent as most, and backed with good interest, I found myself, at the age of thirty-four, a captain of chasseurs, when I met you at Lille, at the Café de la Montagne. There I associated with an individual whose honest appearance prepossessed me in his favour, and our intimacy ripened into so close a friendship that he introduced me to his house. It was one replete with comfort and elegance, and I received every attention and token of amity; so good a fellow was M. Lemaire, so charming a woman was madame Lemaire. A jeweller, travelling about with his articles of trade, he made frequent absences of six or eight days; but still I visited his wife, and you may guess that I soon became her lover. Lemaire did not perceive, or would not perceive it. I led, to be sure, a most agreeable life, when one morning I found Josephine in tears. Her

Q

husband, she told me, had just been apprehended, with
his clerk, for having sold unstamped plate, and as it
was probable that his house would be soon visited,
all its contents must be speedily removed.   The most
valuable goods were then packed in my portmanteau,
and conveyed to my lodgings. Josephine then entreated
me to go to Courtrai, where the influence of my rank
might be of avail to her husband.   I did not hesitate
for a moment, for so deeply was I enamoured of this
woman that I would have given up the exercise of my
faculties if I did not think as she thought, and wish
what she wished.

    " Having obtained my colonel's permission, I sent
for horses and a post chaise, and set out with the express who had brought the news of Lemaire's arrest.
I did not at all like this man's face, and what preju-
diced me against him was, to hear him thee and thou
(tutoyer) Josephine, and treat her with much familiarity.   Scarcely had I got into the carriage, when he
installed himself at ease in one corner and slept till
we reached Menin, where I stopped to take some refreshment. ' Captain, I do not wish to get out,' said
he familiarly and rousing himself; ' be so good as to
bring me a glass of brandy.'   Much surprised at this
tone, I sent what he asked for by the waiting-maid,
who returned to me, saying that he would not answer
her, but was asleep.   I went to the chaise, where I saw
my gentleman motionless in his corner, his face being
covered with a handkerchief, ' Are you asleep?' said
I in a low tone. ' No,' he replied, ' nor do I wish to
be, but why the devil did you send a servant when I
tell you that I do not wish to face these gentry.   I
gave him his glass of brandy and we started again.
As he did not appear disposed for sleep, I asked
him carelessly his reason for preserving so strict an
incognito, and concerning the business which led me
to Courtrai, of which I knew no details.   He then
told me, that Lemaire was accused of belonging to a
band of Chauffeurs, and added, that he had not told

Josephine, for fear of increasing her affliction. We drew near Courtrai, and about four hundred paces from the town my companion called to the postillion to stop for an instant; he then put on a wig, concealed in the crown of his hat, stuck a large plaster on his left eye, took from under his waistcoat a brace of pistols, primed them, returned them to the belt under his vest, opened the door, jumped out and disappeared.

"All these manœuvres, which were perfect mysteries to me, only served to create great uneasiness. Could it be that Lemaire's arrest was only a pretext. Was he laying a snare for me? Did he wish me to play some part in an intrigue of any kind? I could not explain it to myself, nor think it was so. I was still very uncertain what to do, and was pacing the chamber with long strides at the Hotel du Damier, where my mysterious companion had advised me to alight, when the door suddenly opened and I saw—Josephine. At her appearance all suspicions vanished. Her abrupt entrance, her hurried journey made without me and some hours after, whilst she might easily have had part of my chaise and my protection, ought rather perhaps to have excited them. But I was in love, and when Josephine told me that she could not endure an absence, I thought her argument and explanation admirable and unanswerable. It was four o'clock in the afternoon, and Josephine dressed herself, and, going out, did not return till ten o'clock. She was accompanied by a man dressed like a peasant of Liège, but whose manner and expression of countenance did not agree with his costume.

"Some refreshments were brought in, and the servants then leaving us, Josephine immediately throwing herself on my neck, begged me to save her husband, repeating, that it only depended on me to do this. I promised all she asked, and then the pretended peasant, who had till this time been perfectly silent, spoke in very good language, and unfolded to me what I was

required to do. Lemaire, he said, reached Courtrai,
with several travellers, whom he did not know, and
had only met on the road, when they were surrounded
by a body of gendarmes, who summoned them to surrender. The strangers stood on the defensive, and
pistol shots were exchanged, and Lemaire, who, with
his clerk, had remained neuter on the field of battle,
had been seized without making any effort to escape,
feeling a consciousness of innocence, and that he had
nothing to fear. But very serious charges had been
produced against him; he was unable to give a very
precise account of his business in the district, because,
said the assumed countryman, he was then smuggling;
besides, they had found in a bush two pair of pistols,
which it was asserted had been thrown there by himself and clerk, at the moment they were apprehended,
and finally, a woman swore that she had seen him the
week before on the road to Ghent, with the identical
travellers, whom he said he had not met before the
morning of the engagement with the gendarmes.

" ' Under these circumstances,' added my peasant
interlocutor, ' we must find means of proving—

" ' 1st. That Lemaire has only left Lille three days,
and that he had then been there for the entire month
previously.

" ' 2nd. That he never carries pistols.

" ' 3rd. That before starting he received sixty louis
from some person.'

" This confidence ought to have opened my eyes as
to the nature of the steps required of me; but, intox-
icated with Josephine's caresses, I drove away all
thoughts, and compelled myself not to think of what
might be the results. We all three sat out the same
night for Lille, and on arriving I ran about all day
making the necessary arrangements, and by evening all
my witnesses were ready.* Their depositions had no

---

* This may appear surprising, but astonishment will cease
when we learn by how many testimonies of such a nature

sooner reached Courtrai, than Lemaire and his clerk were set at liberty. We may imagine their joy; and it was in fact so excessive, that I could not help thinking that the case must have been critical indeed, if their liberation could occasion such transports. The day after his arrival, dining with Lemaire, I found in my napkin a rouleau of a hundred louis. I was weak enough to accept them, and from that hour my ruin was decreed.

Playing high, treating my comrades, and having habits of luxury, I soon spent this sum. Lemaire daily made me fresh offers of service, by which I profitted to borrow several sums of him, amounting to two thousand francs, without being any the richer or more moderate. Fifteen hundred francs borrowed of a Jew, on a post obit for a thousand crowns, and twenty-five louis which the quarter-master advanced me, disappeared with the same alacrity. At last I spent even a sum of five hundred francs which my lieutenant had begged me to keep for him until the arrival of his horse-dealer, to whom he owed this sum. This I lost on one evening at the Café de la Montagne, with a man named Carré, who had already ruined half the regiment.

" The night that followed was a fearful one; agitated by the shame of having abused the confidence of the lieutenant, by squandering what was his little all; enraged at being duped, and tormented with the desire of still playing on; I was twenty times tempted to blow my brains out. When the trumpets sounded the turn-out, I had not closed my eyes; it was my week, and I went out to go through the examination of the stables; the first person I met was the lieutenant, who told me that the horse-dealer had arrived, and he

the course of justice is perverted. We have recently seen, at the court of assize at Cahors, half the inhabitants of a corporation state a plain fact in direct opposition to the assertion of the other half.

would send his servant for the five hundred francs. My agitation was so great that I answered I scarcely knew what, and the obscurity of the stable alone prevented him from observing my confusion. There was not a moment to lose, if I would not forfeit my good name with my superiors and brother officers.

" In this horrid situation I did not even think of applying to Lemaire, so much I already imagined that I had abused his friendship; but I had no other resource, and, at length, I resolved on writing him a note, stating the embarrassment in which I was placed. He came to me instantly, and laying on the table two gold snuff boxes, three watches and twelve engraved spoons, he told me that he had no ready money at the moment, but that I could easily procure it by taking these valuables to the pawnbrokers, and he left them at my disposal. After overwhelming him with thanks, I sent the whole to be pledged by my servant, who brought me twelve hundred francs for them. I first paid the lieutenant, and then led by my unlucky star, I flew to the Café de la Montagne, when Carré, after much persuasion, was induced to give me my revenge, and the remaining seven hundred francs passed from my purse to his.

" Aghast at this last stroke of fortune, I wandered for some time about the streets of Lille, whilst a thousand mad ideas flashed through my brain. It was in this mood that I imperceptibly drew near to Lemaire's house, which I entered mechanically; they were sitting down to dinner, and Josephine, struck by my extreme paleness, questioned me with interest concerning my affairs and my health; I was in one of those dejected moods whence the consciousness of his weakness makes the most reserved more communicative. I confessed all my extravagancies, adding that within two months I must pay more than four thousand francs, of which I had not a single sous.

" At these words Lemaire looked fixedly at me, with a gaze I can never forget all my life, be it long or short.

'Captain,' said he, 'I will not forsake you in your difficulties, but one confidence deserves another; nothing should be kept from a man who has saved you from—' and with a horrid smile he passed his hand across his throat. I trembled, and looked at Josephine. She was perfectly calm! It was a horrible moment! Without seeming to notice my perturbation, Lemaire continued his fearful confidence. I learnt that he was one of Sallambier's band, and that, when the gendarmes had apprehended him near Courtrai, they were returning from a party of plunder in a country-house in the vicinity of Ghent. The servants had defended themselves, and three had been killed, and two wretched women were hung up in a cellar. The valuables I had pawned were the produce of the robbery which had followed these atrocities! After having explained to me how he had been apprehended near Courtrai, whilst making off, Lemaire added that henceforward it was only for me to repair my losses and better my fortune by accompanying him in two or three expeditions.

"I was annihilated! Up to this period the conduct of Lemaire, the circumstances of his arrest, the nature of the service which I had rendered him, appeared to me very suspicious; but I carefully drove from my thoughts all that could convert my suspicions into reality. As if tormented by a frightful nightmare, I waited till I should awake, and my waking was more horrible still!

" 'Well,' said Josephine, with an inquiring tone, 'you do not answer—Ah! I see, we have lost your friendship; and I shall die!' She burst into tears: my head was in a whirl: forgetful of Lemaire's presence, I threw myself on my knees like a madman, crying out, 'I quit you? no, never, never!' Tears choked my utterance, and I saw a tear in Josephine's eyes, but she instantly resumed her firmness. For Lemaire, he offered us orange-flower water with as much

calmness as a cavalier presents an ice to his partner at
a ball.

"I was thus enlisted in this band, the terror of the
departments of the North, la Lys and l'Escaut. In less
than fifteen days I was introduced to Sallambier, in
whom I recognized the peasant of Liège; to Duhamel,
Chopiné, Calandrin, and the principal Chauffeurs. The
first business in which I took a share was in the environs of Douai. Duhamel's mistress, who accompanied
us, introduced us to the house, in which she had been
waiting-maid. The dogs having been poisoned by a
wood-cutter employed on the premises, we only waited
until the family should be asleep, to commence our
operations. No locks could resist Calandrin, and we
reached the drawing room with the utmost silence.
The family, consisting of the father, mother, great
aunt, two young persons, and a relation on a visit,
were playing at Bouillotte. We only heard the words,
'Pass, I hold; I play Charlemagne,' &c.; when Sallambier, opening the door quickly, appeared, followed
by ten men with blackened faces, and pistols and dag-
gers in their hands. At this sight the cards fell from
the hands of all; the females shrieked for mercy, until, with a motion of his hand, Sallambier compelled
silence, whilst one of our band, jumping like a monkey
on the mantlepiece, cut the ropes of the bells. The
women fainted, but were not heeded. The master of
the house alone retained some presence of mind.
After having opened his mouth at least twenty times
without uttering a word, he at length contrived to ask
what we wanted? 'Money,' said Sallambier, whose
voice seemed to me entirely changed; and taking the
candle from the card-table, he made signs to the
master of the house to follow him into the next room,
where we knew that the money and jewels were deposited. It was precisely Don Juan preceding the
statue of the Commandant.

"We remained in the dark, motionless at our posts,

only hearing the stifled sobs of the females, the chink of money, and these words, 'More, more,' which Sallambier repeated from time to time in a sepulchral tone. At the end of twenty minutes he returned with a red handkerchief, tied together by the corners and filled with pieces of money; the jewels were in his pockets. To neglect nothing, they took from the old aunt and the mother their earrings, as well as the watch of the relation who had so well chosen the time to make his visit. We set out at last, after having carefully locked up the whole party, without the servants, who had been for some time in bed, being at all disturbed or aware of the attack in the château.

"I had a share also in several other enterprizes, more hazardous than that I now mention. We were resisted, or else the proprietors had concealed their money, and to make them produce it they were put to most dreadful tortures. At first they confined themselves to burning the soles of their feet with red-hot shovels; but adopting more expeditious measures, they began to tear out the nails of those who were obstinate, or blow them as large as balloons with bellows. Some of these unfortunates, having really no money, as was supposed, died in the midst of these tortures. See, my friend, on what a career I had entered; I, an officer well born, for whom twelve years of active service, some exploits of bravery, and the testimony of my comrades, had created an universal esteem, which he had ceased to deserve for a very long time, and which he was about to lose for ever."

Here Villedieu paused and dropped his head upon his breast, like one overwhelmed by his recollections. I left him undisturbed for a moment, but the names he mentioned were too well known to me not to excite the most lively curiosity in my mind to hear the whole of his recital. A few glasses of champagne restored his energy, and he thus continued :—

"But crimes multiplied so alarmingly, that the gen-

darmes not being sufficiently powerful to check them,
columns of the military were taken from the various
garrisons. One was placed under my command. You
may suppose that this measure had an entirely contrary effect to that intended; for warned by me, the
Chauffeurs avoided the places that I was to watch with
my division. Thus matters went on worse than ever,
and the authorities were at a loss what plans to adopt,
when they learnt that the majority of the Chauffeurs
resided at Lille, and the order was given for redoubling
the superintendence (surveillance) at the gates. We
found means however to render all these precautions
useless. Sallambier procured at a broker's of the
town, who clothed a regiment, fifteen uniforms of the
13th chasseurs. and disguised with them that number
of Chauffeurs, who, with me at their head, went out
at twilight, as if going on a detachment of a secret
enterprize.

" Although this stratagem completely answered, I
thought I perceived myself to be the object of particular surveillance. A report spread about that there
were men in the vicinity of Lille disguised as horse
chasseurs. The colonel appeared to mistrust me, and
one of my brother officers was appointed alternately
to direct the moving columns before entrusted to my
charge alone. Instead of giving me the watch-word, as
to the other officers of gendarmes, I was not informed
of it until the moment of departure. At length I was
so directly accused, that I was under the necessity of
enquiring of the colonel, who, without any disguise,
told me that I was reported to have communication
with the Chauffeurs. I defended myself as well as I
could, and thus matters remained, only that I left the
service of the moving columns, which began to be so
active that the Chauffeurs scarcely durst show themselves.

" Sallambier, unwilling to remain long in inaction,
redoubled his audacity in proportion as obstacles multiplied about us. In one night he committed three

robberies in the same district. But the proprietors of
the first of the houses a ttacked having divested themselves of their gags and bonds, gave the alarm. The
tocsin was sounded for two leagues round, and the
Chauffeurs only owed their safety to the fleetness of
their horses. The two brothers Sallambier were
hotly followed, and it was only on approaching
Bruges that they distanced their pursuers. In a large
village where they were, they hired a chaise and two
horses, to go, as they said, some leagues and return in
the evening.

" A coachman drove them, whom, on getting to the
water's edge, the elder Sallambier struck from behind
with his knife, and knocked him from his seat. The
two brothers then threw him into the sea, hoping that
the waves would retain the corpse. Masters of the
conveyance, they went on their journey, when, towards
the close of day, they met a countryman who bade
them good evening. As they did not answer, the man
approached, saying, ' Ah! Vandeck, do you not know
me? It is I—Joseph.' Sallambier then told him that
he had hired the carriage for three days without a
conductor. The tone of this answer, the condition of
the horses, covered with sweat, and which their master
would never have let without a driver, all made the
interrogator suspicious. Without prolonging the
conversation, he ran to the adjacent village and gave
the alarm ; seven or eight men on horseback pursued
the carriage, which they soon perceived travelling
slowly along. They increased their speed and overtook it. It was empty. Rather disappointed, they
drove it into an auberge where they intended to pass
the night; but scarcely were they seated, when a great
noise was heard, occasioned by a crowd conveying
before the magistrate two travellers accused of the
murder of a man whom some fishermen had found
with his throat cut on the sea shore. All ran out,
and Joseph recognized the individuals whom he had
seen in the carriage, and which they quitted because

the horses could go no farther. They (the two Sallambiers) appeared greatly disconcerted when confronted with Joseph. Their identity was soon settled. Under a suspicion that they might belong to some band of Chauffeurs, they were transferred to Lille, where they were recognized on reaching the Petit Hotel.

" There the elder Sallambier, pressed by the agents of police, denounced all his companions, and pointed out when and where they might be taken. In consequence of this information forty-three persons of both sexes were apprehended. Amongst them were Lemaire and his wife. At the same time an order of arrest was issued against me; but informed by a quarter-master of gendarmes, whom I had served, I escaped and reached Paris, where I have been these ten days. When I met you I was looking for the house of an old sweetheart, where I intended to conceal myself, or obtain some means of escape to a foreign country, but I am now easy, since I meet with Vidocq."

CHAPTER XII.

Journey to Arras—Father Lambert—Vidocq a schoolmaster—
Departure for Holland—The " sellers of souls"—The mutiny
—The corsair—Catastrophe.

THE confidence of Villedieu flattered me very much;
but yet I thought my rencontre with him might lead
me into danger. I therefore told him a false tale
when he enquired about my mode of life and domicile.
For the same reason I took care not to be at the
rendezvous which he had appointed for the next day;
for it would have been attended with much risk to
myself and no advantage to him. On leaving him, at
eleven o'clock in the evening, I took the precaution of making many detours before I entered my
auberge, for fear of being dogged by any police agents.
My master, who had gone to bed, aroused me early in
the morning to tell me to set out with him for Nogent
le Rotrou, whence we were to proceed to his own
farms, situated in the environs of this city.

In four days we arrived at the termination of our
journey, and although received in the family as a
hardworking and faithful servant, I still persisted in
the intention I had formed for some time, of returning
to my own country, whence I received neither information nor money. On returning to Paris with some
cattle, I told my master of my determination, and he
let me go with much reluctance. On quitting him, I
entered a café in the Place du Chatelet, to procure a
porter to fetch my luggage, and there taking up a
newspaper, the first intelligence that met my eyes was
an account of Villedieu's capture. He had not allowed
himself to be taken before he had prostrated two of
the agents of police, who had orders to apprehend
him, and was himself severely wounded. On being
executed, two months afterwards at Bruges, the last

of eighteen, all his accomplices, he contemplated their
headless and bleeding bodies as they fell one by one
by his side, with a calmness and fortitude that never
wavered for an instant.

This circumstance gave me reason to be satisfied
with the step that I had taken.   Had I staid with the
cattle-dealer, I was under the necessity of coming
twice a week to Paris; and the police, directing its
attention against all plots and foreign agents, was
assuming an extent and energy which might have
brought detection on me, as they minutely watched
individuals, who, perpetually called by business from
the departments of the west, might serve as agents
between the Chouans and their friends in the capital.
I therefore set out without delay, and on the third
day reached Arras, which I entered in the evening, at
the time when the workmen were returning home
from labour.   I did not go directly to my father's
house, but to one of my aunts, who informed my
parents.   They thought me dead, not having received
any of my last letters; and I have never been able to
discover how and by whom they were intercepted.
Having related all my adventures at length, I asked
news of my family, which necessarily led to my enquiring for my wife.   I was told that my father had
for some time received her at his house, but that her
conduct was so scandalous, that she had been dis-
gracefully expelled thence.   She was, I was informed,
pregnant by an attorney, who supplied most of her
wants; but that for some time nothing had been heard
of her, and they had ceased to trouble themselves
concerning her.

I gave myself no care about her, for I had matters
of much greater import which demanded my attention.
I might be discovered at any moment; and if apprehended at my parents' house they would be involved
in difficulties.   It was imperative on me to find an
asylum where the vigilance of the police was not so
active as at Arras, and I threw my eyes upon a village

in the vicinity, Ambercourt, where there resided a quondam carmelite friar, a friend of my father, who agreed to receive me. At this period (1798) priests were compelled still to say mass in secret, although direct hostilities towards them had ceased. Father Lambert, my host, celebrated his divine functions in a barn; and as he had no assistance but from an old man, feeble and impotent, I offered to fulfil the duties of sacristan, which I did so satisfactorily, that one would have supposed it had been my calling all the days of my existence. I also became father Lambert's assistant in giving lessons to the children of the neighbourhood. My skill in teaching made some noise in the district, for I had taken an excellent method to advance my pupils rapidly; I traced the letters with a lead pencil, which they wrote over with the pen, and the Indian rubber effected the rest. The parents were delighted; only it was rather difficult for my scholars to perform without their master; but the Artesian peasants, however cunning in the common transactions of business, were good enough not to find this out.

This sort of life was rather agreeable to me. Clothed as a wandering friar, and tolerated by the authorities, I had no fear of detection or suspicion; on the other hand, my animal tastes, which I have always held in consideration due, were well supplied, the parents sending us perpetually, beer, poultry, and fruit. I had in my classes some pretty peasant girls, who were very teachable. All went on well for some time, but at length a distrust of me was evinced; I was watched, and it was discovered that I pushed my instructions occasionally rather too far, and complaint was made to father Lambert, who told me of the charges against me, which I stoutly denied. The complainants were silenced, but redoubled their vigilance; and one night, when, impelled by classic zeal, I was about to give a lesson in a hay-loft to a female scholar about sixteen years of age, I was seized by four brewers' men, dragged into a hop-ground, stripped of my clothes, and scourged, till the blood flowed copiously, with rods of nettles and thistles. The pain was so acute, that I lost my senses, and on reviving, found myself in the streets, naked, and covered with blisters and blood.

What was to be done? To return to father Lambert would be to incur fresh dangers. The night was not much advanced, and although eaten up with excess of fever, I determined to go on to Mareuil, to an uncle's house, and arrived there at two o'clock in the morning, worn out with fatigue, and only covered with a ragged mat which I had found near a pond. After having laughed unsparingly at my mishap, they rubbed my body all over with cream mixed with oil; and at the end of eight days I set out quite well for Arras, but it was impossible for me to remain there. The police might get information at some unlucky moment that I was there, and I therefore decided on starting for Holland, and fixing myself there, taking with me a supply of money which enabled me to remain at my ease until something should occur that would employ me usefully.

I passed through Brussels (where I learnt that the baroness d'I—— had settled in London), Anvers, and Breda, and then embarked for Rotterdam, in which city I put up at an inn that had been specially recommended to me. I there met with a Frenchman who was remarkably attentive and civil to me, and frequently invited me to dinner. I received all his advances with mistrust, knowing that all means were resorted to by the Dutch government to recruit their navy. In spite of all my caution, my companion contrived to intoxicate me with a particular liquor, and on the next morning I awoke on board a Dutch brig of war. All doubt was at an end; intemperance had given me up as a prey to the " sellers of souls."

Lying near the shrouds, I was reflecting on my singular destiny, which multiplied so many incidents of my wayward career, when one of the crew, pushing

me with his foot, desired me to rise and get on my
sailor's clothes. I pretended not to understand him,
and then the boatswain gave me the same orders in
French. On my replying that I was not a sailor,
since I had signed no agreement, he seized a rope's
end to strike me with; on which, I grasped a knife
belonging to a sailor, who was breakfasting at the foot
of the main-mast, and, placing my back against a gun,
I swore I would rip up the first man who should
assault me. This occasioned much disturbance in the
ship, and brought up the captain, who was a man
about forty, of good appearance, and whose manners
were free from that coarseness so usual with seafaring
people. He listened to me with kindness, which was
all he could do, for it was not in his power to change
the maritime organization of his government.

In England, where the duty on board a man-of-war
is more severe, less profitable, and, above all, less free
than in the merchants' ships, the royal navy was manned, and is still manned by the press. In war time
the press is carried into effect at sea, on board the
merchants' ships, with whom they exchange useless
or invalid sailors for vigorous and able-bodied men.
On shore it is carried on in the midst of large cities,
but it is customary only to press those individuals
whose appearance and costume bespeak that they have
not been unaccustomed to the sea. In Holland, on
the contrary, at the period I now allude to, they acted
in pretty nearly the same manner as at Turkey, where
in time of need, they seize on and send to the ships of
the line, masons, grooms, actors, barbers, &c. &c.;
persons, as we may suppose, of the most useful kind.
Thus, if on leaving port, a ship be compelled to engage
with another, she fails in every manœuvre; and this
circumstance may perhaps account for the number of
Turkish frigates that have been captured or destroyed
by the Greek pirates.

We had then on board men whose inclinations and
habits of life were so totally foreign from naval service,

that the very idea of compelling them to enter it was
essentially ridiculous. Of the two hundred individuals
pressed, like myself, there were not perhaps twenty
who had ever set foot on shipboard before.   The majority had been carried off by main force, or trepanned
by drunkenness: they had inveigled others by a promise of a free passage to Batavia, where they wished
to settle; amongst these were two Frenchmen, one a
book-keeper from Burgundy, and the other a gardener
of Lemosin, who, it is evident, were admirably calculated to make sailors.   To console us, the crew told
us that, for fear of desertion, we should not go ashore
for six months, which is likewise a plan practised in
the English fleets, where the sailor may be whole years
without seeing any other land than the main-top-gal-
lants of his ship: trustworthy men are made the boats'
crews, and foreigners are sometimes employed amongst
the crew.   To soften the severity of this usage, they
allow some of those women who swarm in all the sea-
ports, and whom they call, I know not why, queen
Caroline's daughters (les filles de la reine Caroline)
to come on board.   The English sailors, from whom I
have since learnt these details, which we are not to
consider as precisely true in every particular, add, that
to disguise in some measure the immorality, some
puritanical captains occasionally require that these
lady visitors should assume the names of sister or
cousin.*

   To me, who had so long intended to enter the
navy, the situation was not so repugnant, if I had
not been constrained to it, and if I had not had in
perspective the slavery which threatened me; added
to which, was the ill treatment of the boatswain, who
could not forgive my first essay with him. On the
least false manœuvre or mistake, the rope's end descended on my back in a style so argumentative and

   * Certainly M. Vidocq's statement, as he himself says,
must be taken ' cum grano salis!'—*Translator.*

convincing, that I even regretted the cudgel of the
galley-serjeant at the Bagne. I was in despair, and
twenty times resolved to let fall from the maintop a
wooden pulley on the head of my tormentor, or else
to fling him into the sea when I was on the watch. I
should certainly have done one or the other of these,
if the lieutenant, who had taken a liking to me because
I taught him to fence, had not in some measure alle-
viated my sufferings. Besides, we were forthwith going
to Helvoetsluys, where the Heindrack lay, of whose
crew we were to form a part, and in the passage an
escape might be effected.

The day of transhipment came, and we embarked,
to the number of two hundred and seventy, in a small
sloop, manned by twenty-five sailors, and with twenty-
five soldiers to guard us. The weakness of this detachment determined me to attempt to disarm the soldiers and compel the sailors to conduct us to Anvers.
One hundred and twenty of the recruits, French and
Belgians, entered into the plot, and we resolved on
surprising the men on guard at the moment their comrades were at dinner, whom we could then easily secure. This enterprise was executed with the more
success, as they suspected nothing. The commandant
of the detachment was seized at the moment he was
taking his tea, but was not at all mal-treated. A young
man of Tournai, engaged as supercargo, and reduced
to work as a sailor, explained to him so eloquently the
motives that led to our revolt, as he called it, that he
allowed himself to be conducted into the hold, with
his soldiers, unresistingly. As for the sailors, they
were neutral; a man of Dunkirk only, who was in our
plot, took the helm.

Night came on, and I wished to lie to, lest we
should encounter any guard-ship, to which the sailors
would make signals; but the Dunkirker obstinately
refused, and we kept on our course, and at day-break
we were under the cannon of a fort near Helvoetsluys.
The Dunkirker then announced his intention of land-

ing, to see if we could get on shore safely, and I saw
then that we were sold; but it was impossible to recede: signals had doubtlessly been made, and, on the
least movement, the guns of the fort could blow us
out of water.   It was compulsory then that we should
await the event.   Soon a boat, with twenty men on
board, left the shore and approached the sloop: three
officers who were in it came on deck, without testifying
any fear, although it was the scene of a busy struggle
between our comrades and the Dutch sentry, who
wanted to free the soldiers from the hold.   The first
word of the eldest officer was to ask for the ringleader,
and all remaining mute, I spoke in French:—" Indeed
that there had been no plot, but that it was by a simultaneous movement that we had resolved on throwing
off the slavery imposed on us; we had ill-treated no
one, as the captain and sailors could testify, who knew
it was our intention to have left them in possession of
the vessel, after we had landed at Anvers."   I know
not what effect my harangue produced, for I was not
allowed to finish it; only, whilst we were piled up
in the hold, in the place of the soldiers whom we
had confined there on the previous evening, I heard
some one say to the pilot, " that more than one
would swing at the yard-arm next morning."   The
sloop was then turned towards Helvoetsluys, and
we reached that place the same day, at about four
o'clock in the afternoon.   In the roadstead was anchored the Heindrack.   The commandant of the fort
went in his cutter, and in an hour afterwards I was
conducted thither also.   I found there assembled a
sort of maritime council, who questioned me as to the
particulars of the mutiny, and the part I had taken in
it.   I asserted, as I had already done to the fort governor, that having signed no articles of engagement,
I thought myself justified in effecting my escape by
any means that presented.

I was then ordered to retire, to make way for the
young man of Tournai, who had seized the captain.

We were looked on as the leaders in the enterprize, and we know that in such cases it is the ringleaders who undergo the punishment, and we were to suffer nothing more or less than hanging; fortunately, the young man, who had had time for consideration, corroborated my statement, and asserted firmly that no one had suggested it, but that the idea had come across us all at the same moment; besides, we were quite sure of not being betrayed by our comrades, who showed much concern for us, and swore that if we were condemned, the ship on board which they should be placed, should jump like a rocket; that is, that they would fire the powder magazine, although they should be blown up with it; and these were lads who would have dared to do what they ventured to talk about. Whether they feared the results of these menaces, and the bad example that it would afford to the sailors of the fleet, who had been recruited in a similar way; or whether the council held that we were entrenched behind a rampart of legitimate defence, in seeking to withdraw ourselves from a compulsory service; they promised to ask for our pardon from the admiral, on condition that we kept our comrades in due subordination, which appeared not to be their favorite virtue. We promised all that they desired, for nothing makes one so easy to be persuaded or to promise, as the feeling a cord about one's neck.

These preliminaries agreed upon, our comrades were transferred on board the ship, and went between decks with the crew, whose complement they were to make up: all was done with the greatest order, neither was any complaint heard, nor was there the smallest disorderly symptom to be repressed. It is right to say, that we were not ill-treated, as we had been on board the brig, where our old friend the boatswain did all with the rope's end in his hand. Besides, by giving the marines instruction in fencing, I was treated with some attention, and was even made bombardier, with a

pay of twenty-eight florins per month. Two months
passed away thus, whilst the vigilance of the English
cruisers would not allow of our quitting anchorage.
I became reconciled to my new employment, and had
no thoughts of leaving it, when news was brought
that the French authorities were searching for all
Frenchmen who were forming part of the Dutch
crews.   It was a good opportunity for those amongst
us who disliked the service, and yet none cared to
avail themselves of it, for they only wanted to em-
body us into French ships of the line, a change which
presented no advantage; and besides, the greater part
of my companions had, I believe, good reasons, as well
as myself, not to be anxious to display themselves before the agents of the metropolis.   All then were
silent, and when they demanded from the captain the
list of his crew, the examination of it had no other
result, for the simple reason that we had all assumed
false names.   We thought we had weathered the
storm.

Researches, however, were continued; only, instead
of making inquiries, they stationed agents at the ports
and taverns, who examined those men who landed by
permission or otherwise.   In one of my excursions, I
was apprehended.   I have long preserved my gratitude
for it towards the ship's cook, who honored me with
his personal animosity ever after that, I had found
fault with his giving us swipes for beer, and stinking
cod for fresh fish.   Taken before the commanding
officer, I said I was a Dutchman, and my knowledge
of the language sufficed for me to keep up my assertion; and besides, I demanded to be taken back to my
ship with a guard, that I might procure papers to substantiate my assertion, than which nothing could be
more natural.   A subaltern was ordered to accompany me, and we set out in the skiff that had conveyed
me ashore.   On getting near the ship, I made my friend
with whom I had been talking very familiarly, get up
alongside first; and when I saw him entangled amongst

the rigging, I thrust off suddenly from the ship's side, calling to the boat's crew to pull their hardest, and that they should have something to drink. We were cutting through the water whilst my subaltern friend was jostled about amongst the crew, who did not or pretended not to know him. On getting ashore, I ran to conceal myself in a house which I knew, determined on quitting the vessel, in which it would be difficult for me to appear without being apprehended. My flight would confirm all suspicions raised against me, and therefore the captain gave me his authority, tacitly, to do what I might think best for my own security.

A Dunkirk privateer, the Barras, captain Fomentin, was in the roads. At this period, vessels of this kind were seldom overhauled, as they had in a measure a sort of asylum; and as it suited me to get on board it, I got a lieutenant, to whom I applied, to introduce me to Fomentin, who, on my own statement, admitted me on board as master-at-arms. Four days afterwards, the Barras set sail for a cruise in the Sound. It was at the beginning of the winter of 1799, when the tempestuous weather destroyed so many vessels on the coast of the Baltic. Scarcely were we at sea, when a northerly wind rose, quite contrary to our destination. We were compelled to put about, and the roll of the ship was so great, that I was excessively ill; so much so, that for three days I could take nothing but weak brandy and water, and half the crew were in the same state, so that a fishing-boat might have taken us without our striking a blow. At length the wind abated, and turned suddenly to the south-west; and the Barras, an admirable sailer, going ten knots an hour, all hands aboard soon recovered. At this moment, the man at the mast-head cried out, " A sail on the larboard tack !" The captain took his glass, and declared it to be an English coaster, under a neutral flag, and which the squalls had separated from the convoy.

We bore down on her, with the wind on our bow, after hoisting French colours. At the second discharge of our guns she struck, before we could board her; and, putting the crew down into the hold, we made for Bergen in Norway, where our cargo of mahogany was soon disposed of.

I remained six months on board the Barras, and my share of the prizes was pretty considerable, when we went to lay up for a time at Ostend. We have already seen that this city was always unpropitious to me; and what now happened to me almost made me a convert to fatalism. We had scarcely got into the basin, when a commissary, gendarmes, and police agents, came on board to examine the papers of the crew; and I afterwards learnt that the object of this unusual visitation was, that a murder having been committed, it was conjectured that the assassin might have taken refuge with us.

When my turn came for examination, I asserted that I was Auguste Duval, born at l'Orient; and added, that my papers were at Rotterdam, in the office of the Dutch marine department. No notice was taken, and I thought I had well got rid of the affair. When the three hundred men who were on board had been questioned, eight of us were called, and told that we must go to the register-office, to give the requisite explanation. Not liking this, I turned off at the first angle of the street, and had already gained thirty yards on the gendarmes, when an old woman, who was washing the steps of a house, put her broom between my legs and I fell. The gendarmes came up to me and put on handcuffs, besides belabouring me pretty well with the butts of carbines and the flat sides of swords, and I was conducted thus to the commissary, who, after hearing me, asked me if I had not escaped from the hospital of Quimper. I saw that I was caught, for there was equal danger as Duval or Vidocq. However, I decided on the first

name, which offered less unfavourable chances of the
two; since the road from Ostend to l'Orient is longer
than from Ostend to Arras, and thus afforded more
opportunities and time for escape.

CHAPTER XIII.

I see Francine again—My re establishment in the prison of
Douai—Am I, or am I not, Duval?—The magistrates embar-
rassed—I confess that I am Vidocq—Another residence at
Bîcetre—I find captain Labbre there—Departure for Toulon—
Jossas, the famous robber—His interview with a great lady—
A tempest on the Rhone—The marquis of St Armand—The
executioner of the Bagne—The plunderers of the wardrobe—
A family of Chauffeurs.

EIGHT days elapsed, during which I only once saw the
commissary, and was then sent with a party of prisoners, deserters, &c. who were to be conveyed to
Lille.   It was to be expected that the uncertainty of
my identity would terminate in reaching a city where
I had so often dwelt; and therefore, informed that we
should pass through that place, I took such precautions
that the gendarmes who had already conducted me
did not recognize me; my features, concealed under a
thick mask of dust and sweat, were, besides, completely
altered by the swelling of my cheeks, almost as large
as those of the angels which on the frescoes of churches
are seen blowing the trumpet of the last judgment.   It
was in this state that I entered the Egalité, a military
prison, where I was to stay for some days, there to
charm away the weariness of my seclusion.   I risked
several visits to the canteen, in the hope that mingling
with the visitors I might find an opportunity of escape.
Meeting with a sailor whom I had known on board the
Barras, I thought I might make him instrumental to
my project.   I asked him to breakfast with me, and,

S

our meal finished, I returned to my chamber, where I remained for three hours, reflecting on the means of recovering my liberty, when the sailor came to ask me to share the dinner which his wife had just brought him. The sailor, then, had a wife,—and the thought crossed me, that to elude the vigilance of the jailors, she might procure me female attire or some disguise. Full of this idea, I went down to the canteen and drew near the table, when I heard a piercing cry, and a woman fainted. It was my comrade's wife. I ran to raise her—Good heavens, 'twas Francine! Alarmed at my own imprudence, which had allowed an expression of astonishment to escape from me, I tried to repress the emotion which I had unavoidably testified. Surprised and astonished, the spectators crowded round us, and overwhelmed me with enquiries; and, after some moments' silence, I told them that it was my sister, whom I had so unexpectedly met.

This incident passed without any consequences, and next day at early dawn we set off: and I was in consternation at finding that the convoy, instead of following as usual the road to Sens, took that of Douai. Why change the direction of our journey? I attributed this to some indiscretion of Francine; but I soon learnt that it resulted simply from the necessity of leaving at Arras some of the refractory prisoners from Cambrai.

Francine, whom I had so unjustly suspected, was awaiting me at our first halt. In spite of the gendarmes she would speak to and embrace me. She wept bitterly, and joined my tears with hers. With what bitterness did she reproach herself for the infidelity which was the cause of all my misfortunes! Her repentance was sincere, and I sincerely forgave her: and when, on the order of the brigadier, we were compelled to separate, she slipped into my hands two hundred francs in gold as the only recompense in her power.

At length we reached Douai, and at the gate of the

prison of the department a gendarme rang the bell.
Who answered the summons ? Dutilleul, the turnkey,
who, after one of my attempts to escape, had dressed
my hurts for a month afterwards. He did not appear
to know me. At the office I found another person
whom I knew, the guard Hurtrel, in such a state of
inebriety that I flattered myself his memory had entirely left him. For three days nothing was said to
me ; but on the fourth I was led before the examining
magistrate, in the presence of Hurtrel and Dutilleul,
and was asked if I were not Vidocq ? I replied that
I was Auguste Duval, which might be confirmed by
sending to l'Orient; and besides, the motive of my
apprehension at Ostend proved it, as I was only
charged with having deserted from a ship of war. My
straight-forward tale seemed to weigh with the judge,
who hesitated ; but Hurtrel and Dutilleul persisted in
asserting that they were not mistaken. Rausson, the
public accuser, came to see me, and also said he knew
me ; but as I was not disconcerted, he remained in
doubt, and to clear up the affair they devised a stratagem.

One morning I was told that a person wanted me at
the office, and on going thither I found my mother,
whom they had sent for from Arras ; with what intention may be easily divined. The poor woman hastened to embrace me, but I saw through the snare,
and putting her from me quietly, I said to the magistrate who was present, that it was an unmanly thing
to give the unfortunate woman any hopes of seeing
her son, when they were, at least, uncertain of their
ability to produce him. My mother, who was put
on her guard by a signal which I managed to communicate to her, pretending to examine me attentively,
at length declared that a wonderful likeness had deceived her, and then retired, uttering many bitter
reproaches against those who had taken her from home
only to afford her but a fallacious joy.

The magistrate and turnkeys were then reduced to

their original state of dubiety, when a letter which
arrived from l'Orient seemed to put the matter beyond a doubt. It mentioned a drawing pricked on
the left arm of Duval, who had escaped from the
hospital at Quimper, as a thing which would at once
dispel every doubt as to the identity of the individual
detained at Douai. I was again summoned before the
examining-judge, and Hurtrel, already triumphing in
his penetration, was present at the interrogation. At
the first words I saw what was coming, and stripping
my coat sleeve above my elbow, I showed them the
drawing, which they scarcely expected to find, and
which exactly coincided with the description sent from
l'Orient. All were in the clouds again, and what yet
made the situation more complicated, was that the
authorities of l'Orient demanded me as a deserter
from the fleet. Fifteen days were thus spent without
any decision having been made concerning me; then
tired with the severities used towards me, and hoping
to procure approbation, I wrote to the president of
the criminal tribunal, declaring that I was really Vidocq. I had determined on this, under the idea
that I should be sent forthwith to Bicêtre with a party,
and that was actually the result. It was utterly impossible, however, for me to make the least effort to
escape by the way, as I was guarded with unremitting
vigilance.

I made my second entry at Bicêtre on the second of
April 1799, and there found some old prisoners, who,
although galley-slaves, had obtained permission to
have their sentence to the Bagne remitted, and it was
an advantageous commutation for them, as the duration of their punishment took date from the day of
their actual apprehension. These kinds of favours are
occasionally granted at the present day; and if only
conferred on persons whom peculiar circumstances of
condemnation, or repentance, rendered worthy of it,
we should give it a tacit consent; but deviations from
the general principle arise ordinarily from the sort of

struggle which exists between the police of the provinces and the general police, each of which has its favourites. The convicts, however, always belonging to the general police, it can remove at will any prisoner from the Bicêtre, or other prison, to the Bagne, and this is convincing with regard to the observation I have just made. The convict, who up to this time had conducted himself with apparent piety, throws off the mask, and shows himself one of the most depraved of malefactors.

I saw at Bicêtre captain Labbre, who, it may be recollected supplied me, when at Brussels, with papers, by means of which I had deceived the baroness d'I——. He had been sentenced to sixteen years at the galleys, for being concerned in an extensive robbery committed at Ghent, at the house of Champon, the aubergiste. He was, with us, to depart with the first chain, the near approach of which was disagreeably announced to us. Captain Viez, knowing the gentlemen who were to be confided to him, had declared, that to prevent any chance of escape, he would put us on wrist-cuffs and collars until we reached Toulon. However, our promises induced him to forego this formidable project.

After the rivetting of the fetters was done (in a similar way to that in which it had been performed at my first departure) I was put at the head of the first cordon, with Jossas, one of the most celebrated robbers of Paris and the provinces, better known as the marquis de Saint-Armand de Faral, which he constantly bore. He was a man about thirty-six years old, with a gentlemanly appearance, and able to assume at will the most perfect suavity of manners. His travelling costume was that of a dandy leaving his bed-room for his boudoir. With pantaloons of silver-gray knit materials, he wore a waistcoat and cap trimmed with Astracan fur, of the same colour, and the whole covered with a large cloak lined with crimson velvet. His expenditure equalled his appearance, for not contented with living sumptuously at the places of repose, he also supported three or four others of the cordon.

Jossas never had any education, but having entered when very young into the service of a rich colonel, whom he accompanied in his travels, he had acquired manners sufficiently good not to disgrace any circle. Thus his comrades seeing him introduce himself into the first society, named him " Passe-par-tout." He was so completely identified with this character, that at the Bagne, when confined in double irons, and mingling indiscriminately with men of the most miserable appearance, he still kept up a portion of his grandeur, though disguised in a convict's cassock. Having provided himself with a splendid dressing-box, he bestowed an hour daily on his toilet, and was extremely particular about the appearance of his hands, which were certainly very handsome.

Jossas was one of those thieves, of whom, fortunately, but few are now in existence. He meditated and prepared an enterprise sometimes as long as a year beforehand. Operating principally by means of false keys, he began by taking first the impression of the lock of the outer door. The key made, he entered the first part; if stopped by another door, he took a second impression, had a second key made; and thus in the end attained his object. It may be judged, that only being able to get on during the absence of the tenant of the apartment, he must lose much time before the fitting opportunity would present itself. He only had recourse to this expedient when in despair, that is, when it was impossible to introduce himself to the house; for if he could contrive to procure admittance under any pretext, he soon obtained impressions of all the locks, and when the keys were ready, he used to invite the persons to dine with him, in the Rue Chantereine, and whilst they were at table, his accomplices stripped the apartments, from whence he had also contrived to draw away the servants, either by asking their masters to bring them to help to wait at table, or by engaging the attention of the waiting-maids and cooks by lovers who were in the plot. The porters saw nothing, because they seldom took any-thing but jewels or money. If by chance any large parcel was to be removed, they folded it up in dirty linen, and it was thrown out of window to an accom-plice in waiting with a washerwoman's wheel-barrow.

A multitude of robberies committed by Jossas are well known, all of which bespeak that acute observa-tion to invention which he possessed in the highest degree. In society, where he passed as a Creole of Havannah, he often met inhabitants of that place, with-out ever letting anything escape him which could be-tray him. He frequently led on families of distinction to offer him the hand of their daughters. Taking care always, during the many conversations thereon, to learn where the dowry was deposited, he invariably carried it off, and absconded at the moment appointed for signing the contract. But of all his tricks, that played off on a banker at Lyons it perhaps the most astonishing. Having acquainted himself with the ways of the house, under pretext of arranging accounts and negociations, in a short time an intimacy arose, which gave him the opportunity of getting the impression of all the locks except that of the cash chest, of which a secret ward rendered all his attempts unavailing. On the other hand, the chest being built in the wall, and cased with iron, it was impossible to think of break-ing it open. The cashier, too, never parted from his key; but these obstacles did not daunt Jossas. Having formed a close intimacy with the cashier, he proposed an excursion of pleasure to Collonges; and on the day oppointed, they went in a cabriolet. On approaching Saint Rambert, they saw by the river side a woman apparently dying, and the blood spouting from her mouth and nostrils; beside her was a man, who appeared much distressed, assisting her. Jossas, testi-fying considerable emotion, told him that the best method of stopping the effusion of blood was to apply a key to the back of the female. But no one had a key, except the cashier, who at first offered that of his apartment. That had no effect. The cashier, alarmed at seeing the blood flow copiously, took out the key of his cash-chest which was applied with much success between the shoulders of the patient. It has been already guessed that a piece of modelling wax had been placed there previously and that the whole scene had been preconcerted. Three days after, the cash-box was empty.

As I have already stated, Jossas playing off the high and mighty, spent money with the facility of a man who comes easily by it. Besides, he was very charitable; and I could cite many instances of his whimsical generosity, which I leave to the examination of moralists. Amongst others, the following: One day he penetrated into an apartmant in the Rue du Hazard, which he had been informed would yield a rich booty. At first the wretchedness of the furniture surprised him, but the proprietor might be a miser. He went on searching, burst open all, broke everything, and only found in a desk a bundle of pawnbrokers' duplicates. He took from his pocket five louis, and placing them on the mantel-piece, wrote on the glass these words, "Payment for broken furniture;" he then retired, after closing the doors carefully, lest any other robbers, less scrupulous, should carry off what he had respected.

When Jossas set out with us for Bicêtre it was his third journey. He afterwards escaped twice, was retaken, and died at the Bagne at Rochefort in 1806.

On our way to Montereau, I was witness of a scene which may as well be known, as it may prevent a similar recurrence. A convict, named Mauger, knew a young man of the city, who was believed by his parents to be sentenced to the gallies; and recommending his next neighbour to hide his face with his handkerchief, he told several persons we met on our way,

that the persons who thus concealed himself was the
young man in question. The chain went onwards, but
scarcely were we a quarter of a league from Montereau,
when a man, running after us, gave the captain fifty
francs, produced by a collection made for the 'man
with the handkerchief.' These fifty francs were in the
evening distributed amongst the plotters of the scheme,
without any other persons but themselves knowing the
cause of such liberality.

At Sens, Jossas played another comedy. He had
sent for a man, named Sergent, who kept the auberge
de l'Ecu; and on his arrival, this man testified the
most excessive grief. "What!" he exclaimed, with tears
in his eyes, "you here, my noble marquis! You, the
brother of my old master! I, who thought you on
your return to Germany! Oh heavens! what a misfortune." It may be guessed that in some expedition,
Jossas, being at Sens, had passed himself for an emigrant, returned clandestinely, and the brother of a
count with whom Sergent had been cook. Jossas
explained to him how, being apprehended with a forged
passport at the moment he was gaining the frontier, he
had been sentenced as a forger. The good aubergiste
did not confine himself to empty lamentations, but
sent the galley slave an excellent dinner, which I partook, with an appetite greatly contrasted with my
wretched situation.

Save and except a tremendous chastisment inflicted on
two convicts who had tried to escape at Beaume, nothing extraordinary occurred till we reached Châlons,
when we were put on board a large boat, filled with
straw, very similar to those which convey charcoal to
Paris; the whole covered with a thick cloth. If, to
cast a glance over the country, or breathe a purer air,
a convict ventured to raise a corner, a shower of blows
rained instantly on his shoulders. Although freed from
such treatment, I was not the less affected at my situation; scarcely could the gaiety of Jossas, who was never downcast, avail in making me for a moment for-

get, that, on reaching the Bagne, I should be the object of a special vigilance that must frustrate every hope of escape. This idea doubly depressed me when we reached Lyons.

On seeing the Ile Baslie, Jossas said to me, " You are going to see something new." I saw, on the quay of the Seine, an elegant carriage, which seemed to be awaiting the arrival of the boat. As soon as it came in sight, a female put her head from the window, and waved a white handkerchief. " It is she," said Jossas, who replied to the signal. The boat having been moored to the quay, the lady descended, and mixed in the crowd of lookers-on; I could not see her face, which was concealed by a very thick black veil. She remained there from four in the afternoon till evening, and the crowd then dispersing, Jossas sent lieutenant Thierry to her, who soon returned with a sausage, in which were concealed fifty louis. I learnt that Jossas, having made a conquest of this lady under his title of marquis, had informed her by letter of his condemnation, which he doubtlessly accounted for as he had done with the aubergiste at Sens. These sort of intrigues, now very rare, were at this period very common, in consequence of the disorders which sprung from the revolution; an event which shook to the very centre the structure of social order and good conduct in society. Ignorant of the stratagem plotted to deceive her, the veiled lady reappeared the next day on the quay, and remained there until our departure, to the great satisfaction of Jossas, who not only was recruited in finance, but was assured of an asylum in the event of effecting his escape.

We had nearly reached the termination of our navigation, when two leagues from Pont St Esprit, we were overtaken by one of those terrific storms so common on the Rhone. It was announced by distant rumblings of thunder. Soon afterwards, the rain descended in torrents; gusts of wind, such are only experienced under the tropics, blew down houses, uprooted

trees, and drove the waves mountain high, which
threatened at each moment to overwhelm us with destruction. At this moment, the spectacle that presented itself was horrific ; by the rapid flashes of lightning were to be seen two hundred men, chained so as
to deprive them of the remotest hope of safety, and
expressing by fearful cries the anguish of approaching
death, rendered inevitable by the weight of their fetters :
on their sinister countenances might be read the desire
to preserve a life disputed by the scaffold, a life henceforward to be spent in misery and degradation. Some
of the convicts evinced an absolute passiveness, many,
on the contrary, delivered themselves up to a frantic
joy. If any unfortunate wretch, mindful of his innocent youth, muttered out the fragment of a prayer, his
next companion would perhaps shake his fetters, whilst
he howled an obscene song, and the prayer expired in
the midst of lengthened howls and shrieks.

What redoubled the general consternation was, the
despair of the mariners, who seemed to have given
all over for lost. The guards were not more confident,
and even gave symptoms of an intention to quit the
boat, which was visibly filling fast with water. Then
matters took a fresh turn, and they urged on the argousins, crying,"Make the shore ; let all make for shore."
The darkness, added to the confusion of the moment, affording an opportunity with impunity, the most
intrepid of the convicts rose, declaring that no person
should quit the boat until it reached the bank. Lieutenant Thierry was the only one who appeared to have
preserved his presence of mind ; he put on a bold front,
and protested that there was no danger, as neither he
nor the sailors had any intention of quitting the vessel.
We believed him the more as the weather was gradually becoming more moderate. Daylight appeared,
and on the surface of the waters, smooth as ice, there
would have been nothing to recall the disasters of the
night, if the muddy tide had not been strewn with dead
cattle, trees, and fragments of furniture and houses.

Escaped from the tempest, we landed at Avignon, and were confined in the castle. There commenced the vengeance of the argousins; they had not forgotten what they were pleased to term our insurrection; refreshing our memories with it by blows from their cudgels, and then preventing the public from giving the convicts that assistance which the end of the journey prevented from passing through their hands. " Alms to these vagabonds!" said one of them, called father Lami, to some ladies who wished to bestow some aid; " it would be money lost. Besides, ask the captain."

Lieutenant Thierry, who ought not to be mentioned with such brutal and inhuman beings, and of whom I have already spoken, gave permission; but, by a refinement of villany the argousins made the signal for departure before the distribution was finished. The rest of the journey had no features of interest; and at length, after thirty-seven days of most painful travel, the chain entered Toulon.

The fifteen carriages arrived at the port, and drawn up in front of the rope-yard, the convicts were ordered to alight, and were then escorted to the court-yard of the Bagne. On the way thither, those who had clothes worth anything made all possible haste to take them off and sell or give them to the crowd which assembled at the arrival of a new chain. When the clothing of the Bagne was distributed, and the manacles had been rivetted, as I had seen it done at Brest, we were conveyed on board a cut-down frigate, called le Husard (now le Frontin) used as the floating Bagne. As soon as the 'payots' (convicts employed as writers) had written down our descriptions, the " return horses" (escaped convicts) were rivetted to the double chain. Their escape added three years additional confinement to the original sentence.

As I was thus circumstanced, I was sent to No. 3, where the most suspected convicts were placed. Lest they should find an opportunity for escaping in going to the harbour, they never went to labour. Always fettered to the 'banc,' lying on the bare plank, eaten up by vermin, and worn out by brutal treatment and want of nourishment and exercise, they presented a most lamentable appearance.

What I have already said concerning the abuses of every kind, of which the Bagne at Brest was the theatre, precludes the necessity of making any remarks on that at Toulon. Here was the same mixture of convicts ; the same inhumanity of argousins ; the same pilfering of the government property ; only the importance of the armaments afforded more scope for plunder to the galley-slaves, who were employed in the arsenals or magazines. Iron, lead, brass, hemp, pease, beans, oil, rum, smoked beef, and biscuit, disappeared daily ; and the men easily found receivers, as the convicts had very active auxiliaries in the marines and free workmen of the dock-yard. The rigging procured by these means served to equip a multitude of boats and fishing smacks, whose owners got them very cheaply, and were borne out, in case of inquiry, by saying that they had bought them at a sale of refuse stores.

A convict of our ward, who being a prisoner in England, had worked as a carpenter in the dock-yards of Chatham and Plymouth, told us that the plunder was there very great. He assured us that in all the villages along the banks of the Thames and Medway, there were persons perpetually occupied in untwisting the cordage of the royal navy, to take out the marks and stamps put in to make it known ; others were employed in effacing the 'broad arrow' stamped on all the metal materials used in the arsenals. These thefts, however considerable, are not at all comparable to the robberies on the river Thames, so very injurious to trade. Although the establishment of a river police has in great measure repressed these abuses, I think it will not be uninteresting to give some details concerning the frauds exercised still in some parts at the expence of the cargoes of vessels.

The thieves here alluded to are divided into many classes, each of which has its particular province or department; they are called the river pirates (pirates de rivière); light horsemen (chevaux legers); heavy horsemen (gendarmes); game watermen (bateliers chasseurs); game lightermen (gabariers chasseurs); mud-larks (hirondelles de vase); scuffle hunters (tapageurs); and copmen (receleurs). The river pirates consist of the boldest and most desperate of the robbers who infest the Thames: they carry on their operations in the night against all vessels badly watched, and whose crews are sometimes murdered that they may the more easily pillage the vessel. More frequently they confine themselves to taking the cordage, oars, poles, and bales of merchandize. The captain of an American brig, anchored off Castlane-Ter,* hearing a noise, went on deck to look out, he saw a boat row away, and found they were pirates, who, wishing him good evening, told him that they had just raised his anchor and cable. Having an understanding with the watchmen charged with taking care of the cargoes at night, they plunder with the greatest facility. When they cannot effect such collusions, they cut the cables of the lighters and let them drift until they get to a place where they can effect their object without any fear of discovery. Small coal barges have been thus found entirely emptied during the night. Russia tallow, which from the difficulty of moving the enormous barrels containing it, would seem to be safe, is not so; for an instance has been known of the noc-

* We give M. V.'s own spelling of this word, but such a place on the banks of the Thames is not known to us, nor, we believe to any one else in London: but in reference to Colquhoun's ' Police of the Metropolis,' we find this and the following anecdotes, whence M. Vidocq must have literally copied them; and the ' Castlane Ter' is ' East Lane Tier.' So much for accuracy!—*Translator.*

turnal removal of seven of these casks, each weighing between thirty and forty hundred weight.

The light horsemen also plunder during the night, but principally those vessels coming from the West Indies. This species of robbery arises from a concerted plan between some of the crew and the receivers, who buy the scrapings, that is, the samples of sugar, the refuse of the coffee, or the drippings of the spirits, and which remain in the hold when the cargo has been discharged. It is an easy matter to encrease these by piercing the sacks, and loosening the hoops of the barrels. This, a Canadian merchant, who sent a great deal of oil annually, discovered to his great astonishment. Always finding a deficit much greater than could arise from common leakage, and unable to get, on this head, a satisfactory solution from his correspondents, he determined on making a voyage to London, to penetrate the mystery. Resolved to pursue his investigations with the most minute research, he was in the quay waiting with much impatience for a lighter laden the previous evening, and whose delay seemed very extraordinary. At length it appeared, and the merchant saw a pack of fellows of very bad appearance jump on board with as much eagerness as a crew of corsairs into a prize. He also went down into the hold, and was completely stupified on seeing the barrels placed with their bungs downwards. When they begun to unload the lighter, he found as much oil left floating in the hold as would fill nine barrels. The proprietor having had a few planks taken up, there was found as much more as filled five casks, so that the load of one lighter had made a diminution of fourteen barrels. It would be scarcely credited, that the crew, far from being ashamed of this, had the impudence to assert that they had a right to this as a profit that belonged to them.

Not content with these thefts, the light horsemen, united with the lightermen, opened, during the night, barrels of sugar, which they entirely emptied, carrying them off in black bags which they call "black straps"

(bandes noires).   Some constables sent to Paris, and
with whom I was associated in an affair, assured me
that in one night there had been carried off from
various vessels as much as twenty hogsheads of sugar,
and also of rum drawn of by means of a pump, called a
jigger, and which was conveyed away in bladders.   The
ships, on board which this traffic is carried, were called
" game ships" (vaisseaux à gibier).   At this period,
the robberies of liquors and spirits were, besides, very
common, even in the royal navy.   A very remarkable
instance occurred on board the Victory, which brought
to England the dead body of Nelson, killed, as we
know, at the battle of Trafalgar.   To preserve the
remains, they were put into a puncheon of rum.   On
reaching Plymouth, the puncheon on being opened
was entirely empty and dry.   During the voyage, the
sailors, very certain that the purser would not visit
this cask, had drank up all the rum by straw pipes, or
jiggers.   They called this " tapping the admiral"
(mettre l'amiral en perce).

The game boatmen are on board vessels unloading
their cargoes, and receive, and instantly carry off, all
stolen goods.   As they are the parties who treat with
the receivers, they make a profitable business of it,
and spend a great deal of money.   I heard of one
who, from the fruits of his industry, kept a very elegant woman, and a saddle horse.

By mud-larks, are meant those men who grope
about on the shores at low tide, under the bottoms
of vessels, pretending to look for old pieces of cord,
iron, coals, &c., but in fact to receive and conceal
various articles thrown over to them.

The scuffle-hunters, are workmen with long aprons,
who pretend to ask for work, go in a body on shipboard, and find opportunities of ' prigging' something
during the confusion.

Last of all are the receivers, who not content with
buying all that the thieves bring to them, sometimes
have understandings with the captain, or some of the
crew, whom they find out to be not indisposed to deal

with them. These transactions are made in slang terms, intelligible only to the parties concerned. Sugar was "sand;" coffee, "beans;" pepper, "small pease;" rum, "vinegar;" tea, "hops;" so that they could deal for them even in the presence of the supercargo of the ship, whilst he was not aware that it was his cargo that was the subject of such roguery.

I found in the cell, No, 3, all the most abandoned scoundrels that ever assembled at the Bagne. I saw there one named Vidal, who even struck the convicts themselves with horror. Apprehended at fourteen years of age, in the midst of a band of brigands, whose crimes he participated, his age alone redeemed him from the scaffold. He was sentenced to imprisonment for twenty-four years; but scarcely had he reached the prison when, at the conclusion of a quarrel, he killed a comrade with a blow of his knife. A sentence of twenty-four years' hard labour, was then substituted for that of imprisonment only. He had been for some years at the Bagne, when a convict was sentenced to death. There was not an executioner to be found in the city, and Vidal eagerly offered his services, which were accepted, and the execution was carried into effect, but they were compelled to put Vidal on the bench with the galley-guards, or else the convicts would have knocked him on the head with their fetters. The threats which menaced him did not prevent him from fulfilling his new office again, some time afterwards. Besides, he undertook to administer the sentences of bastinado on the prisoners. At length, in 1794, the revolutionary tribunal having been installed at Toulon, after the taking of that town by Dugommier, Vidal was employed to carry their sentences into effect. He then thought he was liberated, but when the terror had ceased, he was remanded to the Bagne, where he was placed under a special surveillance.

On the same bench with Vidal, was the Jew Deschamps, one of the principal of the party concerned

in robbing the royal wardrobe (garde-meuble), to the
details of which the convicts listened with a sinis-
trous pleasure. At the enumeration of the diamonds
and jewels carried off, their eyes sparkled, their
muscles contracted by a convulsive motion ; and by
the expression of their countenances, inferences might
unerringly have been drawn of the first uses they
would have made of their liberty. This disposition
was particularly discernible in those men only convicted of petty offences, who were taunted and ban-
tered as only having stolen objects of small value;
and then, after estimating the plunder of the wardrobe,
at twenty millions of francs, Deschamps, added,
with an air of contempt towards a poor devil sentenced for stealing vegetables, " Ah! ah! this was
cabbage."

From the moment when the robbery was perpetrated it became the subject of multiplied comments,
which circumstances and agitation of mind rendered
very singular. It was during the meeting of the re-
presentatives on the Sunday evening (16th of September 1792), that Roland, minister of the interior,
announced the event to the tribune of the convention,
complaining bitterly of the inefficient surveillance of
the agents and the military guards, who had forsaken
their posts, under pretext of the "severity of the
cold." Some days afterwards, Thuriot, who was one
of the commission charged with searching out the
matter, in his turn accused the minister of carelessness, who answered drily, that he had something else
to do beside watching the wardrobe. The discussion
rested here, but these debates had aroused the public
attention, and the sole public theme was of guilty
collusions, and plots framed for robbery, of which the
produce was devoted to keeping the police agents in
pay ; they went so far as to say, that the government
had robbed itself; and what gave a consistency to
such a report, was the reprieves granted on the 18th
of October to some individuals condemned for this

affair, and from whom confessions were expected.
However, on the 22nd of February 1797, in a report
to the Conseil des Anciens, on a proposal to grant a
reward of five thousand francs to a madame Corbin,
who had facilitated the discovery of a great quantity
of the plundered property, Thiebault declared, in the
most formal manner, that this event was not the result of any political measure, and had all been in-
curred by the defective vigilance of the police, and
by the mismanagement which pervaded every department of the administration.

At the beginning, the Moniteur had heated the ima-
ginations of the most wary, by speaking of forty
armed robbers who had been surprised in the wardrobe. The truth is, that no one was surprised; and
when they first discovered the loss of " the regent," the
dauphin's coral, and a vast many other jewels valued
at seventeen millions of francs, for four successive
nights, Deschamps, Bernard Salles, and a Portuguese
Jew, named Dacosta, had in their turns entered the
apartments, without any other arms than the tools requisite to extract the jewels set in the plate, which
they disdained to carry off; and thus they removed
with the greatest precaution the magnificent rubies
which formed the eyes of the ivory fishes.

Deschamps, to whom belongs the honour of the
invention, first got into the gallery by climbing a window, by means of a lamp-post, which still stands at the
angle of the Rue Royale, and the place of Louis XV.
Bernard Salles and Dacosta, who kept watch, were
at first his only comrades; but on the third night,
Benôit Naid, Philipponeau, Paumettes, Fraumont,
Gay, Monton, lieutenant of the National Guard, and
Durand, called ' le Turc,' a jeweller in the Rue Saint
Sauveur, were added to the gang, as well as many first-
rate ' cracksmen,' who had been, in a friendly way, invited to come and participate in the spoil.   The rendezvous was at a billiard-room in the Rue de Rohan;
and, besides, they made so little mystery of the rob-

béry, that the morning after the first booty, Paumettes, dining with some girls at a cook shop, in the
Rue d'Argenteuil, threw on the table to them a handful of rose and small brilliant diamonds.   The police
however got no information.   To detect the principal
authors it was necessary that Durand, arrested for
forging assignats, should confess to obtain his own
pardon, and on his information " the regent" was discovered and seized at Tours, sewn up in the head-
dress of a woman named Lebiène, who, unable to
reach England in consequence of the war, was about
to sell it at Bordeaux to a Jew, known to Dacosta.
They had attempted to get rid of it in Paris, but the
value of the gem, estimated at twelve millions of francs,
would have awakened dangerous suspicions; they had
also given up the idea of cutting the stone, lest the
lapidary should betray them.

The majority of the robbers were in turns apprehended, and sentenced for other offences, amongst
whom were Benôit Naid, Dacosta, Bernard Salles,
Fraumont, and Philipponeau; this last, arrested in
London at the close of the year 1791, at the moment
he was engraving a plate of assignats of 300 francs,
was taken back to France, and shut up in La Force,
whence he escaped by favour of the massacres of the
2d of September.

Before having been sentenced for the robbery of the
wardrobe, Deschamps had been implicated in a capital
affair, whence he was extricated, although so guilty,
as he boasted to us, by giving details not to be doubted.
He had been concerned in the double murder of the
jeweller Deslong and his servant maid, committed with
his accomplice, the broker Fraumont.

Deslong had an extensive business, and besides
private purchases, he also bartered diamonds and
pearls; and as he was known to be an honest man, he
often had valuable gems entrusted to him, either to
sell or unset.   He also frequented auctions, where
Fraumont first knew him, who was constantly at sales

to buy the ropes, altar cloths, and other pillaged church ornaments (1793) which he burnt to get the metal from the gold lace. From the custom of meeting together so frequently in business, a sort of acquaintance sprung up between the two men, which soon became a close intimacy. Deslong had no concealment with Fraumont, and consulted him in all his undertakings, informed him of the worth of all the deposits entrusted to him, and even confided to him the secret of a hiding-place in which he kept his most valuable articles.

Informed of all these particulars, and having free access at all times to Deslong's house, Fraumont conceived the project of robbing him whilst he and his wife were at the theatre, which they frequented. He wanted an accomplice to keep watch; and besides it would have been dangerous for Fraumont, whom everybody knew, to be seen on the premises on the day of the robbery. He first selected a locksmith, a fugitive convict, who made the false keys necessary for entering Deslong's house; but this man being pursued by the police, was forced to leave Paris, and he then substituted Deschamps.

On the day fixed for the perpetration of the robbery, Deslong and his wife having gone to the Theatre de la Republique, Fraumont concealed himself at a vintner's to watch for the return of the servant maid, who usually took advantage of the absence of her master and mistress to go and see her lover. Deschamps went up to the apartment, and opened the door gently with one of his false keys. What was his astonishment to see in the hall the maid servant whom he thought absent, (her sister, who was much like her, having in fact left the house a few minutes before!) At the sight of Deschamps, whose surprise made his countenance even more frightful, the girl let fall her work and shrieked. Deschamps sprang upon her, threw her down, seized her throat, and gave her five blows with a clasp knife, which he had about him, in

the right-hand pocket of his trowsers. The unhappy
creature fell bathed in blood, and whilst the death
rattle was yet sounding in her throat, the ruffian
ransacked every corner of the room : but whether this
unexpected event disturbed him, or that he heard
some noise on the staircase, he only carried off some
pieces of plate which came to hand, and returned to
his accomplice at the vintner's, and told him the
adventure. He (Fraumont) was much grieved, not
at the murder of the servant, but at the little information and clumsiness of Deschamps, whom he
reproached with not having discovered the secret
closet which he had so plainly pointed out; and what
put the cope-stone on his discontent was, that he
foresaw that after such a catastrophe Deslong would
be more careful of his property, and it would be impossible ever again to get such an opportunity.

In fact, Deslong did change his lodging after this
event, which inspired him with the most excessive
fright, and the few persons whose visits he allowed
were received with the greatest precaution. Although
Fraumont did not present himself, yet he had no
suspicion of him. How could he suspect a man who,
if he had perpetrated the crime, would not have failed
to have ransacked the closet, of which he knew the
secret? Meeting him at the end of a few days on the
Place Vendôme, he pressed him strongly to come and
see him, and became more intimate with him than ever.
Fraumont then began plotting again; but, despairing
of breaking open the new place of security, which
besides was carefully guarded, he determined on
changing his plan. Led to Deschamps' house, under
pretence of bargaining for a large lot of diamonds,
Deslong was assassinated and robbed of seventeen
thousand francs, in gold and assignats, with which he
had provided himself by advice of Fraumont, who
dealt him the first stab.

Two days elapsed, and madame Deslong, not seeing
her husband return, who never made so long an

absence without a previous intimation, and knowing
that he had considerable property about him, no
longer doubted but that some misfortune had befallen
him. She then went to the police, the confused organization of which was then felt sensibly in every
department; but, however, they contrived to get hold
of Fraumont and Deschamps; and the confession of
the locksmith, which corresponded with the accounts
of the robbery, and who was apprehended soon after,
would have had an unpropitious termination for them,
had not the authorities refused to give this man the
liberty they had promised to reward him with; and the
police agent, Cordat, who had been the go-between,
unwilling that his promises should be broken, aided
his escape on the way from La Force to the Palace.
This circumstance removing the only witness who
could be brought forward, Deschamps and Fraumont
were set at liberty.

Condemned afterwards to eighteen years' imprisonment for other robberies, Fraumont set out for the
Bagne at Rochefort on the first Nivose, year eight;
but he was not yet out of courage, and by means of
money, produced by his plunder, he had bribed several
persons who were to follow the chain to aid his
escape, in case he should attempt it, or even to carry
him off by force, if need should be. The use he proposed to make of his liberty was, to assassinate M.
Delalande, high president of the tribunal which had
condemned him, and commissary of the police of the
Section de l'Unité, who had brought such overwhelming charges against him. All was ripe for the execution
of this plot, when a common woman, who had learned
the details from the lips of one of the accomplices,
made a spontaneous confession, and measures were
accordingly taken. The escort was informed of it;
and when the chain left Bicêtre, Fraumont was put in
extra chains, which were not removed until his arrival
at Rochefort, where he was an object of special vigilance; and I was told that he died at the Bagne. As

for Deschamps, who escaped from Toulon soon after, he was apprehended at the end of three years, as concerned in a robbery committed at Anteuil, sentenced to death by the criminal tribunal of the Seine, and executed at Paris.

In cell, No. 3, I was only separated from Deschamps by a burglar named Louis Mulot, son of that Cornu who so long affrighted the people of Normandy, where his crimes are still unforgotten. Disguised as a horse-dealer, he frequented the fairs, watched the merchants who had large sums about them, and taking the cross roads, laid in wait for and assassinated them. Married, for the third time, to a young and pretty woman of Bernai, he had at first carefully concealed from her his infernal trade; but he was not slow in discovering that she was entirely worthy of him, and thenceforward she accompanied him in all his expeditions. Frequenting all the fairs as a peripatetic mercer, she easily introduced herself to the rich graziers of the valley of Auge, and more than one met his death at the appointed spot of gallant rendezvous. Often suspected, they brought forward *alibis*, always successful, and for which they were indebted to the fleetness of the excellent horses with which they were always provided.

In 1794, the Cornu family consisted of the father, mother, three sons, two daughters and their lovers, all of whom had been habituated to crime from their earliest childhood, either in keeping watch or setting fire to barns, &c. The youngest, Florentine, having at first testified some repugnance, they had cured her delicacy by compelling her to carry in her apron, for two leagues, the head of a farmer of the environs of Argentin!

At a later period, entirely devoid of any tender scruples, she had, as her lover, the assassin Capelle, executed in 1802. When the family formed itself into a band of Chauffeurs to infest the country (Caen and Falaise) it was she who put to torture the

wretched farmers, by putting a lighted candle under
their armpits, or placing blazing tinder on their
toes.*

Hotly pursued by the police of Caen, and particularly by that of Rouen, who had apprehended two of
the juniors of the family at Brionne, Cornu resolved
on retiring for some time to the vicinity of Paris,
trusting thus to elude enquiry. Installed with his
family in a lone house, on the road to Sevres, he did
not fear to take his walks in the Champs-Elyseés,
where he met nearly all the robbers of his acquaintance. "Well, father Cornu," said they to him one
day, "what are you about now?"—"Oh, always
administering the last consolation (assassination), my
sons—the last consolation."—"That is droll, father
Cornu; but discovery may ensue."—"Oh! no fear
where no witnesses. If I had done for all the corn-
threshers (farmers) whom I have only singed, I should
have nothing to funk about now."

In one of his excursions, Cornu met an old comrade,
who proposed to him to break into a villa, situated in
the wood of Ville d'Avray. The robbery was committed and the booty shared, but Cornu found that he
had been duped. On reaching the middle of the
wood, he let fall his snuff-box whilst offering it to his
companion, who stooped to pick it up, and at that
very instant Cornu blew out his brains with a pistol-
shot, plundered him, and regained his own house,
where he told the tale to his family with bursts of
laughter.

Apprehended near Vernon, at the moment he was
breaking into a farm, Cornu was conducted to Rouen,
tried before the Criminal Court, and sentenced to
death. Soon after this, his wife, who was still at
liberty, came every day to bring him food and console

* Whence the name of Chauffeurs, or burners.—
Translator.

VOL. I. U

him. " Listen," said she to him one morning, when
he appeared more dejected than usual, " listen,
Joseph: they say that death affrights you,—don't
play the noodle, at all events, when they lead you
to the scaffold. The lads of the game will laugh at
you."

" Yes," said Cornu, " all that is very fine, if one's
scrag was not in danger; but with Jack Ketch on one
side, and the black sheep (clergyman) on the other,
and the traps (gendarmes) behind, it is not quite so
pleasant to be turned into food for flies."

" Joseph, Joseph, do not talk in this way; I am
only a woman, you know; but I could go through it
as if at a wedding, and particularly with you, old lad!
Yes, I tell you again, by the word of Marguerite, I
would willingly accompany you."

" Are you in earnest?" asked Cornu. " Yes, quite
in earnest," sighed Marguerite. " But what are you
getting up for? What are you going to do?"

" Nothing," replied Cornu; and then going to a
turnkey who was in the passage, " Roch," said he to
him, " send for the jailor, I want to see the public
accuser."

" What!" said his wife, " the public accuser! Are
you going to split (confess)? Ah, Joseph, consider
what a reputation you will leave for our children!"

Cornu was silent until the magistrate arrived, and
he then denounced his wife; and this unhappy woman,
sentenced to death by his confessions, was executed at
the same time with him. Mulot, who told me all this,
never repeated the narrative without laughing till he
cried. However, he thought the guillotine no subject
for joking; and for a long time avoided all crimes that
could send him to rejoin his father, mother, one of his
brothers, and his sister Florentine, all executed at
Rouen. When he spoke of them, and the end they
had made, he frequently said, " This is the fruits of
playing with fire; they shall never catch me at such

work :" and in fact, his tricks were not so redoubtable; he confined himself to a species of robbery in
which he excelled. His eldest sister, whom he had
brought to Paris, aided him in all his enterprizes.
Dressed as a washerwoman, with a pannier at her
back and a basket on her arm, she went to all the
houses where there was no porter, and, knocking at
the doors, if she learnt that the occupants were from
home, she returned and told Mulot. Then he, disguised as a journeyman locksmith, went, and with his
bunch of picklocks in his hand, opened with the
greatest ease the most complicated locks. Frequently,
that suspicion might not be aroused, in case any one
should pass, his sister, with her apron and a modest
cap on, and with the disturbed appearance of a nurse
who had lost her key, aided his operations. Mulot,
as we may see, did not want foresight, but yet was
one day surprised in the very act, and soon after
condemned to imprisonment.

CHAPTER XIV.

Father Mathieu—I enter on a new line of business—Ruin of my establishment—I am supposed to be paralyzed in my limbs —I am assistant major—Ecce Homo, or the psalm-seller—A disguise—Stop him! he is a fugitive convict—I am added to the double chain—The kindness of the commissary—I tell him a made-up tale—My best contrived escape—The lady of the town and the burial—I know not what—Critical situation—A band of robbers—I detect a thief—I get my dismissal—I promise secrecy.

I NEVER was so wretched as after my entry at the Bagne at Toulon. Cast at twenty-four years of age amongst the most abandoned wretches, and necessarily in contact with them, although I would have preferred a hundred times to be reduced to living in the midst of people infected with the plague,—compelled only to see and hear degraded beings, whose minds were incessantly bent on devising evil schemes, I feared the dire contagion of such vicious society. When, day and night, in my presence, they openly practised the most vile and demoralized actions, I was not so confident in the strength of my own character as not to fear that I might become but too much familiarised with such atrocious and dangerous conversation. In fact, I had resisted many dangerous temptations; but want, misery, and the thirst of liberty, will often involuntarily tempt us to a step towards crime. I had never been in any situation where it was more positively incumbent on me to attempt an escape; and henceforward all my ideas and thoughts were turned to the compassing of this measure. Various plans suggested themselves, but that was not sufficient; for to put any of them into execution I must await a favourable opportunity, and until then, patience was the only remedy for my woes. Fastened to the same bench with robbers by profession, who had already escaped several times, I was

as well as they, an object of special surveillance, which
it was difficult to divert. In their cambrons (watch-
boxes) at a short distance from us, the argousins were
always on the look-out, and observed our least motions. Father Mathieu, their chief, had the eyes of a
lynx, and such a knowledge of the men he had to deal
with, that he could tell at the slightest glance if they
were scheming to deceive him. This old fox was
nearly sixty years of age; but having a vigorous constitution, which seemed proof against the attacks of
time, he was still hale and hearty. He was one of
those square figures which never wear out. I have
him now in "my mind's eye," with his little tail, his
grey and powdered locks, and his face in wrinkles
so congruous with the business of his calling. He
never spoke without mentioning his cudgel; it was a
never-ending theme of pleasurable recital to talk of
the many bastinadoes he had inflicted personally, or
ordered to be done. Always at war with the convicts,
he knew every one of their tricks. His mistrust was
so excessive, that he often accused them of plotting
when they were not at all thinking of it. It may
be supposed that it was no easy matter to make a
sop for this Cerberus. I tried however to procure
his favour, an attempt in which no one had as
yet succeeded: but I soon found that I had not
essayed in vain; for I perceptibly gained on his
good will. Father Mathieu sometimes talked to
me; a sign, as the experienced told me, that I had
made some way with him. I thought I might ask
something from him on the strength of this, and I
asked him to allow me to make children's toys with
the pieces of wood brought in by the working convicts.
He granted all I asked, provided I was steady; and
the next day I began my work. My companions cut
out roughly, and I finished the toys. Father Mathieu
approved of my productions; and when he saw that I
had assistance in my work, he could not forbear testifying his approbation, which he had not expressed for

u 2

a long time previously. "Well, well!" said he, "how I like people to amuse themselves; it would be well if you all did the same; it would pass time away; and, with the profits, you might purchase some small comforts." A few days afterwards, the bench was a perfect workshop, where fourteen men, equally anxious to drive away ennui and to earn a little money, worked away with much industry. We had all some goods ready, which were sold by the assistance of the convicts who gave us the materials. For a month, our trade was very brisk, and every day we had abundant returns, not a sous of which was reserved. Father Mathieu had authorized us to appoint as our treasurer a convict named Pantaragat, who sold provisions in the room in which we were. Unfortunately there are goods which cannot be multiplied without the necessary balance between produce and consumption being destroyed. This is a fact in political economy, that there is a point when the production must terminate for lack of demand. Toulon was replete with toys of every description, and we must thenceforward sit with folded arms. No longer knowing what to do, I feigned a complaint in my legs, that I might be sent to the hospital. The doctor, to whom I was recommended by father Mathieu, whose protegé I had become, actually believed that I was unable to walk. When one would attempt to escape, it is impossible to manage better than to contrive to excite such an opinion. Doctor Ferrant did not for an instant suspect me of any intent to deceive him; he was one of those disciples of Esculapius, who, like many of the Hippocrates of the school of Montpellier, whence he came, think that bluntness is a part of their profession; but still he was a humane man, and behaved very kindly to me. The chief surgeon had also a liking for me, and to me he trusted the care of his surgery chest; I scraped his lint, rolled his bandages, and made myself generally useful, so that my willingness procured for me his kindness: every one, even to the argousin of the infirmary, behaved well to me, although no one could exceed in sternness M. l'Homme (that was his name), whom they called, jokingly, " Ecce Homo," because he had been formerly a seller of psalms and canticles. Although I had been pointed out to him as a daring fellow, M. l'Homme was so much pleased with my good behaviour, and still more with the bottles of mulled wine which I shared with him, that he perceptibly became more humanized. When I was pretty well assured that I should not excite his suspicions, I unmasked my battery, to overpower his vigilance, as well as that of his fellow guards. I had already procured a wig and black whiskers, and had besides concealed in my mattress an old pair of boots, which, when well waxed, seemed as good as new; but that was only an equipment for my head and feet: to complete my toilet, I relied on the head surgeon, who used to lay on my bed his great coat, hat, cane, and gloves. One morning, whilst he was engaged in amputating an arm, I saw that M. l'Homme had followed him to assist in the operation, which was performed at the extremity of one of the wards: the opportunity for a disguise was admirable, and I hastened to complete it; and, in my new costume, I went straight to the door. I had to pass through a crowd of argousins, but I ventured boldly, and none of them appeared to pay any attention to me, and I already thought myself out of danger, when I heard a cry, " Stop him, stop him; a prisoner has escaped!" I was not more than twenty steps from the arsenal, and, without losing my presence of mind, I redoubled my speed, and having got to the door, I said to the guard, pointing to a person who was just entering the city, " Run with me, he has escaped from the hospital."

This would, perhaps, have saved me; but, just as I stepped over the wicket, I was seized by the wig, and, on turning round, saw M. l'Homme: resistance would have been certain death; and I therefore quietly followed him back to the Bagne, where I was put to the double chain. It was evident that I was to undergo punishment, and to avoid it, I cast myself on my knees before the commissary, saying, "Oh, sir, do not let me be beaten; that is the only favour I ask; I would rather undergo three years' additional confinement." The commissary, however touching my petition might have been, could not keep his countenance; but told me, that he would pardon me on account of my boldness and ingenuity, on condition that I would point out the person who had procured me the disguise. "You must be aware," I replied to him, "that the people who guard us are wretches, who will do anything for money, but nothing in the world shall induce me to betray those who serve me." Pleased with my frankness, he ordered me to be released from the double chain; and when the argousin murmured at so much indulgence, he desired him to be silent, adding, "You ought to like, rather than be angry with him; for he has just given you a lesson, which you would do well to profit by." I thanked the commissary, and the next moment was conducted to the fatal bench to which I was to be fastened for the next six years. I then flattered myself with the hopes of returning to my trade of toy-making, but father Mathieu refusing me, I was compelled unwillingly to remain unemployed. Two months elapsed without any change in my circumstances, when, one night, being unable to sleep, there flashed through my brain one of those luminous ideas which only occur in darkness. Jossas was awake, and I mentioned it to him. It may be surmised that he was always intent on effecting his escape, and he thought it admirably wonderful as I had devised it, and begged me not to fail putting it into execution. It will be seen that I did not neglect his advice. One morning, the commissary of the Bagne going his rounds, passed near me, and I begged leave to speak to him in private. "What do you want?" said he. "Have you any complaint to make? Speak, my man; speak out, and I will do you justice."

Encouraged by the kindness of this language, I said, " Good sir, you see before you a second example of an honest criminal. You may perhaps remember that on coming here, I told you that I was put in my brother's place. I do not accuse him; I am even pleased at thinking he was ignorant of the crime imputed to him; but it was he, who, under my name, was condemned by the court at Douai; he escaped from the Bagne at Brest, and now, having reached England, he is free; and I, the victim of a sad mistake, must submit to punishment. Alas! how fatal to me has been our resemblance!

" Without this circumstance, I should not have been taken to Bicêtre; the keeper would not have sworn to my person. In vain have I begged for an inquiry; it is because their testimony has been received, that an identity is allowed which does not exist. But the error is consummated, and I have much to bewail! I know that it is not with you to alter a decision from which there is no appeal, but it is a favour you may grant to me: to be sure of me, I am placed in a cell with suspected men, where I am with a herd of robbers, assassins, and hardened ruffians. At every moment I tremble at the recital of crimes which have been committed, as well as at the hopes of those who are plotting others, to be perpetrated the moment, if it ever arrives, they shall get free from their fetters. Ah! I beg you, in the name of every sentiment of humanity, to leave me no longer amongst a set of such abandoned miscreants. Put me in a dungeon, load me with chains, do with me whatever you will, but do not leave me any longer with them. If I have endeavoured to escape, it has been only that I might get away from such a sink of infamy. (At this moment I turned towards the convicts.) You may see, sir, how ferociously they gaze at me; they already prepare to make me repent of what I am saying to you; they pant, they burn, to bathe their hands in

my blood: once more I conjure you, do not give me
up to the vengeance of these atrocious monsters."

During this discourse, the convicts were petrified
with astonishment; they could not conceive that one
of their comrades would thus upbraid them in their
very teeth; the commissary himself did not know what
to think of such a step; he was· silent, and I saw that
I had touched him deeply. Then throwing myself at
his feet, with tears in my eyes, I added. "Pity me;
if you refuse me, if you go without removing me from
this room, you shall never see me again." These words
produced the desired effect. The commissary, who
was a worthy man, had me unloosed in his presence
and gave orders that I should be placed with the
working convicts (à la fatigue). I was yoked with a
man named Salesse, a Gascon, as knavish as a convict
may be. The first time we were alone he asked me
if I intended to escape. "I have no thoughts of it,"
replied I, "I am but too glad that they allow me to
work. But Jossas possessed my secret, and he arranged all for my escape. I had a plain dress which
I concealed under my galley clothes without the knowledge even of my yoke-fellow. A moving screw had
supplied the place of the rivet in my fetters, and I was
ready to start. The third day after leaving my companions I went out to labour, and presented myself
before the argousin; "Get along, good-for-naught,"
said Father Mathieu, "it is not time." I was in the
rope-room, and the place appeared propitious. I told
my companion that I had a call of nature, and he
pointed out some pieces of wood behind which I could
go, and he was scarcely out of sight, when throwing
off my red shirt, and taking out the screw, I ran towards the basin. The frigate la Meuron was then
under repair, which had brought Buonaparte and his
suite from Egypt. I went on board and asked for
the master carpenter, whom I knew to be in the hospital. The cook, whom I accosted, took me for one

of the new crew. I was rejoiced at this, and to confirm the idea, as I knew him to be a man of Auvergne, by his accent, I began conversing with him in his own provincial dialect, and in a tone of much assurance, although I was on thorns the whole time; for forty couples of convicts were at work close to us. They might recognize me in a moment. A cargo soon set off for the town, and I jumped into the boat, when seizing an oar, I rowed away like an old sailor, and we soon reached Toulon. Anxious to reach the country I went to the Italian gate, but no one was allowed to go out without a green card given by the magistrates, and I was refused egress, and whilst I was thinking how I could get out, I heard the three reports of the cannon which announced my escape. At this moment a tremor pervaded all my limbs; already did I see myself in the power of the argousins, and all the police of the Bagne. I pictured myself in presence of the excellent commissary, whom I had so basely deceived. If I were taken I must be lost. These sad reflexions coming over me, I walked away in haste, and that I might avoid a crowd, betook myself to the ramparts.

On reaching a solitary spot, I walked very slowly like a man who not knowing whither to bend his steps, is full of consideration, when a female accosted me, and asked me in provincial French what the hour was; I told her that I did not know, and she then began talking of the weather, and concluded by asking me to accompany her home; it is only a few yards hence, she added, and no one will see us. The opportunity of finding a place of refuge was too propitious to be refused, and I followed my conductress to a sort of small inn, when I sent for some refreshment. Whilst we were conversing together, three other cannon shots were heard. " Ah !" cried the girl, with an air of satisfaction, " there is a second escape to-day." " What ! " said I, " my lass, does that please you ? Should not you like to get the reward ? " " I, why

you cannot know much of me." "Bah, bah," I replied, "fifty francs are always worth earning, and if I
swear to you that if one of these fellows fall into my
clutches ———." " You are a wretch !" she said,
making a gesture of indignation. " I am only a poor
girl, but Celestine would never eat the bread earned
by means so despicable." At these words, pronounced
with an accent of truth which left no doubt on my
mind of her sincerity, I did not hesitate to confide my
secret to her. As soon as I had informed her that I
was a convict, I cannot express how much she appeared interested in my fate. " Mon Dieu !" said she,
" they are so much to be pitied; I would save them
all, and have already saved many ;" then, after pausing
for an instant, as if to consider. "Let me manage it,"
she then added, " I have a lover who has a green card,
I will borrow it from him and you shall use it, and,
once out of the city, you can deposit it under a stone
which I will point out to you, and, in the interim, as
we are not in security here, I will take you to my
apartment." On reaching this, she told me that she
must leave me for a moment. " I must tell my lover,"
said she, " and will speedily return." Women are
sometimes most admirable actresses, and, in spite of
her kind protestations I feared some treachery. Perhaps Celestine was going to denounce me; she had
not reached the street, when I ran down the staircase ;
" Well, well." cried the girl, " do not fear. If you
mistrust me, come along with me." I thought it
most prudent to watch her, and we walked away
together, whither I knew not. Scarcely had we gone
ten yards, when we met a funeral procession. " Follow
the burial," said my protectress, " and you will escape ;"
and before I had time to thank her, she disappeared. The
followers were numerous, and I mixed amongst the
crowd of assistants, and that I might not be thought
a stranger at the ceremony, I entered into a conversation with an old sailor, from whose communications
I soon learnt how to utter a few well-timed remarks on

the virtues of the defunct. I was soon convinced that
Celestine had not betrayed me. When I left the ramparts behind me, which it had been of such paramount
importance for me to pass, I almost wept for joy; but
that I might not betray myself, I still kept up a strain
of suitable lamentations.

On reaching the cemetery I advanced in my turn
to the edge of the grave, and after having cast a handful of earth on the coffin, I separated from the company by taking a circuitous path. I walked on for
many hours without losing sight of Toulon, and about
five o'clock in the evening, just as I was entering a
grove of firs, I saw a man armed with a gun. As he
was well clad, and had a game-bag, my first thought
was that he was a huntsman; but observing the butt
of a pistol projecting from his girdle, I feared that I
had met with one of those provençals, who at the
sound of the cannon, always scour the country in
search of the runaway galley-slaves. If my fears
were just, flight was unavaling; and it was perhaps
best to advance rather than retreat. This I did, and
on approaching him sufficiently close to be on my
guard in case he should show any hostilities, I asked
the road to Aix.

"Do you want the high road or the bye-way?"
said he with peculiar emphasis.

"Oh either, no matter which," I answered; hoping
by my indifference to remove his suspicions.

"In that case, follow this path, it leads to the
station of the gendarmes; and if you do not like travelling alone, you can avail yourself of the escort."

At the word 'gendarmes' I turned pale, and the
stranger perceiving the effect his words had produced,
added, "Come, come; I see you are not over anxious
to travel on the highway. Well, if you are not in a
very great hurry, I will conduct you to the village of
Pourières, which is not two leagues from Aix."

He seemed so well acquainted with the localities,
that I availed myself of his offer, and consented to

x

follow him. Then, without stirring, he pointed out a clump of bushes, where he bid me await his joining me. Two hours passed before he finished his guard, and he then came to me—" Get up," said he. I obeyed, and when I thought myself in the thickest of the wood, I found myself at the borders of it, about fifty paces from a house, in front of which were seated several gendarmes. At the sight of their uniforms, I started. " What ails you, man," asked my guide ; " do you think I would betray you ? If you fear anything, take these and defend yourself;" at the same time offering me his pistols, which I refused. " Well, well ;" he added, and squeezed my hand, to testify how much he was satisfied with my confidence.

Concealed by the bushes which skirted our path, we stopped. I could not comprehend the motive of a halt so near the enemy. Our stay was protracted till nightfall, when we saw approaching from Toulon a mail, escorted by four gendarmes, who were relieved by the same number from the brigade whose vicinity had so much alarmed me. The mail proceeded on its journey, and was soon out of sight. My companion then taking my arm, said in an under-tone, " Let us start, nothing can be done to-day."

We then walked away in an opposite direction for about an hour, and my guide going up to a tree, clasped the trunk in his hands, and I saw that he was counting the number of notches cut by a knife—" Good, good ;" he ejaculated with an air of satisfaction, which was to me inexplicable, and taking from his game-bag a piece of bread, which he divided with me, he then gave me a bottle, whence I drank with pleasure. The collation could not have been more opportune, for I was in want of something to recruit my strength. In spite of the darkness, we walked so fast that I was tired, and my feet, long unused to exercise, had become so painful that I was going to declare it impossible for me to proceed further, when a village clock struck three. " Gently," said my guide, stooping and

placing his ear on the ground; "do as I do, and listen;
with this cursed Polish legion one must be always on
the watch. Did you hear nothing?" I replied that I
thought I heard the footsteps of a body of men.
" Yes," he added, it is they; stir not on your life, or
we shall be taken." He had scarcely spoken, when a
patrol guard came towards the thicket in which we
were concealed. " Did you see anything, you fellows?" said some one in a low tone.—" Nothing,
serjeant."

" Parbleu! I thought so; it is as dark as an oven.
This devil of a Roman, whom heavens thunders crush!
To make us travel all night like wolves in a wood!
Ah, if ever I find him, or any of his gang!"

" Qui vive? (who goes there?)" cried a soldier suddenly.

" What do you see?" said the serjeant.—" Nothing; but I heard a breathing on this side," and he
indicated the spot where we were.

" Stuff! you are dreaming. You are so much alarmed about Roman, that you think that you always have
him in your cartridge-box."

Two other soldiers asserted that they had heard the
same.

" Hold your tongues," replied the serjeant. " I see
there is nobody, and we must once more, according to
custom, return to Pourières without having trapped
our game. Come, my lads, it is time to be off." The
patrol seemed disposed to retreat. " It is a *ruse de
guerre*," said my companion. " I know they will beat
the wood and return upon us in a semi-circle."

It was now necessary that I should be firm and composed. " Are you fearful?" said my guide.

" This is no time for fear," I replied.

" Well then, follow me: here are my pistols; when
I fire, do you the same, so that the four shots only
sound like one report. Now, fire!"

The four shots were fired, and we then ran with all
speed, without being pursued. The fear of falling into

an ambuscade had made the soldiers come to a halt, but we did not pause from our flight. On getting near an isolated hut, the stranger said to me, " It is now daylight, and we are safe :" and then leaping the pales of the garden, he took a key from the hollow trunk of a tree, and opening the door of the cot we immediately entered.

An iron lamp, placed on the mantel-piece, lighted up a plain and rustic apartment. I only observed in a corner a barrel containing, as I thought, gunpowder, and near it on a shelf was a quantity of gun-cartridges. A woman's attire placed on a chair with one of those large black hats worn by the provençal peasants, indicated the presence of a sleeping female, whose heavy breathing reached our ears. Whilst I threw a rapid glance about me, my guide produced from an old trunk a quarter of a kid, some onions, oil, and a bottle of wine : he invited me to partake of a repast, of which I felt in the greatest need. He seemed very desirous of interrogating me, but I ate with so much appetite that I believe he felt a scruple of conscience in interrupting me. When I had finished, which was not whilst anything remained on the table, he led me to a sort of loft, assuring me that I was in perfect safety, and then left me before I could ask if he was going to stay in the hut ; but scarcely had I stretched myself out on the straw when a heavy sleep took possession of all my faculties.

When I awoke I judged by the height of the sun that it was two o'clock. A female peasant, doubtlessly the same whose apparel I had seen, warned by my movements, showed her head at the opening of the door of my garret—" Do not stir," said she in a provincial dialect, " the environs are full of sapins (gendarmes) who are examining every place." I did not know what she meant by ' sapins,' but I guessed that it did not refer to anything very propitious for me.

At twilight I saw my new friend of the previous evening, who, after some trifling conversation, asked me point-blank who I was, whence I came, and whither I was going. Prepared for these unavoidable questions, I replied that I was a deserter from the ship Ocean, then in the roadstead at Toulon, that I was going to Aix, whence I hoped to get to my own country.

"That is all very good," said my host. "I see who you are; but do you know who I am?"

"I 'faith, to tell the honest truth, I first took you for a patrol; afterwards I took you for a leader of smugglers—and now I do not know what to think."

"You shall know then. In our country we are brave enough, you see, but object to be made soldiers on compulsion—so we did not comply with the requisition when we could do anything to avoid it. The quota selected in Pourières even refused to march at all when called upon. The gendarmes came to compel the refractory, and they resisted. Men were killed on both sides: and all the townsmen who participated in the affray, betook themselve to the woods to escape a court-martial. We thus met sixty in number, under the orders of M. Roman and the brothers, Bisson de Tretz: if you like to remain with us I shall be glad, for last night's experience tells me that you are a man of mould, and I advise you not to be in any fear about gendarmes. Besides, we want for nothing, and run but little risk. The country people inform us of all that passes, and give us provisions in time of need. Come, will you join us?"

I did not judge it wise to reject the proposition: and without reflecting on the consequences, I answered as he wished. I stayed two days at the hut, and on the third set out with my companion, armed with a carbine and two pistols. After many hours' walking over mountains covered with wood, we reached a hut larger than that we had quitted: it was the head-quarters of Roman. I waited a moment at the door for my guide to announce me. He soon returned, and introduced me to a large apartment, where I saw about forty persons, the greater number of whom were

grouped about a man who, by his appearance, half
rustic, half citizen, might have passed for a rich country proprietor.   I was presented to this personage, who
said to me, " I am delighted to see you: I have heard
of your coolness, and know your worth.   If you will
share our perils, you shall find friendship and freedom :
we do not know you, but you have a face which would
command friends everywhere.   To sum up all, our
men are honourable and brave—for probity and honour
are our mottos."   After this discourse, which could
only be addressed to me by Roman, the brothers Bisson,
and then all the troop, gave me the embrace of brotherhood.

Such was my reception in this society, to which its
leader attributed a political intent; but it is certain,
that after beginning, like the Chouans, to stop the diligences which conveyed the state monies, Roman had
began to plunder travellers.   The mutineers who composed his band had at first much reluctance in committing these robberies; but habits of an unsettled
life, idleness, and especially the difficulty of returning
to their homes, soon removed all scruples.

The day after my arrival, Roman appointed me to
conduct six men to the environs of Saint Maximin.   I
did not know the purport of the mission.   About midnight, on reaching the borders of a small thicket that
skirted the road, we ensconced ourselves in a ravine.
Roman's lieutenant, Bisson de Fretz, recommended
absolute silence.   The wheels of a carriage were soon
heard, and it passed us.   Bisson looked out cautiously,
and said, " It is the Nice diligence; that will not do
for us : it has more soldiers than ducats."   He then
ordered us to retreat, and we regained the hut : when
Roman, enraged at seeing us return empty-handed,
swore loudly, exclaiming, " Well, well! they shall pay
for this tomorrow."

It was no longer possible for me to deceive myself
as to the association to which I belonged : I had decidedly fallen in with that famous band of highwaymen

who were spreading terror throughout Provence. If I fell into the hands of justice—a fugitive galley-slave—I could hardly hope for that pardon which might be granted even to the troop with which I was mingled. Reflecting on all the difficulties of my situation, I was tempted to escape them by flight; but, so recently enrolled, how was it possible to evade the strict scrutiny with which they regarded me? On the other hand, to express any desire of withdrawing myself from the confederacy would only have provoked a suspicion fatal to my purpose or safety. Might I not be considered as a spy, and be shot as such? Death and infamy threatened me whichever way I turned. In the midst of these perplexities to which I was a prey, my only idea was to sound the man who had first effected my introduction amongst my comrades; and, with as much apparent indifference as I could assume, I enquired if it would not be possible to obtain from our captain leave of absence for a few days? The man looked at me with an air of cunning and suspicion: " Yes, friend," said he, " such favours are sometimes obtained, when our chief knows well the person to whom he grants them." This said, he turned upon his heel, and left me to rack my brain anew for some happier device to effect my liberty than this had proved.

I had now been upwards of eleven days with these bandits, each day more fully resolved to withdraw myself from the honour of their exploits, when, one night that I had fallen asleep through excessive fatigue, I was suddenly aroused by an extraordinary noise; I listened, and discovered that the confusion which had broken my rest was occasioned by one of the troop having been robbed of a purse heavy with many years' booty: to my consternation I found that, as being the last comer amongst them, their suspicions were directed to me. They surrounded me, and formally accused me of having stolen the purse; the cry was unanimously against me, and drowned my protestations of innocence; they insisted upon searching my person. I had lain down in my clothes, which a hundred hands were ready to strip off me. What was their surprise, anger, and astonishment, at preceiving on my shoulder the brand of a galley-slave! "A galley-slave!" exclaimed the captain. "A galley-slave amongst us! He can only be here as a spy; knock him on the head, or shoot him, that will be soonest done." I heard the click of the muskets preparing to obey this last order. "One moment," exclaimed the chief; "let him, before he dies, make restitution of the lost money." "Yes," said I to him, "the money shall be restored, but on condition that you grant me a few minutes' private conversation." He consented to listen to what I had to say, under the idea that now I should make a full confession; but the moment I found myself alone with him, I protested anew that I was entirely innocent of the affair, and suggested an expedient for discovering the culprit, the idea of which was drawn from a work I had read of Berquin's. My plan was acceded to, and the captain returned to his men, holding as many straws in his hand as there were individuals present. "Observe me well," said he to them; "the longest of these straws will fall into the hands of him who is guilty."

The drawing began, each man in silence plucked out a straw; but when it had concluded, the straws were returned to the captain, and his troop looked with curious eagerness for the result.

One alone was found shorter than the others. A man named Joseph d'Osiolles presented it. "You are then the thief!" exclaimed the captain. "Every straw was of the same length; you have shortened yours, and thus criminated yourself."

Joseph was searched, and the stolen purse found hid in his belt.

My justification was complete; the whole troop acknowledged my innocence; and the captain, whilst he sought to excuse the violence to which I had been subjected, added, that I must no longer form part of his band. "It is a sad piece of ill luck for you," said

he; " but you must feel that, having been at the gallies —— " He did not complete the sentence; but,
putting fifteen louis in my hands, he compelled me to
promise silence as to all I had seen or heard for the
next twenty-five days.

I was prudent, and faithful to my engagement.

END OF THE FIRST VOLUME.

LONDON:

PRINTED BY C. AND W. REYNELL, BROAD ST. GOLDEN SQ.

MEMOIRS

OF

VIDOCQ,

PRINCIPAL AGENT OF THE FRENCH POLICE

UNTIL 1827:

AND NOW PROPRIETOR OF

THE PAPER MANUFACTORY AT ST MANDÉ.

WRITTEN BY HIMSELF.

TRANSLATED FROM THE FRENCH.

"Que l'on m'approuve ou non, j'ai la conscience d'avoir fait mon devoir; d'ailleurs, lorsqu'il s'agit d'atteindre des scélérats qui sont en guerre ouverte avec la société, tous les moyens sont bons sauf la provocation."

MÉMOIRES, VOL. II.

IN FOUR VOLUMES.

VOL. II.

LONDON, 1829:

PRINTED FOR HUNT AND CLARKE,

YORK STREET, COVENT GARDEN.

LONDON:

C. AND W. REYNELL, PRINTERS, BROAD STREET, GOLDEN SQ.

CONTENTS.

———

CHAPTER XV.

Page

A receiver of stolen goods—Denouncement—First treaty
with the police—Departure for Lyons—A mistake ..   1

CHAPTER XVI.

Residence at Arras—Disguises—The false Austrian—
Departure—Residence at Rouen—Arrest.........   11

CHAPTER XVII.

The camp at Boulogne—The rencontre—The recruiters
of the ancien regime—M. Belle-Rose   23

CHAPTER XIX.

Page

Continuation of the same day—The Cotemporaine—An
adjutant de place—The daughters of mother Thomas
—The Silver Lion—Captain Paulet and his lieutenant
—The pirates—The bombardment—Departure of
lord Lauderdale—The disguised actress—The executioner—Henry the Ninth and his ladies—I embark
—Sea-fight—Paulet's second is killed—Capture of
a brig of war—My Sosia—I change my name—
Death of Dufailli—Twelfth-day—A frigate sunk—I
wish to save two lovers—A tempest—The fishermen's
wives 74

CHAPTER XX.

I am admitted into the marine artillery—I become a
corporal—Seven prisoners of war—Secret societies
of the army, 'The Olympiens'—Singular duels—
Meeting with a galley-slave—The count de L——, a
political spy—He disappears—The incendiary—I am
promised promotion—I am betrayed—Once more in
prison—Disbanding of the Armée de la Lune—The
pardoned soldier—A companion is sentenced to be
shot—The Piedmontese bandit—The camp fortune-
teller—Four murderers set at liberty............ .. 81

CHAPTER XXI.

Page

I am conducted to Douai—Application for pardon—
My wife marries again—The plunge in the Scarpe
—I travel as an officer—Reading the dispatches—
Residence at Paris—A new name—The woman of
my heart—I am a wandering merchant—The commissary of Melun—Execution of Herbaux—I denounce a robber; he denounces me—The galley-
slaves at Auxerre—I am settled in the capital—Two
fugitives from the Bagne—My wife again—Receiving
stolen goods.................................... 109

CHAPTER XXII.

Another robber—My wicker car—Arrest of two galley-
slaves—Fearful discovery—St Germain wishes to
involve me in a robbery—I offer to serve the police—
Horrid perplexities—They wish to take me whilst in
bed—My concealment—A comic adventure—Disguises on disguises—Chevalier has denounced me—
Annette at the Depôt of the Prefecture—I prepare
to leave Paris—Two passers of false money—I am
apprehended in my shirt—I nm conducted to the
Bicêtre 127

CHAPTER XXIII.

Page

A plan of escape—New proposal to M. Henry—My
   agreement with the police—Important discoveries—
   Coco-Lacour —A band of robbers—The inspectors
   under lock and key—The old clothes woman and the
   assassins—A pretended escape 147

CHAPTER XXIV.

M. Henry, surnamed the Evil Spirit—MM. Bertaux and
   Parisot—A word respecting the police—My first capture—Bouhin and Terrier are arrested upon my information 165

CHAPTER XXV.

I again meet St Germain—He proposes to me the murder of two old men—The plunderers—The grandson
   of Cartouche—A short account of instigating agents—
   Great perplexities—Annette again aids me—An attempt to rob the house of a banker in the Rue Hauteville—I am killed—Arrest of St Germain and his
   accomplice Boudin—Portraits of these two assassins .. 172

CHAPTER XXVI.

Page

I continue to frequent places of bad resort—The inspectors betray me—Discovery of a receiver of stolen goods—I arrest him—Stratagem employed to convict him—He is condemned 188

CHAPTER XXVII.

Gueuvive's gang—A girl helps me to discover the chief—I dine with the thieves—One of them takes me to sleep at his house—I pass for a fugitive galley-slave—I engage in a plot against myself—I wait for myself at my own door—A robbery in the Rue Cassette—Great surprise—Gueuvive with four of his men are arrested—The girl Cornevin points the others out to me—A batch of eighteen............................. 194

CHAPTER XXVIII.

The agents of the police chosen from amongst liberated galley-slaves, thieves, bullies and prostitutes—Theft tolerated—Degeneracy of the inspectors—Coalition of informers—They denounce me—Destruction of three classes of thieves—Formation of a new species—The brothers Delzève—How discovered—Delzève the younger arrested—The perquisites of a préfet of police—I free myself from the yoke of the peace officers and inspectors—My life is in danger—A few anecdotes.. 202

CHAPTER XXIX.

Page

I seek two celebrated thieves—The music mistress, or
another "mother of robbers"—A metamorphosis, which
is not the last—Scenes of hospitality—The false keys
Ramifications of an admirable plot—Perfidy of an
agent—The plan detected—Mother Noel accuses me
of having robbed her—My innocence recognized—My
female accuser sent to St Lazarre................ 214

CHAPTER XXX.

The police-officers sent in pursuit of a celebrated robber
—They are unable to discover him—Great anger of
one of them—I promise another new-year's gift to the
préfet—The yellow curtains and the hump-backed
female—I am a good citizen—A messenger puts me on
the right scent—The chest of the prefecture of police—I
am a coal-man—The fright of a vintner and his wife
—The little Norman in tears—The danger of giving
Eau-de-Cologne—Carrying off of mademoiselle Tonneau—A search—The thief takes me for his mate—
Thieves laugh at locksmiths—The jump from the
window—The effects of a long slide, or broken
stitches 227

CHAPTER XXXI.

Page

A general clearance at la Courtille—The white cross—
—I am called a spy—The popular opinion concerning
my agents—Summary of the results of the Brigade de
Sureté—Biography of Coco-Lacour—M. Delavau, and
the Trou-Madame—The grant of my pardon—Retrospective glance over these Memoirs—I can speak, I
will speak.................................... 244

MEMOIRS OF VIDOCQ

CHAPTER XV.

A receiver of stolen goods—Denouncement—First treaty with the police—Departure for Lyons—A mistake.

AFTER the dangers I had undergone whilst remaining with Roman and his band, some idea may be formed of the joy which I experienced on quitting them. It was evident that the government, once determinately settled, would adopt the most efficacious measures for ensuring the safety of the interior. The remains of the bands, which, under the name o. "Chevaliers du Soleil, or the Compagnie de Jésus," owed their formation to a political re-action, deferred indefinitely, could not fail to be destroyed as soon as was desired. The only honest excuse for their brigandage—royalism—no longer existed; and although Hivèr, Leprêtre, Boulanger, Bastide, Jansein, and other 'sons of the family,' made a boast of attacking the couriers, because they found their profit in it, it began to be no longer in good taste to think that it was quite correct to appropriate to one-self the money of the state. All the *incroyables* who had thought it a service to check, pistol in hand, the circulation of dispatches and the collection of the im-posts, withdrew now to their fire-sides, and those who had profited by their exertions, or wished for other reasons to be forgotten, betook themselves to a distance from the scene of their exploits. In fact, order was re-established, and the time was at hand when robbers, whatever might be their pretext or motive, were no longer to be tolerated. I should have been very desirous, under such circumstances, to have enrolled myself in a band of robbers, only, the infamy of such a procedure apart, I should have been kept from it by the certainty of being speedily brought to the scaffold. But another thought animated me; I wished to avoid, at any cost, the opportunities and means of committing crimes: I wished to be free. I knew not how this wish was to be realised, or did it matter; my determination was made, and I had, as they say, marked a cross on the prison. In haste to get at a considerable distance, I took the road to Lyons, avoiding the high roads, until I reached the environs of Orange; there I fell in with some Provençal waggoners, whose packages soon revealed to me that they were about to take the same road as myself. I entered into conversation with them; and as they appeared to me to be hearty jovial fellows, I did not hesitate to tell them that I was a deserter, and that they would serve me materially if, to aid me in avoiding the vigilance of the gendarmes, they would agree to bestow their patronage on me. This proposal did not surprise them, and it even seemed as if they had suspected that I should claim their protection and secresy. At this period, and particularly in the south, it was not rare to meet with fine fellows, who had left their colours and committed themselves to the care of heaven. It was then very natural to take my word, and the waggoners received me kindly; and some money which I displayed, as if by chance, completed the interest which I had already excited. It was agreed that I should pass for the son of the person who had these conveyances in charge. I was accordingly clothed with a smock-frock, and was supposed to be making my first journey. I was decorated with ribands and nosegays, emblems which at each public-house, procured for me the congratulation of all the inmates.

A new 'John of Paris,' I filled my part very well; but the donations necessary to support it adequately

made such inroads on my purse, that, on reaching
the guillotiere, where I was to leave my party, I had
only twenty-eight sous left. With resources so ineffe-
cient, I had no thoughts of fixing my abode at the hotels of the Place des Terreaux. Having wandering about
for some time in the dirty and dark streets of the second city in France, I remarked, in the Rue des Quatre-
Chapeaux, a sort of tavern where I thought that I
might procure a supper commensurate with my finances. I was not mistaken; the supper was light enough,
and soon dispatched. To remain hungry is indeed a
disagreeable thing; and not to know where to find
shelter for one's head is equally annoying. When I
had wiped my knife, which, however, had not been
much engaged, I was reflecting, that I must pass the
night under the canopy of heaven, when, at a table
near to mine, I heard a conversation in that bastard
German so much spoken in some districts of the Netherlands, and with which I was well acquainted. The
speakers were a man and woman about to retire, and
whom I found to be Jews. Informed that at Lyons,
as in many other towns, these people kept furnished
houses, in which they received smugglers, I asked if
they could direct me to a public house. I could not
have addressed myself to better persons; for they were
lodging-keepers, and offered to become my hosts, which,
on agreeing to, I accompanied them to the Rue Tho-
massin. Six beds were in the room in which I was
placed, none of which were occupied, although it was
ten o'clock, and I fell asleep under the idea that I
should have no companions in my room.

On awaking, I heard the following conversation in
a slang language which was familiar to me.

"It is half past six," said a voice, which was not
unknown to me, "and you lie snoring still."

" Well, and what then? We wanted to break open
the old goldsmith's shop to night, but he was on his
guard, and we ought to have given him a few inches of
cold steel, and then the blood would have flowed."

" Ah ha! but you fear the guillotine too much. But
that is not the way to go to work to get the money."

" I would rather murder on the highway, than
break open shops; the gendarmes are always at your
heels."

"Well, then, you have got no booty; and yet there
were snuff-boxes, watches, and gold chains enough. The
Jew will have no business to day."

" No; the false key broke in the lock, the citizen
cried for help, and we had to run for it. . . ."

" Holla!" said a third person; " do not wag your
tongue so fast; there is a man in bed, who may be
listening."

The advice was too late, but it silenced them, and
I half-opened my eyes to see the faces of my companions; but my bed being very low, I could not perceive them. I remained quiet, that they might suppose me asleep; when one of the speakers having
arisen, I recognised him as an escaped prisoner from
Toulon, named Neveu, who had left some days before
me. His comrade jumped out of bed, and him I knew
to be Cadet-Paul, another fugitive; a third, and then
a fourth arose, and I knew them all then to be galley-
slaves.

I almost fancied myself in my room, No. 3. At
length I got up from my bed, and scarcely had I
put foot on the floor, when they all exclaimed " 'Tis
Vidocq!" They surrounded and congratulated me.
One of be robbers, Charles Deschamps, who had escaped a few days after me, told me, that the whole
Bagne were fall of admiration at my boldness and success. Nine o'clock having struck, they conducted me to
breakfast, where we joined the brothers Quinét, Bonne-
foi, Robineau, Metral, and Lemat, names well known
in the south. They overwhelmed me with kindnesses,
procured me money, clothes, and even a mistress.

I was here situated precisely as I had been at
Nantes, but I was not more desirous of following the
profession of my friends than I had been in Bretagne;

but until I had a remittance from my mother I must live somehow. I thought I might manage to support myself for a time without labour. I proposed most determinately only to receive subsistence from the robbers; but man proposes and God disposes. The fugitives, discontented that I, under various pretexts, always avoided joining their daily plundering parties, at once denounced me, to get rid of a trouble-some witness, who might become dangerous. They imagined that I should escape, as a matter of course, and relied, that once known by the police, and having no refuge but with their band, I should then unite myself to their party. In this circumstance, as in all others of a similar kind, in which I have been found, if they were so desirous of my companionship, it was because they had a high opinion of my penetration, my adroitness, and particularly of my strength,—a valuable quality in a profession in which profit is too often attained by peril.

Arrested at Adele Buffin's, in the passage Saint Come, I was taken to the prison of Roanne, where I learnt from my examination that I had been sold. In the rage which this discovery threw me into, I took a sudden step, which was in a measure my introduction to a career entirely new to me. I wrote to M. Dubois, commissary-general of the police, requesting a private interview, and the same evening I was conducted to his private closet. Having explained my situation to him, I offered to put him in the way of seizing the brothers Quinet, then pursued for having assassinated the wife of a mason of the Rue Belle-Cordaire. I proposed besides to point out the means of appre-hending all the persons, lodging as well at the Jew's as at Caffin's, the joiner's, in the Rue Ecorche-Bœuf. In return, I only asked for liberty to quit Lyons. M. Dubois had doubtless been before the dupe of such proposals, and I saw that he hesitated to trust me. "You doubt my word," said I to him: "should you still suspect me if I should escape on my way back to prison, and return and surrender myself as your prisoner?"—"No," he replied. "Well, then, you shall soon see me again, provided that you consent not to give my guards any additional orders for my security." He agreed, and I went away; but on arriving at the corner of the Rue de la Lanterne, I knocked down the two tipstaffs, who had each an arm of mine, and regained the Hotel de Ville with all possible speed, where I found M. Dubois, who was greatly surprised at my prompt re-appearance; but certain from that that he might rely on me, I was allowed to go at liberty.

The next day I saw the Jew, whose name was Vidal, who directed me to a house in the Rue Croix Rousse, where, he said, my friends had gone to live, and thither I went. They knew of my escape; but as they had no idea of my understanding with the commissary-general of police, and did not think that I knew who had directed the blow which struck me, they gave me a very cordial reception. During the conversation, I gathered details from the brothers Quinet, which I transmitted to M. Dubois the same evening, and who, convinced of my sincerity, reported my conduct to M. Ganier, secretary-general of the police, and now commissary at Paris. I gave this gentleman all necessary information, and must say that he acted on his part with much tact and activity.

Two days before they commenced operations, as I had advised on Vidal's house, I thought it expedient that I should be again arrested. I was again conducted to the prison of Roanne, where the next day Vidal, Coffin, Neveu, Cadet Paul, Deschamps, and many others, whom they had caught in the same snare, were brought in. I was at first kept from communicating with them, because I had thought it best that I should be put 'au secret.' When I was released from it, at the end of several days, to join the other prisoners, I pretended much surprise at finding all the party here; none appeared to have the least idea of the part which I had played. Neveu alone regarded me with distrust; and on my demanding the cause, he said, that by the way in which they had been pursued and interrogated, he could not help suspecting that I was the denouncer. I feigned much indignation, and fearing that this opinion might be disseminated, I assembled the prisoners, and informing them of Neveu's suspicions, I demanded if they thought me capable of selling my comrades? and on their answering in the negative, Neveu was compelled to apologise to me. It was important to me that these suspicions should be thus destroyed; for I knew that certain death would be my doom if they had been confirmed. There had been many instances at Roanne of this distributive justice, which the prisoners exercised towards one another. One named Moissel, suspected of having given information relative to a robbery of church plate, had been knocked on the head in the court, without the assassin being detected. More recently, another individual accused of a similar indiscretion, had been found one morning hung with a straw band at the bars of his window, and the perpetrator was never discovered.

In the mean time, M. Dubois sent for me to his closet, where, to avoid suspicion, the other prisoners were conducted with me, as if about to undergo an examination. I entered first, and the commissary-general told me that many very expert robbers had arrived at Lyons, from Paris, and the more dangerous, as being supplied with regular credentials, they might wait in safety for the opportunity of making some decided stroke, and then immediately go away: their names were Jaillier, called Boubanec, Bouthey, called Cadet, Buchard, Garard, Mollin, called the Chapellier, Marquis, called Main d'Or, and some others less notorious. These names, by which they were mentioned, were then entirely new to me; and I told M. Dubois so, adding, that possibly they might be false. He wished to release me immediately, that by seeing these individuals in some public place, I might assure myself whether I had ever seen them

before; but I observed to him, that so abrupt a liberation would certainly compromise me with the prisoners,
in case that the good of the service should require me
again to be entered as prisoner on the jailor's books.
The reflection appeared just; and it was agreed that
they should devise a means of sending me away the
next day without incurring suspicion.

Neveu, who was amongst the prisoners, was also
examined after me in the commissaries' closet. After
some minutes he came out in a rage, and I asked him
what had happened?

"What do you think?" said he, "the old covey
wanted me to turn nose on the cracksmen who have
just arrived. If they find no one to blow them but me
they are all right."

"Why, I did not think you such a flat," said I, the
idea flashing on my mind, that I might turn this to
advantage, "I have promised to blow the gang, and
ensure them a lodging in the stone jug."

"What! you turned nose? Besides, you are not fly
to the gang."

"What matters that? I shall get out of quod, and
show them my heels, whilst you are still clinking the
darbies."

Neveu appeared struck with the idea, and expressed
much regret for having refused the offers of the commissary-general; and as I could not get rid of him,
I begged him to return to M. Dubois and recall his
refusal. He agreed; and as I had arranged, we were
one evening conducted to the great theatre; then to
the Celestins, where Neveu pointed out to me all the
men. We then retired, escorted by the police agents,
who kept close upon us. For the success of my plan,
and to avoid suspicion, it was expedient to make the
attempt to escape, which would at least confirm the
hope which I had given to my companion, and I told
him of my intention. On passing Rue Merciere, we
entered abruptly into a passage and closed the door;
and whilst the officers ran to the other end, we went
out quietly by the way we had entered. When they

returned, ashamed of their stupidity, we were already at a considerable distance.

Two days afterwards, Neveu, who was no longer wanted, and could not suspect me, was again arrested. I, knowing then the robbers whom we wanted, pointed them out to the police-officers, in the church of Saint Nizier, where they had one Sunday assembled, in the hope of making a good booty on the termination of the prayers. Being no longer useful to the authorities, I then quitted Lyons to go to Paris, where, thanks to M. Dubois, I was sure of arriving in safety.

I set out on the Burgundy road by the diligence, which then only travelled by day. At Lucy-le-Bois, where I slept with the other travellers, I was forgotten; and on waking, learnt that the vehicle had been gone two hours. I trusted to overtake it, in consequence of the ruggedness of the road, which is very steep in these districts; but on reaching Saint Brice, I was convinced that it was too much in advance to allow of my overtaking it, and I accordingly slackened my pace. A person who was travelling in the same direction, seeing me in a great heat, looked attentively at me, and asked me if I had come from Lucy-le-Bois; and on my replying in the affirmative, our conversation rested there. This man stopped at Saint Brice, whilst I pushed on to Auxerre. Spent with fatigue, I entered an inn, where, after having dined, I desired to be conducted to a bed.

I slept for several hours, when I was awakened by a great noise at my door, at which some persons were knocking violently. I got up, half dressed, and my eyes, heavy from sleep, gazed, as I opened the door, on tri-coloured scarves, yellow trowsers, and red facings. It was the commissary of police, attended by the quarter-master and two gendarmes, a sight which I could not see without some emotion. " See how pale he turns," said one of them; " it is he." I raised my eyes, and recognised the man who had spoken to me at Saint Brice; but nothing explained to me as yet the motive of this sudden invasion.

" Let us proceed methodically," said the commissary; " five feet five inches (French measure), that is
right; brown hair—eye-brows and beard, idem—common forehead—grey eyes — prominent nose — good
sized mouth—round chin—full face—good colour—
tolerably stout."

" It is he," said the quarter-master, the two gendarmes, and the man of Saint Brice.

" Yes, it is indeed," said the commissary in his turn.
" Blue surtout—trowsers of grey casimere—white
waistcoat—black cravat."

This was my dress, certainly.

" Well, did I not say so," said the officious guide
of the police: " he is one of the robbers!' "

The description tallied exactly with mine. But I
had stolen nothing; and yet in my situation I could
experience all the disquiets of having done so. Perhaps it was a mistake; perhaps also.... The party
were transported with joy. " Peace!" said the commissary; and turning over the leaf, he continued, " We
shall easily recognise his Italian accent. He has
besides the thumb of the right hand injured by a
shot." I spoke, and showed my right hand, which
was in a perfectly sound state. All the party stared;
and particularly the man of Saint Brice, who appeared
singularly disconcerted: as for me, I felt relieved of
an enormous weight. The commissary, whom I questioned in my turn, told me, that on the preceding
night a considerable robbery had been committed at
Saint Brice. One of the suspected individuals wore
clothes similar to mine, and there was a similarity
of description. It was to this combination of circumstances, to this strange sport of fortune, that I was
indebted for the disagreeable visit which I received.
They made excuses, which I accepted with a good grace,
very happy at getting off so well; but yet, in the fear
of some new catastrophe, I put myself the same
evening into a packet-boat, which conveyed me to
Paris, whence I started immediately for Arras.

CHAPTER XVI.

Residence at Arras—Disguises—The false Austrian—Departure
—Residence at Rouen—Arrest.

MANY reasons which may be divined, did not allow of
my proceeding at once to my paternal abode; and,
alighting at the house of one of my aunts, I learnt the
death of my father, which sad intelligence was soon
confirmed by my mother, who received me with a
tenderness widely contrasting with the treatment I
had experienced during the two years of my absence.
She was extremely anxious to keep me with her; but
it was absolutely necessary that I should be constantly
concealed, and I did not leave the house for three
months. At the end of that time my confinement
began to weary me, and I went out, sometimes under
one disguise and sometimes under another. I
thought I had not been recognised, when suddenly
a report spread through the town that I was there,
and the police began to search for me, making
constant visits to my mother, without, however, discovering the place of my concealment, which was not
very large, being only ten feet long and six wide; but
I had so well contrived it, that a person, who afterwards purchased the house, lived in it nearly four
years without suspecting the existence of this place,
and would probably never have known it had I not
revealed it to him.

Secure in my retreat, out of which I thought it
would be difficult to surprise me, I soon took fresh
excursions. One day, on Shrove Tuesday, I even
carried my daring to such an extent as to appear at a
ball, in the midst of upwards of two hundred persons.
I was dressed as a marquis; and a female, with whom
I had been on intimate terms, having recognized me,

told another, who thought that she had a cause of complaint against me; so that in less than a quarter of an hour everybody knew under what disguise Vidocq was concealed. The report reached the ears of two police serjeants, Delrue and Carpentier, who were on duty at the ball; and the former, coming up to me, said in a low voice that he wished to speak with me in private; a refusal would have been dangerous, and I followed him into the court, where Delrue asked my name. I did not hesitate to give him a false one; and proposing politely that he should untie my mask if he doubted me. "I do not require that," said he, "but I shall not object to look at you." "Well, then, untie my mask, which has got entangled with my hair." Full of certainty, Delrue went behind me, and at that instant I upset him with a forcible motion of my body backwards, and with a blow of my fist I sent his satellite rolling, beside him on the earth. Without waiting until they arose, I fled with the utmost speed in the direction of the ramparts, relying on being able to climb over them, and get into the country; but scarcely had I run many paces, when I found myself in an alley which had been blocked up at one end since I had quitted Arras.

Whilst I was thus wandering out of my way, a noise of iron heels announced that the two serjeants were at hand; and I soon saw them approach me, sword in hand. I was unarmed; and seizing the large house key, as if it had been a pistol, I presented it at them, and compelled them to make way for me. "Pass quietly, François," said Carpentier, with a tremulous voice, "do not play any nonsense with us." I did not want to be told a second time, and in a few minutes reached my retreat.

This adventure was noised about, and in spite of the efforts which the two serjeants made to conceal it, they were laughed at by everybody. What was most annoying to me was, that the authorities redoubled their vigilance, so that it was almost impossible for me to go out. I remained thus immured for two months, which to me seemed as many centuries. Being no longer able to endure it, I resolved on quitting Arras, and they made me up a pack of lace; and one fine night, provided with a passport, which Blondel, one of my friends, had lent to me, I set out. The description did not answer; but for want of a better, I was compelled to put up with that; and, in fact, no objection was made to me on my route.

I reached Paris. Whilst engaged in disposing of my commodities, I made indirectly some steps towards finding out if it were not possible to obtain some reversal of my sentence. I learnt that I must, in the first instance, give myself up as a prisoner, but I could never resolve on again mixing with the wretches whom I knew so well. It was not the confinement that I dreaded; I would willingly have submitted to have been enclosed alone between four walls; and what proves this is, that I then requested leave from the minister to finish the term of my sentence in the madhouse at Arras; but my application remained unanswered.

My lace was sold, but with so little profit that I could not think of turning to this trade as a mode of life. A travelling clerk, who lived in the Rue Saint Martin, in the same hotel as I did, and to whom I partly stated my situation, proposed that I should enter the service of a seller of finery, who visited the fairs. I procured the situation, but only kept it for ten months, as we had some disagreements which determined me again to return to Arras. I was not long in returning to my nightly excursions. In the house of a young person to whom I paid some attentions, I frequently met the daughter of a gendarme, and endeavoured to learn from her all that was plotting against me. The girl did not know me; but as in Arras I was the constant subject of conversation, it was not extraordinary to hear her speak of me, and frequently in singular terms. " Oh," said she to me

c

one day, " we shall soon catch that vagabond; there is our lieutenant (M. Dumortier, now commissary of police at Abbeville) who wants him too much not to catch him soon; I will bet that he would give a day's pay to get hold of him."

" If I were your lieutenant, and wanted to take Vidocq," replied I, " I would contrive that he should not escape me."

" You! Oh yes, you and everybody! He is always completely armed. You know they said that he fired twice at Delrue and Carpentier; and that is not all, for he can change himself into a bundle of hay whenever he likes."

" A bundle of hay!" cried I, surprised at the novel endowment assigned to me— " A bundle of hay! How ?"

" Yes, sir; my father pursued him one day; and at the moment he laid his hand upon his collar, he found that he only held a handful of hay. He did not only say it, but all the brigade saw the bundle of hay, which was burnt in the barrack-yard."

I could not make out this history; but learnt afterwards that the police-officers, not being able to lay hold of me, had given circulation to this tale amongst the credulous citizens of Arras. With the same motive they obligingly insinuated that I was the double of a certain loup-garou, whose wonderful appearances froze with fear the superstitious inhabitants of the country. Fortunately, these terrors were not shared by some pretty women, whom I had interested in my favour; and if the demon of jealousy had not suddenly seized on one of the number, the authorities would not perhaps have given themselves so much trouble about me. In her anger she was indiscreet; and the police, who did not clearly know what had become of me, again learnt that I was certainly in Arras.

One evening, as, without mistrust and only armed with a stick, I was returning through the Rue d'Amiens, on crossing the bridge at the end of the Rue des

Goquets, I was attacked by seven or eight individuals. They were constables disguised; and, seizing my garments, were already assured of their prize, when, freeing myself by a powerful jerk, I leapt the parapet, and threw myself into the river. It was in December; the tide was high, the current rapid, and none of the police-men had any inclination to follow me: they thought besides, that by waiting for me on the bank I should not escape them; but a sewer that I found enabled me to deceive them, and they were still waiting for me when I was at my mother's house.

Every day I experienced fresh dangers, and every day the most pressing necessity suggested new expedients for my preservation. However, at length, according to my custom, I grew weary of a liberty which the compulsion of concealment rendered illusory. Some nuns of the Rue —— had for some time harboured me; but I resolved on quitting their hospitable roof, and turned over in my mind the means of appearing in public without inconvenience. Some thousands of Austrian prisoners were then in the citadel, whence they went out to work with the citizens, or in the neighbouring villages, and the idea occurred to me, that the presence of these strangers might be useful to me. As I spoke German, I entered into conversation with one of them, and inspired him with sufficient confidence to confide to me his intention of escaping. This project was favourable to my views; the prisoner was embarrassed with his Kaiserlik uniform, and I offered to exchange it for mine; and for some money which I gave him to boot, he was glad to let me have his papers also. From this moment I was an Austrian, even in the eyes of the Austrians themselves, who, belonging to different corps, did not know all their body.

Under this new disguise, I joined a young widow, who had a mercery establishment in the Rue de ——: she found that I had ability, and wished that I would instal myself at her house; and we soon visited the fairs and markets together. It was evident that I could not aid her, unless I could understand the buyers, and I formed gibberish, half Teutonic, half French, which they understood wonderfully well, and which became so familiar to me, that I insensibly forgot that I knew any other language. Besides, the illusion was so complete, that after cohabiting together for four months, the widow did not suspect any more than the rest of the world, that the soi-disant Kaiser-lik was one of the friends of her childhood. However, she treated me so well, that it was impossible to deceive her any longer; and one day I told her who I really was, and never was woman more astonished. But, far from its injuring me in her estimation, the confidence in some sort only made our intimacy the closer; so much are women generally smitten by any thing that bears the appearance of mystery or adventure! And then, are they not always delighted with the acquaintance of a wicked fellow? Who, better than myself, can know how often they are the providence of fugitive galley-slaves and condemned prisoners?

Eleven months glided away, and nothing occurred to disturb my repose. The frequency of my being in the streets, my constant meetings with the police officers, who had not even paid attention to me, all seemed to augur the duration of this tranquillity, when, one day as we were sitting down to dinner in the back shop, the faces of three gendarmes were visible through a glass door. I was just helping the soup; the spoon fell from my hands; but recovering soon from the stupor into which this unlooked-for visit had thrown me, I darted towards the door, which I bolted, and then jumping out of the window, I got into a loft, whence I gained the roof of the next house, and running down the staircase which led into the street, I found, on reaching the door, two gendarmes. Fortunately, they were but novices, who did not know me: " Go up," said I to them, " the brigadier has got him, but he resists; go up, and lend your aid, whilst I run for the guard." The two gendarmes ascended quickly, and I made off.

It was plain that I had been sold to the police. My friend was incapable of such a black deed, but she had, without doubt, been guilty of some indiscretion. Now that the cry was raised against me, ought I to tarry longer at Arras? It would be in vain to say, that I would always remain in my place of concealment; I could not reconcile myself to a life so wretched, and I determined on quitting the city. My little lady mercer insisted on accompanying me; she had means of conveyance; her commodities were soon packed, and we set out together, and, as usually happens in such cases, the police was informed last of the disappearance of a female, whose measures they ought not to have been in ignorance of. According to some old notions, they imagined that we should go towards Belgium, as if Belgium had still been the country of refuge; and whilst they were pursuing us in the direction of the old frontier, we were quietly progressing towards Normandy, by cross roads, which my companion had obtained a knowledge of in her mercantile journies.

It was at Rouen that we had made up our minds to fix our abode. Arrived in this city, I had with me the passport of Blondel, which I had procured at Arras: the description which it gave was so different from mine, that it was indispensably necessary to make myself a little more like it.

To achieve this, it was necessary to deceive the police, now become the more vigilant and inquisitive, as the communications of the emigrants in England were made through the Normandy coast. Thus did I contrive it. I went to the town-hall, where I had my passport *visé* for Havre. A *visa* was obtained without difficulty; it was sufficient that the passport was not entirely contradictory, and mine was not so. The formality gone through, I departed, and two minutes afterwards I entered the office, and asked if any person had found a pocket-book. No one could give me any tidings of it, and then I was in despair; pressing business called me to Havre, and I wanted to start that very evening, but what was to be done without a passport?

"Is it only that?" said a clerk. "With the register of the *visà* you can get a duplicate passport. This was what I needed; the name of Blondel was kept but this time, at least my description was correctly given. To complete the effect of my stratagem, not only did I set out for Havre, but I advertised my pocketbook by little bills stuck about, although it had only passed from my hands to that of my companion.

By means of this little bit of good management, my reinstatement was complete; and, provided with fitting credentials, I had only to lead an honest life, and I actually began to think of it; and took, in Rue Mortainville, a repository for mercery and bonnets, in which we did so well, that my mother, whom I had informed secretly of my success, determined on coming to join us. For a year I was really happy, my business increased, my connexions extended, my credit was established, and more than one banking-house in Rouen may perhaps remember when the signature of Blondel was well respected in the place. At length, after so many storms, I thought I had reached port; when an incident, which I had never contemplated, involved me in a fresh series of vicissitudes. The lady mercer with whom I lived, this woman who had given me the strongest proofs of devotion and love, began to burn with other fires than those which I had kindled in her heart. I was desirous of persuading myself that she was not unfaithful, but the fault was so flagrant that the offender had not even the resource of those well-supported denials which enable the convenient husband to persuade himself that he is not wronged. At another time, I would not have submitted to such an affront without putting myself into a transport of rage, but how time had changed me! Witness of my misfortune, I coldly signified my deter-

mination to separate; prayers, supplications, nothing
could bend me; I was immutable.   I might have pardoned her, it is true, if only out of gratitude; but who
would convince me that she who had befriended me
would break off with my rival ? And might I not have
cause to fear, that, in a moment of tenderness, she
would compromise my safety by some disclosure ?
We then divided our stock of goods, and my companion quitting me, I never heard of her after.

Disgusted with my residence at Rouen, through this
adventure, I took to my old trade of travelling merchant; my journies comprised the circuit of Nantes,
Saint Germain, and Versailles, where, in a short time,
I formed an excellent connexion; my profits became
sufficiently considerable to allow of my renting at Versailles, in the Rue de la Fontaine, a warehouse, with a
small apartment, which my mother inhabited during
my journies.   My conduct was then free from any
stigma ; I was generally esteemed in the circle which
I had formed; and again I hoped that I had overcome
the fatality which so often cast me into the path of
dishonour, whence all my efforts were now used to
free myself; when, denounced by an early friend, who
thus revenged himself for some disagreement we had
once had together, I was arrested on my return from
the fair of Nantes.   Although I obstinately asserted
that I was not Vidocq, but Blondel, as my passport
proved, I was sent to St Denis, whence I was to be
sent to Douai.   By the extraordinary care taken to
prevent my escape, I perceived that I was recommended ; and a glance which I threw over the book
of the gendarmerie, revealed to me a precaution of a
very particular nature.   I was thus designated—

" SPECIAL SURVEILLANCE.

" VIDOCQ (Eugene François), *condemned to death for
   non-appearance.* This man is exceedingly enterprising and dangerous."

Thus, to keep the vigilance of my guards on the
alert, I was described as a great criminal. I set out

to St Denis in a car, pinioned, so that I could not move, and to Louvres the escort never took eyes off me. These arrangements announced the rigours in store for me, and I roused all the energy that had already so often procured me my liberty.

We had been put into the clock-house of Louvres, now transformed into a prison, where they brought me two mattresses, a counterpane, and sheets, which, cut and fastened together, would help us to descend into the church-yard. A bar was cut with the knives of three deserters confined with us, and at two o'clock in the morning I made the first attempt, and having reached the extremity of the rope, I perceived that it was nearly fifteen feet from the ground; hesitation availed nought, and I let go, but, as in my fall at the ramparts at Lille, I sprained my left leg so severely, that I could scarcely walk; however, I attempted to climb the walls of the churchyard, when I heard the key turn quietly in the lock. It was the jailor and his dog, who had noses alike for following a scent: the jailor, at first, passed beneath the cord without seeing it; and the mastiff near a ditch in which I lay, without smelling me. Having gone the round, they retired, and I thought that my companions would follow my example, but no one appearing, I climbed the wall and got into the plain. The pain of my foot became more and more acute, but I bore the pain, and courage giving me strength, I made considerable progress. I had nearly advanced a quarter of a league, when I suddenly heard the sound of the tocsin. It was in the middle of May. At the earliest dawn, I saw several armed peasants go out of their dwellings and spread themselves over the plains. They were probably ignorant of what was the cause of disturbance, but my sore leg was a token that might make me suspected. My face was unknown: in all probability, the first persons who met me would secure my person. Had I been in full possession of my limbs, I could have distanced all pursuit; I must yield at present; and scarcely had I got on two hundred paces, when, overtaken by the gen-

darmes who were scouring the country, I was seized
and conveyed back to the cursed clock-house.

The unpropitious result of this attempt did not dis-
courage me. At Bapaume we were placed in the
citadel, an old police station, guarded by a detachment of conscripts of the 30th regiment of the line;
one sentinel only was placed over us, and he was under
the window, and near enough for me to enter into conversation with him, which I did. The soldier, to whom
I addressed myself, appeared a good fellow enough,
and I thought I could easily bribe him. I offered him
fifty francs, to let us escape whilst he was on guard.
He refused at first; but, by the tone of his voice, and
by a certain twinkling of his eyes, I thought I saw his
impatience to get such a sum, only that he was afraid
of consequences. To encourage him, I increased the
dose, and showed him three louis, when he said he
would aid us; at the same time adding, that his round
would be from midnight till two o'clock. Having made
our arrangements, I commenced operations; the wall
was pierced so as to allow us a free egress, and we
only waited until the opportunity should arrive. At
length, midnight struck; the soldier announced to me
that he was there, and I gave him the three louis, and
made the necessary dispositions. When all was ready,
I called out. " Is it time?" I said to the sentinel.
" Yes, make haste;" he answered, after a trifling
hesitation. I thought it singular that he did not
answer instantly, and imagining that his conduct was
somewhat dubious, I listened. He seemed to be
marching; and, by the moonlight, I also perceived the
shadow of several men in the ditch, and had no longer
any doubt but that we were betrayed. However, as I
might have been mistaken, to make quite sure, I took
some straw, which I stuffed into some clothes, and put
it at the aperture which we had made; and at the same
instant, a sabre blow that would have cleft an anvil,
informed me that I had well escaped, and confirmed

me more and more in the opinion, that we must not always trust to conscripts. The prison was soon filled with gendarmes, who drew up a statement of facts: they examined us, wishing to know all, and I declared that I had given the conscript three louis, which he denied ; he was examined, and on their being found in his shoes, he was put in the black-hole.

As for us, we were threatened most menacingly; but as they could not punish us, they contented themselves with doubling the guard. There was now no method of escape, without one of those opportunities for which I watched incessantly, and which presented itself earlier than I expected. The next day was the day of our departure, and we had descended into the barrack-yard, which was in great confusion from the arrival of a fresh number of prisoners and a detachment of conscripts from Ardennes, who were going to the camp at Boulogne. The adjutants were squabbling with the gendarmes about room for forming three divisions, and making the muster-call. While each were counting their men, I glided cautiously in at the tail of a baggage-waggon just leaving the court, and thus passed through the city, motionless, and in as small a compass as possible, to elude detection. Once beyond the ramparts, I had only to steal away; and I seized the opportunity whilst the waggoner, thirsty, as these people always are, had gone into an ale-house to refresh himself; and whilst his horses awaited him on the road, I lightened his conveyance of a load, of which he was not aware. I slept in a field of maize, and when night arrived, directed my steps eastward.

CHAPTER XVII.

The camp at Boulogne—The rencontre—The recruiters of the ancien regime—M. Belle Rose.

I TRAVELLED through Picardy towards Boulogne. At this period, Napoleon had abandoned his intention of a descent on England, and was about to make war against Austria with his vast army, but had left many battalions on the shores of the British channel. There were in the two camps, that on the left and that on the right, depôts of almost every corps, and soldiers of every nation in Europe; Italians, Germans, Piedmontese, Dutch, Swiss, and even Irish.

The uniforms were various, and this variety might be useful in concealing me; but I thought that it would be bad policy to disguise myself by only borrowing a military garb. I thought for a moment of becoming actually a soldier, but then to enter a regiment it would have been necessary to have certain papers, which I had not. I then gave up the intention, and yet my abode at Boulogne was dangerous, until I should decide on something.

One day that I was more embarrassed and more unquiet than usual, I met on the walks a serjeant of marine-artillery, whom I had met at Paris, and who was, as well as myself, a native of Arras; but having embarked when very young in a ship of war, he had passed the greater portion of his life in the colonies, and on his return to his native country had learnt nothing of my doings. He only looked on me as a bon vivant; and a public-house row, in which I energetically espoused his cause, had given him a high opinion of my courage.

"What, is it you," said he, "Roger Bontemps; and what are you doing at Boulogne?" "What am I doing! why, seeking employment in the train of the army." " Oh, you want employment; do you know that it is devilish difficult to get a berth now? But, if you will listen to my advice—though this is not the place for such conversation; let us go to Galand's."

We then went to a sort of suttler's booth, which was modestly stationed in one of the angles of the street. " Ah! good day, Parisian," said the serjeant to the host. " Good day, father Dufailli—What will you have this morning?—a dram?—mixed or plain." " Five-and-twenty gods! papa Galand, do you take us for blackguards? It is the best pullet and super-excellent wine that we want, do you hear?" Then addressing me,—" Is it not true, old boy, that the friends of our friends are our friends? That you must agree to;" and, taking my hand, he led me into a small room, where M. Galand admitted his favorite customers.

I was very hungry, and saw with lively satisfaction the preparations for a repast, of which I was to partake. A waiting-maid, from twenty-five to thirty years, well made, and with a face and good humour which such girls have, who can constitute the felicity of a whole regiment, brought in the dishes. She was a native of Liege; lively, agreeable, chattering her patois, and uttering every moment such low witticisms as excited greatly the mirth of the serjeant, who was delighted with her. " She is the sister-in-law of our host," said he to me; " what cat-heads she has; she is as plump as a ball, and as round as a buoy—a dainty lass, upon my faith." At the same time, Dufailli, pulling her about, began to play all sorts of naval tricks; sometimes drawing her on his knees, sometimes applying to her shining cheeks one of those hearty smacks which bespeaks more love than discretion.

I confess I was annoyed at this coquetry, which delayed our meal, when mademoiselle Jeannette (so was the nymph called), having abruptly broken from the

arms of my Amphitryon, returned with part of a devil-
led turkey and two bottles, which she placed before
us.

"Well done," said the serjeant; "here is wherewithal
to moisten our food, and increase the juices. I shall
play my part. After that we shall see; for here, my
boy, it is all as I wish. I have only to make a signal.
Is it not so, Jeannette? Yes, my comrade," continued he, "I am master here."

I congratulated him on so much good fortune, and
we began to eat and drink with might and main. It
was long since I had been at such a festival, and I
played my part manfully. Abundance of bottles were
emptied; and we were about, I believe, to uncork the
seventh, when the serjeant went out, and soon returned,
bringing with him two new guests, a forager and a serjeant-major, "Five and twenty gods! I like good
fellowship," cried Dufailli. "By Jove, I have made
two recruits. I know how to go recruiting; ask
these gentlemen."

"Oh yes," said the forager, "he is the cock, father
Dufailli, to invent plots to seduce conscripts; when I
think of them, I remember my own adventure."—"Ah
you still remember that!"—"Yes, yes, my old lad, I
remember it, and the major also, when you were deep
enough to enlist him as secretary to the regiment."

"Well! has he not done well? A thousand thunders!
Is it not better to be the first accountable man in an
artillery company then sit scratching away on paper in
a study? What say you, forager?"—"I agree with
you; but"—"But, but, you will tell me perhaps, you,
that you were happier, when with your old dog of a
master, your were obliged to lay hold of the watering-
pot, and make yourself dripping wet with throwing
frogs' spawn over your tulips. We were going to embark at Brest, on board 'l'Invincible;' and you would
only go out as a flower-gardener.—Well then," said
I, "go as flower-gardener; the captain likes flowers;

D

every man to his taste, but also every man to his trade; and I carried on mine. I think I see you now; you were rather disappointed when, instead of employing yourself in cultivating marine plants, as you expected, you were sent to man the shrouds of a thirty-six: and when you were ordered to fire a bomb-shell! that was a nosegay for you! But no more of that; and let us drink a measure of wine. Come, lads, here's to our comrades."

I filled all the glasses, and the serjeant continued— " You see that I am not wanted now, therefore let us make of all of us but a pair of friends. This is easily done; I have caught these nicely in my snare, but that is nothing; we recruiters of the marines are but fools to the recruiters of earlier days; you are still but green-horns—Ah, you never knew Belle-Rose; he was the lad for taking in the knowing ones! Such as I am, I was not a thorough noodle, and yet he twisted me completely round his finger. I think I have already told you the tale; but at all events I will give it you again for the general good.

" Under the ancient regime, do you see, we had co-lonies, the isle of France, Bourbon, Martinique, Gua-daloupe, Senegal, Guyana, Louisiana, St Domingo &c.; now they are ours no longer; we have only the isle of Oleron left; it is little more than nothing; or, as somebody said, it is a foot of earth whilst we wait for the rest. The descent would have restored us all the others; but bah, the descent—we must no longer think of that, that is settled; the flotilla will rot in the port, and they will make fire-wood of the hulls. But I am getting out my latitude, steering seaward, instead of landward; now then for Belle-Rose! for I believe it was of Belle-Rose that I was speaking.

" As I told you, he was a spark who had cut his wisdom-teeth, and in his time young fellows were not of the same kidney with those of the present day.

" I had left Arras at fourteen, and been at Paris for six months, apprentice to a gunsmith, when,
one morning, my master desired me to carry to the colonel of the carabineers, who lived in the Place Royale,
a pair of pistols which he had been repairing. I soon
performed this commission, and unfortunately these
cursed pistols should return eighteen francs to the
shop, and the colonel counted out the money, adding
a trifle for myself. So far, so good ; but, lo and be-
hold, in crossing the Rue du Pelican I heard somebody
knock at a window ; I raised my eyes, supposing that I
should see some acquaintance, when what should I see
but a madame de Pompadour, who, with all her charms
displayed, was tapping at a window, and who, by an
inclination of her head, accompanied with a charming
smile, invited me to go up to her. She might have
been called a picture moving in its frame. A magnificent neck, a skin white as snow, a wide chest, and
above all a delightful countenance, combined to enflame
me. I went up the stairs four at a time, and on introducing myself to my princess, I found her a divinity.
'Approach, my little one,' said she to me, tapping my
cheek lightly ; ' you are going to make me a little present, are you not ? '

" I put my trembling hand into my pocket, and taking out the piece of money given me by the colonel—
' Well, my child,' continued she, ' I think you are a
Picardy lad, and I am your country-woman—Oh you
wish to treat your townswoman to a glass of wine.'

" The request was urged so sweetly, that I had no
power of denial left, and the eighteen francs of the colonel were trenched upon. One glass produced another,
that generated a third, which begot a fourth, and so
on, until I was drunk with wine and delight. Night
arrived, and I know not how, but I awoke in the
street on a heap of stones at the gate of the hotel des
Fermes.

" My surprise was great on looking about me, and

still more when on looking in my purse, the birds were flown.

"How could I return to my master's? Where sleep? I determined to walk about till day-break, I had only to kill time, or rather torment myself about the consequences of a first fault. I turned mechanically towards the market of the Innocents. Mind how you trust your country-women! said I to myself; I am nicely fleeced! If I had only some money left—

" I confess that at this moment some droll ideas crossed my brain. I had often seen pasted up on the walls of Paris—"Pocket-book Lost," with one thousand, two thousand or even three thousand francs reward for the person who would bring it back. I thought I might find one of these, and looking carefully about me on the pavement, and walking like a man who is looking for something, I was seriously intent on the probability of finding so good a windfall, when I was aroused from my reverie by a blow of a fist, which encountered my back. 'What! my boy, you out so early this morning?'—'Ah! is it you, Fanfan; and by what chance in this quarter at this hour?'

" Fanfan 'was a pastry-cook's apprentice, whom I knew, and in a moment he told me that he had left the oven for the last six weeks; that he had a mistress who fitted him out; that, for a short time, he was from home, because the intimate friend of his mistress had chosen to sleep with her. ' As for the rest,' said he, ' I wink at it. If I pass a night at the Sourcière, I return to my haunt next morning, and recover myself during the day. Fanfan the pastry-cook appeared to me a keen fellow; and thinking that he might devise some plan to extricate me from my embarrassment, I told him the whole of it.

" ' Is that all?' said he. ' Come to me at mid-day at the public-house at the Barriere des Sergents; and I may give you some useful counsel : under any circumstances we'll dine together.'

" I was punctual at the rendezvous, and Fanfan did not keep me waiting; he was there before me, and on my entrance, I was led into a small room, where I found him seated before a tub of oysters, with a female on each side of him, one of whom, on perceiving me, burst out into a loud fit of laughter. ' Ah, what is that for ?' said Fanfan. ' Oh heaven, it is my towns-man.'—' It is my towns-woman,' said I confused. ' Yes, my little one, it is your towns-woman.' I was going to complain of the trick she had served me on the previous evening, but embracing Fanfan, whom she called her *pet*, she laughed more heartily than before, and I saw that the best thing I could do was to join the laugh like a jolly fellow.

" ' Well,' said Fanfan, pouring out a glass of white wine, and helping me to a dozen oysters, ' you see, you must never despair of Providence. We have some pigs'-feet on the gridiron, do you like pigs'-feet ?' And before I could answer his question, they were put on the table. The appetite I displayed was so much in the affirmative, that Fanfan had no further occasion to ask my opinion of them. The Chablis soon put me in spirits, and I forgot the disagreeables which had given me such cause of dreading my master; and, as the companion of my towns-woman had cast a gracious eye on me, I did not hesitate to make desperate love to her. By the honour of Dufailli ! she was soon won, and gave me her hand.

" ' You really love me then,' said Fanchette—so was my damsel named :—' Love you ?' said I. ' Why, if you like we will be married.' ' That is right,' said Fanfan. ' Marry; and to commence, I will wed you at once. I marry you, my boy; do you understand ? so, embrace;' and at the same time, he united our hands and drew our faces towards each other. ' Poor child,' said Fanchette, giving me a second kiss without the aid of my friend. ' Be easy; I will instruct you.'

" I was in paradise, and spent a delightful day. In

the evening I went to bed with Fanchette, and we were
mutually pleased with each other.

" My education was soon perfected. Fanchette was
delighted at having met with a pupil who profited so
well from her instructions, and recompensed me generously.

" At this period the Notables had just assembled,
and they were good pigeons. Fanchette plucked them,
and we shared the spoil. Each day we banquetted
without limit. These Notables supplied our throats as
well as exerting their own ! And I had always a well-
supplied purse.

" Fanchette and I denied ourselves nothing ; but
how brief are the moments of happiness ! Oh, how
brief !

" Scarcely had a month of this charming life elapsed, when Fanchette and my towns-woman were apprehended and taken to prison. What had they done ?
I do not know, but evil tongues said something about
the abstraction of a repeating-watch. I, who had
no particular wish to make acquaintance with the
lieutenant-general of police, thought it best to make
as few enquiries as possible.

" This arrest was a blow which we had not looked
for. Fanfan and I were overwhelmed at it. Fanchette
was such a dear girl ! and then how was I to carry on
the war ? My kettle was upset ; farewell oysters, farewell chablis, farewell hours of love! I should have
stuck to my anvil; and Fanfan reproached himself for
having quitted his patty-pans.

" We were walking sorrowfully on the Quai de la
Ferraille, when we were suddenly aroused by a sound
of military music, two clarionets, a large drum and
cymbals. The crowd had gathered round this band,
stationed in a car, above which floated colours and
plumes of all colours. I think they were playing the air
' Où peut on être mieux qu'au sein de sa famille ? '
(Where can we find joys equal to those at home ?) When
the musicians had finished, the drums beat a roll, and

a gentleman covered with gold lace, got up and spoke,
showing a large representation of a soldier in full uniform. ' By the authority of his majesty,' said he,
' I am here to explain to the subjects of the king of
France the advantages which he offers in admitting
them to his colonies. Young men who are round me,
you must have heard of the land of Cocagne, and it is
to India that we must go to find this fortunate country. There we must go, if we would live in clover.'
" ' Would you have gold, pearls, or diamonds? the
roads are paved with them; you have only to stoop
and pick them up, and not even that, for the savages
will collect them for you.

" ' Do you love women? There they are for all
tastes; negresses, who belong to all the world; then
creoles, white as you or I, and who dote to madness
on white men, which is natural enough in a country
where the men are all black; and note particularly
that every one of them is as rich as Crœsus; which,
between ourselves, is very advantageous in marriage.

" ' Do you love wine? It is like the women, of all
sorts; Malaga, Bourdeaux, Champagne, &c. For instance,—you must not often expect to meet with Burgundy, I will not deceive you, it will not bear sea carriage; but ask for any other that is made throughout
the world, at sixpence a bottle, and believe me, you
will find them but too happy to procure it for you.
Yes, gentlemen, for sixpence; and that cannot surprise you, when you learn that sometimes one, two,
or three hundred ships, loaded with wines, arrive at
the same time in one single harbour. Picture to yourself the embarrassment of the captains; in haste to
return, they quickly unload, and announce that they
shall esteem it a favour from any who will empty the
casks gratis.

" ' That is not all. Do not you think it would be a
sweet life always to have sugar in plenty? I have not
mentioned coffee, lemons, pomegranates, oranges, pine-
apples, and the millions of delicious fruits which grow

here as wild as they did in Paradise; I say nothing of the liqueurs of these islands, which are so much in esteem, and which are so agreeable, that, saving your presence, they may be called the emanations of the good God and the holy angels.

" 'If I were addressing women or children, I might expatiate on all these delicacies, but I am speaking to men.

" 'Sons of family, I am not ignorant of the efforts usually made by parents to restrain young people from the path which must lead to fortune; but be more rational than the papas, and particularly the mammas.

" 'Do not listen to them, when they tell you that the savages eat the Europeans with only a little salt: that was all very well in the days of Christopher Columbus and Robinson Crusoe.

" 'Do not listen to them, when they endeavour to terrify you about the yellow fever. The yellow fever? Gentlemen, if it was as terrible as people say, there would be nothing but hospitals in the country, and God knows that there is not a single one.

" 'Doubtless they will frighten you about the climate, I am too frank not to confess it; the climate is warm, but nature is so prodigal in giving refreshments, that, in truth, we must attend to the thing, or we should not perceive it.

" 'They will alarm you about the sting of the musquitoes, and the bite of rattle-snakes. But have you not slaves always about you, expressly to drive away the former; and does not the noise of the latter sufficiently inform you of its approach?

" 'They will talk to you of shipwrecks. Know that I have crossed the sea fifty-seven times; that I have again and again crossed the line; that I look on going from one pole to the other, like drinking a glass of water; and although on the ocean, there is neither wooden sledges nor nurses, I think myself more secure on board a seventy-four, than in the inside of the coach to Auxerre, or on the conveyance

from Paris to St Cloud. That must be enough to
dissipate all fears. I might add a variety of delights;
I might talk of the chase, sporting, fishing; imagine to
yourself forests, where the game is so tame that it
never thinks of running away, and so timid that if you
only call to it, it falls down; imagine rivers and lakes,
where fish are so abundant that they choke the waters.
This is all very wonderful, but perfectly true.

" ' I had nearly forgotten to talk to you of horses.
Horses, gentlemen; you cannot take a step without
meeting with thousands of them; you might call them
flocks of sheep, only that they are larger; are you
fond of them? do you like riding? Only take a rope
in your pocket, which should be rather long, and you
must make a running knot in it; you seize the moment when the animals are grazing, and afraid of
nothing, you then approach quietly, and make your
choice; and when your choice is made, you throw the
cord, the horse is your's, you have only to back him
and lead him where you please and think proper; for,
remember, that here every man is uncontrolled in his
actions.

" ' Yes, gentlemen, I repeat it, it is all true, very true;
the proof is, that the king of France, his majesty Louis
XVI, who can almost hear me in his palace, authorizes
me on his part to offer you these advantages. Should
I dare to lie so near to him?

" ' The king desires to clothe you, the king wishes to
support you, he wishes to make you rich men; in return, he asks but little from you; no labour, and good
pay; good nourishment; to rise up and lie down at
pleasure; exercise once a month, at the parade of St
Louis; this, for I will conceal nothing, cannot be dispensed with, unless you get leave, which is never refused. These obligations done, your time is your own.
What more can you desire? a good engagement? you
shall have it: but hasten, I advise you, tomorrow will
perhaps be too late, the ships are about to start, and

only wait for a fair wind to set sail. Hasten, then,
near to Paris; hasten. If, perchance, you should
grow tired of doing well, you shall have dismissal
when you please; a bark is always in port, ready to
conduct to Europe those who are home sick; it is expressly used for that purpose. Let those who desire
to have further particulars, come to me; I have no
occasion to tell my name; I am very well known; my
residence is only a few paces distant, at the first lamp,
at the house of a wine-merchant. Ask for M. Belle-
Rose.'

    " My situation made me attentive to this harangue,
which I have remembered, although it is twenty years
since I heard it, and I do not think that I forget a
single word.

    " It made no less impression on Fanfan, and we
were consulting together, when a shabby-looking fellow, whom we had not at all offended, gave Fanfan a
blow, which knocked his hat off. ' I will teach you,'
said he, ' you puppy, to grin at me.' Fanfan was bewildered by the blow, and I defended him, when the
blackguard raised his hand against me; we were soon
surrounded, and the quarrel was growing warm, and
the people flocked round, trying who should see most
of it. Suddenly, some one separated the crowd; it
was M. Belle-Rose. ' What is all this?' said he; and
looking at Fanfan, who was crying, ' I think this gentleman has been struck—that cannot be put up with;
but the gentleman is brave, and that will settle the
business.' Fanfan was desirous of showing that he
had done nothing wrong, and then that he had not
been struck. ' It is all the same, my friend,' replied
Belle-Rose; ' it cannot be settled that way.' ' Certainly,' said the bully, ' it cannot be decided in this
way. The gentleman insulted me, and shall give me
satisfaction; one of us must fall.'

    " ' Well, well, be it so; he will give you satisfaction,'
replied Belle-Rose: ' I will answer for these gentle-

men; what is your hour?'—' Your's.'—' Five in the morning, behind the bishop's palace;— I will bring weapons.'

" Upon this, the blackguard retired; and Belle-Rose striking Fanfan on the stomach, heard some pieces chink in the waistcoat pocket, where he carried his money, the last relics of our former splendour. ' Really, my lad, I take an interest in you,' said he; ' you must come with me; our friend here must go with us :' and so saying, he gave me a poke, similar to that he had bestowed on Fanfan.

" M. Belle-Rose conducted us into the Rue de la Juiverie, to a wine-merchant's, where he made us enter. ' I will not enter with you,' said he to us; ' a man like me must preserve decorum: I am going to pull off my uniform, and will join you in a minute. Ask for a red seal and three glasses.' He left us. ' A red seal,' said he, turning round; ' mind the red seal.'

" We executed the orders of M. Belle-Rose, who was not long in returning, and whom we received cap-in-hand. ' Ah! my boys,' said he, ' put on your hats; no ceremonies between us; I am going to sit down: where is my glass? the first come, the first served. (He drank it down at a gulp.) I am devilish thirsty, and the dust sticks in my throat.'

" M. Belle-Rose poured out a second, whilst he spoke, and then wiping his forehead with a handkerchief, he leant his two elbows on the table, and assumed a mysterious air, which began to disquiet us.

" ' Ah! my young friends, it is tomorrow that we are to have the brush. Do you know,' said he to Fanfan, ' that you have a devil to meet?—one of the best fencers in France: he pinked St George.' ' He pinked St George,' repeated Fanfan, looking most piteously at me. ' Ah! indeed, he pinked St George; but that is not all,—he has a most unlucky hand.' ' And so have I, ' said Fanfan.' What you, too?'—' By Jove, I think a day never passed, when I was at my master's, that I did not break something, if only a plate or two.' ' Oh, you misunderstand me, my boy,' said Belle-Rose; ' we say that a man has an unlucky hand, when he always kills his man when he fights.'

" The explanation was but too clear. Fanfan trembled in every limb, the sweat ran down his forehead in large drops, white and blue clouds pervaded the red cheeks of the pastrycook's apprentice, his face lengthened, his heart beat, and he would have suffocated, had he not heaved an enormous sigh.

" ' Bravo!' cried Belle-Rose, taking his hand in his own, ' I like men who have no fear. You are not afraid.' Then, striking the table, ' Waiter, another bottle of the same; mind you, my friend, here pays. Get up a little, my friend; move yourself—stir about —stretch out your arm—circulate your blood—thrust out: that's it,—splendid! admirable! superb!' And during this time Belle-Rose emptied his glass. ' On the honour of Belle-Rose I could make a fencer of you. Do you know you have an excellent idea of it? You would do well at it; there are more than four of our masters not so well made for it as you. What a pity you were never taught; but nothing is impossible, you have frequented the schools?'—' Oh, I swear not,' replied Fanfan. ' Come, confess that you fight well.'—' No, not at all.'—' No modesty; why conceal your talent that way, I can easily perceive it.'— ' I protest to you,' said I, ' that he never handled a foil in his life.'—' Since you attest it, sir, I must believe; but, ah! you are two deep fellows; you must not teach old apes how to grin; tell me the truth, and do not fear that I would betray you : am not I your friend? If you have no confidence in me, I may as well go. Farewell, gentlemen,' continued Belle-Rose, with a provoked air, going towards the door, as if about to depart.

" ' Oh, M. Belle-Rose, do not forsake us,' cried Fanfan. ' Rather ask my friend if I have deceived you. I am a pastrycook by trade, and I cannot help my fate. I have handled the rolling pin, but—'

" ' I saw you had handled something,' said Belle-Rose. ' I like sincerity, such sincerity as yours; it is the chief of military virtues; with that we may go to any extent. I am sure you would make an admirable soldier. But that is not our present business. Waiter, a bottle of wine. Since you tell me you never did fight, I will believe nothing again—(after a moment's silence)—Never mind, my delight is to confer happiness on young people. I will teach you a thrust—a single thrust. (Fanfan stared.) You must promise me not to show it to anybody.'—' I swear it,' said Fanfan. ' Well, you will be the first to whom I ever showed it. I must love you! It is a thrust unequalled; one which I kept only to myself. Never mind, I will initiate you at daylight tomorrow.'

" From this moment Fanfan appeared less alarmed, and overpowered M. Belle-Rose with thanks. We drank a few more glasses, during a multitude of protestations on one side and gratitude on the other; and then as it was growing late, M. Belle-Rose took leave of us like a man who knew the world. Before he left us he showed us a place where we could sleep. ' Say that you come from me,' said he, ' at Griffon's, in the Rue de la Mortellerie; sleep in peace, and you shall find all go well.' Fanfan paid the bill, and then Belle-Rose said, ' Good night, tomorrow I shall come and wake you.'

" We went to Griffon's, where we procured beds. Fanfan could not close an eye, and was perhaps impatient to learn the thrust which M. Belle-Rose had promised to teach him; or he might be frightened; perhaps he was.

" At the first peep of day the key turned in the lock, and some one entered. It was Belle-Rose. ' Come, boys; what, still asleep? Hear the muster-call, my lads,' cried he. In a moment we jumped up. When we were ready, he went out a moment with Fanfan, and they soon afterwards returned. ' Let us go,' said Belle-Rose: ' mind, no nonsense; you have nothing to do but give the twisting thrust, and he will pink himself.'

" In spite of his lesson, Fanfan was not quite tranquil; and having reached the ground, he was more dead than alive. The adversary and his second had arrived already. 'Here we are,' said Belle-Rose, taking the foils which he had given to me; and breaking off the buttons, he measured the blades. 'Neither of them is six inches longer than the other. Come, take this,' said he to M. Fanfan, giving him one of the foils.

" Fanfan hesitated; and on the second offer, seized the handle so clumsily that he let it fall. 'That is nothing,' said Belle-Rose, picking it up, and putting it in Fanfan's hand: he then placed him opposite his adversary. 'Mind, guard! We shall see who will tickle his man.'

" ' One moment,' said the second of the opponent; ' I have a question to ask first, sir,' said he, addressing Fanfan, who could scarcely support himself, ' are you either master or provost?'—' What do you say,' replied Fanfan, with the voice of a man half dead. ' According to the laws of duelling,' responded the second, ' my duty compels me to summon you to declare on your honour, are you master or provost?' Fanfan was silent, and looked at Belle-Rose as if to ask him what he should say. ' Speak, sir,' said the second to Fanfan. 'I am—I am—I am only an apprentice,' stammered Fanfan. ' Apprentice means amateur,' added Belle-Rose. ' In this case,' continued the second, ' the gentleman amateur must undress; for our business is with his skin.'—' That is just,' said Belle-Rose, ' I did not think of that; he will undress himself: quick, quick, M. Fanfan, off with coat and shirt.'

" Fanfan cut a scurvy figure; the sleeves of his doublet were very tight, and he unbuttoned at one end and buttoned up at the other. When he had taken off his waistcoat, he could not undo the strings

of the neck of his shirt, and was compelled to cut
them; and at last, except his breeches, was as naked
as a worm. Belle-Rose again gave him the foil.
' Now, my friend,' said he, ' mind your guard!'—' Defend yourself,' cried his adversary; swords were
crossed. Fanfan's blade shook and trembled; the
other weapon was motionless. Fanfan seemed about
to faint.

" ' Enough,' suddenly cried Belle-Rose and the
second, ' you are two brave fellows; enough, you
must not cut each other's throats; be friends, embrace,
and let there be no further dispute. Good God! all
that is good need not be killed. But he is a gallant
young lad. Be appeased, M. Fanfan.'

" Fanfan breathed again, and plucked up when his
courage was mentioned; his opponent made some
difficulties about consenting to an arrangement, but
at length was softened; and they embraced, whilst it
was agreed that the reconciliation should be completed
by breakfasting at a drinking house, near Notre Dame,
where there was good wine to be had.

" When we reached the place, the breakfast was
spread and ready.

" Before we sat down, M. Belle-Rose took Fanfan
and myself aside. ' Well,' said he, ' you know now
what a duel is; it is not an out of the way matter;
I am content with you, my dear Fanfan, you behaved
like an angel. But you must be great throughout:
you understand me—you must not allow him to pay.'

" At these words Fanfan turned very red; for he
knew the depth of our purse. ' Oh, good Lord, let
the mutton boil,' added Belle-Rose, who saw his embarrassment. ' If you are out of cash I will take care
of all that; here, do you want money? Will you have
thirty francs?—or sixty? Amongst friends, that is
nothing.' And so saying, he drew a dozen crowns
from his pocket—' With you they are in good keeping,
and will bring good luck.'

" Fanfan hesitated. ' Accept them, and pay me
when you can.   On these terms there can be no
hesitation in borrowing.'   I jogged Fanfan's elbow,
as much as to say, ' Take it.'   He obeyed; and we
pocketed the crowns, touched at the kindness of
Belle-Rose.

" He was soon, however, to skin us of them.   Experience is a great teacher, and M. Belle-Rose was a
deep fellow !

" Breakfast went off with spirit; we talked much of
the avarice of parents—the brutalities of apprentices'
masters—of the blessings of independence—the immense wealth amassed in the Indies : the names of
the Cape, Chandernagor, Calcutta, Pondicherry, and
Tipoo-Saib were adroitly introduced; examples were
quoted of the vast fortunes made by the young men
whom Belle-Rose had recently engaged.   ' It is not
to boast,' said he, ' but I am not an unlucky fellow:
it was I who enlisted little Martin; and now he is a
nabob, rolling in gold and silver.   I will bet that he
has grown proud; and perhaps if he saw me would
not recognise me.   Oh, I have found many ingrates
in my time !   But what of that ?   It is the fate of
man !'

" Our sitting was a long one.   At the dessert, M.
Belle-Rose again brought on the carpet the fine fruits of
the Antilles : whilst he drank the wine, ' Cape wine for
ever,' said he; ' how delicious that is :' with the coffee
he expatiated on the Martinique : when they brought
the cognac, ' Ah ! ah !' said he, making a grimace,
' this is not equal to the rum, and still less the excellent pine-apple of Jamaica :' they poured out some
parfait amour : ' This is drinkable,' said he, ' but still
it is not even small beer in comparison with the
liqueurs of the celebrated madame Anfous.'

" Belle-Rose was seated between Fanfan and myself,
and during the whole repast took great care of us.
He kept up the incessant song of ' Empty your

glasses,' and he filled them incessantly. 'Who made you such half-wet birds,' said he at intervals, 'Come, another glass, look at me, and do as I do.'

"These phrases, and many others, had due effect. Fanfan and I were pretty well done up; he particularly. 'M. Belle-Rose, is it very far to the colonies, Chanbernagor, Seringapatam? Are they very far off?' he repeated, from time to time, and he imagined himself already embarked, so completely was he imbued with the flourishing accounts. 'Patience,' said Belle-Rose, at length, 'and we shall get there; and in the mean time I am going to tell you a story. One day, when I was on guard at the governor's——'—'One day, when he was governor,' said Fanfan. 'Hold your peace,' said Belle-Rose, putting his hand upon his mouth—'it was only when I was a private,' he continued. 'I was quietly seated in front of my sentry-box, reposing on a sofa, when my negro, who carried my gun,—you must know that in the colonies every soldier has his male and female slave, as we might here have domestics of both sexes; only that you may do with them what you please; and if it be your pleasure, you may kill them as you would a fly; for you have power of life and death over them. As for the woman, you do what you please with her;— I was on guard, as I just told you, and my negro was carrying my gun——'

"M. Belle-Rose had scarcely got so far, when a soldier in full dress entered the room, and gave him a letter, which he opened with haste. 'It is from the minister of the marine,' said he; 'M. de Sartine tells me, that the service of the king summons me to Surinam. The devil!' added he, addressing Fanfan and me, 'how awkward it is; I did not think of quitting so soon; but as they say, he who reckons without his host, reckons twice: never mind.'

"Belle-Rose then taking his glass in his right hand, knocked several times on the table, and whilst the other guests withdrew, a waiting-maid entered. ' The bill, and send your master ;' and the master came with the bill of our expenses. ' Astonishing how soon it mounts up,' observed Belle-Rose: ' one hundred and ninety livres, twelve sous, six deniers ! Ah ! M. Nivet, do you want to skin us alive ? Here is an item I will not pass by—-four lemons, twenty-four sous. We only had three—reduction the first. Peste, papa Nivet, I am not surprised at your making a fortune. Seven half-glasses, that is very fine; but how do you make it out, when there were only six of us ? I shall find other mistakes, I am convinced. Asparagus, eighteen livres; that is too much.'—' In April,' said M. Nivet, ' and so early !'—' Well, that is right; young peas, arti-chokes, fish, lettuces, strawberries, twenty-four livres —that is correct. The wine is fair enough : now I will add it up. Put down nought and carry one—the total is correct, deducting the twelve sous and the six deniers there remains one hundred and ninety livres. Well, will you give me credit for the amount, papa Nivet ?'—' Oh ! ' replied the landlord, ' yesterday, yes ; today, no ; credit on land as long as you please, but once at sea, how am I be repaid ? at Surinam ? Devil take the sea-going creditors. I tell you money I want, and you shall not go out till I am satisfied ; otherwise I shall send for the watch, and we shall then see ——"

" M. Nivet went out in an apparent rage.

" ' He is a man of his word,' said Belle-Rose to us. ' But an idea strikes me, in great distresses, great re-medies. Doubtlessly you have no greater wish than myself to be led before M. Lenoir between four guards. The king gives 100 francs a man for recruits ; there are two of you, that makes 200 francs : sign your en-rolment ; I will go and get the cash, then return and free you. What say you ? '

" Fanfan and I looked at each other in silence. ' What ! do you hesitate ? I had a better opinion of you. I, who would cut myself in quarters—and then

I do not ask you to do an unpleasant thing. Heavens! that I was of your age, and knew what I know! We have always resources whilst we are young. Come,' he added, presenting the paper to us, ' now is your time to coin money: put your name at the bottom of this paper.'

" The persuasions of Belle-Rose were so pressing, and we were so fearful of the watch, that we signed. ' That is right,' said he, ' now I will go and pay; if you are vexed there is always time : you will have nothing to do but return the money; but we shall not come to that. Patience, my friends, I will soon return.'

" Belle-Rose soon went out and quickly returned.

" ' The embargo is removed,' said he, ' and now we are free to go or stay; but you have not yet seen madame Belle-Rose yet, I wish to introduce you to her : she is a woman with wit to the end of her nails.'

" M. Belle-Rose conducted us to his house, his lodging was not over brilliant ; two rooms on the back of a mean-looking house a little distance from the Arch-Marion. Madame Belle-Rose was in a recess at the end of the second room, her head resting on a heap of pillows. Near her bed were two crutches : and at a little distance, a night table, a spitting-box, a shell snuff-box, a silver goblet, and a bottle of brandy nearly emptied. Madame Belle-Rose was about forty-five or fifty : she was attired in a stylish morning gown, with top-knot and head-dress of lace. Her face was distorted as we entered by a violent fit of coughing. ' Wait till she has done,' said Belle-Rose to us : and at length, her cough ceasing, ' Can you talk, my duck ?' —' Yes, my precious,' she answered.—' Well, you will oblige me by informing my friends here what fortunes are made in the colonies.'—' Immense ! M. Belle-Rose, immense ! ' — ' What alliances ? '—' What alliances ? Superb ! M. Belle-Rose, superb ! the meanest heiress has millions of piastres.'—' What life do they lead ? '—' The life of a prince, M. Belle-Rose.'

" ' You see,' said the husband, ' I did not make her say so.'

" The farce was thus performed. M. Belle-Rose offered us the refreshment of a glass of rum: we drank to his wife, and she drank to our good voyage. ' For I suppose,' she added, ' that these gentlemen are ours. My dear fellow,' said she to Fanfan, ' you have the face they like in those parts; square shoulders, wide chest, well-made leg, nose à la Bourbon.' Then turning to me, ' And you too; oh! you are well-limbed fellows.'—' And lads too, who will not allow themselves to be trampled on,' added Belle-Rose; ' this gentleman has been at it already this morning.' ' What, already! I congratulate him. Come here, my dear sir, and let me kiss you; I always liked young fellows, that is my taste: every one has their inclination. Do not be jealous, Belle-Rose.'—' Jealous of what? My friend behaved like a second Bayard, as I shall tell the regiment; the colonel shall know it, and advancement must follow—corporal at least, if not an officer. Ah, when you have the epaulette on your shoulders you will be a noted brave man!' Fanfan jumped for joy. As for me, sure that I was no less brave than him, I said to myself, ' If he advances, I shall not hang back.' We were both very happy.

" ' I ought to tell you one thing,' pursued the recruiter: ' recommended as you are, you must excite jealousy; there are envious people everywhere, in regiments as well as elsewhere; but remember that if they use a word of abuse I shall take it up—once under my protection—enough. Write to me.'— ' What!' said Fanfan, ' do not you go with us?'— ' No,' replied Belle-Rose, ' to my great regret: the minister has need of me. I shall join you at Brest. Tomorrow at eight o'clock I expect you here, not later: today I have no leisure to remain longer with you; duty must be done. Adieu till tomorrow.'

We took leave of madame Belle-Rose, who embraced us. Next day we were, at half-past seven,

aroused by the bugs which lodged with us at Griffon's.
' Give me punctual men!' said Belle-Rose, when he
saw us. ' I am one myself.' Then assuming a more
serious air: ' If you have any friends and acquaintances, you have the rest of the day for leave-taking.
Now this is your route; your allowance is three sous
per league, with lodging, firing, and candle. You may
start as soon as you like; that is no affair of mine; but
do not forget, that, if you are found in the streets of
Paris tomorrow evening, the police will conduct you
to your place of destination.'

" This threat cut us up root and branch; but as we
had baked, so we must brew; and we started. From
Paris to Brest is a famous long walk, but, in spite of
blisters, we made ten leagues a day. We arrived at
last, but not without having a thousand times cursed
Belle-Rose. A month afterwards we embarked. Ten
years afterwards, day for day, I was made corporal,
and Fanfan also promoted; he was knocked on the
head at St Domingo, during Leclerc's expedition. He
was a devil amongst the negro women. As for me, I
have yet a steady foot and good eye; my chest is well
lined, and I may have the luck to bury you all. I have
passed many rough days in my life; been thrown from
one colony to another; I have rolled my ball as I went,
and I have not been a loser; never mind, the children
of glee will never die;—and then, when they are no
more here, they are to be found elsewhere," continued
the serjeant Dufailli, striking the pockets of his uniform; and then lifting up his waistcoat, exposed a
leather belt, apparently well lined. " I say, there is
yet butter in the churn, and yellow enough too, without counting what we may chance to borrow from the
English. The India-Company owe me a balance still,
which some three-masters will bring."—" In the meantime, all goes well with you, father Dufailli," said the
forager. " Very well," said the serjeant-major. Yes,
very well, indeed, thought I; determining to cultivate
an acquaintance which chance rendered so propitious
for me.

CHAPTER XIX.

Continuation of the same day—The Cotemporaine—An adjutant
de place—The daughters of mother Thomas—The silver lion—
Captain Paulet and his lieutenant—The pirates—The bombard-
ment—Departure of Lord Lauderdale—The disguised actress—
The executioner—Henry the Ninth and his ladies—I embark—
Sea-fight—Paulet's second is killed—Capture of a brig of war—
My Sosia—I change my name—Death of Dufailli—Twelfth-day
—A frigate sunk—I wish to save two lovers—A tempest—The
fishermen's wives.

Whilst giving us the scene of the recruiters, father
Dufailli had drank at every sentence. He was of opinion that words flowed best when moistened. He
might, to be sure, have used water; but he had a great
horror of that, he said, ever since he fell into the sea,
which was in 1789. Thus it happened, that, partly
through drinking and partly through talking, he got
drunk imperceptibly. At last he reached a point, at
which he found it impossible to express himself, but
with the utmost difficulty; his tongue became what we
call thick. And then the forager and serjeant-major
retired.

Dufailli and I remained alone: he was asleep and
leant on the table, and begun to snore; whilst I coolly
gave myself up to a train of reflexions. Three hours
elapsed, and he had not finished his sleep. When he
awoke, he was quite surprised to find any one near
him; at first, he looked at me as through a thick fog,
which did not allow him to distinguish my features,
but insensibly the vapour disappeared, and he recognized me, which was all he could do. He stumbled as
he arose; and ordering a basin of coffee, without milk,
into which he emptied a salt-cellar, swallowed the
liquid with small gulps; and having got rid of his
short sword, he took my arm, dragging me towards
the door. My aid was most needful to him; it was
the vine twining about the elm. " You are going to

tow me," said he, " and I will pilot you. Do you see
the telegraph? What does it say, with its arms in the
air?"—"It makes signals that the Dufailli is lying to."
" The Dufailli,—thousand Gods! a ship of three hundred tons at least. Do not fear; all's right with Dufailli." At the same time, without letting go my arm,
he took off his hat, and placing it on the end of his
finger, spun it round. " See my compass; attention—
we go as the cockade points—weather the cape of the
Rue des Prêcheurs; forward, march!" ordered Dufailli; and we took together the road to the lower
town, after he had put on his hat with much noise.

Dufailli had promised to advise me, but he was not
in a state to do it. I anxiously desired that he
should recover his reason, but, unfortunately, the air
and exercise produced a precisely opposite effect. On
going down the main street, we were obliged to enter
every public-house, with which the residence of the
army had filled the place; everywhere made a stay,
shorter or longer. I endeavoured to make them as
brief as possible. Each shop, Dufailli said, was a port,
into which we must put, and each port encreased the
cargo, which he had already so much difficulty to carry.
" I am as full as a beggar," said he to me, in broken
words; " and yet I am not a beggar, for beggars never
get drunk, do they my boy?"

Twenty times I resolved on leaving him; but Dufailli, when sober, might aid me; I remembered his
full girdle, and even without that, I knew well that he
had other resources than his serjeant's pay. Having
reached the church in the Place d'Alton, he took it
into his head to have his shoes brushed, which, when
done, he lost his balance in moving from the stool;
and, thinking he would fall, I approached to support
him. " What, countryman, don't fear because I make
a reel or two; I have a sailor's foot." In the mean
time the brush had given brightness to his shoes; and
when they were completely blackened, " Come, the
finishing touch," said Dufailli; " or is that for tomor-

row?" At the same time he gave him a sous.
" You will not make a rich man of me, serjeant."—
" What, do you grumble?—mind I don't kill you."
Dufailli made a gesture, but his hat fell off, and,
blown by the wind, rolled along the pavement; the
shoe-black ran after it and brought it back. " It is
not worth twopence," cried Dufailli; " never mind,
you are a good fellow." Then thrusting his hands
into his pockets, he took out a handful of money:
" Here, drink to my health."—" Thanks, my colonel,"
said the shoe-black, who proportioned his titles to the
generosity he met with.

" I must now," said Dufailli, who seemed by degrees
to recover his senses, " lead you into good quarters."
I had made up my mind to accompany him wherever
he went. I had witnessed his liberality, and I was
not ignorant that drunkards are the most grateful
persons possible to those who give them their company. I allowed myself then to be piloted as he
wished, and we reached the Rue des Prêcheurs. At
the door of a new house, of elegant appearance, was
a sentry and several soldiers. " This is it," said he.
" What, here? Are you going to take me to the staff-
major?"—" The staff-major!—nonsense; I say it is
the beautiful and fair Magdelaine's; or, if you like it
better ' madame quarante mille hommes ' (madam
forty thousand men) as they call her."—" Impossible,
Dufailli, you are under some mistake."—" Oh, I see
double, do I? Is not that the sentinel?" Dufailli
advanced whilst speaking, and asked for admittance.
" Go back," said a quarter-master, roughly; " you
ought to know well enough that this is not your day."
Dufailli persisted. " Go away, I tell you," said the
subaltern, " or I will take you to the black hole."
This threat made me tremble all over.

Dufailli's obstinacy might be fatal to me, and yet
it would not have been prudent to tell him my fears;
at all events not where we then were; and I therefore
only made some observations to him, which were

however entirely lost upon him in his present state.
" Let the fellow go and be ——, the sun shines
equally for us all : liberty, equality, or death," he
repeated, whilst struggling to escape the hold I kept
on him, that he might not commit himself in any way.
" Equality, I tell you ; " and in an attitude better
conceived than described, he looked at me with that
stupid no-meaning stare which a man has when he
has ' put an enemy into his mouth to steal away his
brains,' and reduce him to the level of a brute.

I was in despair, when, at the cry " Present arms! "
followed by this warning, " Cannoneer, mind what you
do; here is the adjutant, here is Bevignac," he suddenly
seemed quite to come to himself. A shower-bath falling from a height of fifty feet, upon a maniac's head,
has not so sudden an effect in restoring his senses.
The name of Bevignac made a singular impression on
the soldiery, who had ranged themselves in front of
the ground floor of the fair Magdelaine's house. They
looked at one another without, as it seemed, daring to
breathe, so much were they alarmed. The adjutant,
who was a tall meagre-looking man, having arrived,
began to count them, whilst he made motions with his
cane. I never saw a face so deeply furrowed; on his
thin and lank jaws were two small unpowdered curls;
on the whole countenance might be traced a certain
something, which declared that adjutant Bevignac was
a perfect martinet, and determinately opposed to anything like want of discipline. Anger was visible in his
face, his eyes were blood-shot, and a horrible convulsion of his jaws announced that he was about to speak.
" By the devil's nest! Well! All quiet! You know
orders. None but officers! By satan's nest! and every
man in his turn." Then perceiving us, and advancing
with uplifted cane, " What are you doing here, you
serjeant of powder-monkies?" I thought he was about
to strike us. " Oh, I see," he added, " it is nothing;
only drunk;" addressing Dufailli. " Well, a jovial
cup is excusable; go to bed, and do not let me meet

F

you again."—" Yes, commandant," replied Dufailli, at this order, and we went away down the Rue des Prêcheurs.

There is no occasion to mention the profession of the fair Magdelaine le Picarde; it must have been already guessed. She was a tall woman, about twenty-three years of age, remarkable for the bloom of her complexion, as well as the beauty of her figure. It was her boast, that she belonged to no one person. She devoted herself, from a principle of conscience, entirely and solely to the army—the whole army—but nothing but the army: fifer or field-marshal, all who wore the uniform were equally well received by her; but she professed great contempt for what she called the snobs (pequins). There never was a citizen who could boast of her favours : she was somewhat tenacious with marines, whom she called " tar-buckets," and fleeced at pleasure, because she could not make up her mind to look on them as soldiers; and she used to say, that the navy filled her purse, and the army was her lover. This lady, whom I had occasion to visit at a subsequent period, was, for a long time, the delight of the camp, without her health being at all impaired, and was supposed to be rich. But whether Magdelaine (as I know) was not mercenary, or whether as the old proverb goes, " What is got over the devil's back is spent under his belly," Magdelaine died in 1812, at the hospital of Ardres, poor, but true to her flag : but two years more, and, like another nymph well known in Paris, after the disaster of Waterloo, she would have had the grief of calling herself the " widow of the grand army."

The memory of Magdelaine still lives all over France, I might say Europe, amongst the remnants of the old phalanxes. She was the " cotemporaine" of that period; and, if I did not well know that she is no more, I should fancy that I had again found her in the " cotemporaine" of this period. However, I must remark, that Magdelaine, although her features were

rather masculine, had nothing vulgar in her look; the
shade of her hair was not of the sickly hue of heckled
hemp; the golden reflexion of her silken tresses was
in perfect harmony with the tender azure of her eyes;
her nose was not ill formed, in the angular curve of
its aquiline prominence. There was something of
Messalina about her mouth, but yet it was kind and
frank; and, besides, Magdelaine only carried on her
business: she never wrote *; and, amongst all the police, only knew the city serjeants, or the night guard,
whom she paid to leave her in quiet.

The pleasure I have, after a lapse of more than
twenty years, in tracing the portrait of Magdelaine,
has made me for an instant forget Dufailli.

It is very difficult to eradicate an idea from a brain
troubled with the fumes of wine. Dufailli had resolved
on finishing the day in female society, and nothing could
turn him from it. Scarcely had we taken half-a-dozen
steps, than, looking back, " He has disappeared," said
he; " come along, this way;" and, leaving my arm, he
advanced towards a door, at which he knocked; and
which, after a few minutes, was half opened, and an
old woman's head appeared. " What do you want?"—
" What do we want," answered Dufailli; " don't you
know me! Do not you recognize friends?"—" Ah! ah!
is it you, father Dufailli; there is no room for you."
" No room for friends! You're joking, mother; you
are playing off some trick upon us."—" No, on the
word of an honest woman, you know, my old lad,
that no one is more welcome than yourself; but my
eldest daughter is engaged, and so is Pauline; but we
shall be glad to see you bye and bye."—" Well, if it
must be so, mother Thomas," said Dufailli, putting a
piece of money on his eye, " it cannot be helped, but
you must get us something to drink meanwhile; you
have some little spare corner to put us into."—" Aye,
aye, always a wag, always a wag, father Dufailli; it is

* This alludes to a work recently published in Paris, called
' Memoires d'une Cotemporaine.'—*Translator*.

impossible to refuse your insinuating requests. Come!
quick, quick, let no one see you coming in; hide yourselves there, my boys, and mum."

Madame Thomas had placed us behind an old screen,
in a low room, through which all persons going out
must pass. We did not wait long alone. Mademoiselle
Pauline came to us first, and, having whispered to her
mother, came and sat down with us to a flask of
Rhenish.

Pauline was not fifteen years of age, and yet she
had already acquired the dissipated air, the bold look,
the loose discourse, the hoarse voice, and the disgusting manners of the common courtezan. This early
prey to dissipation was destined for my amusement,
and was lavish in her endearments. Therèse was
better suited to the bald head of my companion, who
waited until she should be at leisure; and, at length,
the quick step of a hussar boot, garnished with spurs,
announced that the cavalier was taking leave of his
lady fair. Dufailli, who was somewhat impatient, rose
abruptly from his seat, but his short sword getting between his legs, he fell, knocking down the screen, table,
bottles, and glasses. " Excuse-me, captain," he stammered out, whilst endeavouring to rise; " it was the
fault of the wall."—" Oh, it is of no consequence,"
said the officer; who, although rather confused, very
readily aided in lifting him up, whilst Pauline, Therèse,
and their mother, were seized with a fit of irrepressible
laughter. When Dufailli had recovered his feet, the
captain departed; and, as the fall had produced no
bruise nor wound, nothing checked our mirth. I shall
throw a veil over the remaining scenes of this evening.
We were in a place where Dufailli was well known,
and my readers may guess the rest; suffice it to say,
that, about one o'clock in the morning, I was buried in
profound sleep, when I was suddenly awakened by a
most tremendous uproar. Without suspecting the
cause, I dressed myself iu haste, and some cries of
" Guard! guard! Murder! murder!" from the shrill

lungs of mother Thomas, warned me that the danger was not far off. I was unarmed, and ran immediately to Dufailli's room, to ask for his tinder-box, of which I knew I should make a better use than he would. It was time, for our castle was invaded by five or six marines, who, sword in hand, were endeavouring to get our berths. These gentlemen were threatening, neither more nor less than to force us to jump out of the windows; and, as they swore besides, to put everything to fire and sword in the house, mother Thomas, with her squeaking pipe, was pealing the tocsin of alarm with a noise that aroused the whole neighbourhood. Although a man not easily frightened, I confess I felt a sensation of fear which I could not repress. The event, whatever it might be, would probably end seriously for me.

I was, however, determined to take a resolute part. Pauline earnestly besought me to shut myself up with her. " Fasten the bolt," said she; " I beseech you to fasten the bolt." But the garret in which we were was not impregnable. I might be blockaded; and preferred defending the approach to the place, rather than run the risk of being taken like a rat in a trap. In spite of Pauline's efforts to detain me, I attempted a sortie, and was soon engaged with the assailants. I darted amongst them from the end of a narrow gallery, and with so much impetuosity, that, before they could recover themselves, upset and thrust headlong from a ladder, by which they were attempting to gain an entrance, they were laid sprawling on the ground, bruised and wounded severely. Then Pauline, her sister, and Dufailli, to render the victory more decisive, flung upon them all that came to hand; chairs, tables, stools, and various et ceteras, to detail which would be tedious. At every missile that struck them, the enemy, prostrate on the pavement, cried out with pain and rage. In a moment the passage was filled. This nocturnal brawl could not fail to arouse all in the vicinity; and the night-guard, police agents, and patrole, entered the domicile of madame Thomas;—there must have been at least fifty men, all armed, and making a tremendous hubbub. Madame Thomas endeavoured to testify that her house was quite tranquil, but they would not hear her; and these words, some of which were pretty significant, reached our ears from the ground floor—" Take this woman off." —" Come, old ——, follow us; or shall we get a wheelbarrow to bundle you in, old duchess. Come, no nonsense." " Sweep off the whole party; take every one; seize their arms. I will teach you, you blackguards, to make a row." These words, pronounced in a provincial accent, and mixed with occasional interjections, which, like the garlic and pepper, are fruits of his country, we learnt that adjutant Bevignac was at the head of the party. Dufailli had no inclination to get into his clutches; and, as for me, I had excellent reasons for wishing to escape. " The staircase—go up the staircase, and guard the passage," roared out Bevignac. But whilst he thus bellowed and vociferated, I had time to tie a sheet to the window-bar, and the obstacles which separated us from the armed force had not been removed, when Pauline, Thérèse, Dufailli, and myself, were already out of reach. This threat, " Do not trouble yourselves—I will follow you," which we heard at a distance, only moved our laughter. The danger was over.

We consulted as to where we should pass the night. Thérèse and Pauline proposed that we should quit the city, and make a pastoral excursion into the country. " No, no," said Dufailli; " let us go to the Silver Lion, to Boutrois;" and this was agreed on. M. Boutrois, although it was an untimely hour, opened his doors with much politeness. " Ah," said he to Dufailli, " I learnt that you had received your prize-money, and you are both right and welcome to pay us a visit. I have some admirable claret. What will the ladies please to take? A two-bedded room, I see." At the same time M. Boutrois, armed with a bunch of keys, and with a candle in his hand, led us to the room destined for us. " You will find yourselves quite at home here. No one will disturb you; where we purvey for the lieutenant of the marine, the commandant in chief, and the commissary-general of police, you know no one dare to interfere. Madame Boutrois now, does not like a joke, so I shall take care and not say that you are not alone. Madame B. is a very good woman—a very good woman; but her manners, you see—her manners are very formal; and on this point she is strictness personified. Women here! If she only had the slightest suspicion of such a thing, she would think herself lost for ever; she has such an opinion of the sex in general! Oh, mon Dieu! must we not live with the living?—the jolly?—the vivacious? I am a philosopher myself, provided —mind, I say provided—that there is no ground for scandal; and suppose there were, why every one to his liking, as the elderly gentlewoman said when she embraced her cow; every person to his own way of thinking and doing; the only point being, that it does not offend or prejudice any one."

M. Boutrois treated us to a great many more equally brilliant aphorisms; after which he told us that he had a well-stocked cellar, all of which was at out service. " As for the boiler," he added, " that at the present hour has got rather cool, but your worships have only to order, and in a brace of seconds all shall be ready." Dufailli ordered some claret, and a fire, although it was quite warm enough to have done without.

The claret was brought, five or six logs were cast on the fire, and an ample collation spread before us. Some cold poultry occupied the centre of the table, and formed the resisting point of an unprepared repast where all had been calculated for an enormous appetite. Dufailli desired that nothing should be wanting; and M. Boutrois, sure of being well paid, was most complying. Thérèse and her sister devoured all with their eyes, and I was not in a bad humour for commencing the attack and carrying on the war.

Whilst I was cutting up the fowl, Dufailli tasted the claret. " Delicious, delicious!" he repeated, smacking his lips, and then began to drink heartily; and scarcely had we began to eat, than an unconquerable drowsiness nailed him to his chair, when he snored away most comfortably until the dessert came in. He then woke, crying out, " The Devil—it blows hard—where am I? Does it freeze? I feel a sort of an all-overish, I-don't-know-howishness." " Oh," cried Pauline, who took me for a sapper of the guards, " his supper has not well digested."—" The papa's legs and back are asleep," said Therese, in her turn, and opening a sort of sweetmeat box, in which was some snuff, " Take a pinch, my venerable; that will clear your eyes." Dufailli took a pinch; and if I mention this circumstance, trifling in itself, it is because I have before neglected to say, that Pauline's sister was more than thirty, and from the simple fact that she took snuff like a lawyer or commissary's clerk, we may easily imagine that she was not in the freshness and bloom of youth and beauty.

However that may be, Dufailli made much of her. " I like the little thing," he said occasionally, " she is a good girl."—" Oh, that is nothing new," replied Therese, " whenever a vessel anchors in our roads, I have gone through the scrutiny of all the crew; and I defy any sailor to say ' black's the white of my eye.' When one knows how to behave as one should, one—" —" The wench says right," interrupted Dufailli. " I like her because she is open, and so I will give her a good turn."—" Ah, ah, ah, cried Pauline, laughing, and then addressing me, " And you, will you give me a similar turn?"

Thus ran on our conversation, when we heard, coming from the road leading to the harbour, a body of men, whose boots made a great noise as they

walked. " Captain Paulet for ever ! " they cried out,
" Captain Paulet for ever ! "   The troop soon stopped
in front of the hotel.   " Hallo ! father Boutrois, father
Boutrois ! " they roared out all together.   Some tried to
force the door ; others thumped with the knocker in a
most energetic manner ; some pulled the bell with incredible violence ; and others threw stones at the shutters.

At this uproar I started, imagining that our asylum
was to be again attacked ; Pauline and her sister were
not quite at ease ; and at length somebody running
hastily down stairs, four steps at a time, the door was
opened, and there was a rush, as if the embankments
of a ditch had given way.   The torrent was headlong ;
a mixture of voices uttered sounds quite unintelligible
to us. " Peter, Paul, Jenny, Eliza, house, everybody,
wife, get up !   By Jove, they sleep like dormice."
One might have thought that the house was on fire.
We soon heard doors opening and shutting ; there
was a noise of tables, an inconceivable uproar, a female
servant who was bitterly complaining of indecent
treatment, shouts of riotous laughter, and bottles
rattling and breaking.   Plates, dishes, and glass clash-
ing together, and the winding up of the jack, added to
the din ; a chinking of money, oaths in English and
French occasionally heard amidst this infernal clatter,
all made the place a perfect bedlam broke loose.
" By Jove it is joy, or I never heard it before," said
Dufailli. " What are all these rejoicings for ?   What
does it all mean ?   Have they captured the Spanish
Galleons ?   But this is not the track for them."

Dufailli cudgelled his brain to make out the cause of
all the uproar, which was to me equally inexplicable,
when M. Boutrois, with a radiant face, entered, to
ask leave to light a fire. " You do not know," said
he, " that the ' Revanche ' has just come into port.
Our Paulet has been carrying on the war in his old
way ; is he not a fortunate fellow ?   A capture of three
millions (francs) beneath the very cannon of Dover."
—" Three millions ! " cried Dufailli, " and I not

there!"—"Do you hear that, sister? Three millions!" added Pauline, jumping like a young kid.
" Three millions!" echoed Thérèse, " I am delighted!
We shall come in for a share!"—"Ah, woman,
woman," interrupted Dufailli, "interest before all;
you should rather think of your mother, who is perhaps at this moment in darkness and distress."—
" Mother Thomas is an old ——" (what I will not
sully my pages by repeating) added Thérèse. " Come,
that is neat, very neat," observed Boutrois, "for a
daughter. ' Honour thy father and thy mother, that
thy days may be long,' &c."—" I cannot swallow that
three millions," said Dufailli. " Tell us, father Boutrois, all about it." Our host excused himself on the
plea of business; " besides," he added, " I do not well
know the particulars, and am in a great hurry."
    The riot continued; I heard them ranging chairs,
and the silence that followed betokened that their
jaws were filled. As it was probable that there
would be some suspension of these noises, I proposed
that we should go to bed, which was agreed on; and
as day-break was near at hand, that we might not be
disturbed by the light, and make up for lost time, we
drew the curtains close.
    However, we were not aroused so soon as I had
anticipated: sailors eat fast and drink long. Songs,
which shook the very glasses, at length disturbed our
repose; forty discordant voices joining in the chorus
of the celebrated hymn of Roland. " Devil take the
singers!" cried Dufailli, " I had the most agreeable
dream;—I was at Toulon: were you ever at Toulon,
old fellow?" I answered Dufailli, that I knew Toulon, but could not see what relation there could be
between his agreeable dream and that city. " I was a
galley-slave," he replied, "and I had just escaped."
Dufailli perceived that this statement made an unpleasant impression on me, which I could not conceal.
" Well, what is the matter with you countryman? I
had just escaped, and that's no bad dream, I think,

for a prisoner. It was only a dream, to be sure; but that is not all, for I entered amongst the corsairs, and got as much gold as I could carry."

Although I have never been superstitious, I must confess I took Dufailli's dream as a prediction on my future lot; it was perhaps a warning from heaven, to determine the course I should pursue. However, said I to myself, at present I do not deserve heaven's interposition, and perhaps I only fancy it. I soon made another reflection. It occurred to me, that the old serjeant might have been venting his suspicions of me, and the idea vexed me. I rose; and Dufailli saw that I had an air more serious than usual, "What ails you," said he, "why, you look as moping as an owl."—"Has anybody sold you pease which you cannot boil?" asked Pauline, taking me by the arm, and swinging me round to disturb my reverie. "Is he in the doldrums," enquired Therese. "Hold your tongue," replied Dufailli, "and speak when you have leave to do so; in the mean time, sleep, sluts, sleep, and do not move till we return."

He then beckoned me to follow him; and in obeying he conducted me to a little parlour, where we found captain Paulet and his crew, the majority of whom were drunk with wine and joy. As soon as we appeared, there was an unanimous shout of "Dufailli! Dufailli!"—"Hail to mine ancient!" said Paulet; and then offering my companion a seat beside him, added, "Anchor here my old cock, we may well say that providence is good. M. Boutrois, Boutrois, bring more 'bishops,' as if it rained wine. Come, we will have no sorrow here, from this time henceforward," he added, pressing Dufailli's hand. Paulet then looked attentively at me, and said, "I think I know you, we have met before; you have handled a marlin-spike, my hearty."

I told him that I had been on board the privateer, 'Barras,' but that I did not recollect having ever met him before. "Well, then, we will make acquaintance

now. I do not know," he added, " but you look like
a jolly dog—a lad for all sorts of weathers, as we say.
I say, my boys, has he not the look of a hearty chap ?
I like the cut of his jib.   Sit here, on my right hand ;
by my fist, what a back and loins ; here are shoulders !
You are just the lad for fishing for Englishmen."   On
finishing these words, he put on my head his red
cap.   " It does not look amiss on the lad," he added,
with a knowing look, but in which there was much
kindness.

I saw at once that the captain would not be sorry to
number me amongst his crew.   Dufailli, who had not
yet become speechless, exhorted me most energetically to profit by the opportunity ; this was the good
advice he had promised me, and I followed it.   It was
agreed that I should go a voyage, and that the next
day I should go to the owner, M. Choisnard, who would
advance me some money.

It must not be doubted but that I was well received
by my new comrades ; the captain had placed a thousand crowns to their credit at the hotel, and many of
them had other resources in the city.   I never witnessed
such profusion.   Nothing was too dear or delicate for
the privateers.   M. Boutrois, to satisfy them, was compelled to put the whole city and environs in requisition,
and even dispatched couriers to nourish their luxurious
palates, the duration of which was not limited to a single day.   It was on Monday, and my companion was
not sobered by the following Sunday ; as for me, my
stomach and head agreed delightfully, and neither received the slightest check.

Dufailli had forgotten his promise to the ladies, and
I reminded him of it ; and quitting our party for a moment, I returned to them, presuming that they were
growing impatient at our absence.   Pauline was alone,
her sister had gone to learn what was become of their
mother ; she soon returned, and throwing herself on
the bed, she exclaimed with an air of despair, " We are
undone for ever."—" What is the matter ?" I asked.

" We are lost," she answered, with her face bathed in tears. " Two men have been carried to the hospital with broken ribs, a guard has been wounded, and the commandant has ordered the house to be shut up. What will become of us ? where can we find a home ?"

" A home," said I, " you shall always find; but where is your mother ?" Therèse answered that her mother was first led to the guardhouse, and afterwards to the city prison, and the report was that she would not very easily get out again.

This information gave me some uneasiness : mother Thomas would be questioned, and perhaps had already been examined at the police office, or by the commissary-general ; and she doubtless had mentioned, or would mention, Dufailli's name ; and if he were questioned I should be so also. It was important to prevent this ; I returned with haste to concert with the serjeant the measures necessary to be pursued. Fortunately, he was not so far gone as not to hear reason. I talked only of the danger which threatened him ; he understood me, and taking twenty guineas from his pocket, " Here," said he, " is wherewithal to stop mother Thomas's blabbing tongue ;" and then calling a waiter to him, he gave him the money, desiring him to carry it forthwith to the prisoner. " He is the jailor's son," said Dufailli, " and has admittance everywhere ; and, moreover, is a close and discreet lad."

Our messenger returned quickly, and told us that mother Thomas, though twice examined, had mentioned no names, and had received the bribe with gratitude ; vowing that she was determined, if she died for it, to say nothing that could injure us ; and thus I was assured that I had nothing to fear on this head. " And as to the wenches, what must we do with them ?" said I to Dufailli. " Oh, we must export them to Dunkirk, and I will pay the expenses," he replied ; and we then returned to prepare them for their departure. At first they appeared astonished ; but after some arguments, proving that it was the best method they could adopt,

G

and that there was danger in remaining longer at Bou-logne, they resolved to leave us. The next day we started them off, and the parting did not cost us much pain. Dufailli had put them well in cash, and we hoped for future meetings, &c. In fact, we did meet again at a later period, in a certain house kept by a namesake of the celebrated Jean-Bart, a female descendant of whom, in the bosom of his very country, consecrated herself to the pleasures of the rivals of her great ancestor.

Mother Thomas recovered her liberty after six months' confinement; Pauline and her sister then returning to the maternal bosom, though torn from their native soil, renewed the courses of their former lives. I know not whether they made a fortune; it is not impossible. But for want of accurate information, I here end their history, and resume my own.

Paulet and his crew had scarcely noticed our absence, before we rejoined them; we sang, drank, and eat alternately without stirring, until midnight; thus confounding all repasts in one lengthened meal. Paulet, and Fleuriot his second in command, were the heroes of the feast; physically, as well as morally, they were the perfect antipodes of each other. The former was a stout short man, strong backed, square set, with a neck like a bull; wide shoulders, a full face, and his features like that of a lion, his aspect either fierce or gentle; in fight he was pitiless, elsewhere he was humane and compassionate. At the moment of boarding he was a perfect demon; in the bosom of his family, and with his wife and children, except a little roughness of manner, he was as mild as a dove; then he was the jolly, simple, bluff, and rough farmer; a perfect patriarch, whom it was impossible to discern in the pirate. Once on shipboard, his manners and language entirely changed, and he became harsh and coarse to excess; his will was as despotic as that of an oriental pasha; abrupt and rude, he had an iron arm and will, and woe to him who opposed either. Paulet was a daring and good man, sensible though brutal; no one ever possessed more frankness and loyalty.

Paulet's lieutenant was one of the most singular beings I ever met with : endowed with a most robust constitution, although yet very young, he had tried it with every sort of excess; he was one of those libertines who by dint of anticipating the pleasures of life's stores, spends his revenue before he gets it, eats his calf in the cow's belly. Headstrong, with vivid passions, and a heated imagination, he had early abandoned himself to premature excesses. He had not reached his twentieth year, when the decay of his lungs, together with an universal sinking of his whole frame, had compelled him to quit the artillery, into which he had entered at eighteen years of age; and now this poor fellow had scarcely a breath of life in him; he was frightfully thin; two large eyes, whose blackness made more apparent the melancholy paleness of his complexion, were apparently all that remained of this carcase, in which, however, was a soul of fire. Fleuriot was not ignorant that his days were numbered. The most able physicians had pronounced his sentence of death, and the certainty of his approaching dissolution had suggested to him a strange resolution. This is what he told me upon the subject: " I served," said he, " in the fifth regiment of light artillery, where I was entered as a volunteer. The regiment was quartered at Metz. A gay life and hard work had exhausted me, and I was as dry as parchment. One morning the turn-out was sounded, and we set off. I fell sick by the way, and received an hospital order; and a few days afterwards, the doctors, seeing that I spit blood abundantly, declared that my lungs were not in a state to be subjected to the exercise of a horse, and consequently I was advised to enter the foot artillery; and scarcely was I well, when I did so. I left one berth for another, the small for the large, the six for twelve, the spur for the spatterdash. I had no longer to gallop hard, but I had to turn my body about on the platform; to jump up and down like a goat, to roll gun-

carriages about, to dig trenches, to strap up artillery
geer, and, worse than that, to carry on my back the infernal knapsack, that eternal calf's skin which has killed
more conscripts than the guns of Marengo. The calf's
skin gave me a knock-down blow. I could not resist
its attack. I offered myself to the depôt, and was admitted. I had only to undergo the inspection of the
general. He was that martinet Sarrazin. He came
to me. ' I will wager that he is still weak-chested : are
you not ?' ' Consumption in the second degree,' replied the major. 'Is it so ? I thought it. I said so.
They are all narrow-shouldered, hollow-chested, lanky
limbed, thick visaged. Show your legs. Why there are
four campaigns in them yet,' continued the general,
striking me on the calf. ' And now what would
you ? Your dismissal ? You shan't have it. Besides,' he added, ' death only comes to him who
pauses : go your way.' I wished to speak. ' Begone,'
repeated the general, ' and be silent.'

" The inspection concluded; I went and threw
myself on my camp-bed, and whilst I reclined on my
four-feet-long mattrass, reflecting on the harshness of
the general, it occurred to me that I might find him more
tractable if I were recommended by one of his brother
officers. My father had been intimate with general Legrand, who was then at the camp at Ambleteuse, and
I thought I might find a protector in him. I saw him,
and he welcomed me as the son of an old friend, gave
me a letter to Sarrazin, and sent one of his aide-de-
camps to attend me. The recommendation was pressing,
and I made sure of success. We arrived at the camp,
and making for the general's abode, a soldier pointed
it out to us, and we found ourselves at the gate of a
dilapidated barrack, which bore no marks of being a
general's residence; no sentinel, no inscription, no
centry-box. I knocked with my sabre-hilt, and a voice
cried ' Enter,' with the accent and tone of displeasure.
A packthread, which I pulled, drew up a wooden
latch, and the first object that met our eyes on penetrating this asylum, was a woollen covering, under

which, lying side by side on the straw, were the general
and his negro. In this posture he gave us audience.
Sarrazin took the letter, and having read it, without
changing his position, he said to the aide-de-camp :
' General Legrand takes an interest in this young man.
Well, what would he have ? that I put him on half-
pay ? Oh ! he cannot think such a thing.' Then addressing me—' How much fatter should you be, if I
put you on half-pay ? Oh, you have a fine prospect
at home : if you are rich, to die gradually with over-
nursing ; if you are poor, to encrease the misery of
your parents, and finish your days in an hospital. I
am a doctor for you : and my prescription is a bullet,
and then your cure will follow ; if you escape that, the
knapsack will do for you, or marching and exercise will
put you to rights ; these are additional chances. Besides, do as I do, drink tar-water : that is worth all your
jalaps, and gruels, and messes.' At the same time, he
stretched out his arm, he seized a large pitcher, which
was near him, and filled a can, which he offered to
me, and all refusal was in vain. I was compelled to
swallow some of the nauseous stuff, as was also the
aide-de-camp ; the general drank after us, and his negro, to whom he handed the can, finished what was
left.

" There was then no hope of his recalling the decision against which I had appealed, and we withdrew
greatly discontented. The aide-de-camp returned to Am-
bleseuse and I to Fort Chatillon, which I entered more
dead than alive. From this moment I became the prey
to an apathetic sadness, which absorbed all my faculties:
I then obtained an exemption from service : night and
day I remained on my couch, indifferent to all
around me ; and I think I should have remained in
that position till now, if one winter's night the English
had not determined to burn our flotilla. An inconceivable fatigue, although I did nothing, seizing on my
senses, had induced a profound sleep. Suddenly I
was aroused by the report of cannon. I arose, and

through the panes of my window, I saw a thousand fires
crossing each other in the air. On one side were immense trains of fire like rainbows; on the other side
were vast stars, which seemed to grow larger and
redder, and my first idea was that I saw fireworks.
At length a noise like that of torrents, which precipitate themselves in cascades from the tops of rocks, gave
me a sort of shuddering feeling: at intervals darkness
usurped the place of the ruddy light, which I can only
compare to daylight in hell. The very earth seemed
scorched by it. I was already agitated by fever, and I
thought my head was swelling larger and larger. The
muster-call was beaten, I heard the cry 'To arms!' and on
the ground the trampling of horses feet. Terror siezed
me, and delirium possessed me. I got my boots, and tried
to pull them on; it was impossible; they were too tight,
my legs were entangled in them; I tried to pull them
off again; I could not. During my exertions each moment increased my fears, all my comrades were dressed;
the silence which reigned about me warned me that
I was alone, and whilst, from all parts, persons were
running together, without thinking of the inconvenience
of my boots, I fled with haste across the country, carrying my clothes under my arms.

"Next day I reappeared amidst all the people whom
I found living. Ashamed of a cowardice at which I was
myself astonished, I had trumped up a story, which,
if I could ensure belief, would have given me the reputation of a hero. Unfortunately the tale was not
swallowed so easily as I could have desired; no one
was the dupe of my lies: sarcasms and rude jokes
without end were thrown out, until I almost burst with
spite and rage; in any other circumstances I would have
fought the whole regiment, but I was in a state of
weakness, from which I did not rouse till the following
night, when I recovered a little of my wonted energy.

"The English had again commenced the bombardment
of the city, and were so close to the shore, that we could
even hear their voices, and the balls of the thousand

cannons on the coast passed over their heads. Move-
able batteries were then erected, which to approach
them as closely as possible, floated according to the
ebb and flow of the tide. I was ordered to the command of a twelve-pounder, which having stationed at
the extremity of the rafts, we anchored. At that very
moment, a shower of bullets were directed at us: our
howitzers were observed under the waggons, and
amongst the horses. It was evident that in spite of the
obscurity of the night, we had become an object of aim
to the enemy. We were about to return the compliment, and had altered the level of our gun, when my
corporal, almost as much alarmed as I had been the
previous evening, desirous of seeing if the trunnions
had got loose in shifting the gun, placed his hand on
them, and suddenly uttered a piercing shriek which was
re-echoed all along the bank. His fingers were crushed
beneath twenty hundred weight of metal. He attempted to disengage them, but the incumbent mass
only pressed the more heavily, and he was still held
fast, and when enabled to disengage himself he fainted.
A dram of brandy revived him, and I offered to lead
him to the camp, which was no doubt set down as a
pretext for absenting myself.

" The corporal and I walked away together; but the
moment of entering the artillery warren, which we had
to cross, a burning hand grenade fell between two chests
filled with powder. The danger was imminent, and in
a few seconds the whole ammunition would have blown
up. By running away I could have escaped safely, but
a change came over me, and death was no longer fearful. Quicker than lightning I seized on the metal tube
whence brimstone and fiery matter were escaping, and
attempted to extinguish the flame; but this being impossible, I carried it in my hand, blazing as it was, to a
distance; and the instant I threw it on the earth, it
burst with a violence that shivered the metal to pieces.

" There was a witness of this deed; my hands, my
face, my burnt garments, the sides of the powder

boxes already blackened with fire, all testified my courage.   I might have been proud, but I was only satisfied : my companions would henceforward have no
right to taunt me with their offensive jokes.   We went
onwards, and scarcely had we advanced a single step,
when the whole atmosphere seemed one blaze of fire ;
the flames appeared in seven places at once, and the
brilliant and horrible light seemed at the harbour : the
slates cracked, whilst the roofs were burning, and we
thought we heard the report of musquetry.   Some detachments, deceived by this, scoured about to discover
the enemy.   Nearer to us, at a short distance from the
ship building yard, clouds of smoke and flame rose from
a thatch, whence the burning straw was driven in all
directions by the wind.   We heard a cry of distress—
the voice of a child—which struck to my heart ; it was
perhaps too late, but I determined to attempt its rescue, and succeeded in restoring the infant to its mother,
who having left it for an instant, was returning to it in
an agony of distress.

   " My honour was now redeemed, and cowardice
could no longer be charged upon me.   I returned to
the battery, when every person congratulated me.   A
chief of a battalion promised me a cross, which, he
had, however, been unable to procure for himself for
forty years, because he had always had the bad luck to
get always behind, and never in front of, the cannon.
I was now in a fair way of getting renown, and opportunities presented perpetually.   There were mediators
appointed between England and France to negociate for
peace.   Lord Lauderdale was in Paris as plenipoten-
tiary, when the telegraph announced the bombardment
of Boulogne, which was but the second act to the attack
of Copenhagen.   At this information, the emperor, in-
dignant at a causeless renewal of hostilities, sent for
lord L., reproached him with the perfidy of his cabinet,
and ordered him to quit France instantly.   A fortnight
afterwards, lord Lauderdale arrived here at the *Canon
d'Or.* He was an Englishman, and the exasperated

people were desirous of revenging themselves on him :
they surrounded him, mobbed him, and pressed upon
him; and in defiance of the protection of two officers
who were attending him, they showered stones and
mud upon him from all sides. Pale, trembling, and
faltering, the peer thought he was about to fall a sacrifice, when sword in hand, I cleared my way through the
rabble, crying ' Destruction to whoever strikes him!'
I harangued the multitude, dispersed them, and led the
way to the harbour, where, without being subjected to
further insult, he embarked on board a flag of truce
boat. He soon reached the English squadron, which
the next evening renewed the bombardment. The following night we were again on the shore, and at one
o'clock the English, after throwing a few Congreve
rockets, suspended their firing; and I, worn out with
toil, threw myself on a gun carriage, and slept soundly.
I know not how long my sleep lasted, but when I
awoke I was up to my neck in water, my blood was
frozen, my limbs stiffened, and my sight and memory
bewildered. Boulogne had changed its situation, and
I took the fire of the flotilla for that of the enemy.
It was the commencement of a lengthened malady,
during which I obstinately refused to go to the hospital. At length I was convalescent; but as I only recovered slowly, I was again named for the half-pay, and
this time was reduced against my own wish; for I had
now adopted the opinion of general Sarrazin.

" I had no longer any wish to die in my bed, and
applying to myself the sense of the words, ' There is
only death for him that pauses,'—that I might not pause,
I commenced a career in which, without too painful
labours, there is a never-ceasing activity requisite.
Persuaded that I have but a short time to live, I am determined to employ that time. I have turned privateer,
and what risk do I run? I can but be killed, and
have but little to lose; in the mean while I want for
nothing, emotions of every sort; perils and pleasures;
and now I never *pause*."

The reader will now judge what sort of men were captain Paulet and his lieutenant. Scarcely had this latter a breath left in his body, and yet in fight, as everywhere else, he was the leader. Sometimes he was lost in dull thought, whence he roughly aroused himself, his head giving the impetus to his system, and he evinced a turbulence which was restrained by no bounds. There was no extravagance, no wild sally of which he was not capable; and in this reckless state of excitation, all was dared by him. He would have scaled heaven itself. I cannot tell all the pranks he played at the first banquet to which Dufailli had presented me. Sometimes he proposed one scheme, sometimes another; at length he bethought him of the theatre. "What do they play to night?"—"'Misanthropy and Repentance.'" * "I prefer the 'Two Brothers.' Comrades! which of you is in a snivelling mood? The captain weeps every year at his festival, we fellows know nothing of such joys. They are confined to the fathers of families? Do you ever go to the play, captain? You should go; for there will be all the world there. All the fashionables, shrimp girls in silken gowns; the nobility of the land. Oh God! heaven itself is struck to see sows in ruffles. Never mind; these ladies must have their play, though it would be as well if they understood French. Oh, do go and see them. I remember some ladies at the last ball, who being asked to dance answered 'I'm axed already.'"—"Come, come, will you never hold your gabble?" said Paulet to his lieutenant, whom none of the men had interrupted. "Captain," he replied, "I have made a motion, and no one has answered me; nobody wants to snivel. Well, good by; I will go and blubber alone."

Fleuriot immediately went out, and the captain then commenced his eulogy. "He has," said he, "a burning brain, but for courage he is not equalled by

* The 'Stranger' of the English Stage.—*Translator.*

any man under heaven." He then informed us how he was indebted to the daring of Fleuriot for the capture he had just made. The recital was animated and well told, in spite of Paulet's manner, who had a strange way of pronunciation, and who informed us that he had knocked out the brains of a dozen Englishmen with a hand-spike. The evening advanced, and Paulet, who had not seen his wife and children, was about to retire, when Fleuriot returned. He was not alone. " Captain," said he, entering, " what think you of this agreeable sailor I have just engaged ? I think that red cap was never placed over a prettier countenance."—" True," replied Paulet, " but is it a cabin-boy you have brought us ? He has no beard. Parbleu ! " he added, raising his voice, " it is a woman ! " Then continuing, with more strongly expressed astonishment, " If I am not mistaken, it is the Saint ——" *—" Yes," replied Fleuriot, " it is Eliza, the amiable and better half of the manager of the company which now enchants Boulogne ; she has come to congratulate us upon our late good fortune."— " Madame amongst privateers ! " said the captain, casting on the disguised actress a look of contempt but too expressive of his thoughts. " I compliment her taste ; she will hear agreeable conversation ; the devil must possess her ! A woman, too ! "—" Come, come, captain," cried Fleuriot, " privateers are not cannibals, they will not eat her up. Besides, you know, the old ditty :

  ' She loves a laugh ; she loves a glass ;
  ' She loves a song ; a jolly lass.'

What harm is there in it ?"—" None ; only the season is propitious for a cruise ; my crew are all well, and we were in no want of madame to improve their health."

---

* The name had nearly escaped my pen ; but the husband of the lady in question has been for some time manager of one of our theatres in the capital. He is living, and my discretion will be commended.

At these words, significantly uttered, Eliza cast her eyes on the ground. " My dear girl, do not blush," said Fleuriot, " the captain is only jesting."—" Not I, by Neptune; I never jest; I remember the Saint Napoleon, when the whole staff, beginning with marshal Brune, was in commotion; there was no small battling in that day : madame knows all about it, the how, the when, the why, and the wherefore, and will not wish me to be more explicit."

Eliza, humbled by this language, did not repent however of having accompanied Fleuriot; during her agitation, she attempted to justify her appearance at the ' Lion d'Argent ' with that softness of tone, those insinuating manners, that mildness of countenance, which seem so foreign to licentious behaviour; she talked of admiration, glory, valour, heroism, &c., that she might make way in Paulet's estimation; she appealed to his gallantry, and called him a ' chevalier Français.' Flattery has more or less influence over every mind, and Paulet's language became more polished; he excused himself as well as possible, obtained Eliza's pardon, and took leave of his comrades, recommending them to amuse themselves, though there was no fear of growing dull. As for me, I could not keep my eyes open, and I went to my bed, where I heard and saw nothing. Next day I arose, recruited and in spirits, and Fleuriot took me to the owner, who, on the strength of my appearance, advanced me a few five-franc pieces. A week afterwards, seven of our comrades were in the hospital. The name of the actress, Saint ——, had disappeared from the play-bill, and we learnt that she had profitted by the offer of part of a post-chaise, belonging to a colonel who, tormented by a thirst of gaming even to the risking the very epaulets of his uniform, had gone off express to Paris,

I awaited with anxiety the moment of our embarkation. The five-franc pieces of M. Choisnard were spent, and if they allowed me to live, they scarcely permitted me to cut any figure; besides, on shore I daily ran the risk of some unpleasant rencontre. Boulogne was infested with a great many bad fellows: Mansui, Tribout, Salé, were carrying on their trade in the port, where they despoiled the conscripts under the orders of another thief named Canivet, who, in the face of the army and its commander, ventured to call himself the Decapitator (bourreau des crânes.) I think I still see the legend on his police-cap, where were depicted a death's head, swords, and thigh-bones crossed. Canivet was the collector, or rather lord paramount, and had a large number of sub-agents, cabin-boys, and petty fellows who payed him a tax for the privilege of thieving: he watched them incessantly, and if he suspected them of deceiving him, he generally chastised them with his sword. I thought it likely that in this gang there might be some fugitive from the gallies, and I feared recognition. My apprehensions were the better founded, as I had heard a report that many freed galley slaves had been placed either in the corps of sappers, or that of the military workmen in the fleet.

For some time nothing was talked of but murders, assassinations, robberies; and all those crimes were evidences of the presence of hardened villains, amongst whom, perchance, might be some with whom I had compulsorily associated when at Toulon. It was absolutely necessary to avoid them; for to come again in contact would have given me much trouble, from the difficulty of not compromising myself. Robbers are like women; when we would escape their vices and their society, all league against us to prevent it; all seek to retain the comrade who would fly from evil; and it is a glory for them to keep him in the abject state whence they themselves wish not to be emancipated, nor would allow others to escape. I recalled to mind the comrades who denounced me at Lyons, and the motives that induced them to have me apprehended. As my experience was fresh, I was

very naturally inclined to profit by it, and be on my
guard; and consequently went into the streets as
seldom as possible, and passed nearly all my time in
the lower town, at madame Henri's, where the privateers boarded, and were accommodated with credit
on the strength of their perspective prizes. Madame
Henri, supposing she had ever been a wife, was now
a good-looking widow, and still attractive, though she
owned to thirty-six: she had two charming girls, who,
without forgetting themselves, yet gave hopes to every
jolly lad whom fortune favoured. Whoever spent his
money in the house was a welcome guest, and he who
squandered most was always first in estimation with
the mother and daughters, as long as his profusion
lasted. The hand of these girls had been promised
twenty times; twenty times had they been betrothed,
and yet their reputations for virtue had never been
blown upon. They were free in conversation, but
reserved in manners; and although their purity of
mind was not unsullied, yet no one could boast of
having induced them to commit a faux-pas. Yet how
many naval heroes had been subdued by the power of
their charms! How many aspirants, deceived by
their unmeaning coquetries, had flattered themselves
on a predilection which was to lead them to so much
bliss! And then, how could one not be mistaken
as to the real sentiments of these chaste Dianas,
whose perpetual amiability seemed to give the preference to the person last looked upon? The hero
of to-day was feasted, fondled; a thousand little attentions were evinced, certain little peculiar privileges
permitted,—a kiss, for instance, on the sly; a seducing
glance of the eye: economical advice was freely bestowed, whilst seeking to procure something extra-
vagant; they regulated the expenditure of his money,
and as funds grew low, which was a matter of course,
they learned the fact of approaching penury by the
well-timed proffer of a temporary loan; it was rarely
refused, and without evincing indifference or disgust,

they only expected that necessity and love would send
the inamorato to seek new perils. But scarcely was
the wind in the sail of the ship of the lover, and he
was calculating the happy chances which would ultimately lead to a marriage, and the small loan which
he had vowed to return an hundred fold, when already
was his place filled by some other fortunate mortal;
so that in madame Henri's house, the lovers were constantly succeeding each other, and her two girls were
like two citadels, which, always besieged, and always
on the point of surrender in appearance, yet never
yielded. When one raised the siege, another attacked
the spot; there was illusion for all, and nothing but
illusion. Cecile, one of madame Henri's daughters,
had passed her twentieth year; she was a merry one,
a great laugher, and would listen without blushing to
the broadest joke; and denied only the final surrender
of the fort. Hortense, her sister, was much like her,
only younger, and her character more natural; she
sometimes said strange things; but it seemed as if
honey and orange-flower water flowed in the veins of
these two females, for they were so mild and gentle
on all occasions. There was no inflammable material
in their hearts, although they showed no repugnance
to a pressing proposal, and evinced no astonishment
at the familiarity of a sailor; yet, be it said, they did
not the less deserve the surname bestowed on the
shepherdess of Vaucouleurs, as well as on a little
town of Picardy.

It was at the fire-side of this amiable family that I
seated myself for a month, with a constancy that
astonished myself, dividing my hours between piquet,
cribbage, and mild ale. The inactivity of my life was
irksome, but at last it ceased: Paulet was desirous
of resuming his cruise, and we set sail; but the nights
were not dark enough, and the days had become too
long. All our captures were limited to a few poor
coal-brigs, and a sloop of no value; on board which
we found lord Somebody, who, in the hopes of regain-

ing his appetite, had undertaken a sea voyage, accompanied by his cook. He was sent to spend his money and eat his trout at Verdun.

The dull season was at hand, and we had as yet made no prizes. The captain was as moody and dull as a country whipping-post. Fleuriot was entirely out of patience, swore and raved from morning till night, and from night till morning was in a tempest of rage; all the crew were quite out of sorts (to use a vulgar expression), and I think we were all in a humour which would have led us on to attack a first-rate man-of-war. It was midnight, and we had just left a small bay near Dunkirk, and were steering towards the English coast, when, by the light of the moon, which bursting forth from the thick clouds, cast her brilliant rays on the waves, at a short distance we saw a sail. It was a brig of war which was ploughing the glittering wave. Paulet instantly discerned it. " My lads," he cried, " it is our own; every man lie down on his face, and I will answer for our success." In an instant we boarded her. The English crew fought bravely, and a bloody struggle ensued on the deck. Fleuriot, who according to custom was the first to board, fell amongst the number of the dead. Paulet was wounded, but was avenged; and well avenged his lieutenant also. He struck down all who faced him, and never did I witness such a scene of slaughter. In less than ten minutes we were masters of the ship, and the tri-coloured flag was hoisted in the place of the red flag. Twelve of our crew had fallen in the action, in which an equal desperation was testified on both sides.

Amongst those who fell was one Lebel, whose resemblance to me was so striking, that it daily caused the most singular mistakes. I called to mind that my " Sosia" had regular credentials, and it occurred to me that I should do wrong to let slip so favourable an opportunity. Lebel had become food for the fishes, and consequently had no farther need of a passport, which would stand me in the greatest stead.

The idea appeared to me admirable. I only had one cause of fear, which was that Lebel might have left his pocket-book with the owner of the privateer. I was over-joyed at discovering it about his person, and immediately took possession of it without being discovered by any person; and when they threw into the sea the sacks of sand in which the dead bodies were put that they might the more readily sink, I felt myself lightened of a great weight, thinking that at length I had got rid of that Vidocq who had played me so many scurvy tricks.

However, I was not completely assured, for Du-failli, who was our master-at-arms, knew my name. This circumstance annoyed me; and that I might have nothing to dread from him, I determined to let him into my secret by some pretended confidence. My precaution was useless. I called for Dufailli and sought him in every part of the vessel, but found him not; I went on board the ' Revanche' and looked for him, called to him, but no answer was given; I went down to the powder room, but no Dufailli. What could have become of him? I went to the spirit room; near a barrel of gin and some bottles I saw an extended body; it was he. I shook him, turned him on his back—he was breathless—livid—dead.

Such was the end of my protector: a congestion of the brain, a sudden apoplexy, or instantaneous choking caused by intoxication, had terminated his career. Since the first creation of marine serjeants, never was there one who got drunk with such consistent regula-larity and unremitting perseverance. A single trait cha-racterised him, and this prince of drunkards related the circumstance as the most delighful event of his life. It occurred on Twelfth-day. Dufailli had drawn king; and to honour his royalty, his comrades seated him on a handbarrow borne by four gunners. On each side of him were placed bottles of brandy for distribution; and elevated on this temporary palanquin, Dufailli made a halt before every booth in the camp, where he drank, and made others drink, amidst overwhelming

H 2

shouts. These rejoicings were so often repeated, that
at last his head became giddy; and his ephemeral majesty, introduced to a public house, swallowed without
scarcely tasting it, a pound of bacon, which he mistook
for Gruyère cheese. The meat was indigestible; and
Dufailli, conducted back to his barrack, threw himself
on his bed, when he soon begun to experience a most
violent convulsion of the stomach, and in vain did he
strive to repress the event that followed. The crisis
over, he fell asleep, and was only awakened from his
lethargic stupor by the growling of a dog and the noise
of a cat, who were quarrelling in his room! O dignity
of human nature, where wert thou! Such was the
lesson of temperance which the Spartans gave
their children, by making their slaves drunken, and
then pointing out the effect of their excesses to
them.

I have delayed an instant, to give the last and finishing
touch to my fellow-countryman. He is no more. Peace
be to his manes! Returned on board the brig, where
Paulet had left me with the captain of the prize and five
men of the crew of the ' Revanche,' scarcely had we
closed the hatchways on our prisoners, than we begun
coasting our way into Boulogne; but some reports of
the cannon fired by the English before we had boarded,
had summoned one of their frigates, which bore down
upon us, crowding all sail; and was soon so near
that several shots passed over us, and we were pursued
as far as Calais, when the swell of the sea becoming
very great, and a stormy wind blowing on shore, we
thought she would sheer off for fear of getting
amongst the breakers; but she was no longer under
control, and driven towards land had to contend at
once with all the violence of the elements. To run
aground was her only chance of safety, but that was
not attempted. In a moment the frigate was impelled
beneath the cross fires of the Batteries de la Côte de Fer,
of the jetty, and of Fort Rouge; and from every quarter
there came a shower of bombs, chain-shot and grape.

Amidst the horrible noise of a thousand shots, a cry of distress was heard, and the frigate sank without any possibility of succour being afforded.

An hour afterwards it was daylight; and in the distance we saw several fragments floating. A man and woman were tied to a mast, and waved a hand-kerchief, which we saw just as we were doubling Cape Grenet. I thought we could rescue these unfortunate beings, and proposed the attempt to the commander of the prize; and on his refusal to allow us the use of the jolly-boat, in a rage, I threatened to break his skull. "Well," said he, with a disdainful smile, and shrugging his shoulders, "captain Paulet is more humane than you; he has seen them, but does not stir about it because it is useless. They are there, and we are here, and every one for himself in bad weather; we have suffered quite loss enough, if it were only Fleuriot."

This answer restored me to my natural coolness, and made me understand that we ourselves were in greater danger than I had imagined. In fact, the waves evinced it; over our heads were gulls and divers, mingling their piercing cries with the shrill whistling of the north wind; in the horizon, darkening more and more, were long black and red streaks; the face of heaven was disfigured, and all betokened the impending tempest. Fortunately, Paulet had skilfully calculated time and distance; we failed in reaching Boulogne harbour, but found shelter and anchorage at Portel, not far from thence. On going ashore here, we saw lying on the strand the two unfortunates whom I would have succoured; the flow of the tide had cast them lifeless on a foreign shore, on which we gave them burial. They had been lovers perhaps, and I was touched at their fate; but other cares diminished my regrets. All the population of the village, women, children, and old men, were assembled on the coast. The families of a hundred and fifty fishermen were in despair at seeing their frail barks

fired upon by six English ships of the line, whose
solid hulks were furrowing the waves. Each spectator,
with an anxiety more easily imagined than described,
followed with his eyes the bark in which he was most
interested, and, according as it was sunk or escaped
from peril, were cries, tears, lamentations, or transports
of rapturous joy evinced. Mothers, daughters, wives,
and children, tore their hair, rent their clothes, threw
themselves on the earth, uttering imprecations and
blasphemies. Others, without reflecting how much
they insulted distress, without thinking of rendering
thanks to heaven, towards which their suppliant
hands had been raised the instant before, danced,
sung, and, with faces shining through forgotten tears,
manifested every symptom of the most overpowering
joy. Fervent vows, the patronage of Saint Nicholas,
the efficacy of his intercession, all was forgotten.
Perhaps, next day, recollection might have returned,
and a little more compassion been evinced for a suffering
neighbour; but during the storm egotism was paramount; and, as I was answered, " every one for
himself."

CHAPTER XX.

I am admitted into the marine artillery—I become a corporal—
Seven prisoners of war—Secret societies of the army, 'The
Olympiens'—Singular duels—Meeting with a galley slave—
The count de L—— a political spy—He disappears—The incendiary—I am promised promotion—I am betrayed—Once more
in prison—Disbanding of the armeé de la Lune—The pardoned
soldier—A companion is sentenced to be shot—The Piedmontese
bandit—The camp fortune-teller — Four murderers set at
liberty.

I RETURNED to Boulogne the same evening; where I
learnt that, in consequence of an order from the
general in command, all the individuals who, in each
corps, were marked as black sheep, were to be immediately arrested, and sent on board the cruisers. It
was a sort of press which was intended to purge the
army, aad to check its demoralization, which had
increased to an alarming extent. Thus I judged it
best to quit the 'Revanche,' on board which, to repair the losses of the late fight, the owner did not
fail to send some of the men whom the general had
deemed it expedient to get rid of. Since Canivet and
his myrmidons were no longer in the camp, I thought
there could be no ill result if I again turned soldier.
Furnished with Lebel's papers, I entered a company
of gunners, then employed in coast service; and as
Lebel had formerly been a corporal in this division,
I obtained that rank on the first vacancy; that is, a
fortnight after my enrolment. Regular behaviour,
and a perfect knowledge of my duties, with which I
was well acquainted, as an artillery-man of the old
school, soon acquired for me the favour of my officers;
and a circumstance which might have gone greatly
against me, still farther conciliated them towards me.

I was on guard at the fort of Eure, during the
spring-tides, and the weather was excessively bad;

mountains of water were dashed over the platform with so much violence, that the thirty-six pounders were shaken from the embrasures, and, at the dash of every wave, it seemed as if the whole fort was rent to pieces.   Until the Channel should be calmer, it was evident that no ship would dare to venture out; and night having come on, I did not station sentinels, but allowed the soldiers to remain in bed until next day. I watched for them, or rather I could not sleep, as I had no need of repose; when, about three in the morning, some words which I knew to be English, struck on my ear; at the same time, a knocking commenced at a door under the steps, leading to the battery.   I thought we were surprised, and immediately roused everybody.   I put them under arms, and had already determined on selling my life dearly, when I heard a woman's voice, who supplicated our aid.   I soon heard distinctly these words in French: " Open, we have been shipwrecked!"   I wavered an instant, and then with due precaution and a determination to sacrifice the first who on entering should betray any hostile intent, I opened the door and saw a woman, an infant, and five sailors, all more dead than alive. My first care was to have them all placed before a roaring fire, for they were dripping with wet and almost motionless from cold.   My men and I lent them shirts and clothing; and as soon as they were a little revived, they told us the accident to which their visit to us was attributable.   Having sailed for the Havannah, in a three-masted vessel, and on the point of finishing a prosperous voyage, they had dashed upon the mole of our pier, and only escaped death hy throwing themselves on our battery from the main-top. Nineteen of their crew, amongst whom was the captain, had perished in the waves.

The sea still blockaded us for several days, without any boat daring to venture out to us.   At the end of the time, I was rowed on shore with my wrecked sailors, whom I conducted myself to the chief officer of the naval service, who congratulated me, as if I had taken so many prisoners. If it were so brilliant a capture, I could really have said that it had only caused me one single fright. However that may be, in the company, it procured for me a very high opinion.

I continued to fulfil my duties with exemplary punctuality, and three mouths glided away, during which I had nothing but praise. This I determined always to deserve, but an adventurer's career was still to be my lot. A fatality which I was compelled to submit to unresistingly, and often unknowingly, perpetually threw me in contact with persons and things which were most in opposition to the destiny I was attempting to cut out for myself. It was to this singular fatality, that, without being enrolled in the secret societies of the army, I was indebted for being initiated into its mysteries.

It was at Boulogne that these societies were first formed. The first of all, notwithstanding what M. Nodier says in his " History of the Philadelphes,"* was that of the Olympiens, whose founder was one Crombet of Namur. It was at first only composed of a few young naval officers, but it rapidly increased, and all military men were admitted; principally, however, those of the artillery corps.

Crombet, who was very young (only a volunteer of the first class), laid aside his title of " chief of the Olympiens," and returned to the ranks of the brotherhood; who elected a " Vénérable," and formed themselves into a masonic order.

The society had not at first any political motive; or if it had, it was only known to the influential members. The avowed intent was mutual advancement.

---

* " Histoire des Sociétés secretes de l'Armée et des Conspirations Militaires qui ont eu pour objet la destruction du gouvernement de Bonaparte."—2nd ed. Paris.

The Olympien who got promotion was to exert all his influence to ensure the promotion of the brother Olympiens who were in inferior ranks. To be received, if belonging to the navy, it was necessary to be at least a volunteer of the second class; and at most, captain of a ship : if serving on land, the limits were, from a colonel to an adjutant, subaltern inclusive. I have never understood that, in their societies, the Olympiens ever discussed questions concerning the conduct of the government; but they proclaimed equality and brotherhood; and pronounced discourses which greatly contrasted with the imperial doctrines.

At Boulogne, the Olympiens constantly met at the house of a madame Hervieux, who kept a kind of coffee-house, but little frequented. It was there that they kept their meetings, and installed their members in a room consecrated to that purpose.

There was at the Military as well as at the Polytechnic Schools, lodges which were united with the Olympiens. In general, the initiation was confined to pass-words, signs, and tokens, which were taught to the members on entrance; but the real adepts knew and looked for other things. The symbol of the society sufficiently explains their intentions:—an arm, with the hand grasping a dagger, was emerging from a cloud; above was a bust reversed. It was that of Cæsar. This symbol, which is easily explained, was imprinted on the seal of their diplomas. This seal had been modelled in relief by an artillery-man named Beaugrand, or Belgrand; and the brass stamp was procured by means of welding and cutting.

To be received as an Olympien, a proof of courage was required, as well as of talent and discretion. Soldiers of distinguished merit were those who had the preference of enrolment. As much as possible it was endeavoured to attract to the society the sons of patriots who had protested against the erection of the imperial throne, or who had been persecuted. Under the empire, it was enough to belong to a family of non-contents, to be at once placed on the list of admissibles.

The real chiefs of the association were in the shade, and never communicated their projects. They plotted the overthrow of despotism, but admitted no person to their confidence. It was necessary that the men, by whose intervention they hoped to accomplish their ends, should be conspirators without knowing it. No one was ever to propose to them to join a conspiracy, but they were voluntarily to lend their power and inclination. It was by virtue of this combination, that the Olympiens at length included in their numbers the lowest ranks of the army and navy.

If a subaltern or soldier evinced talent, energy, firmness, independence, and spirit, the Olympiens sought him as a recruit, and he soon entered the brotherhood, or was bound by the influence of an oath to afford to them, as far as in him lay, "help and protection." The reciprocal support which was promised seemed to be the sole bond of the fraternity; but there was, beneath this seeming, a concealed but no less determined premeditation. It was found, after long experience, that out of one hundred individuals admitted, scarcely ten obtained a promotion proportioned to their merits: thus, amongst a hundred individuals, it was probable that, in a few years, ninety at least would be found opposed to the order of things in which it was impossible to advance a step. It was the sum of wisdom to have such men classed under a common denomination; men amongst whom it was certain that sooner or later a spirit of discontent would arise; men quite irritated and worn out by neglect or injustice, who would not hesitate to seize with eagerness on any opportunity of revenge. Thus was a league fomented, which had an existence of which it was itself unconscious. The elements of conspiracy were brought together, perfected themselves, and became more and more developed; but no conspirators were to be known or thought of until

I

the conspiracy should be ripe for perpetration. They awaited a propitious moment.

The Olympiens preceded the Philadelphes by many years, and were at length united with them. The origin of their society is somewhat prior to the coronation of Napoleon. It is said that they were first united on the occasion of the disgrace of admiral Truguet, who was deprived because he had voted against the perpetual consulate. After the condemnation of Moreau, the society, constituted on a more extended basis included a great many men of Britanny and Franche Compté. Amongst these latter was Oudet, who unfolded to the Olympiens the first idea of Philadelphy.

The Olympiens existed for two years without giving any cause of uneasiness to the government. At length, in 1806, M. Devilliers, commissary-general of police at Boulogne, wrote to Fouché to denounce their meetings. He did not signalize them as dangerous; but he thought it his duty to have them watched, and having no agent with him to whom he could confide such a duty, he consequently begged the minister to send to Boulogne one of those expert spies which a politic police always has in pay. The minister replied to the commissary-general, thanking him cordially for his zeal for the emperor's service, but stating that he had long had his eye on the Olympiens, as well as on many similar fraternities; that the government was sufficiently strong not to fear any conspiracies they might engender; and that, besides, they could not have any schemes but some crotchets of ideology, for which the emperor cared nothing; and that, according to all appearances, the Olympiens were but dreaming speculists, and their union only one of those masonic puerilities invented by some fools to amuse others.

This security of Fouché was but feigned; for scarcely had he received the information which M. Devilliers had transmitted, than he sent for the young comte de L***, who was initiated into the secrets of nearly every society in Europe. He thus addressed him.

" They write me from Boulogne, that a sort of secret association has been formed in the army under the title of ' Olympiens.' I am not informed of the objects of the society, but they tell me that its ramifications are most extensive. Perhaps they have some bond of union with the ' Conciliabules ' who met at the houses of Bernadotte and de Staël. I know well enough what passes there : Garat, who thinks me his friend, and who has the goodness to suppose me still a patriot as I was in 93, tells me everything. There are some Jacobins who imagine that I regret the republic, and would do all in my power to restore it : they are the fools whom I exile or place as may suit me,—Truguet, Rousselin, Ginguené form no plan, say no word, of which I am not informed. They are gentry not very formidable ; like all the Moreau gang, they talk much, and do little. However, for some time, they think they must have a party in the army ; and it is necessary that I should know their plans : the Olympiens are perhaps their creation. It would be well that you should become an Olympien ; you will disclose to me the secrets of these gentlemen, and I shall then know what steps to take."

The count de L*** told Fouché, that the proposed mission was a delicate affair ; that the Olympiens would probably only receive members after they had been convinced of their fidelity and fitness ; and that, besides, no one would be admitted to the brotherhood, who did not belong to the army. Fouché reflected a moment on these obstacles, and then said—" I have hit on a mode of causing you to be instantly admitted. Go to Genès ; you will there find a detachment of Ligurian conscripts, who are under orders for Boulogne, to be incorporated in the eighth regiment of foot artillery. Amongst them is a count Boccardi, for whom his family have vainly endeavoured to procure a substitute. You shall offer to supply the place of the noble Genèse ; and, to remove all difficulties, I give you a certificate, stating that you have, under the name of Bertrand, satisfied the laws of conscription. Thus you will be put in a straightforward path, and will march with the detachment. On reaching Boulogne, you will see your colonel,* a fanatic in masonry, illuminatism, hermetism, &c. You must tell him who you are; and, as you have rank, he will be sure to protect you. You can then tell him all concerning your origin that you may choose, and that may aid your plans. This confidence will at first do away with the sort of mistrust that is usually shewn to a substitute, and will ultimately procure you the regard of the other officers. But it is indispensable that you should make them believe that you have turned soldier on compulsion. Under your real name you were exposed to persecution from the emperor; and, to escape proscription, you had concealed yourself in a regiment. This is your tale, which will circulate throughout the camp, and no one will doubt but that you are the victim and enemy of the imperial system. I have no occasion to enter into longer details; the consequences will naturally ensue;—besides, I rely much,—entirely, on your sagacity."

Thus instructed, the count de L*** set out for Italy, and soon afterwards he entered France with the Ligurian conscripts. Colonel Aubry received him like a brother after a long absence, dispensed with his military drillings, assembled the lodge of the regiment to receive and feast him, and showed him every attention; authorising him to wear plain clothes; and treated him, in a word, with the greatest distinction.

In a few days the army knew that M. Bertrand was a " somebody." They could not give him epaulets, but he was nominated sergeant; and the officers forgetting, in his case only, that he was in the inferior ranks of a military hierarchy, did not hesitate to admit

* Colonel Aubry, inspector-general of artillery, who fell in his thirty-third year. He died a few days after the battle of Dresden, in which his two legs were carried off by a shot.

him to an intimacy. M. Bertrand was the oracle of the corps: he was intelligent and full of information, and they were disposed to consider him more witty and well-informed than he really was. However, he soon got acquainted with several Olympiens, who each desired the peculiar honour of introducing him to the fraternity. M. Bertrand was initiated, and as soon as he succeeded in establishing a communication with the Olympien leaders, he forwarded his reports to the minister of the police.

What I have related of the society of the Olympiens and of M. Bertrand, was told me by M. Bertrand himself; and to confirm the veracity of my statement, it will not, perhaps, be superfluous to say, how he was led to confide to me the mission with which he was charged, and to reveal to me those circumstances, of which mention is here made for the first time.

Nothing was more common at Boulogne than duelling; and the mania had extended even to the dull and peaceable Netherlanders of the flotilla, under the orders of admiral Werhwel. There was not far from the camp on the left, at the foot of a hill, a small wood, which could be passed at no hour without observing on the turf a dozen individuals engaged in what they called an affair of honour. It was here that a celebrated amazon, the demoiselle Div***, fell under the sword of a quondam lover, colonel Camb***, who, not recognizing her in her male attire, had accepted from her a challenge to single combat. The demoiselle Div***, whom he had forsaken for another, had wished to perish beneath his hand.

One day I was casting my eyes on this scene of bloody encounter, from the extremity of the left camp which peopled the extensive plain, when I saw at some distance from the little wood two men, one of whom was advancing towards the other, who was retreating across the plain. By the white trowsers I knew the champions were Hollanders, and I paused a moment to look at them. Soon the assailant retrograded in his turn, and then, mutually alarmed, they both retreated, brandishing their sabres; one, plucking up a little courage, made a thrust at his adversary, and then pursued him to the brink of a ditch which he was unable to leap. Both then throwing down their swords, a pugilistic combat commenced between the heroes, who thus decided their quarrel. I was greatly amused at this comic duel, when I saw near a farm where we sometimes went to eat ' codiau' (a kind of white soup made with flour and eggs) two individuals who, stripped to the skin, were already prepared, sword in hand, attended by their seconds, who were respectively a quarter-master of the tenth regiment of dragoons and a forager of artillery. The weapons soon crossed, and the smaller of the two combatants, who was an artillery serjeant, skipped about in a very singular manner, and having traversed in a strange way at least fifty paces, I thought he must be infallibly run through, when in an instant he disappeared, as if the earth had opened and swallowed him up, and a loud burst of laughter succeeded. After the first shoutings of this noisy mirth, the seconds approached, and I observed that they stooped down. Impelled by a feeling of curiosity, I went towards the spot, and arrived just in time to help them in pulling out from a hole dug for the formation of a large hog-trough, the poor devil whose sudden disappearance had so greatly astonished me. He was almost lifeless, and covered with mire from head to feet. The air soon brought him back to his senses, but he was afraid to breathe; he dared not open his eyes or mouth, so foul was the liquid in which he had been plunged. In this woful plight, the first words that saluted his ears were jokes. Feeling disgusted at such unfeeling conduct, I yielded to my just indignation, and darted at his antagonist one of those significant glances which between soldier and soldier need no interpreter. " Enough," said he, " I am ready for you;" and scarcely was I on my guard, when on the arm which

held the foil, to which I had opposed mine, I saw a
tattooing which I thought was not unknown to me.
It was the figure of an anchor, of which the stem was
encircled by the folds of a serpent. "I see the tail,"
I exclaimed, "take care of the head;" and with this
word of advice I thrust at my man, and hit him on the
right breast. "I am wounded," he then said, "that
is first blood."—"It is," said I, "first blood;" and
without another word I began to tear my shirt to
staunch the blood that flowed from his wound. I
necessarily exposed his breast, where, as I had judged,
I saw the head of the serpent, which was delineated
as if gnawing the extremity of his bosom.

Observing how earnestly I alternately examined his
features and this mark, my adversary seemed to grow
uneasy; but I hastened to assure him, by these words
which I whispered in his ear: "I know you; but fear
nothing, I am discreet."—"I know you too," he replied, squeezing my hand, "and I will be also silent."
He who thus promised secrecy was a fugitive galley-
slave from the Bagne of Toulon. He told me his
assumed name, and stated that he was principal
quarter-master of the 10th dragoons, where in expense he surpassed all the officers of his regiment.

Whilst this mutual recognition was taking place,
the individual whose cause I had espoused as the
champion of his wrongs, was endeavouring to wash
off in a rivulet the thickest of the filth which covered
him, and he soon returned to us, and all were now
quiet and well behaved, so that there were no longer
any grounds of difference, and the inclination for
laughter was turned into an uncommon wish for
reconciliation.

The principal quarter-master, whom I had wounded
but slightly, proposed that we should ratify articles of
peace at the Canon d'Or, where they had always
ready excellent stewed eels and ready-plucked poultry.
He there gave us a princely breakfast, which was kept
up till supper came, for which his adversary paid.

On our separation, the quarter-master made me promise to meet him again, and the serjeant would not be contented unless I accompanied him home.

This serjeant was M. Bertrand, who lodged in the upper town, in the house of a superior officer. As soon as we were alone, he testified his gratitude with all the warmth of which he was capable; for after drinking, a coward who has been rescued from peril may evince some feeling. He made me offers of any kind of service, and as I would accept of none, he said, " You think, perhaps, that I have no influence; I should be but a paltry protector, certainly, comrade, if I had only the power of a subaltern; but that is because I do not wish to be otherwise. I have no ambition, and all the Olympiens are like me; they despise the miserable distinction which rank confers." I asked who the Olympiens were? " They are," he replied, " men who adore liberty, and seek equality : will you be an Olympien? For if so, say the word, and you shall be admitted instantly."

I thanked M. Bertrand, adding, that I did not see any necessity to enrol myself in a society to which the attention of the police would be drawn sooner or later. " You are right," he replied, and then with earnestness added, " do not enter, for it will go badly with them." He then gave me details concerning the Olympiens, which I have already inserted in these Memoirs; and, as if impelled by the feeling of confidential communication which champagne so peculiarly excites, he told me, under the seal of secresy, the object of his mission to Boulogne.

After this first interview, I continued to see M. Bertrand, who remained for some time in his office of ' spy,' until the period having arrived when he was sufficiently instructed, he asked and procured a months' leave of absence, being about, as he said, to obtain a considerable estate; but at the expiration of the month M. Bertrand did not return, and the report spread that he had carried off the sum of 12,000 francs, which had been confided to his care by colonel Aubry, for whom he was to have brought back an equipage and horses; another sum, destined for purchases on account of the regiment, had also been carried off by the active M. Bertrand. It was known that in Paris he had alighted at the Rue Notre-Dame des Victoires, at the Hotel de Milan, where he had pushed his credit to the very utmost extent.

All these particulars caused a mystification, of which even the sufferers by it dared not openly to complain. It was only settled that M. Bertrand had disappeared: he was tried and condemned, as a deserter, to five years' labour. A short time afterwards, an order arrived for the arrest of the principal Olympiens, and for the dissolving of their society. But this order could be but partially enforced; as the leaders, aware that government was about to interfere with them, and cast them into the dungeons of Vincennes, or some other state prison, preferred death to a miserable existence, and five suicides took place on the same day. A serjeant-major of the twenty-fifth regiment of the line, and two other serjeants of another regiment, blew out their brains. A captain, who had the previous evening received his commission and a company, cut his throat with a razor. He lodged at the Lion d'Argent; and the innkeeper, M. Boutrois, astonished that he did not, as usual, come down to breakfast with the other officers, knocked at his door. The captain was stooping over a large basin which he had placed to receive the blood; he put on his cravat hastily, opened the door, and fell dead in the effort of speaking. A naval officer, who commanded a brig laden with powder, set fire to it, which communicated to another brig, which also blew up. The earth shook for several miles round, and all the windows in the lower town were broken; the fronts of several houses on the harbour were shaken down; pieces of wood, broken masts, and fragments of carcases, were hurled to a distance of eighteen hundred toises.

The crews of the two ships perished. One man only was saved, and that most miraculously. He was a common sailor, and at the time of the explosion in the main-top; the mast to which he clung was carried almost to the clouds, and then fell perpendicularly into the basin of the harbour, which was dry, and planted itself to a depth of more than six feet. The sailor was found alive, but had lost both sight and hearing, which he never after recovered.

At Boulogne, these coincidences were the theme of general conversation. The doctors pretended that these simultaneous suicides were the result of a peculiar affection emanating from the atmosphere. They appealed, by way of proof, to an observation made at Vienna, where, the previous summer, a great many young girls, impelled by a sort of frenzy, had thrown themselves into the river on the same day.

Some persons thought they could explain what appeared most extraordinary in this circumstance, by saying, that most commonly one suicide, when very generally talked of, is followed by two or three others. In fact, the public understood the cause the less, inasmuch as the police, which feared to allow any-thing to appear that could characterise the opposition to the imperial regime, designedly circulated the wildest reports; and precautions were so well taken, that in this instance the name of Olympien was not once pronounced in the camps: but the real origin of these tragic events was in the denunciations of M. Bertrand. Doubtless, he was recompensed, al-though I know not in what manner; but what appears most probable is, that the minister of police, satisfied with his services, continued to employ him; for, some years afterwards, he was in Spain, in the regiment of Isembourg, where, as a lieutenant, he was no less thought of than Montmorenci, Saint-Simon, and other offsprings of some of the most illustrious houses of France, who had been placed in this corps.

A short time after the disappearance of M. Bertrand, my company was sent to St Leonard, a small village, at a league from Boulogne. There our duties consisted in guarding a powder magazine, in which was kept a large quantity of warlike stores and ammunition. The service was not arduous, but the fort was thought dangerous, as many sentinels had been murdered on duty; and it was thought that the English had a design of blowing up this depôt. Some such attempts, which had taken place in various posts, left no doubt on the matter; and we had sufficient reason, therefore, for exercising unremitting vigilance.

One night, when it was my turn to keep guard, we were suddenly roused by the report of a musket, and every one was instantly on foot. I hastened, according to custom, to relieve the guard, who was a conscript, of whose courage there was some doubt; and, on being questioned, I thought, from his answers, that he had been needlessly alarmed. I then went round the magazine, which was an old church; I had all parts and places examined, but nothing was observable, —no trace of any person. Persuaded, then, that it was a false alarm, I reprimanded the conscript and threatened him with the black-hole. However, on the return of the relief-piquet, I interrogated him afresh; and, from the assured tone with which he asserted that he had seen some one, and by the details he gave, I began to think that his terror was not so causeless as I had imagined, and I consequently went out, and going a second time towards the magazine, of which I found the door ajar, I pushed it open, and on entering, my eyes were struck with the faint glimmering of a light which projected from between two rows of boxes filled with cartridges. I dashed along the passage, and on reaching the extremity, I saw a lighted lamp beneath the lowest cask, the flames of which already had smoked the wood, and a smell of turpentine pervaded the place. There was not a moment to lose, and without hesitation I overturned the lamp, and stamped out all the other appearances of sparks, &c. The profound darkness that ensued, guaranteed to me the certainty that I had prevented the explosion, but I was not at ease until the smell was entirely dissipated, and then I went away. Who was the incendiary? This I knew not; but there arose in my mind strong suspicions of the magazine-keeper, and to arrive at the truth I went forthwith to his residence. His wife was then alone, and told me that, kept at Boulogne on business, he would sleep there, and would return on the next morning. I asked for the keys of the magazine, but he had taken them with him; and this removal of the keys confirmed me in the opinion that he was guilty: but, before I made any report, I again visited his house at ten o'clock, to convince myself, and he had not then returned.

An inventory, which was made the same day, proved that the keeper must have the greatest interest in destroying the depôt entrusted to his care, as the only mode by which he could conceal the extensive robberies he had committed. Six weeks elapsed before we learnt what had become of him; and then some reapers found his dead body in a wheat field, with a pistol lying beside him.

As it had been my presence of mind which had prevented the blowing up of the powder magazine, I was promoted to the rank of serjeant; and the general, who desired to see me, promised to recommend me to the consideration of the ministry. As I thought I was now in a fair way to do well, I was very careful to lose as Lebel all the bad qualities of Vidocq; and, if the necessary duty of attending to the distribution of rations had not led me to Boulogne occasionally, I should have been a most exemplary fellow; but every time I went to the city, I had to visit the quarter-master-in-chief of dragoons, against whom I had espoused the cause of M. Bertrand: not that he exacted this from me, but I thought it needful to be on good terms with him. Then, however, the whole day was consecrated to Bacchus; and, in spite of myself, I lapsed from my good intentions of reform.

By the help of a supposititious uncle, a man of wealth and influence, whose property, he said, was secured to him, my old colleague of the Bagne led a very agreeable life; and the credit he obtained from the reputation of being a person of family, was unlimited. There was not a Boulognese citizen of wealth, but cultivated the acquaintance of a personage of such distinction most sedulously. The most ambitious papas desired nothing more ardently than to have him for a son-in-law; and, amongst the young ladies, it was the general wish to catch him: thus he had facilities of dipping into the purses of the one, and obtaining the good graces of the other. He had an equipment like a colonel,—dogs, horses, and servants; and affected the tone and manners of a nobleman; possessing, in a supreme degree, the art of throwing powder in people's eyes, and making himself appear a man of consequence: so much so, that the officers themselves, who are generally so extremely jealous of the prerogatives belonging to an epaulet, thought it very natural that he should eclipse them. In any place but Boulogne, the adventurer would have been soon detected as a swindler, as he had not received any education; but in a city where the citizens of a recent establishment were as yet genteel in costume only, it was an easy matter to carry on such an imposition.

Fessard was the real name of this quarter-master, who was only known at the Bagne as Hippolyte. He was, I believe, from Low Normandy; and, with an exterior of much frankness, an open countenance, and the haughty air of a young rake, he combined that sly character which slander has attributed to the inhabitants of Domfront: in a word, he was a shrewd man of the world, and gifted with all that was necessary to inspire confidence. A rood of land in his own country would have been to him sufficient

K

to have produced a thousand actions at law, and
quite a sufficient possession to have enabled him to
make his fortune by ruining his neighbour; but Hippolyte really had nothing in the world, and unable to
turn pleader, he became a swindler, then a forger,
then —— we shall learn what, and must not anticipate.

Every time I visited the town, Hippolyte paid for
dinner; and one day, between dessert and cheese, he
said to me, " Do you know I am astonished at you;—
to live in the country like an anchorite; to be content
with a daily pittance; to have just twenty-two sous
per diem. I cannot conceive how a person can endure
such a lot; as for me, I would rather die at once.
But you have your pickings somewhere, slily; you are
not the lad to live without some such additions." I
told him that my pay sufficed for me; and, besides, I
was fed, clothed, and in want of nothing. " All very
fine," he replied; " but yet we have some priggers
(grinchisseurs) here: you have no doubt heard of the
' minions of the moon' (l'armée de la Lune)—You
must be one; and, if you like, I will quarter you;—
take the environs of Saint Leonard."

I was told that the army " de la Lune" was a band
of malefactors, the leaders of whom were, up to this
period, concealed from the scrutiny of the police.
These brigands, who had organized a system of murder and robbery for a circuit of more than ten leagues,
all belonged to various regiments. At night they
ranged about the camps, or concealed themselves on
the roads, making pretended rounds, and patroles
stopping any person who presented the least hope of
booty. That they might not be impeded, they provided themselves with uniforms of every denomination.
At a time of need they were captains, colonels, gene-
rals, and used all the proper words of regimental order
and discipline,—pass-words, countersigns, &c.; with
which some trusty friends took care to inform them,
from time to time, as they were altered.

From what I knew, the proposal of Hippolyte was
well calculated to alarm me; for either he was one of
the leaders of this army de la Lune, or he was one of
the secret agents employed by the police to effect the
breaking up of this army: perhaps he was both. My
situation with him was most embarrassing, and the
thread of my destiny was again entangled; nor could
I, as at Lyons, extricate myself from this business by
denouncing him; and then, what would it have availed
me to have denounced him, had he been an agent?—
This idea made me cautious of the mode in which I
should reject his proposition, which I did by saying
with firmness, that I was resolved to become an honest
man. "Did'n't you see," said he, "that I was only
joking, and you take up the matter seriously; I only
wanted to try you. I am charmed, my comrade, to
find in you such a determination. I have formed a
similar one," he added, "and am on the highway to
it; and the devil shall not again turn me from it."
Then, turning the conversation, we left all farther
mention of the army de la Lune.

Eight days after this interview, during which Hippolyte had made me this proposal, so promptly retracted, my captain, on going through the inspection,
condemned me to four-and-twenty hours' confinement,
for a spot, which, he said, was on my uniform. This
cursed spot, although I opened my eyes as widely as
possible, I was unable to perceive; but be it as it may,
I went to the guard-house without a murmur. Four-
and-twenty hours soon pass away! The next morning
would terminate my sentence;—when, at five o'clock
in the morning, I heard the trot of horses, and soon
afterwards I heard the following dialogue:—"Who
goes there?"—"France."—"What regiment?"—"The
imperial corps of gendarmerie." At the word gendarmerie I felt an involuntary shudder, and suddenly
my door opened and some one called "Vidocq." Never
did this name, falling suddenly on the ears of a troop
of villains, disconcert them more effectually than it

did myself at this moment. "Come, follow us," cried
out the officer; and, to prevent any possibility of escape, he fastened a rope round me. I was instantly
conducted to prison, where I had a tolerable bed, on
paying for it. I found a numerous and goodly assemblage. "Did I not say so?" cried a soldier of artillery,
whom, by his accent, I knew to be a Piedmontese.
"We shall have all the camp. Here is another. I will
bet my head that he owes his imprisonment to that
thief of a quarter-master. Will no one cut that villain's throat!"—"Go, look for him, then, your quarter-master;" interrupted a second prisoner, who also
seemed to be a new comer. "Whatever he may have
done, he is now at a distance; he has made himself
scarce a week since. But, my lads, you must own
that he is a crafty chap. In less than three months,
forty thousand francs in debt in the city. What a
lucky dog! And then how many little boys and girls
has he left behind—I should be sorry to father all his
flock. Six young ladies, daughters of our leading bur-
gesses, are in a fair way of becoming mammas! Each
thought she had him to herself; but he seems to have
cut his heart into small pieces, and shared it amongst
them!"—"Oh! yes," said a turnkey, who was preparing my bed, "he has spent like a prodigal, and now
must mind what he is about; for, if they catch him,
handcuffs are the word. He is marked as a deserter.
He will be caught, I think."—"Do not make too sure,"
I replied; "they will catch him as they caught M.
Bertrand."—"Well, suppose he should be taken," resumed the Piedmontese, "would that prevent my being
guillotined at Turin? Besides, I repeat it, I will bet
my head ——"—"What does the fool say about his
head?" cried a fourth. "We are here in prison, and
as it was to be, what consequence through whose
means!" This reasoner was right. It would have
been useless to lose oneself in a field of conjectures,
and we must all have been blind not to have recognized Hippolyte as the author of our arrest. As for

me, I could not be deceived, for he was the only person in Boulogne who knew that I had escaped from
the Bagne.

Many soldiers of different ranks came against their
will to fill up a chamber in which were assembled the
principal leaders of the army de la Lune. Very seldom in the prison of so small a town, was there seen a
more singular assemblage of delinquents; the ' prevôt,'
that is, the elder of our room, named Lelievre, was a
poor devil of a soldier, who condemned to death three
years before, had perpetually before him the chance of
the termination of the respite by virtue of which he
still existed. The emperor, to whose mercy he had
been recommended, had pardoned him; but as the
pardon had not been registered, and as the indispensable official papers had not been transmitted to the
chief judge, Lelievre continued a prisoner; and all that
could be done in favor of this unfortunate being, was
to suspend the execution until the moment when an
opportunity should present itself of again calling the
emperor's attention to his case. In this state, in which
his life was uncertain, Lelievre deliberated between the
hope of freedom and the fear of death; he laid down to
sleep with the one, and awoke with the other. Every
evening he thought himself sure of his liberty, and
every morning he expected to be shot; sometimes gay
even to folly, sometimos dull and spiritless, he never
enjoyed a moment of equable calm. If he played a
game of draughts or matrimony, he paused in the midst
of it, threw down the cards, and striking his forehead
with his clenched hands, jumped from his seat, and
raving like a madman, he ended by flinging himself on
his bed, where lying on his face, he remained for hours
in a state of mental depression. The hospital was
Lelievre's house of pleasure; and if he got wearied, he
went there for consolation from sister Alexandrine,
who had a most tender heart, and sympathised
with all the wretched. This compassionate sister was
deeply interested in the prisoner, and Lelievre deserved

it, for he was not a criminal but a victim; and the sentence against him was the unjust result of a feeling but too common in councils of war, that the innocent should even suffer if there are disorders to repress. The conscience and humanity of judges ought to be silent when necessity calls for exemplary punishment. Lelievre was one of the few of those men who, steeled against vice, can without danger to their morality remain in contact with the most contaminated. He acquitted himself in his duties of steward (prevôt) with as much equity as if he had been endued with all the powers of a licensed magistrate; he never let off a new comer, but explained to him his duties as a prisoner, endeavouring to render as easy as possible the first days of his captivity; and rather might be said to do the honours of the prison than to enforce his authority.

Another character also attracted the regard and affection of the prisoners, Christiern, whom we called the Dane. He did not speak French, and only understood by signs; but his intelligence seemed to penetrate our very thoughts: he was melancholy, thoughtful, and gentle; in his features there was a mixture of nobleness, candour, and sadness, which insinuated and touched at the same time. He wore a sailor's dress; but the flowing curls of his long black hair, his snowy white linen, the delicacy of his complexion and manners, the beauty of his hand, all announced a man of exalted condition. Although a smile was often on his lips, yet Christiern appeared a prey to the deepest sorrow; but he kept his grief to himself, and no one knew even the cause of his detention. One day he was summoned whilst he was engaged in tracing on the glass with a flint the drawing of a fleet, which was his sole amusement, except occasionally sketching the portrait of a female, whose resemblance he seemed delighted to be perpetually depicting. We saw him go out; and soon afterwards being brought back, scarcely was the door closed upon him, than taking from a leathern bag a prayer book, he was soon engrossed in its perusal.

At night he slept as usual until day-break, when the round of a drum warned us that a detachment was entering the prison yard, and he then dressed himself hastily, gave his watch and money to Lelievre, who was his bedfellow; and having frequently kissed a small crucifix which he always wore round his neck, he shook hands with all us. The gaoler, who was present, was very deeply affected; and when Christiern left us, said, " They are going to shoot him; all the troops are assembled, and in less than a quarter of an hour all his misfortunes will terminate. This sailor, whom you all took for a Dane, is a native of Dunkirk; his real name is Vandermot; he served in the corvette Hirondelle, and was taken prisoner by the English, and placed in the hold of a prison ship with many others; when, exhausted with breathing infectious air and almost starving, he consented to a proposal of being removed from this living tomb, on condition that he would embark in a vessel belonging to the East India Company. On the return of the ship it was captured by a privateer, and Vandermot was brought here with the rest of the crew. He was to have been sent to Valenciennes, but at the moment of departure, an interpreter interrogated him, and it was found by his answers that he was not conversant with the English language; this gave rise to suspicions, and he declared that he was a subject of the king of Denmark; but as he had no proof of this assertion, it was decided that he should remain here until the whole affair should be cleared up. , Some months elapsed, and Vandermot seemed to have been forgotten, when one day a woman and two children came to the gaol, and asked for Christiern. ' My husband!' she cried, seeing him. ' My wife! my children!' he exclaimed, embracing them with ardour. ' How imprudent you are!' said J in a whisper to Christiern; ' it is well that only I am with you!' I promised to be secret, but it was useless. In the joy of having news from him, his wife, to whom he had written, and who thought him dead, had shown his letters to her neighbours, and some of the most officious of them had already denounced him—the wretches! it is their deed which this day destroys him. For some old howitzers which the ship mounted, they have treated him as one taken in arms against his country. Are not such laws unjust?"

" Yes, yes, the laws are unjust," said a number of fellows who were sitting round a bed, playing at cards and drinking spirits. " Come, push round the glass," said one, handing it to his neighbour. " Holla!" said a second, who remarked the air of consternation expressed in Lelievre's features, and shook his arm; " do not put yourself in a fright about it! His turn to-day, our's to-morrow."

This conversation, horribly prolonged, degenerated into unfeeling jokes, until the sound of a drum and fifes, which the echo of the river repeated in various quarters, indicated that the detachments of various corps were marching back to the camp. A death-like silence pervaded the prison for several minutes, and we thought that Christiern had already undergone his sentence; but at the instant when his eyes were covered with the fatal bandage, and on his knees he awaited the execution of his sentence, an aid-de-camp had stopped the fire of the musquetry. The prisoner again saw the light of heaven, and was to be restored to his wife and children, whose prayers and supplications to marshal Brune had been the means of saving his life. Christiern, led back to confinement, was still full of joy, as he had been assured of his speedy freedom. The emperor had been petitioned for his pardon, and the request made in the name of the marshal himself, was so generously urged, that it was impossible to doubt of success.

The return of Christiern was an event on which we did not fail to congratulate him: we drank to the health of the returned prisoner; and the arrival of six new prisoners, who payed their entrance fees with much liberality, was an additional incentive to rejoicing.

These men, whom I had known as a part of Paulet's crew, were sentenced to a few days' confinement, as a punishment for having in boarding a prize, in defiance of the articles of war, plundered the English captain. As they had not been compelled to refund, they brought their guineas with them, and spent them freely. We were all satisfied : the gaoler, who collected even to the very smallest portions of this golden shower, was so pleased with his new guests, that he relaxed his vigilance, although there were in one room three prisoners under sentence of death, Lelievre, Christiern, and the Piedmontese Orsino, a chief of barbets, who having encountered near Alexandria a detachment of conscripts marching towards France, had got into their ranks, where he had supplied the place and name of a deserter. Orsino, whilst serving under this flag, had conducted himself irreproachably, but had marred all by an indiscretion. A price was set upon his head in his own country, and the sentence was to be put into execution at Turin. Five other prisoners were under the weight of charges of the gravest nature. Four were marines; two of them Corsicans and two Provençals, charged with the assassination of a woman from whom they had stolen a golden cross and silver buckles; the fifth had been, as well as they, of the army de la Lune, and to him were attributed very peculiar powers : the soldiers asserted that he could render himself invisible, and metamorphose himself as he pleased; he had, besides, the gift of ubiquity; in fact, he was a sorcerer; and that because he was hump-backed, facetious, severe, a great tale-teller, and having been a sharper all his days, was clever in many tricks of legerdemain. With such company, most gaolers would have used the greatest precaution, but our's considered us as only skilful practitioners, and constantly associated with us. Besides, for ready cash he provided for all our wants, and had no idea that we could have any wish to leave him; and he was correct to a certain point ; for Lelievre and Christiern had not the least wish to escape; Or-

sino was resigned; the marines did not anticipate a
very severe sentence; the sorcerer relied on the insuf-
ficiency of evidence; and the privateers, always drinking,
felt no sort of melancholy. I alone nourished the idea
of getting away; but that I might not be suspected, I
affected to be undisturbed; and so well did I conceal
my intent, that it seemed as if the prison were my
natural element, and all thought that I was there as
comfortable as a fish in water. I did not drink but on
one occasion, that of Christiern's return amongst us.
That night we were all somewhat in liquor, and about
two in the morning I felt a burning thirst which seemed
to inflame my whole body; and on getting out of bed
half awake, I groped about for the pitcher, and on
drinking I found a most horrible mistake; I had taken
one vessel for another, and was almost poisoned. By
day-break I had scarcely repressed the violent commo-
tions of my stomach, when one of the turnkeys came
to tell us that there was some work to be done: as
this afforded an opportunity for getting a little air,
which I thought would revive me, I offered myself as
substitute for a privateer, whose clothes I put on; and
crossing the court-yard, I saw a subaltern officer of my
acquaintance who came in with his cloak on his arm.
He told me that he was sentenced to a month's imprisonment for having created an uproar in the theatre,
and had just been entered on the prison book. " In
that case," said I, " you can begin your work at once;
here is the trough." The subaltern was accomodating,
and did not require a second hint; and whilst he went
to work, I passed boldly by the sentinel, who took no
notice of me.

Leaving the prison, I made my way into the
country, and did not stop till I reached the bridge of
Brique, where I paused in a small ravine, whilst I
reflected on the best mode of escaping pursuit;
and at first resolved on going to Calais, but my
unlucky stars suggested my return to Arras. In the
evening I went to sleep in a barn, in which tra-

vellers rested. One of them, who had left Boulogne three hours after me, told me that the whole city was plunged in grief at the execution of Christiern. " It is the only thing they can talk about," said he. " It was expected that the emperor would pardon him, but the telegraph signalled that he was to be shot. He had once narrowly escaped, but to-day he has suffered. It was piteous to hear him cry ' Pardon, pardon,' whilst endeavouring to raise himself after the first fire, amidst the howlings of some dogs behind him, whom the shots had struck! It went to the very heart, but yet they finished their work. It was his destiny!' "

Although this information caused me great affliction, I could not help thinking that Christiern's death would effect a diversion in favour of my escape; and as he told me nothing which seemed as if I had been missed on the general muster-call, I thought myself in security. I reached Bethune without mishap, and went to lodge with an old regimental acquaintance, who received me kindly. But however prudent one may be, there are always some unexpected occurrences : I had preferred the hospitality of a friend to a lodging at an auberge, and I had thereby placed myself in the jaws of danger; for my friend was recently married, and his wife's brother was one of those obstinate brutes, whose hearts, insensible to glory, only desires inglorious peace. As a natural consequence, the abode I had chosen, as well as those of all the young fellow's relations, were frequently visited by the gendarmes; and these very agreeable gentlemen invaded the residence of my friend long before day-break, and, without any respect to my slumbers, demanded to see my papers. For want of a passport, I endeavoured to enter into certain explanations with them, which was but lost labour. The brigadier, after viewing me attentively, cried out, " I am not mistaken, 'tis he; I have seen him at Arras; 'tis Vidocq!" I was compelled to get up, and in less than a quarter of an hour found myself in the prison of Bethune.

Perhaps, before I proceed, my reader will not be sorry to learn the fate of my companions in captivity, whom I had left at Boulogne; and I can satisfy their curiosity with respect to some of them. We have learnt that Christiern was shot, brave, good fellow, as he was! Lelievre, who was equally worthy, lingered on between hope and fear till the year 1811, when the typhus fever terminated his existence. The four sailors, the murderers, were one night liberated, and sent to Prussia, where two of them received the cross of honour under the walls of Dantzic; and the Sorcerer was released without any sentence having been passed. In 1814 he called himself Collinet, and was the quarter-master of a Westphalian regiment, of which he hoped to get the chest for his own particular profit. This adventurer, not knowing how to dispose of his booty, went on the wings of haste to Burgundy, where, in the neighbourhood, he fell in with a troop of Cossacks, who compelled him to surrender, and give an account of himself. This was the last day of his life, for they ran him through with their lances.

My stay at Bethune was brief; for the day after my capture I was forwarded to Douai, whither I was conducted under good escort.

CHAPTER XXI.

I am conducted to Douai—Application for pardon—My wife marries again—The plunge in the Scarpe—I travel as an officer—
Reading the dispatches—Residence at Paris—A new name—
The woman of my heart—I am a wandering merchant—The commissary of Melun—Execution of Herbaux—I denounce a robber; he denounces me—The galley slaves at Auxerre—I am
settled in the capital—Two fugitives from the Bagne—My wife
again—Receiving stolen goods.

I HAD scarcely set foot in the prison, when the attorney-general Rauson, whom my repeated escapes
had irritated against me, appeared at the grating, and
said—" What, Vidocq has arrived?   Have they put
him in fetters?"—" What have I done, sir," said
I, " that you should wish to be so severe with
me?   Is it a great crime because I have so frequently
escaped?   Have I abused the liberty which I hold so
precious?   When I have been retaken, have I not been
found exerting myself to procure honorable modes of
livelihood?   I am less guilty than unfortunate! Have
pity on me,—pity my poor mother; if I am condemned
to return to the Bagne, she will die!"

These words, pronounced with accents of sincerity,
made some impression of M. Rauson, who returned in
the evening, and questioned me at length of the mode
of my life since I had left Toulon; and as in proof of
what I told him, I offered indubitable testimony, he
began to evince some kindness towards me.   " Why
do you not draw up," said he, " an application for
pardon, or at least for a commutation of the sentence?
I will recommend you to the chief justice "   I thanked
the magistrate for his proffered kindness to me, and
the same day a barrister of Douai, M. Thomas, who
took a real interest in me, brought for my signature
a petition, which he had been so kind as to draw up
for me.

I was in expectation of the answer, when one morning I was sent for to the police-office. Imagining that it was the decision of the minister which was to be communicated to me, and impatient to know it, I followed the turnkey with the haste of a man who anticipates agreeable intelligence. I relied on seeing the attorney-general, but—my wife appeared, accompanied by two strangers. I endeavoured to guess the purport of her visit, when, with the most unembarrassed tone in the world, madame Vidocq said to me, "I have come to tell you that the sentence of our divorce has been pronounced. I am going to be married again, and therefore I have judged it best to go through this formality. The clerk will give you a copy of the judgment for perusal."

Except obtaining my freedom, nothing could be more agreeable to me than the dissolution of this marriage, as I was for ever embarrassed with a creature whom I loathed. I do not know if I had sufficient command of myself to restrain my joy, but certainly my countenance must have betokened it; and if, as I have cogent reasons to believe, my successor was present, he retired with a conviction that I did not at all envy him the treasure he was about to possess.

My detention at Douai was painfully prolonged. I was in suspense for five whole months, and nothing arrived from Paris. The attorney-general had evinced much interest for me, but misfortune engenders distrust, and I began to fear that he had led me on with a vain hope, that I might form no plans of escape before the departure of the galley-slaves; and struck with the idea, I again plotted deeply-laid projects for escape.

The jailor, named Wettu, viewing me as gained over and peaceable, showed me various little favours ; we frequently dined together tête-a-tête in a small room with one window, which looked on to the Scarpe. It struck me, that with the aid of this opening, which was not grated, some day, after dinner, I could easily take French leave, and depart ; only it was absolutely necessary that

I should secure some disguise, which, when I had effected my escape, would effectually conceal me from all
pursuit.   I confided my intentions to some friends, and
they provided for me the uniform of an artillery officer,
of which I resolved to avail myself at the very first opportunity.   One Sunday evening I was at table with
the jailor, and the agent Hurtrel; the wine had made
them very merry, for I had pushed it about briskly.
" Do you know, my hearty," said Hurtrel to me, " that
it would have been no safe business to have put you
here seven years ago.   A window without bars !   By
Jove, I would not have trusted you."—" And further,
Hurtrel," I replied, " one should be made of cork to
risk a plunge from such a height; the Scarpe is very
deep for a person who cannot swim."—" True," said
the jailor; and there the conversation rested, but my
determination was taken.   Some friends arrived, and
the jailor sat down to play with them; and fixing on
the moment when he was most intent on his game, I
threw myself into the river.

At the noise of my fall, all the party ran to the window, whilst Wettu called loudly to the guard and
turnkeys to pursue me.   Fortunately, twilight rendered
it scarcely possible to discern objects; and my hat,
which I had thrown designedly on the bank, seemed to
indicate that I had immediately got out of the river,
whilst I had continued swimming towards the Water-
gate, under which I passed with great difficulty, in consequence of being very cold, and my strength beginning
to fail.   Once out of the city, I gained the bank, my
clothes full of water, not weighing less than an hundred
weight; but I had made up my mind not to delay, and
pushed on at once for Blangy, a village two leagues
from Arras.   It was four in the morning; and a baker
who was heating his oven, gave me leave to dry my
garments, and supplied me with food.   As soon as I
was dried and refreshed, I started for Duisans, where
the widow of an old friend of mine, a captain, resided.
A messenger was to bring to me there the uniform

which had been provided for me at Douai; and no sooner had I obtained it, than I went to Hersin, where I stayed a few days with a cousin of mine. The advice of my friends, which was very rational, urged me to depart as quickly as possible; and as I learnt that the police, convinced that I was in the vicinity, were beating up every quarter, and were approaching the place of my abode, I determined not to wait for them.

It was evident that Paris only could afford me a refuge; but to get to Paris it was indispensable I should pass through Arras, where I should be infallibly recognised. I cogitated on the means of obviating this danger; and prudence suggested to me to get into the wicker calash of my cousin, who had a famous horse, and was the cleverest fellow in the world for his knowledge of the cross roads. He pledged himself on the reputation of his talent as a guide, to carry me in safety by the ramparts of my native town; and I wanted no more at his hands, trusting to my disguise to effect the rest. I was no longer Vidocq, unless I was examined very closely; and on reaching the bridge of Gy, I saw, without the least alarm, eight horses belonging to gendarmes, tied to the door of a public house. I confess I would rather have avoided the rencontre; but it faced me, and it was only by fronting it boldly that I could hope to escape detection. "Come on," said I to my cousin; "here we must make an essay; get down; be as quick as you can, and call for something." He immediately alighted, and entered the public house with the air of a man who had no dread of the eye of the brigade. "Ah!" said they, "it is your cousin Vidocq that you are driving?"—"Perhaps, it may be," he answered with a laugh; "go and see." A gendarme did approach the calash, but rather from curiosity than suspicion. At the sight of my uniform, he respectfully touched his hat, and said, "Your servant, captain;" and soon afterwards mounted his horse with his comrades. "Good journey," cried my cousin, cracking his whip; "if you lay hold of him, perhaps you will write

üs word."—" Go your way," said the quarter-master
who commanded the troop, " we know his haunt ; Hersin is the word ; and to-morrow by this time, he will be
again between four walls. "

We continued our journey very quietly, but yet one
thing made me somewhat uneasy; my military dress
might expose me to some difficulties which would have
an unpleasant result. The war with Prussia had begun,
and there were but few officers in the interior, unless
they were confined there by some wound. I determined on carrying my arm in a sling as an officer
who had been disabled at Jena; and if any questions
were asked, I was prepared to give all particulars on
this subject, which I had learnt from the bulletins ; and
to add those which I could pick up by hearing a multitude of accounts, some true and some false, from witnesses either ocular or not. In fact, I was quite *au fait*
concerning the battle of Jena, and could speak to all
comers with perfect knowledge of the subject ; nobody
knew more of it than I did. I acquitted myself in admirable style at Beaumont, when the weariness of our horse
which had conveyed us thirty-three leagues in a day and
a half, compelled us to halt. I had already begun conversing in the inn, when I saw a quarter-master of gendarmes
go straight up to an officer of dragoons, and ask for his
papers. I went up to the quarter-master, and asked
him the motive of this precaution. " I asked for his
route," he answered, " because when every one is with
the army, a healthy officer would not be left in France."
" You are right, comrade," said I, " duty must be performed ;" and at the same time, that he might not take
a fancy to ask me a similar question, I asked him to
dine with us; and during the meal I so far gained his
confidence, that he requested me, on reaching Paris,
to use my interest in procuring him a change of quarters. I promised all he asked, which much pleased
him; as I was to use my own influence, which was
great, and that of others still more powerful. We are
generally prodigal in bestowing that which we have

not. However it may be, the flask circulated rapidly; and my guest, in the enthusiasm of having secured an interest which was so desirable to him, began to talk that voluble nonsense which usually precedes drunkenness, when a gendarme brought him a packet of dispatches. He opened them with an unsteady hand, and attempted to read them, but his eyes refused their office, and he begged me to peruse them for him. I opened a letter, and the first words which struck my sight were these : " Brigade of Arras." I hastily read it, and found that it was advice of my travelling towards Beaumont, and adding that I must have taken the diligence of the Silver Lion. In spite of my agitation, I read the letter to him, omitting or adding particulars as I pleased. " Good! very good !" said the sober and vigilant quarter-master; " the conveyance will not pass until to-morrow morning, and I will take due care." He then sat down with the intention of drinking more, but his strength did not equal his courage, and they were obliged to carry him to bed, to the great scandal of all the lookers-on, who repeated with much indignation; " What! the quarter-master ! A man of rank to behave so shamefully !"

As might be conjectured, I did not wait the uprising of the man of rank ; and at five o'clock got into the Beaumont diligence, which conveyed me safely to Paris, where my mother, who had remained at Versailles, rejoined me. We dwelt together for some months in the faubourg Saint-Denis, where we saw no one except a jeweller named Jacquelin, whom I was compelled, to a certain extent, to make my confidant, because he had known me at Rouen under the name of Blondel. It was at his house that I met a madame de B——, who holds the first rank in the affections of my life. Madame de B——, or Annette, for so I call her, was a very pretty woman, whom her husband had abandoned in consequence of his affairs turning out unfortunate. He had fled to Holland, and had not been heard of for a considerable time. Annette was then quite free; she pleased me; I liked her wit, un-derstanding, kindly feeling, and ventured to tell her so; she saw soon, and without much trouble, my assiduity and regard; and we found that we could not exist without each other. Annette came to live with me, and as I resumed the trade of a travelling seller of fashionable commodities, she resolved to accompany me in my perambulations. The first journey we un-dertook together was excessively fortunate. I learnt, however, at the moment I was leaving Melun, from the landlord of the inn at which I had put up, that the commissary of police had testified some regret at not having examined my papers; but what was deferred was not ended, and that at my next visit, he meant to pay me a visit. The information surprised me, for I must consequently have been in some way an object of suspicion. To go on might lead to danger, and I therefore returned to Paris, resolving not to make any other journeys, unless I could render less unfavorable the chances which combined against me.

Having started very early, I reached the faubourg Saint Marceau in good time; and at my entrance, I heard the hawkers bawling out, " that two well-known persons are to be executed to-day at the Place de Grêve." I listened, and fancied I distinguished the name of Herbaux. Herbaux, the author of the for-gery which caused all my misfortunes! I listened with more attention, but with an involuntary shudder; and this time the crier, to whom I had approached, repeated the sentence with these additions: " Here is the sentence of the criminal tribunal of the department of the Seine, which condemns to death the said Ar-mand Saint Leger, an old sailor, born at Bayonne, and César Herbaux, a freed galley-slave, born at Lille, accused and convicted of murder," &c.

I could doubt no longer; the wretch who had heaped so much misery on my head was about to suffer at the scaffold. Shall I confess that I felt a sentiment o joy, and yet I trembled ? Tormented again, and agi-

tated with a perpetually renewing uneasiness, I would
have destroyed all the population of the prisons and
Bagnes, who, having been the means of casting me into
the abyss of misery, had kept me there by their vile disclosures. It will not excite wonder, when I say that
I ran with haste to the palace of justice to assure
myself of the truth; it was not mid-day, and I had
great trouble in reaching the grating, near which I
fixed myself, waiting for the fatal moment.

At last four o'clock struck, and the wicket opened.
A man appeared first on the sledge. It was Herbaux.
His face was covered with a deadly paleness, whilst
he affected a firmness which the convulsive workings
of his features belied. He pretended to talk to his
companion, who was already incapacitated from hearing him. At the signal of departure Herbaux, with a
countenance into which he infused all the audacity he
could force, gazed round on the crowd, and his eyes
met mine. He started, and the blood rushed to his
face. The procession passed on, and I remained as
motionless as the bronze railings on which I was
leaning; and I should probably have remained longer,
if an inspector of the palace had not desired me to
come away. Twenty minutes afterwards a car, laden
with a red basket, and escorted by a gendarme, was
hurried over the Pont-au-Change, going towards the
burial-ground allotted for felons. Then, with an oppressed feeling at my heart, I went away, and regained
my lodgings, full of sorrowful reflections.

I have since learnt, that, during his detention at the
Bicêtre, Herbaux had expressed his regret at having
been instrumental in getting me condemned, when
innocent. The crime which had brought this wretch
to the scaffold was a murder committed, in company
with Saint Leger, on a lady of the Place Dauphine.
These two villains had obtained access to their victim
under pretence of giving her tidings of her son, whom
they said they had seen in the army.

Although, in fact, Herbaux's execution could not

have any direct influence over my situation, yet it alarmed me, and I was horror-struck at feeling that I had ever been in contact with such brigands, destined to the executioner's arm : my remembrance revealed me to myself, and I blushed, as it were, in my own face. I sought to lose the recollection, and to lay down an impassable line of demarcation between the past and the present; for I saw but too plainly, that the future was dependant on the past; and I was the more wretched, as a police, who have not always due powers of discernment, would not permit me to forget myself. I saw myself again on the point of being snared like a deer. The persuasion that I was interdicted from becoming an honest man drove me to despair; I was silent, morose, and disheartened. Annette perceived it, and sought to console me; she offered to devote herself for me, pressed me with questions, and my secret escaped me; but I never had cause to regret my confidence. The activity, the zeal, and presence of mind of this woman became very useful to me I was in want of a passport, and she persuaded Jacquelin to lend me his, and to teach me how to make use of it; she gave me the most complete accounts of her family and connexions. Thus instructed, I set out on my journey, and traversed the whole of Lower Burgundy. Almost everywhere I was examined as to my passport, which if they had compared with my person, would have at once detected the fraud; but this was nowhere done, and for more than a year, with trifling exceptions not worth detailing, the name of Jacquelin was propitious to me.

One day that I had unpacked at Auxerre, and was walking peaceably on the quay, I met one Paquay, a robber by profession, whom I had seen at the Bicêtre, where he was confined for six years. I would rather have avoided him, but he addressed me abruptly, and from his first salutation, I found that it would not be safe to pretend no acquaintance with him. He was

too inquisitive about what I was doing; and as I saw
from his conversation that he wished me to join him
in his robberies, I thought it best to get rid of him, to
talk of the police of Auxerre, whom I represented as
very vigilant, and consequently much to be dreaded.
I thought I saw that my information made an impression on him, and I coloured the picture still higher,
until at length, after having listened with much, but
unquiet attention, he suddenly cried, " Devil take it !
it appears that there is nothing to be done here; the
packet-boat will start in two hours, and if you like we
will be off together."—" Agreed," said I; " if you are
for starting I am your man." I then quitted him,
after having promised to rejoin him immediately that
I should have made some preparations which were
necessary. How pitiable is the condition of a fugitive
galley-slave, who, if he would not be denounced or
implicated in some evil deed, must be himself the
denouncer. Returned to the public-house, I then
wrote the following letter to the lieutenant of the
gendarmerie, whom I knew to be on the hunt for
the authors of a robbery lately committed at the
coach office :—

" SIR,
" A person who does not wish to be known, informs
you that one of the authors of the robbery committed
at the coach-office in your city, will set out by the
packet-boat to go to Soigny, where his accomplices
most probably are. Lest you should fail, and not
arrest him in time, it would be best for two disguised
gendarmes to go on board the packet-boat with him, as
it is important that he should be taken with prudence,
and not be allowed to get out of sight, as he is a very
active man."

This missive was accompanied by a description so
minute that it was impossible to mistake him. The
moment of departure arrived, and I went on the quays,

taking a circuitous route, and from the window of a
public-house where I stationed myself, I perceived
Paquay enter the packet-boat, and soon afterwards
the two gendarmes embarked, whom I recognized by
a certain air, which may be seen, but cannot be described. At intervals they handed a paper to each
other, which they perused, and then cast their
eyes on the man, whose dress, contrary to the usual
garb of the robbers, was in a bad condition. The
boat moved on, and I saw it depart with the more
pleasure, as it carried with it Paquay, his propositions,
and even his discoveries, if, as I did not doubt, he had
the intention of making any.

The day after this adventure, whilst I was taking
an inventory of my merchandizes, I heard an extraordinary noise, and, looking from the windows, I saw
Thierry and his satellites guarding a chain of galley-
slaves! At this sight, so terrible and inauspicious for
me, I drew back quickly, but in my haste I broke a
pane of glass, and suddenly attracted all looks towards
me. I wished myself in the bowels of the earth.
But this was not all; for to increase my disquietude,
somebody opened my door; it was the landlady of
the Pheasant, madame Gelat. " Here, M. Jacquelin,
come and see the chain passing," she cried. " Oh, it
is long since I saw such a fine one, there are at least
one hundred and fifty, and some of them famous
fellows! Do you hear how they are singing?" I
thanked my hostess for her attention, and pretending
to be much busied, told her that I would go down
in an instant. " Oh, do not hurry yourself," she
answered, "there is plenty of time, they are going to
sleep here in our stables. And then if you wish to
have any conversation with the commandant, they will
put him in the chamber next to you." Lieutenant
Thierry my neighbour! At this intelligence I know
not what passed in my mind; but I think that if
madame Gelat had observed me she would have seen
my countenance grow pale, and my whole frame

tremble with an involuntary shudder.   Lieutenant
Thierry my neighbour!   He might recognize me,
detect me; a gesture might betray me; and it was
therefore expedient to avoid a rencontre if possible.
The necessity of completing my inventory was an
excuse for my apparent want of curiosity.   I passed a
frightful night, and it was not until four o'clock in
the morning that the departure of the infernal procession was announced to me, that I breathed freely
again.

He has never suffered, who has not experienced
horrors similar to those into which the presence of
this troop of banditti and their guards threw me.   To
be again invested with those fetters which I had broken
at the cost of so much endurance and exertion, was
an idea which haunted me incessantly.   I was not the
sole possessor of my own secret, for there were galley-
slaves everywhere, who, if I sought to flee from them
would infallibly betray me : my repose, my very existence was menaced on all sides, and at all times.
The glance of an eye, the name of a commissary, the
appearance of a gendarme, the perusal of a sentence,
all roused and excited my alarm.   How often did I
curse the perverse fate which, deceiving my youth,
had smiled at the disorderly license of my passions;
and that tribunal which, by an unjust sentence, had
plunged me into a gulf whence I could not extricate
myself, nor cleanse myself of the foul imputations
which clung to me; and those institutions which close
for ever the door of repentance!   I was excluded from
society, and yet I was anxious to give it proofs of
good conduct; I had given them; and I attest my
invariable honourable behaviour after every escape,
my habits of regularity, and my punctilious fidelity in
fulfilling all my engagements.

Now some fears arose in my mind concerning Paquay, in whose arrest I had been instrumental; and,
on reflection, it seemed that I had acted inconsiderately in this circumstance; I felt a forewarning

of some impending evil, and the presentiment was realized. Paquay, when conducted to Paris and then brought back to be confronted at Auxerre, learnt that I was still in that city; he had always suspected me of having denounced him, and determined on his revenge. He told the jailor all he knew concerning me, and he reported it to the authorities; but my reputation for probity was so well established in Auxerre, where I remained for three months at a time, that, to avoid an unpleasant business, a magistrate, whose name I will not disclose, sent for me, and gave me notice of what had occurred. There was no occasion for me to avow the truth, my agitation revealed all, and I had only strength to say, " Sir, I seek to be an honest man." Without any reply, he went out and left me alone. I comprehended his generous silence, and in a quarter of an hour I had lost sight of Auxerre; and from my retreat I wrote to Annette, to inform her of this fresh catastrophe. But to remove suspicion, I recommended her to stay for a fortnight at the ' Pheasant,' and to tell everybody that I was at Rouen, making purchases, and on the expiration of the time she was to rejoin me at Paris, where she arrived at the day appointed. She told me, that the day after my departure, disguised gendarmes had called at my warehouse, intending to arrest me, and that not finding me, they had said that they did not mind, for they should discover me at last.

They continued their search; and this deranged all my plans, for, masked under the name of Jacquelin, I saw myself reduced to quit it, and once more renounce the industrious trade which I had created.

No passport, however good, could protect me through the districts which I usually travelled over; and in those where I was unknown, my unusual appearance would most probably excite suspicion. The crisis was horridly critical. What could I do? This was my only thought, when chance introduced me to

M

a tailor of the Cour Saint Martin, who was desirous
of selling his business. I treated with him, persuaded
that I could nowhere be so safe as in the heart of a
capital, where it is easy to lose oneself amid the
crowded population. Eight months elapsed, and
nothing disturbed the tranquillity enjoyed by my
mother, Annette, and myself. My trade prospered,
and every day augmented it; nor did I confine myself,
as my predecessor had done, to the making up of
clothes, but traded also in cloths, and was perhaps
on the road to fortune, when one morning all my
troubles were renewed.

I was in my warehouse, when a messenger came to
me, and said I was wanted at a coffee-house in the
Rue Aumaire, and thinking that it was some matter
of business, I immediately went to the place appointed.
I was taken into a private room, and there found two
fugitives from the bagne at Brest; one of them was
that Blondy who aided my unfortunate escape from
Pont-a-Luzen. " We have been here these ten days,"
said he to me, " and have not a sous. Yesterday we
saw you in a warehouse, that we learnt was your
own, which gave us much pleasure; and I said to my
friend, ' Let us now cast off all care;' for we know
that you are not the man to leave old comrades in
difficulty."

The idea of seeing myself in the power of two
ruffians, whom I knew capable of the vilest deeds,
even of selling me to the police to make a profit of
me, although they injured themselves, was overwhelming. I did not fail to express my pleasure at
seeing them, adding, that I was not rich, and regret-
ting that it was only in my power to give them fifty
francs. They appeared content with this sum; and
on leaving me, expressed their intention to depart at
once for Chalons-sur-Marne, where they said they
had business. I should have been but too fortunate
had they at once quitted Paris, but on bidding me
adieu, they promised soon to see me again, and I

remained tormented with the dread of their return. Would they not consider me as a milch-cow, and make the most of their power over me ? Would they not be insatiable ? Who could answer that their demands would be limited to my means ? I already saw myself the banker of these gentlemen and many others ; for it was to be presumed, that in conformity with the cus• tom of these thieves, if I satisfied them, they would introduce their friends to me, who would also draw upon me, and I shall only be on good terms with them till my first refusal, and after that they would without doubt serve me a villanous trick. With such blood-hands let loose upon me, it may be imagined that I was but ill at ease ! It must be allowed that my situation was a pleasant one, but it was crowned with a rencontre which made it still worse.

It may or may not be remembered that my wife, after her divorce, had married again, and I thought she was in the department of the Pas-de-Calais, entirely occupied in being happy and making her new husband so, when in the Rue du Petit-Carreau, I met her, face to face ; and it was impossible to pass her, for she at once recognized me. I spoke to her, without alluding to the wrongs she had done me ; and as the dilapidation of her dress evinced that she was not in very flourishing circumstances, I gave her some money. She perhaps imagined that it was an interested generosity, but it certainly was not. It never occurred to me that the ex-madame Vidocq would denounce me. In truth, in recurring at a later period to our old wrangles, I thought that my heart had only given me prudential suggestions, and then approved of what I had done ; it appeared most proper that this female, in her distress, should rely on me for some assistance. Detained in or far from Paris, I was anxious to relieve her misery. This should have been a consideration to determine her to preserve silence ; and I at least thought so. We shall see whether or not I was deceived in my expectation.

The support of my ex-wife was an expense to which I reconciled myself; but of this charge I did not as yet know the whole weight. A fortnight had elapsed since our interview; when one morning I was sent for to the Rue de l'Echiquier, and on going there, and at the bottom of a court, in a ground-floor room, very clean, but meanly furnished, I saw again, not only my wife, but also her neices and their father, the terrorist Chevalier, who had just been freed from an imprisonment of six months, for stealing plate. A glance was sufficient to assure me that I had now the whole family on my hands. They were in a state of the most complete destitution; I hated them and cursed them, and yet I could do nothing better than extend my hand to them. I drained myself for them, for to have driven them to despair would have brought on my own ruin; and rather than return to the power of the police, I resolved on sacrificing my last sous.

At this period it seemed as if the whole world was leagued against me; I was compelled to draw my purse-strings at every moment, and for whom? For creatures who, looking on my liberality as compulsory, were prepared to betray me as soon as I ceased to be a certain source of reliance. When I went home from my wife's, I had still another proof of the wretchedness affixed to the state of a fugitive galley-slave. Annette and my mother were in tears. During my absence, two drunken men had asked for me, and on being told that I was from home, they had broke forth in oaths and threats which left me no longer in doubt of the perfidy of their intentions. By the description which Annette gave me of these two individuals, I easily recognized Blondy and his comrade Deluc. I had no trouble in guessing their names; and besides, they had left an address, with a formal injunction to send them forty francs, which was more than enough to disclose to me who they were, as there were not in Paris any other persons who could send me such an intimation. I was obedient, very obedient; only in paying my contribution to these two scoundrels, I could not help letting them know how inconsiderately they had behaved. "Consider what a step you have taken," said I to them; "they know nothing at my house, and you have told all; my wife, who carries on the concern in her name, will perhaps turn me out, and then I must be reduced to the lowest ebb of misery."—"Oh you can come and rob with us," answered the two rascals.

I endeavoured to convince them how much better it was to owe an existence to honest toil, than to be in incessant fear from the police, which sooner or later catches all malefactors in its nets. I added that one crime generally leads to another; that he would risk his neck who ran straight towards the guillotine; and the termination of my discourse was, that they would do well to renounce the dangerous carreer on which they had entered.

"Not so bad!" cried Blondy, when I had finished my lecture, "not so bad! But can you in the mean time point out to us any apartment that we can ransack. We are, you see, like Harlequin, and have more need of cash than advice;" and they left me, laughing deridingly at me. I called them back, to profess my attachment to them, and begged them not to call again at my house. "If that is all," said Deluc, "we will keep from that."—"Oh yes, we'll keep away," added Blondy, "since that is unpleasant to your mistress."

But the latter did not stay away long: the very next day at nightfall he presented himself at my warehouse, and asked to speak to me privately. I took him into my own room. "We are alone?" said he to me, looking round at the room in which we were; and when he was assured that he had no witnesses, he drew from his pocket eleven silver forks and two gold watches, which he placed on a stand. "Four hundred francs for this would not be too much—the silver plate and the gold watches—Come, tip us the needful."—"Four hundred francs!" said I, alarmed at so abrupt a total.

M 2

" I have not so much money."—" Never mind. Go and sell the goods."—" But if it should be known!" " That's your affair; I want the ready; or if you like it better, I'll send you customers from the police office—you know what a word would do—Come, come, the cash, the chink, and no gammon." I understood the scoundrel but too well: I saw myself denounced, dragged from the state into which I had installed myself, and led back to the Bagne. I counted out the four hundred francs.

CHAPTER XXII.

Another robber—My wicker car—Arrest of two galley-slaves—
Fearful discovery—St Germain wishes to involve me in a
robbery—I offer to serve the police—Horrid perplexities—
They wish to take me whilst in bed—My concealment—A
comic adventure—Disguises on disguises—Chevalier has denounced me—Annette at the Depôt of the Prefecture—I prepare to leave Paris—Two passers of false money—I am apprehended in my shirt—1 am conducted to the Bicêtre.

I WAS a receiver of stolen goods! a criminal, in spite
of myself! But yet I was one, for I had lent a hand to
crime.   No hell can be imagined equal to the torment
in which I now existed.   I was incessantly agitated;
remorse and fear assailed me at once, night and day;
at each moment I was on the rack.   I did not sleep, I
had no appetite, the cares of business were no longer
attended to, all was hateful to me.   All! no, I had
Annette and my mother with me.   But should I not
be forced to abandon them?   Sometimes I trembled at
the thoughts of my apprehension, and my home was
transformed into a filthy dungeon; sometimes it was
surrounded by the police, and their pursuit laid open
proofs of a misdeed which would draw down on me
the vengeance of the laws.   Harassed by the family
of Chevalier, who devoured my substance; tormented
by Blondy, who was never wearied with applying to
me for money; dreading all that could occur, that was
most horrible and incurable, in my situation; ashamed
of the tyranny exercised over me by the vilest wretches
that disgraced the earth; irritated that I could not
burst through the moral chain which irrevocably bound
me to the opprobrium of the human race; I was driven
to the brink of despair, and, for eight days, pondered
in my head the direst purposes.   Blondy, the wretch
Blondy, was the especial object of my wrathful indignation; I could have strangled him with all my heart,
and yet I still kept on terms with him, still had a

welcome for him. Impetuous and violent as I was by
nature, it was astonishing how much patient endurance
I exercised; but it was all owing to Annette. Oh!
how I prayed with fervent sincerity, that, in one of his
frequent excursions, some friendly gendarme might
drive a bullet through Blondy's brain! I even trusted
that it was an event that would soon occur; but every
time that a more extended absence began to inspire me
with the hope that I was at length freed from this
wretch, he again appeared, and brought with him a
renewal of all my cares.

One day I saw him come with Deluc and an ex-
clerk, named St Germain, whom I had known at
Rouen; where, like many others, he had barely the
reputation of an honest man. St Germain, who had
only known me as the merchant Blondel, was much
astonished at the meeting; but two words from Blondy
explained my whole history.—I was a thorough rogue.
Confidence then replaced astonishment; and St Germain, who at first had frowned, joined in the mirth.
Blondy told me, that they were going all three to set
out for the environs of Senlis, and asked me for the
loan of my wicker car, which I made use of when
visiting the fairs. Glad to get rid of these fellows on
such terms, I hastily wrote a note to the person who
had charge of it. He gave them the conveyance and
harness, and away they went; whilst for ten days I
heard nothing of them, when St Germain re-appeared.
He entered my house one morning with an alarmed
look, and an appearance of much fatigue. " Well,"
said he, " my comrades have been seized."—" Seized!"
cried I, with a joy which I could not repress; but assuming all my coolness, I asked for the details, with
an affectation of being greatly concerned. St Germain
told me, in few words, that Blondy and Deluc had
only been apprehended because they travelled without
credentials. I did not believe anything he said, and
had no doubt but they had been engaged in some robbery; and what confirmed my suspicions was, that, on

proposing to send them some money, St Germain told
me that they were not in want of any. On leaving
Paris, they had fifty francs amongst them; and certainly, with so small a sum, it would have been a difficult matter to have gone on for a fortnight; and yet
how was it that they were still not unprovided? The
first idea that flashed through my brain, was, that they
had committed some extensive robbery, which they
wished to conceal from me; but I soon discovered
that the business was of still more serious nature.

Two days after St Germain's return, I thought I
would go and look at my car; and remarked, at first,
that they had altered its exterior appearance. On getting inside, I saw on the lining of white and blue
striped ticken, red spots, recently washed out; and
then opening the seat, to take out the key, I found it
filled with blood, as if a carcase had been laid there!
All was now apparent, and the truth was exposed,
even more horrible than my suspicions had foreboded.
I did not hesitate; far more interested than the murderers themselves in getting rid of all traces of the
deed, on the next night I took the vehicle to the
banks of the Seine, and having got as far as Bercy, in
a lone spot, I set fire to some straw and dry wood,
with which I had filled it, and did not leave the spot
until the whole was burnt to ashes.

St Germain, to whom I spoke of the circumstances,
without adding that I had burnt my carriage, confessed that the dead body of a waggoner, assassinated
by Blondy, between Louvres and Dammartin, had
been concealed in it, until they found an opportunity
of throwing it into a well. This man, one of the most
abandoned villains I ever encountered, spoke of the
deed as if it were a most harmless action; and a laugh
was on his lips while he related the facts with the
most unembarrassed and easy tone. I was horrified,
and listened with a sort of stupefaction; and when he
asked me for the impression of the lock of an apartment with which I was acquainted, I reached the cli-

max of my terrors. I made some observations, to
which he replied, " What is that to me?—business
must be done—Because you know him! Why that is
the stronger reason; you know all the ways of the
house; you can guide me, and we will share the
produce!—Come, it is no use refusing; I must have
the impression." I pretended to yield to his arguments. " Such scruples as these—hold your tongue!"
replied St Germain; " you make me sweat (the expression he used was not quite so proper). But come
—all is agreed, and half the plunder is yours." Good
God! what an associate! I had no cause to rejoice at
Blondy's mishap; I really got rid of a fever and fell
into an ague. Blondy would yield to persuasion on
certain terms, but St Germain never; and he was
even more imperious in his demands. Exposed to
see myself compromised from one moment to another,
I determined to see M. Henry, chief of the division of
security in the prefecture of police. I went to
him; and having unfolded my situation to him, declared that if he would tolerate my residence at Paris,
I would give him exact information of a great many
fugitive galley-slaves, with whose retreats and plans I
was well acquainted.

M. Henry received me with much kindness; but
having for a moment reflected on what I had said,
answered that he could not enter into any terms with
me. " That should not prevent your giving the information," he continued, " and we can then judge
how useful it may be; and perhaps ...."—" Ah,
sir, no perhaps, that would risk my life. You are not
ignorant of what those individuals are capable whom
you denounce; and if I must be led back to the Bagne
after some part of an accusation has stated that I have
made communications to the police, I am a dead man."
—" Under these circumstances, let us speak no farther
on the subject;" and he left me, without even asking
my name.

I was deeply grieved at the ill success of my propo-

sition. St Germain was about to return, and demand
the performance of my promise. What was I to do?
Ought I to inform the individual, that we were about
to rob him together? If it had been possible to have
avoided accompanying St Germain, it would not have
been so dangerous to have given such notice; but I
had promised to assist him, and had no pretext for
getting off from my promise, and I waited for him as
I should have done for a sentence of death. One, two,
three weeks passed in these perplexities, and at the
end of this time I began to breathe again; and when
two months had elapsed, was perfectly at my ease,
thinking that he had been apprehended, as well as his
two companions. Annette (I shall always remember
it) made a nine days' vow, and burnt at least a dozen
wax candles in token of joy. " I pray to heaven,"
she sometimes said, " that they may continue where
they are." The torment had been of long duration,
but the moments of calm were brief, and they preceded the catastrophe which decided my existence.

The 3rd of May 1809, at day-break, I was awakened
by several knocks at my warehouse door; and going
down to see, was on the point of opening the door,
when I heard some voices in conversation in a low
tone. " He is a powerful man," said one; " we must
be wary!" There was no doubt concerning the motives of this early visit, and I returned hastily to my
chamber, told Annette what had passed, and opening
the window, whilst she entered into conversation
with the officers, I glided out in my shirt, by a door
which opened on the staircase, and soon reached the
upper story; at the fourth I saw an open door and entered, looked about me, listened, and found I was
alone. In a recess in the wall was a bed, hidden by a
ragged crimson damask curtain. Pressed by circumstances, and sure that the staircase was guarded, I
threw myself beneath the mattress; but scarcely had
I lain down when some one entered, whom I recog-

nized to be a young man named Fossé, whose father, a brass-worker, was lying in an adjacent room, and a dialogue thus began :—

SCENE THE FIRST.

FATHER, MOTHER, AND SON.

Son. "What do you think, father? They are looking for the tailor—they want to seize him—all the house is in an uproar—Do you hear the bell? Hark! hark! they are ringing at the watchmaker's."

Mother. "Let them ring—do not you meddle in business that does not concern you;—(to her husband) Come, father, dress; they will soon be-here."

Father. (Yawning, and as I imagined, rubbing his eyes) "The devil fetch them—what do they want with the tailor?"

Son. "I do not know, father; but there are lots of them—bailiffs and gendarmes, and a commissary with them."

Father. "Perhaps it is nothing at all."

Mother. "But what can they want with the tailor? What can he have done?"

Father. "What can he have done? Since he sells cloth, he may have made clothes of English goods."

Mother. "He may have employed foreign goods! You make me laugh at you. Do you think he would be apprehended for that?"

Father. "Yes, I think they would apprehend him for that, and the continental blockade."

Son. "Continental blockade! What do you mean by that, father? What has that to do with the matter?"

Mother. "Oh yes! Tell us, then, what will be the end of this; and let us know the truth of it all."

Father. "The meaning of all this;—that perhaps they will make the tailor a head shorter."

Mother. "Good God! poor man! I am sure they

will take him away—criminals, like him, are not guilty; and if it only depended on me, I know I would hide them all in my chemise."

Father. " Do you not know the tailor is a large fellow ?—he has a famous body of his own."

Mother. " Never mind, I would hide him. I wish he would come here. Do you remember the deserter?"

Father. " Hush, hush! Here they come."

SCENE THE SECOND.

ENTER THE COMMISSARY, GENDARMES, AND THEIR ATTENDANTS.

(At this moment the commissary and his staff having traversed the house from top to bottom, reached the fourth story.)

Commissary. " Ah! the door is open. I beg pardon for disturbing you, but the interest of society demands it. You have a neighbour, a very bad man, a man who would kill either father or mother."

Wife. " What, monsieur Vidocq ? "

Commissary. " Yes, madam, Vidocq; and I charge you, in case you or your husband have given him shelter, to tell me without delay."

Wife. " Ah, monsieur le commissaire, you may look everywhere if you please. We give shelter to any one who—"

Commissary. " Ah, you should beware, for the law is very severe in this particular. It is a subject on which there is no joking! You would subject yourselves to very severe punishment; for a man condemned to capital punishment, it would be nothing less than——"

Husband (quickly). " We are not afraid of that, monsieur commissaire."

Commissary. " I believe you, and rely on you. However, that I may have nothing to reproach myself with, you will permit me to make a slight search, just a simple formality. *(Addressing his attendants).* Gentlemen, are the egresses well guarded ?"

After a very minute search of the inner room, the commissary returned to that in which I was. " And in this bed," said he, raising the tattered damask curtain, whilst at my feet I felt one of the corners of the mattress shake, which they let fall carelessly, " there is no Vidocq here. Come, he must have made himself invisible; we must give over our search." It may be imagined that I felt overjoyed at these words, which removed an enormous weight from my mind. At length all the alguazils retired, the brass-worker's wife attending them with much politeness, and I was left alone with the father and son, and a little child, who did not think that I was so near them. I heard them pitying me; but madame Fossé soon ran up the staircase, four steps at a time, until she was quite of breath, and I still was the theme of conversation.

SCENE THE THIRD.

THE HUSBAND, WIFE, AND SON.

Wife. " Oh my God! my God! how many people there are in the street. Ah! they say fine things about M. Vidocq; they talk much, and all sorts of things. However, there must be some of it true; never so much smoke without some fire. I knew very well that this monsieur Vidocq was a proud chap for a master-tailor. His arms were crossed much more frequently than his legs."

Husband. " There you go like all the rest with your suppositions; you are a slanderous woman now. Besides, it is no business of ours; and suppose that it did concern us, of what do they accuse him, what do they chatter about? I am not curious."

Wife. " What do they chatter about! Why the very thoughts on't make me tremble, when they say he is a man condemned to death for having killed a man.

I wish you could hear the little tailor who lives lower down."

Husband. " Oh, he speaks from a professional jealousy."

Wife. " And the porteress at No. 27, who speaks of what she knows well, says that she has seen him go out every evening with a thick stick, so well disguised that she did not know him."

Husband. " The porteress says that ?"

Wife. And that he went to lay wait for the people in the Champs Elysées."

Husband. " Are you growing foolish ? "

Wife. " Ah, is that foolish! The cook-shopman, perhaps is foolish, when he says that they were all robbers who came in, and that he had seen M. Vidocq with some very ill-looking fellows."

Husband. " Well! who had ill looks after——"

Wife. " After all, he is, said the commissary to the grocer, a worthless man; and worse than that, for he added that he was a vile criminal, and justice could not get hold of him."

Husband. " And you talk nonsense; you believe the commissary because he is beating up our quarters; but I will never be persuaded that M. Vidocq is a dishonest man. I think, on the other hand, that he is a good fellow, a punctual man. Besides, whatever he may be, it is no business of ours; let us meddle with our own affairs, and time wags onward;—we must to work; come quickly, to work, to work."

The sitting was adjourned; father, mother, son, and little daughter, all the Fossé family, went away, and I remained locked up, reflecting on the perfidious insinuations of the police, who to deprive me of the aid of my neighbours, represented me as an infamous villain. I have often seen, subsequently, this species of tactics employed, the success of which is always founded on atrocious calumnies and measures, revolting, because unjust; clumsy, because they produce an effect entirely contrary to that which is expected; for those persons who would exert themselves personally in the apprehension of a thief, are prevented from fear of struggling with a man whom the feeling of crime and the prospect of a scaffold, drives probably to despair.

I had been shut up for two hours; there was no noise either in the house or in the street, and the groups had dispersed; I was beginning to take courage, when I heard a key thrust into the lock, and whilst I again squatted beneath the coverlid, the father, mother, son, and daughter Fossé entered.

The father and son were quarrelling, and by the interference of the mother I had no doubt but blows would arise, when, throwing aside the tattered curtains, I made my appearance in the midst of the astonished family. It may be imagined how much the good folks were surprised. Whilst they were looking at me without saying a word, I told them as briefly as possible how I had got amongst them; how I had concealed myself under the mattress, &c. The husband and wife were astonished that I had not been stifled in my place of concealment; they pitied me, and with a cordiality not uncommon amongst people of their class, offered me refreshments which were necessary after so painful a morning.

It may be supposed that I was on thorns during the progress of the whole affair; I perspired copiously; at any other moment I should have been amused; but when I reflected on the inevitable results of a discovery, none less than myself could appreciate the burlesque of my situation. Supposing myself lost, I would have expedited the fatal moment, it would have cut short my train of perplexities; a reflection on the mobility of circumstances determined me to wait the event; I knew from more than one hour of experience, that the best contrived schemes of man are disconcerted, and sometimes we triumph over the most desperate cases.

After the reception afforded me by the Fossé family, it was probable that I should have no reason to repent

of having waited patiently for results. However, I was
not yet fully assured: this family was not well off;
and it might happen that the first impression of kindness and compassion which the most perverse persons
sometimes evince, would give place to the hope of obtaining some reward by surrendering me to the police;
and then supposing my hosts to be what is called
'staunch,' yet an indiscreet expression might betray me.
Without being endowed with much penetration, Fossé
guessed the secret of my uneasiness, which he succeeded in dissipating by protestations too sincere to be
doubted.

He undertook to watch over my safety, and began
by disclaiming any return for his kindness, and then
informed me, that the police agents had fixed themselves in the house and the adjoining streets, and
intended to pay a second visit to all the lodgers
of the house. On these statements I judged that it
was imperative on me to get away, for they would
doubtlessly this time ransack all the apartments.

The Fossé family, like many other of the work-people
of Paris, used to sup at a wine-shop in the vicinity,
where they carried their provisions, and it was agreed
that I should seize on that moment to go out with
them. Till night I had time to form my plans, and
was first occupied with thinking how I should obtain
intelligence of Annette, when Fossé undertook this for
me. It would have been the height of imprudence to
have communicated directly with her, and he thus contrived it. He went into the Rue de Grammont, where
he bought a-pie, into which he introduced the note
that follows:

"I am in safety. Be careful of yourself, and trust
no one. Do not attend to promises from persons who
have neither the intention nor the power of serving
you. Confine yourself to these four words: 'I do
not know.' Play the fool, which will be the best proof
of your sense. I cannot meet you; but when you go

out, always go through the Rue St Martin and the Boulevards. Mind, do not return; I will answer for all."

The pie, entrusted to a messenger of the Place Vendôme, and addressed to madame Vidocq, fell, as I
had foreseen, into the hands of the agents, who allowed it to be delivered, after having read the dispatch;
and·thus I attained two ends at once, that of deceiving
them, by persuading them that I was not in that quarter, and that of assuring Annette that I was out of
danger. My expedient succeeded, and emboldened by
my first success, I was more calm in making preparations for my retreat. Some money, which I had
snatched by chance from my night-table, served to
procure me pantaloons, stockings and shoes, a frock,
and a blue cotton cap, intended to complete my disguise.
When supper-hour came, I left the room with all the
family, carrying on my head, as a precaution, a large
dish of harrico mutton, the appetizing fumes of which
sufficiently explained the intent of our excursion. My
heart did not beat less anxiously when I met, face to
face on the second floor, a police-officer, whom I did
not at first perceive, as he was ensconced in a corner.
" Put out your candle," cried he, abruptly to Fossé.
" Why?" replied he, who had only taken a light that it
might not awaken suspicion. " Go along, and ask no
questions," said the fellow, blowing out the candle
himself. I could have hugged him! In the passage
we met several of his comrades, who, more polite than
he, made way for us to pass. At length we got out, and
the moment we turned the angle of the street, Fossé
took the dish from me, and we parted. That I might
not attract attention, I walked very slowly to the Rue
des Fontaines; but when once there, I did not amuse
myself, as the Germans say, in counting my buttons,
but directed my steps towards the Boulevard of the
Temple, and running rapidly, reached the Rue de
Bondy, without thinking of asking where I was.

However, it was not enough to have escaped a first

pursuit; for doubtless other searches more active would be instituted. It was necessary to mislead the police, whose numerous blood-hounds, according to custom, would leave all other business, and occupy themselves solely in hunting for me. At this critical juncture I resolved to make use of those persons for my safety whom I considered as my denouncers. These were the Chevaliers, whom I had seen on the previous evening, and who in conversation had dropped some of those words which make no impression at the time, but which we reflect upon afterwards. Convinced that I had no terms to keep henceforward with these wretched beings, I determined to avenge myself on them, whilst I compelled them to refund all that I could enforce from them. It was on a tacit understanding that I had obliged them; and they had violated the faith of treaties, even against their own interest; they had done wrong; and I intended to punish them for having mistaken their own interest.

The road is not far from the Boulevard to the Rue de l'Echiquier, and I fell like a bomb-shell on Chevalier's domicile, whose surprise at seeing me at liberty confirmed my suspicions. He pretended at first an excuse for going out; but, double-locking the door, and putting the key in my pocket, I seized on a knife lying on the table, and told my brother-in-law that if he uttered a cry it was all over with him and his family. This threat could not fail to produce the due effect: I was with people who knew me, and who feared the violence of my despair. The women were more dead than alive, and Chevalier, petrified and motionless as the stone-vessel on which he leant, asked me, with a faint voice what I wanted from him? "You shall know," answered I.

I began by asking for a complete suit of clothes, with which I had provided him the month previously, and he gave it to me: I made him also give me a shirt, boots and a hat; all of which having been purchased with my means, my demand was only for restitution. Chevalier did all this with a stern look, and I thought I read in his eyes the meditation of some project; it might be that he intended to let his neighbours know by some means the embarrassment into which my presence threw him, and prudence demanded that I should ensure a retreat in case of a nocturnal visit. A window, looking on a garden, was closed by two iron bars; I ordered Chevalier to take one of them out; and as, in spite of my directions, he was exceedingly awkward about it, I took the work in hand myself, without his perceiving that I had laid down the knife which had inspired him with so much fear. The operation ended, I again took up the weapon: "And now," said I to him and the terrified women, "you may go to bed." As for me, I was hardly inclined to sleep, and threw myself into a chair, where I passed a very agitated night. All the vicissitudes of my life passed in review before me, and I did not doubt that a curse hung over me: in vain did I fly from crime, crime came to seek me; and this fatality, against which I struggled with all the energy of my character, seemed to delight in overturning my plans of conduct, in incessantly placing me in contact with infamy and imperious necessity.

At break of day I roused Chevalier, and asked him what money he had, and on his replying that he only had a few pieces of money I desired him to take four silver knives and forks, which I had given him to take his permit of residence, and to follow me. I had no need of him, but it would have been dangerous to leave him at home, for he might have informed the police, and directed them on my route, before I had concerted my plans. Chevalier obeyed, and I was not very fearful of the women, as I took so precious a hostage with me; and as, besides, they did not precisely partake of his feelings. I contented myself on going out by double-locking the door, and we reached the Champs Elysées by the most deserted streets of the capital, even in day-time. It was four o'clock in the morning, and we met nobody. I carried the knives and forks, which I took good care not to trust to my companion, as I wanted to get off without inconvenience in case he should turn upon me or create a disturbance. Fortunately he was very quiet, for I had the terrible knife, and Chevalier, who never reasoned, felt persuaded that at the least motion he should make, I would stab him to the heart; and this salutary dread, which he felt the more deeply as it was not undeserved, kept him in check.

We walked for some time in the environs, and Chevalier, who did not foresee how this was to end, walked mechanically beside me, like one bewildered and idiotic. At eight o'clock I made him get into a coach and conducted him to the passage of the wood of Boulogne, where he pledged, in my presence, and under his own name, the four knives and forks, on which they lent him a hundred francs. I took the sum, and, satisfied with having so conveniently recovered in a lump what he had exorted from me in detail, I got into the coach with him once more, which I stopped at the Place de la Concorde. There I alighted, after having given him this piece of advice—"Mind and be more circumspect than ever; if I am arrested, whoever is the cause, look to yourself." I desired the coachman to drive on to Rue de l'Echiquier, No. 23; and to be sure that he took no other direction, I remained for a short time on the watch; and then jumping into a cabriolet, I went to a clothesman of the Croix-Rouge, who gave me the clothes of a workman in exchange for my own. In this new costume I walked towards the Esplanade des Invalides, to learn if it were possible to purchase a uniform of this etablishment. A wooden-legged man, whom I questioned, directed me to Rue St Dominique, where, at a broker's, I should find a complete outfit. This broker was, it appeared, a chattering fellow. "I am not inquisitive," said he— (that is the preamble to all impertinent enquiries)— "You have all your limbs; I presume the uniform is not for yourself."—" It is," said I; and as he testified astonishment, I added that I was going to act in a play. —" And in what piece ?"—" In l'Amour Filial."

The bargain concluded, I immediately set out for Passy, where, at the house of a friend, I hastened to effect my metamorphose. In less than five minutes I was converted into the most maimed of invalids; my arm laid over the hollow of the breast, and kept close to my body by a girth and the waistband of my breeches, had entirely disappeared; some ribbons introduced into the upper part of one of the sleeves, the end of which was hung to a button in front, joined a stump admirably deceptive, and which made the disguise most efficient; a dye which I used to stain my hair and whiskers black, perfected my disguise, under which I was so sure of misleading the physiognomical knowledge of the observers in the quarter St Martin, that I ventured there that same evening. I learnt that the police not only still kept possession of my abode, but were making an inventory of the goods and furniture. By the number of officers whom I saw going and coming, it was easy to perceive that the search was prosecuted with a renewal of activity very extraordinary at this period, when the vigilant administration was not too zealous unless it were in cases of political arrests. Alarmed at such an appearance of investigation, any one but myself would have judged it prudent to leave Paris without delay, at least for a time. It would have been best perhaps to allow the storm to blow over; but I could not resolve on forsaking Annette in the midst of her troubles, caused by her attachment to me. At this time she must have suffered much; shut up in the depôt of the prefecture, she was placed in solitary confinement for twenty-five days, whence she was only taken to be threatened with being left to rot in St Lazarre, if she would not confess the place of my retreat. But with a dagger at her breast, Annette would not have betrayed me. It may be judged how deeply I was grieved to learn her wretched situation and yet be unable to deliver her. As soon as it depended on me, I hastened to aid her. A friend to whom I had lent a few hundred francs, having returned them to me, I begged him to retain a portion of the sum; and full of hope that the term of her detention would soon expire, since, after all, they had only to reproach her with having lived with a fugitive galley-slave, I prepared to quit Paris, determining, if she was not set at liberty before my departure, that I would let her know, by some means, where I had betaken myself.

I lodged in the Rue Tiquetonne, at the house of a currier, named Bouhin, who undertook, for a compensation, to get for himself a passport which he would give to me. We were exactly alike: he, like me, was fair, with blue eyes, coloured complexion, and, by a singular chance, had on his upper lip a slight cicatrice. He was however shorter than I was, and to increase his height so as to reach mine, he put two or three packs of cards in his shoes. Bouhin had recourse to this expedient; so that, although I could use the strange faculty I had of reducing my height four or five inches, at pleasure, the passport which he procured did not need that I should have recourse to this curtailment of my fair proportions. Provided with this, I was congratulating myself on a resemblance which ensured my liberty, when Bouhin (after I had been at his house eight days) confided to me a secret which made me tremble. He was a forger of false money, and, to give me a sample of his skill, coined in my presence eight five-franc pieces, which his wife passed the same day. It may be believed that the confidence of Bouhin alarmed me.

At first I argued that actually from one moment to another, his passport would become but a bad recommendation in the eyes of the gendarmes; for from the trade he carried on, Bouhin must sooner or later be the object of an arrest; besides, the money I had

given him was but a rash adventure, and it must be
confessed that I had but a small chance of advantage
in personating such a character. This was not all;
considering that this state of suspicion, which, in the
opinion of the judge and of the public is always inse-
parable from the condition of a fugitive galley-slave,
was it not likely that if Bouhin were apprehended as
a coiner, I should be considered as his accomplice?
Justice has committed many errors! Condemned once,
though innocent, who would answer that I should not
a second time be similarly sentenced? The crime
which had been wrongfully imputed to me, inasmuch
as it pronounced me a forger, was nominally the same
species of crime as that which Bouhin had committed.
I saw myself sinking beneath a weight of presumptive
evidence and appearances, such as, perhaps, my counsel, ashamed of undertaking my defence, would conceive necessary to impel him to throw me on the pity
of my judges. I heard my death-sentence pronounced. My fears redoubled when I learnt that Bouhin
had an associate, a doctor, named Terrier, who frequently came to his house. This man had a most
hanging look, and it seemed to me that on only looking at him, all the police-officers in the world would
have suspected and watched him. Without knowing
him, I should have thought that in following him it
would be impossible not to attain the knowledge of
some perpetrated or intended crime. In a word, he
was a bird of ill omen to every place he entered; and
persuaded that his visits would bring mischief to the
house, I persuaded Bouhin to give up a business so
hazardous as that he followed; but the most cogent
reasons prevailed not with him; all I could obtain by
dint of intreaty was, that to avoid giving rise to a search
which would certainly betray me to the police, he
would suspend the making and the passing of money
as long as I should remain with him; but this promise
did not prevent my discovering him two days after.

wards hard at work. This time I thought it best to
address his fellow-labourer, to whom I represented, in
the most glaring colours, the dangers which he ran.
" I see," answered the doctor, " that you are one of
those cowardly fellows of whom there are so great a
number. Suppose we are detected, what then? There
are many others who make their exit at the Place de
Grève, and we are not there yet; for fifteen years I
have used these ' chamber gentlemen' as my bankers,
and nobody has yet doubted me; it will do yet. And
besides, my friend," he added in an ill-humoured tone,
" do you meddle with your own affairs."

After the turn which this discussion took, I saw
that it would be superfluous to continue it, and that I
should do wisely to be on my guard, feeling still more
the necessity of quitting Paris as speedily as possible.
It was Tuesday, and I purposed starting on the following day; but having learnt that Annette would be set
at liberty at the end of the week, I proposed deferring
my departure until her release, when on Friday, about
three o'clock in the morning, I heard a light knock at
the street-door; the nature of the rap, the hour, and
circumstance, all combined to make me think that they
were coming to take me; and saying nothing to Bouhin,
I went out on the staircase, and getting to the top,
I got hold of the gutter, and climbing on the roof,
hastened to conceal myself behind a stack of chimnies.

My presentiments had not deceived me, and in an
instant the house was filled with police-agents, who
searched everywhere. Surprised at not finding me,
and doubtless informed by my clothes, left near my
bed, that I had escaped in my shirt, which would not
allow me to go far, they imagined that I would not
have escaped by the usual way. For want of cavaliers
to send in pursuit of me, they sent for some bricklayers,
who went all over the roof, where I was found and
seized, without the nature of the place allowing me
to offer any resistance, which could only have been

done at the risk of a most perilous leap.   Except a few cuffs, which the agents betowed on me, my arrest offered nothing remarkable.   Conducted to the prefecture, I was interrogated by M. Henry, who remembering perfectly the offer I had made him some months previously, promised to do all in his power to ease my situation; but still I was taken to the Force, and thence to Bicêtre, to await the departure of the next chain of galley-slaves.

CHAPTER XXIII.

A plan of escape—New proposal to M. Henry—My agreement with the police—Important discoveries—Coco Lacour—A band of robbers—The inspectors under lock and key—The old clothes woman and the assassins—A pretended escape.

I BEGAN to grow wearied of escapes and the sort of liberty they procured for me : I did not wish to return to the Bagne ; but I preferred a residence at Toulon to that in Paris, if I were compelled to submit to such creatures as Chevalier, Blondy, Deluc and St Germain. I was in this mood in the midst of a considerable number of these supporters of the galleys, whom I had had but too many opportunities of knowing, when several of them proposed that I should help them in trying for a run through the court of the Bons Pauvres. At any other time the project would have made me smile. I did not decline it; but I studied it like a man who considered localities, and so as to preserve for myself that preponderance which my real successes procured for me, and those which were attributed to me—I might say those which I attributed to myself; for as soon as we live amongst rogues, there is always an advantage in passing for the most wicked and the most clever; and such was my well-established reputation, wherever there were four prisoners, at least three had heard of me;—not at all an extraordinary thing, for there were galley-slaves who assumed my name. I was the general to whom all the deeds of his soldiers is attributed; they did not use the places I had taken by assault, but there was no jailor whose vigilance I could not escape, no irons that I could not break through, no wall that I could not penetrate. I was no less famed for courage and skill, and it was the general opinion that I was capable of any deed of renown in case of need. At Brest, at Toulon, at Rochefort, at Anvers, in fact everywhere, I was considered amongst robbers as the most cunning and most bold. The most villanous sought my friendship, because they thought there was still something to be learnt from me, and the greatest novices collected my very words as instructions from which they could gather profit. At Bicêtre, I had a complete court, and they pressed around me, surrounded me, and made tenders of services and kind offers, and expressed regards of which it would be difficult to form an idea. But now, this prison glory was hateful to me : the more I read the soul of malefactors, the more they laid themselves open to me, the more I pitied society for having nourished in its bosom such offspring. I no longer felt that sentiment of the community of misfortune which had formerly inspired my breast; cruel experience and a riper age had convinced me of the necessity of withdrawing myself from these brigands, whose society I loathed, and whose language was an abomination to me. Decided, at any event, to take part against them for the interest of honest men, I wrote to M. Henry to offer my services afresh, without any other condition than that of not being taken back to the Bagne, resigning myself to finish the duration of my sentence in any prison that might be selected.

My letter pointed out so fully the information I could supply, that M. Henry was struck with it : one only consideration balanced with him; it was the example of many accused or condemned persons, who having engaged to guide the police in its searches, had only given but trifling information, or had even finished themselves by being detected in criminal deeds. To this powerful argument, I opposed the cause of my condemnation, the regularity of my conduct after my escapes, the constancy of my endeavours to procure an honorable existence, and finally I produced my correspondence, my books, my punctuality and credit, and I called for the testimony of all persons with whom I had transacted business, and particularly of my creditors, who had all the greatest confidence in me.

Amongst other papers which I produced was the following, which I here transcribe, because it relates to the reasons of my condemnation, at the same time that it proves the steps taken in my favour by the attorney-general Ranson, during my detention at Douai.

"Douai, le 20 Janvier 1809.

"The Attorney-General Imperial at the court of criminal justice of the department of the North,

"Attests, that the said Vidocq was condemned the 7 Nivose, year 5, to eight years of imprisonment for having forged a pardon.

"That it appears that Vidocq was imprisoned on a charge of insubordination, or other military offence, and that the forgery for which he was sentenced was only intended to aid the escape of a fellow-prisoner.

"The attorney-general attests also, that after the deposition taken by him at the office of the Court, the said Vidocq escaped at the moment they were about to transfer him to the Bagne; that he was retaken and again escaped, and being again retaken, M. Ranson, then attorney-general, had the honor of writing to his excellency the minister of justice to consult him on the question, whether the time elapsed from the condemnation of Vidocq to his re-apprehension might count as freeing him from punishment.

"That a first letter being unanswered, M. Ranson wrote several; and Vidocq interpreting the silence of his excellency as unfavourable, again effected an escape.

"The attorney-general cannot give any of these letters, because the registers and papers of M. Ranson, his predecessor, were removed by his family, who have refused to return them to the archives of the court.

"ROSIE."

These facts and documents militated strongly in my favour. M. Henry submitted my proposal to the prefect of the police, M. Pasquier, who decided on granting it. After a residence of two months at Bicêtre, I was removed to the Force; and, to avoid suspicion, it was stated amongst the prisoners, that I was kept back in consequence of being implicated in a very bad affair, which was to be enquired into. This precaution, joined to my renown, put me entirely in good odour. Not a prisoner dared breathe a doubt of the gravity of the charge against me. Since I had shown so much boldness and perseverance to escape from a sentence of eight years in irons, I must of necessity have a conscience charged with some great crime, capable, if I should be discovered as the author, of sending me to the scaffold. It was then whispered, and at last stated openly at the Force, in speaking of me, " He is a cut-throat!" And as, in the place where I was confined, an assassin inspires great confidence, I took care not to refute an error so useful to my plans. I was then far from seeing that an imposture, which I allowed freely to be charged upon me, would be thence perpetuated; and that one day, in publishing my Memoirs, it would be necessary to state that I had never committed murder. Since I have been a subject of con· versation with the public, how many absurd titles have not been disseminated about me! What lies have not been invented to defame me, by agents interested in representing me as a vile wretch! Sometimes the tale runs, that I had been branded and condemned to perpetual labour at the galleys. Sometimes I was only freed from the guillotine, on condition of giving up to the police a certain number of persons every month; and if one was wanting, the bargain was to be declared void: and that was the reason, they affirm, that for want of real delinquents, I selected them at my pleasure. Did they not go so far as to accuse me of having, at the Café Lamblin, put a silver fork in the pocket of a student? I shall have occasion, at a later period, to revert to some of these calumnies, in several chapters in the following volumes; in which I shall develope the system of police, its means, and mysteries: in fact, all that has been revealed to me,—all that I have known.

The engagement I had entered into was not so easily fulfilled as may be supposed. In fact, I had known a crowd of malefactors; but, incessantly decimated by excesses of all sorts,—by justice, by the horrible discipline of bagnes and prisons, by misery,—this hideous generation had passed away with incredible rapidity: a new race occupied the stage, and I was even ignorant of the names of the actors who composed it; I was not even informed of their exploits. A multitude of robbers were then preying on the capital, and it was impossible to furnish the slightest indication of the principal of them; it was only on my ancient renown that I could rely for obtaining any information of the staff of these Bedouins of our civilization: it availed me, I will not say beyond, but equal to what I could desire. Not a robber arrived at the Force, who did not hasten to seek my company, if he had never seen me, to give himself consequence in the eyes of his comrades; it fed his self-love to appear to be on terms of intimacy with me. I encouraged this singular vanity, and thus insensibly made many discoveries; informations came to me in abundance, and I no longer experienced obstacles in acquitting myself of my undertaking.

To give an idea of the influence I had with the prisoners, it is enough to say, that I inoculated them at will with my opinions, my feelings, my sentiments; they thought by, they swore by me. If they happened to take a prejudice against one of the prisoners, because they thought he was what they called 'a sneak,' I had only to answer for him, and he was at once re-established. I was at once a powerful protector and a pledge of freedom, when it was suspected. The first for whom I gave a guarantee, was a young man, ac-

cused of having served the police as a secret agent.
They said, that he had been in the pay of the inspector-general, Veyrat; and they added, going to his
house with an information, he had carried off a basket
of plate.—To rob the inspector's house, was not the
crime, but to lay an information! Such, however,
was the enormous crime imputed to Coco Lacour,
now my successor. Threatened by the whole prison,
driven about, repulsed, ill-treated, not daring to set a
foot in the courts, where he would certainly have been
knocked on the head, Coco came to solicit my protection; and to influence me the more in his favour, he
began by making disclosures to me, which I knew how
to turn to advantage. At first, I employed my credit
in making his peace with the prisoners, who gave up
their projects of vengeance. I could not have rendered
him a more important service; and Coco, as much from
gratitude as a desire of speaking, had soon no secret
from me. One day, he had been before the judge of
instruction: "Faith," said he, on his return, "I am
lucky; none of the plaintiffs recognized me; yet I do
not consider myself as safe: there is amongst them a
devil of a porter, from whom I stole a silver watch.
As I was obliged to talk with him for some time, my
features must have been fixed on his memory; and, if
he be called, he might do me a mischief, by confront-
ing me; and besides, porters are, from their station,
physiognomists." The observation was true; but I
made Coco observe, that it was not likely that they
would discover this man, and that most probably he
would never come of his own accord, since he had not
already done so; and, to confirm him in this opinion,
I spoke to him of the carelessness or idleness of some
people, who do not like to be disturbed. What I said
about this, induced Coco to mention the quarter in
which the owner of the watch lived, and even told me
the number; and this was all I wanted. I took care
not to get so complete a detail as might induce a suspicion of me, and that given at the investigation ap-

peared to me sufficient. I mentioned it to M. Henry,
who thereupon sent out his spies. The result of the
inquiry was as I had foreseen : they found out the
porter; and Coco being confronted with him, was overwhelmed by the evidence, and sentenced by the tribunal to two years' imprisonment.

At this period there was in Paris a band of fugitive
galley-slaves, who daily perpetrated robberies, without
any hope being entertained of putting a termination to
their plunderings.   Many of them had been apprehended, and acquitted for want of evidence; obstinately
entrenched in absence of witnesses, they had long
braved the attempts of justice, which could neither
oppose to them the testimony of the commission of
crime, nor proofs of guilt. To surprise them properly,
it would have been necessary to know their domicile;
and they were so well concealed, that discovery seemed
impossible.   Amongst them was one named France
(called Tormel), who, on coming to the Force, had
nothing more urgent than to ask me for ten francs, to
pay his footing, and I was not inclined to refuse his
demand. He soon came to join me, and feeling obliged
to me, did not hesitate to give me his confidence.   At
the time of his arrest he had concealed two notes of
a thousand francs, from the police, which he gave to
me, begging me to advance him money, from time to
time, as he needed it.   " You do not know me," said
he, " but these bills speak for me; I trust them to
you, because I know they are better in your hands
than in mine; some time or other we will change
them, which now would be difficult, and we must
wait." I agreed with France, as he wished; I promised to be his banker, as I risked nothing.

Apprehended for violent burglary at an umbrella
shop in the passage Feydeau, France had been often
interrogated, and constantly declared that he had no
residence. However, the police had learnt that he had
an abode; and it was the more interesting to learn it,
as it would lead to discovery of instruments of rob-

bery, as well as a great quantity of stolen goods. It was a detection of the highest importance, since it would adduce most material proofs. M. Henry told me that he relied on me for obtaining this information; I manœuvred accordingly, and soon learnt that at the time of his arrest, France was at the corner of the Rue Montmartin and the Rue Notre-Dame des Victoires, in an apartment let by a female receiver of stolen goods, named Josephine Bertrand.

These proofs were positive, but it was difficult to make use of the information without betraying my share in the business to France, who, having only confessed to me, could only suspect me of betraying him. I, however, succeeded; and so little did he suspect that I had abused his confidence, that he told me all his troubles, in proportion as the plan which I had concerted with M. Henry progressed. Besides, the police was so arranged, that they seemed only to be guided by chance, and thus were the arrangements made.

They gained over to their interest one of the lodgers of the house which France had inhabited; and this lodger told the landlord, that, for about three weeks, no movement was seen in the apartment of madame Bertrand; and this awakened and afforded a wide field for conjecture. It was remembered that a person went frequently in and out of this apartment; his absence was talked of, and it was a matter of astonishment that he was not seen: the word disappearance was mentioned, and thence the necessity of the intervention of the commissary; then the opening the door in presence of witnesses; then the discovery of a great number of stolen property belonging to the neighbourhood, and many of the instruments made use of to consummate these robberies. The next enquiry was, what had become of Josephine Bertrand? and all the persons were visited to whom she had referred when she hired the apartments, but nothing could be learnt of this woman; only that a girl, named Lambert, who had succeeded her in the apartment of the Rue Mont-

martre, had just been apprehended; and as this girl
was known as France's mistress, it was conjectured
that these two had a common residence.   France was
in consequence conducted to the spot, and recognized
by the neighbours. He pretended that he had been taken
by surprise, and that they were mistaken, but the jury
before whom he was taken decided otherwise, and he
was condemned to the gallies for eight years.

France once convicted, it was easy to follow up the
traces of his comrades, two of whom were named Fossard and Legagneur.   They were watched, but the
negligence and want of address in the officers enabled
them to escape the pursuit which I directed.   The
former was a man the more dangerous, as he was very
skilful in making false keys.   For fifteen months he
seemed to defy the police, when one day I learnt that
he resided with a hair-dresser in Rue du Temple,
facing the common sewer. To apprehend him from
home was almost impossible, for he was skilful in disguises, and could detect an officer a hundred paces off;
on the other hand, it would be better to seize him in
the midst of his professional apparatus, and the produce of his robberies.   But the undertaking presented
obstacles : Fossard never answered when they knocked
at his door, and it was most likely that he had a means
of egress and facilities for getting over the roofs.   It
appeared to me, that the only mode of seizing him
was to profit by his absence, and hide in his lodging.
M. Henry was of my opinion; and the door being
broken open in the presence of a commissary, three
agents placed themselves in a closet adjoining a recess.
Nearly seventy-two hours elapsed, and nobody arrived;
at the end of the third day, the officers having exhausted their provisions, were going away, when they
heard a key turn in the lock, and Fossard entered.
Immediately two of the officers, in conformity with
their instructions, darted from the closet and threw
themselves upon him; but Fossard, arming himself
with a knife which they had left on the table,

frightened them so, that they themselves opened the door which their comrade had closed; and, having turned the key upon them, Fossard quickly descended the staircase, leaving the three agents all the leisure necessary for drawing up a report, in which nothing was wanting except the circumstance of the knife, which they were very cautious in mentioning. We shall see, in the progress of these Memoirs, how, in 1814, I contrived to arrest Fossard; and the particulars of this expedition are not the least interesting of these Memoirs.

Before being sent to the Conciergerie, France, who had never ceased to think me staunch, recommended one of his friends to me, named Legagneur, a fugitive galley-slave, arrested in the Rue de la Mortellerie, at the moment when he was executing a robbery by the aid of false keys; and this man, deprived of all resource in consequence of the departure of his comrade, was thinking of sending for the money which he had deposited with a receiver of stolen goods in the Rue St Dominique, at the Gros-Caillou. Annette, who came constantly to see me at the Force, and sometimes ably abetted me in my pursuits, was charged with the commission; but either from distrust, or a desire to retain it for himself, the receiver received the messenger very ungraciously; and as she insisted, he threatened her with an arrest. Annette returned to tell us that she had failed in her errand. At this information Legagneur would have denounced the receiver, but that was only the first impulse of anger. Growing more calm, he judged it most fitting to defer his vengeance; and, moreover, to make it turn to his profit. " If I denounce him," said he to me, " not only shall I get nothing by it, but he may contrive to appear not at all in fault. It will be best to wait until I get out, and then I will make him squeak." Legagneur, having no farther hope from his receiver, determined to write to two accomplices, Marguerit and Victor Desbois, renowned robbers. Convinced of this old truism, that small presents preserve friendship, in exchange for the aid he asked from them, he sent them the impressions of the locks which he had taken for his own private use. Legagneur again had recourse to the mediation of Annette, who found the two friends at Rue Deux-Ponts, on a wretched ground floor, a place where they never met without taking great previous precaution. It was not their residence. Annette, whom I had desired to do all in her power to learn this, had the sense not to lose sight of them. She followed them for two days, under different disguises; and, on the third, informed me that they slept in the small Rue St Jean, in a house with gardens behind. M. Henry, to whom I communicated this circumstance, arranged all the necessary measures which the nature of the place required; but his officers were not more courageous, nor more skilful, than those from whom Fossard had escaped. The two robbers saved themselves by the gardens, and it was not till some time afterwards that they were apprehended in the Rue St Hyacinthe St Michel.

Legagneur having been in his turn conducted to the Conciergerie, was replaced in my room by the son of a vintner at Versailles, named Robin, who united with the thieves of the capital, told me in our conversations, their arrangements, as well concerning all that had been done, as of their present state and intended plans. He it was who pointed out to me the prisoner Mardargent as a fugitive galley-slave, whilst he was only detained in custody as a deserter; for this latter crime he had been sentenced to twenty-four years labour at the galleys: he had passed some time in the Bagne; and by the help of my notes and recollections, we were soon excellent friends: he fancied (and he was not mistaken) that I should be delighted to meet again my old companions in misfortune; he pointed out several amongst the prisoners, and I was fortunate enough to send back to the galleys a considerable number of those individuals whom justice, for want of the necessary

P

proofs for their conviction, might have let loose upon social life.

Never had any period been marked with more important discoveries than that which ushered in my debût in the service of the police; although scarcely enrolled in this administration, I had already done much for the safety of the capital, and even for the whole of France. Were I to relate half my successes in my new department, my readers' patience would be exhausted, I will simply make mention of an adventure which occurred a few months before I quitted the prison, and which deserves to be rescued from the general oblivion.

One afternoon a tumult arose in the court, which terminated in a violent pugilistic combat; at this hour in the day such occurrences were very frequent, but in the present case there was as much ground for astonishment as if a duel had been fought between Orestes and Pylades. The two champions were Blignon and Charpentier, (called Chante à l'heure), known to live in that disgusting intimacy which has no excuse, even the most rigorous seclusion. A violent quarrel had arisen between them; it was said that jealousy had sprung up to disunite them: however this may be, when the action had ceased, Chante à l'heure, covered with contusions, entered the drinking shop to have his bruises fomented. I was there engaged at my game of piquet. Chante à l'heure, irritated with his defeat, was no longer master of himself; and as the brandy he had called for to wash his hurts, found its way almost unconsciously to his mouth instead, he became proportionably energetic; until at last his mind could no longer contain the angry burst of his feelings. " My good friend," said he to me, ("for you are my very good friend) do you see how this beggar of a Blignon has served me? But he shall not go off scot-free !"

" Oh, never heed him," I replied; " he is stronger than you, and you must mind what you are about. Do you wish to be half killed a second time?"

" Oh, that is not what I mean. If I choose, I can put a stop to his beating me, or any one else again. I know what I know!"

" Well, and what do you know?" cried I, struck by the tone in which he pronounced these last words.

" Yes, yes," answered Chante à l'heure, highly exasperated; " he has done well in driving me to this : I have only to blab, and his business is settled."

" Nonsense; hold your tongue," said I, affecting not to believe him; " you are both birds of a feather. When you owe any one a spite, you have only to blow at his head, and he would instantly fall."

" You think so, do you?" said Chante à l'heure, striking the table. " Suppose I told you that he had slit a woman's weasand!"

" Not so loud, Chante à l'heure; not so loud," said I, putting my finger significantly on my lips. " You know very well that at Lorcefée (La Force) walls have ears ; and you must not turn nose against a comrade."

" What do you call turning nose," replied he, the more irritated in proportion as I feigned a wish to stop him from speaking; " when I tell you that it only depends on me to split upon him in another case."

" That is all very well," I replied ; " but to bring a man before the big wigs, we must have proofs !"

" Proofs! Does the devil's child ever want them? Listen. You know the little shopkeeper who lives near the Pont Notre-Dame?"

" An old procuress, mistress of Chatonnet, and wife of the hump-backed man ?"

" The same! Well, three months ago, as Blignon and I were blowing a cloud quietly in a boozing ken of the Rue Planche-Mibray, she came there to us. ' There's swag for you, my lads,' said she, 'not far off, in the Rue de la Sonnerie ! You are boys of mettle, and I will put you on the lay. An old dowager who has been pocketing lots of blunt ; a few days since she received fifteen or twenty thousand francs, in notes or gold; she often comes home in the darkey, and you must slit her windpipe; and when you have prigged the chink, fling her into the river.' At first we did not relish the proposition, and would not hear of it, as we never cared to commit a murder; but the old hag so pestered us by telling us that she was well feathered, and that there was no harm in doing for an old woman, that we agreed to it. It was settled that the procuress should give us notice of the precise right time and hour. However, I felt very I don't-know-howish about it; because, you see, when you are not used to a job of the kind, you feel queerish a bit. But, never mind, all was settled; when next morning, at the Quatre-Cheminées, near Sevres, we met with Voivenel and another pal. Blignon told the business to them, at the same time stating his objection to the murder. They thereupon proposed to give us a hand if we chose. ' Agreed,' replied Blignon: ' where there is enough for two, there is enough for four :' thus we settled it, and they were to be in the rig with us. From that time Voivenel's pal never let us rest, and was impatient for the arrival of the moment. At length the old mother Murder-love told us all was ready. It was a thick fog on the night of the 30th of December. ' Now's the time !' said Blignon. Believe me or not, as you like; but on the word of a thief I would have backed out, but I could not; I was drawn on, and dogged the old woman with the others; and in the evening when, having as we knew, received a considerable sum, she was returning from the house of M. Rousset, a person who let out carriages, in the Alley de la Pompe, we did for her. It was Voivenel's friend who stabbed her, whilst Blignon, having blinded her with his cloak, seized her from behind. I was the only one who did not dabble in her blood, but I saw all, for I was put on the look-out: and I then learnt, and saw, and heard enough to give that scoundrel Blignon his passport to the guillotine."

Chante à l'heure then, with an insensibility which

exceeds belief, detailed to me all the minutest circumstances of this murder. I heard this abominable recital to the close, making incredible efforts to conceal my indignation; for every word which he uttered was of a nature to make the hair stand on end of even the least susceptible person. When the villain had finished retracing, with a horrible fidelity, the agonies of his victim, I urged him anew not to break off his friendship with Blignon: but at the same time I dexterously threw oil on the fire I appeared solicitous to extinguish. My plan was to lead Chante à l'heure to make a public confession of the horrible revelation to which rage and revenge had spurred him on. I was further desirous of being enabled to furnish justice with those means of conviction which would be necessary to punish the assassins. Much yet remained in uncertainty; possibly, after all, this affair was merely the fruits of an over-heated brain, and Chante à l'heure when no longer under the influence of wine and vengeance, might disavow all recollection of it. However the business might terminate, I lost no time in dispatching to M. Henry a report, in which I explained the affair, as well as the doubts I myself entertained of its veracity; he was not long in replying to my communication, that the crime I alluded to was but too true. M. Henry begged I would endeavour to procure for him the precise account of everything which had preceded and followed this murder; and the very next day my plans were laid to obtain them. It was difficult to procure the arrest of any of the guilty party, without their suspecting the hand which directed the blow; but in this dilemma, as well as in many others in which I had been placed, chance came to my assistance. The following day I went to awaken Chante à l'heure, who, still suffering from the intemperance of the preceding night, was unable to quit his bed; I seated myself beside him, and began to speak of the state of complete intoxication in which I had seen him, as well as of the indiscreet actions he had committed, the reproof appeared to astonish him, but when I repeated a few words of the conversation we had held together, his surprise redoubled, and as I had foreseen, he protested the impossibility of his having used such language; and whether he had effectually lost his recollection, or whether he mistrusted me, he tried hard to persuade me that he had not the slightest remembrance of what had passed. Whether he at this moment spoke the truth, or not, I profited by it to tell him that he had not confined his confidential communications to one alone, but had spoken of all the circumstances of the murder in a loud tone, in the presence of several prisoners who were sitting near the fire, and had heard all that had passed as well myself. " What an unlucky fellow I am," cried he, with every sign of sincere distress. " What have I done ? What is to be done to extricate myself from the situation in which it places me?"—" Nothing is more simple," said I; " if you should be questioned as to the scene of yesterday, you can say, ' Upon my word, when I have taken too much drink, I say or do anything; and if I happen to have a spite against a man, I do not now what I might invent about him.' " Chante à l'heure took all this for genuine advice; but on the same morning, a man named Pinson, who passed for a great sneak, was conducted from La Force to the office of the préfet : this exchange could not have occurred more opportunely for my project, and I hastened to acquaint Chante à l'heure with it, adding that all the prisoners believed the Pinson was only removed in the expectation of his making some very important discoveries.

At this intelligence he appeared thunderstruck: " Was he one of those who were present when I was talking the other night?" asked he with strong anxiety. I replied that I had not particularly observed; he then communicated to me more frankly his fears, and I obtained from him fresh particulars, which, sent off without delay to M. Henry, caused all the accomplices in this murder to fall into the hands of justice; the shopkeeper and her husband were of the number. They were all committed to solitary confinement; Blignon and Chante à l heure in the new building, the others in the infirmary, where they remained a very long time. The public authorities had enquired into it, and I no longer troubled myself with the affair. Nothing material resulted from the investigation, which had been badly begun from the first, and finally the accused were pardoned. My abode at Bicêtre and La Force embraced a point of twenty-one months, during which not a single day passed without my rendering some important service. I believe I might have become a perpetual spy, so far was every one from supposing that any connivance existed between the agents of the public authority and myself. Even the porters and keepers were in ignorance of the mission with which I was entrusted. Adored by the thieves, esteemed by the most determined bandits (for even these hardened wretches have a sentiment which they call esteem), I could always rely on their devotion to me ; they would have been torn to pieces in my service, a proof of which occurred at Bicêtre, where Mardargent, of whom I have before spoken, had several severe battles with some of the prisoners who had dared to assert that I had I had only quitted La Force to serve the police. Coco-Lacour and Goreau, prisoners in the same jail as incorrigible thieves, with no less ardour and generous intrepidity undertook my defence. Perhaps at that time they might have taxed me with ingratitude, that I did not evince to them any greater partiality than I showed to others; but my duty was imperious. Let them now receive the tribute of my gratitude ; they have had a more powerful influence than they imagine in the advantages which society has derived from my services.

M. Henry did not allow the préfet to remain in ignorance of the numerous discoveries effected by my sagacity. This functionary, to whom I was represented as a person on whom he might depend, consented at last to put an end to my detention. Every measure was taken that it might not be known that I had recovered my liberty; they sent to fetch me from La Force, and carried me from thence without neglecting any of their rigorous precautions. My handcuffs were replaced, and I ascended the wicker car with the private understanding that I was to escape on the road, and I was not slow in profiting by this permission. The same night my flight was made known, and all the police were in search of me. This escape caused much noise, particularly at La Force, where my friends celebrated it with rejoicings, drank to my health, and wished me a safe and prosperous journey.

CHAPTER XXIV.

M. Henry, surnamed the Evil Spirit—MM. Bertaux and Parisot —A word respecting the police—My first capture—Bouhin and Terrier are arrested upon my information.

THE names of baron Pasquier and M. Henry will never be effaced from my recollection; these two generous men were my liberators; how many thanks do I not owe them! They restored me more than my life; for them I would cheerfully sacrifice it; and the reader will believe me, when he learns that I have frequently exposed it to obtain from them a single word, or a glance of satisfaction. I breathed once more the air of liberty; my blood flowed freely through my veins; I no longer feared anything. The secret agent of government, I had duties marked out, and the kind and respectable M. Henry took upon himself to instruct me in their fulfilment; for in his hands were entrusted nearly the entire safety of the capital : to prevent crimes, discover malefactors, and to give them up to justice, were the principal functions confided to me. The task was difficult to perform. M. Henry kindly guided my first steps; he smoothed the difficulties of it for me; and if in the end I acquired some celebrity in the police, I owe it to his counsels, as well as to the excellent lessons I received from him. Gifted with a cool and reflective character, M. Henry possessed, in its utmost perfection, that tact of observation which can detect culpability under the greatest appearance of innocence : he had an astonishing memory; an acute penetration, from which nothing escaped; added to which, he was an excellent judge of countenances. By thieves he was styled the Evil Spirit; and well did he merit the surname, for with him, cunning and suavity of manners were so conjoined as seldom to fail in their purpose. Rarely indeed did a criminal, interrogated by him, quit his closet without having confessed his crime, or given, unknown to himself, some clue by which to convict him. With M. Henry it was a sort of instinct which conducted him to the discovery of truth; it was not an acquired possession; and whosoever might have sought to assume his manner, to obtain the same results, would find himself continually perplexed and uncertain; for, cameleon-like, he changed with every circumstance, and varied with each character with whom he had to deal. Devoted to the duties of his post, he, in a manner, lived but for it, and was at all times accessible to the public business. It was not necessary under his management to wait till the hour of twelve before his offices were open to receive complaints, or, according to the present practice, to wait for hours in an antichamber ere an audience could be obtained. Industrious and persevering, no species of fatigue disheartened him; and to this undeviating course of life may be attributed the many infirmities with which he was afflicted, when, at the close of thirty-five years hard service, he retired from office. I have frequently seen him passing two or three nights, in the week, and the greater part of his time, meditating upon the instructions he was about to give me, or to effect the prompt repression of crimes of every species. Illnesses (and he had many very severe ones) were scarcely permitted to interrupt his labours; it was only when carried into his study that he would listen to the directions of his physicians. In a word, he was a man, such as there are but very few, if indeed there exist any, like him; his very name was a terror to offenders, and when brought before him, audacious as they were, they trembled and became confused; they blundered in their answers, firmly believing that equivocation or denial was useless with one whom they firmly imagined had the power of reading their most inward thoughts.

One remark which I have often had occasion to make is, that efficient men are always the best seconded; perhaps in verification of the old proverb, that " birds of a feather flock together." I leave the decision of the point to wiser heads than mine; but this I know, that M. Henry had coadjutors worthy of him; amongst the number was M. Bertaux, a cross-examiner of great merit, whose particular talent consisted in sifting a thing to the bottom, however intricate it might appear. The proofs of his talent may be found in the archives of the court. Next to him, I have great pleasure in naming M. Parisot, governor of the prisons. In a word, MM. Henry, Bertaux, and Parisot, formed a veritable triumvirate, which was incessantly conspiring against the perpetrators of all manner of crimes; to extirpate rogues from Paris, and to procure for the inhabitants of this immense city a perfect security: such was their mutual aim, their only thought, and the effects amply repaid them for the attempt. It is true, that there existed at this time amongst the heads of the police, a frankness, an unanimity, and a cordiality, which have disappeared in the last five or six years. In the present day, chiefs or subalterns mistrust each other; they reciprocally fear and hate each other; a continual state of hostilities is kept up; each dreads in his comrade a foe who will denounce him; there is no longer a sympathy of action in the different departments of the administration : and from whence does this proceed ? Because each man's post and duties are not sufficiently definite. Nothing is distinctly defined; and no person, even of those highest in office, is placed in the department for which he is best fitted. Most usually, the préfet himself, on being elected to fill that important situation, is wholly ignorant of the duties of the police, and yet he ascends at once to the highest rank in it, there to pass through his apprenticeship. In his train follow a crowd of protegés, whose least fault is that of being destitute of decided talent, but who, for want of being equal to other employment, occupy themselves with flattering their patrons, and preventing the truth from reaching their ears. Thus have I seen, from time to time, sometimes under one direction and sometimes under another, the police organized, or rather indeed disorganized, each change of a préfet introducing into it fresh novices, and causing the dismissal of experienced officers. I shall hereafter dwell more at length upon the consequences of these changes, which have originated solely in the desire of bestowing appointments upon the creatures of the last comer. Meanwhile I will resume the thread of my narrative.

So soon as I was installed in my new office of secret agent, I commenced my rounds, in order to take my measures well for setting effectually to work. These journies, which occupied me nearly twenty days, furnished me with many useful and important observations, but as yet I was only preparing to act, and studying my ground.

One morning I was hastily summoned to attend the chief of the division. The matter in hand was to discover a man named Watrin, accused of having fabricated and put in circulation false money and bank notes. The inspectors of the police had already arrested Watrin, but, according to custom, had allowed him to escape. M. Henry gave me every direction which he deemed likely to assist me in the search after him; but unfortunately he had only gleaned a few simple particulars of his usual habits and customary haunts; every place he was known to frequent were freely pointed out to me; but it was not very likely he would be found in those resorts which prudence would call upon him carefully to avoid; there remained therefore only a chance of reaching him by some bye path. When I learnt that he had left his effects in a furnished house, where he once lodged, on the boulevard of Mont Parnasse, I took it for granted that, sooner or later, he would go there in search of

his property; or at least that he would send some
person to fetch it from thence; consequently, I directed all my vigilance to this spot; and after having
reconnoitred the house, I lay in ambush in its vicinity
night and day, in order to keep a watchful eye upon
all comers and goers. This went on for nearly a
week, when, weary of not observing anything, I determined upon engaging the master of the house in
my interest, and to hire an apartment of him, where
I accordingly established myself with Annette, certain
that my presence could give rise to no suspicion. I
had occupied this post. for about fifteen days, when
one evening, at eleven o'clock, I was informed that
Watrin had just come, accompanied by another person.
Owing to a slight indisposition, I had retired to bed
earlier than usual; however, at this news I rose
hastily, and descended the staircase by four stairs at
a time; but whatever diligence I might use, I was only
just in time to catch Watrin's companion; him I had
no right to detain, but I made myself sure that I
might, by intimidation, obtain further particulars
from him. I therefore seized him, threatened him,
and soon drew from him a confession, that he was a
shoemaker, and that Watrin lived with him, No. 4
Rue des Mauvais Garçons. This was all I wanted to
know: I had only had time to slip an old great coat
over my shirt, and, without stopping to put on more
garments, I hurried on to the place thus pointed out
to me. I reached the house at the very instant that
some person was quitting it: persuaded that it was
Watrin, I attempted to seize him; he escaped from
me, and I darted after him up a staircase; but at the
moment of grasping him, a violent blow which struck
my chest drove me down twenty stairs. I sprung
forward again, and that so quickly, that to escape
from my pursuit he was compelled to return into the
house through a sash window. I then knocked loudly
at the door, summoning him to open it without delay.
This he refused to do. I then desired Annette (who

Q

had followed me) to go in search of the guard, and whilst she was preparing to obey me, I counterfeited the noise of a man descending the stairs. Watrin, deceived by this feint, was anxious to satisfy himself whether I had actually gone, and softly put his head out of window to observe if all was safe. This was exactly what I wanted. I made a vigorous dart forwards, and seized him by the hair of his head: he grasped me in the same manner, and a desperate struggle took place: jammed against the partition wall which separated us, he opposed me with a determined resistance. Nevertheless, I felt that he was growing weaker; I collected all my strength for a last effort; I strained every nerve, and drew him nearly out of the window through which we were struggling: one more trial and the victory was mine; but in the earnestness of my grasp we both rolled on the passage floor, on to which I had pulled him: to rise, snatch from his hands the shoemaker's cutting-knife with which he had armed himself, to bind him and lead him out of the house, was the work of an instant. Accompanied only by Annette, I conducted him to the prefecture, where I received the congratulations first of M. Henry, and afterwards those of the prefect of police, who bestowed on me a pecuniary recompense. Watrin was a man of unusual address; he followed a coarse clumsy business, and yet he had given himself up to making counterfeit money, which required extreme delicacy of hand. Condemned to death, he obtained a reprieve the very hour that was destined for his execution; the scaffold was prepared; he was taken down from it, and the amateurs of such scenes experienced a disappointment. All Paris remembers it. A report was in circulation that he was about to make some very important discoveries; but as he had nothing to reveal, a few days afterwards he underwent his sentence.

Watrin was my first capture, and an important one too; this successful beginning awoke the jealousy of the peace-officers, as well as those under my orders; all were exasperated against me, but in vain; they could not forgive me for being more successful than themselves. The superiors, on the contrary, were highly pleased with my conduct; and I redoubled my zeal to render myself still more worthy their confidence.

About this period a vast number of counterfeit five-franc pieces had got into general circulation; several of them were shown to me; whilst examining them, I fancied I could discover the workmanship of Bouhin (who had informed against me) and of his friend, doctor Terrier. I resolved to satisfy my mind as to the truth of this; and in consequence of this determination, I set about watching the steps of these two individuals; but as I durst not follow them too closely, lest they might recognise me, and mistrust my observation, it was difficult for me to obtain the intelligence I wanted. Nevertheless, by dint of unwearied perseverance, I arrived at the certainty of my not having mistaken the matter, and the two coiners were arrested in the very act of fabricating their base coin; they were shortly after condemned and executed for it. It has been publicly asserted, in consequence of a report set on foot by the inspectors of the police, that Dr Terrier had been led away by me, and that I had in a manner placed in his hands the instruments of his crime.

Let the reader remember the reply which this man made to me, when, at Bouhin's house, I sought to persuade him to renounce his guilty industry, and he will judge whether Terrier was a man to allow himself to be drawn away.

CHAPTER XXV.

I again meet St Germain—He proposes to me the murder of
two old men—The plunderers—The grandson of Cartouche—
A short account of instigating agents—Great perplexities—
Annette again aids me—An attempt to rob the house of a
banker in the Rue Hauteville—I am killed—Arrest of St
Germain and his accomplice Boudin—Portraits of these two
assassins.

In so populous a capital as that of Paris, there are
usually a vast many places of bad resort, at which
assemble persons of broken fortune and ruined fame;
in order to judge of them under my own eye, I frequented every house and street of ill fame, sometimes
under one disguise and sometimes under another,
assuming indeed all those rapid changes of dress and
manner which indicated a person desirous of concealing himself from the observation of the police, till
the rogues and thieves whom I daily met there firmly
believed me to be one of themselves; persuaded of my
being a runaway, they would have been cut to pieces
before I should have been taken; for not only had I
acquired their fullest confidence, but their strongest
regard; and so much did they respect my situation, as
a fugitive galley-slave, that they would not even propose to me to join in any of their daring schemes, lest
it might compromise my safety.   All however did not
exercise this delicacy, as will be seen hereafter.   Some
months had passed since I commenced my secret investigations, when chance threw in my way St Germain, whose visits had so often filled me with consternation. He had with him a person named Boudin,
whom I had formerly seen as a restaurateur in Paris,
in the Rue des Prouvaires, and of whom I knew no
more than that trifling acquaintance which arose from
my occasionally exchanging my money for his dinners.
He however seemed easily to recollect me, and, ad-

dressing me with a bold familiarity, which my determined coolness seemed unable to subdue, " Pray," said
he, " have I been guilty of any offence towards you,
that you seem so resolved upon cutting me ? "—" By
no means, sir," replied I; " but I have been informed
that you have been in the service of the police."—
" Oh, oh, is that all ?" cried he, " never mind that,
my boy; suppose I have, what then? I had my
reasons; and when I tell you what they were, I am
quite sure you will not bear me any ill will for it."—
" Come, come," said St Germain, " I must have you
good friends; Boudin is an excellent fellow, and I
will answer for his honour, as I would do for my own.
Many a thing happens in life we should never have
dreamt of, and if Boudin did accept the situation you
mention, it was but to save his brother: besides, you
must feel satisfied, that were his principles such as a
gentleman ought not to possess, why, you would not find
him in my company." I was much amused with this
excellent reasoning, as well as with the pledge given
for Boudin's good faith: however, I no longer sought
to avoid the conversation of Boudin. It was natural
enough that St Germain should relate to me all that
had happened to him since his last disappearance,
which had given me such pleasure.

After complimenting me on my flight, he informed
me that after my arrest he had recovered his employment, which he however was not fortunate enough to
keep; he lost it a second time, and had since been
compelled to trust to his wits to procure a subsistence.
I requested he would tell me what had become of
Blondy and Deluc ? " What," said he, " the two who
slit the waggoner's throat ? Oh, why the guillotine
settled their business at Beauvais." When I learnt
that these two villains had at length reaped the just
reward of their crimes, I experienced but one regret,
and that was, that the heads of their worthless accomplices had not fallen on the same scaffold.

After we had sat together long enough to empty several bottles of wine, we separated. At parting St Germain having observed that I was but meanly clad, enquired what I was doing, and as I carelessly answered that at present I had no occupation, he promised to do his best for me, and to push my interest the first opportunity that offered. I suggested that, as I very rarely ventured out for fear of being arrested, we might not possibly meet again for some time. You can see me, whenever you choose, said he; I shall expect that you will call on me frequently. Upon my promise to do so, he gave me his address, without once thinking of asking for mine.

St Germain was no longer an object of such excessive terror as formerly in my eyes; I even thought it my interest to keep him in sight, for if I applied myself to scrutinizing the actions of suspicious persons, who better than he called for the most vigilant attention? In a word, I resolved upon purging society of such a monster. Meanwhile I waged a determined war with all the crowd of rogues who infested the capital. About this time robberies of every species were multiplying to a frightful extent: nothing was talked of but stolen palisades, out-houses broken open, roofs stripped of their lead; more than twenty reflecting lamps were successively stolen from the Rue Fontaine au Roi, without the plunderers being detected. For a whole month the inspectors had been lying in wait in order to surprise them, and the first night of their discontinuing their vigilance the same depredations took place. In this state, which appeared like setting the police at defiance, I accepted the task which none seemed able to accomplish, and in a very short time (to the great disappointment of all the Arguses of the Quai du Nord) I was enabled to bring the whole band of these shameless plunderers to public justice, which immediately consigned them to the gallies. One amongst them was named Cartouche. I do not know whether the name he bore had any particular influence over him, or whether he possessed any quality peculiar to

his family; probably he might be a descendant of the
celebrated Cartouche. I leave to genealogists the
trouble of deciding the question.

Each day encreased the number of my discoveries.
Of the many who were committed to prison, there were
none who did not owe their arrest to me, and yet not
one of them for a moment suspected my share in the
business. I managed so well, that neither within nor
without its walls, had the slightest suspicion transpired.
The thieves of my acquaintance looked upon me as
their best friend and true comrade; the others esteemed
themselves happy to have an opportunity of initiating
me in their secrets, whether for the pleasure of conversing with me, or in the hope of benefiting by my
counsels. It was principally beyond the barriers that
I met with these unfortunate beings. One day that I
was crossing the outer boulevards, I was accosted by
St Germain, who was still accompanied by Boudin.
They invited me to dinner; I accepted the proposition, and over a bottle of wine they did me the honour
to propose that I should make a third in an intended
murder.

The matter in hand was to dispatch two old men,
who lived together in the house which Boudin had
formerly occupied in the Rue des Prouvaires. Shuddering at the confidence placed in me by these villains,
I yet blessed the invisible hand which had led them
to seek my aid. At first I affected some scruples at entering into the plot, but at last feigned to yield to
their lively and pressing solicitations, and it was
agreed that we should wait the favourite moment
for putting into execution this most execrable project.
This resolution taken, I bade farewell to St Germain
and his companion, and (decided upon preventing the
meditated crime) hastened to carry a report of the affair to M. Henry, who sent me without loss of time to
obtain more ample details of the discovery I had just
made to him. His intention was to satisfy himself
whether I had been really solicited to take part in it,

or whether from a mistaken devotion to the cause
of justice, I had endeavoured to instigate those
unhappy men to an act which would render them
amenable to it. I protested that I had adopted no
such expedient, and as he discovered marks of truth in
my manner and declaration, he expressed himself satisfied. He did not, however, omit to impress on me
the following discourse upon instigating agents, which
penetrated my very heart. Ah, why was it not likewise heard by those wretches, who since the revolution
have made so many victims! The renewed era of le-
gitimacy would not then in some circumstances have
recalled the bloody days of another epoch. "Remember well," said M. Henry to me in conclusion, " remember that the greatest scourge of society is he who
urges another on to the commission of evil. Where there
are no instigators to bad practices, they are committed
only by the really hardened ; because they alone are
capable of conceiving and executing them. Weak
beings may be drawn away and excited : to precipitate
them into the abyss, it frequently requires no more
than to call to your aid their passions or self-love ;
but he who avails himself of their weakness to procure their destruction, is more than a monster—he is
the guilty one, and it is on his head that the sword of
justice should fall. As to those engaged in the police,
they had better remain for ever idle, than create matter
for employment."

Although this lesson was not required in my case,
yet I thanked M. Henry for it, who enjoined me not
to lose sight of the two assassins, and to use every
means in my power to prevent their arriving at the
completion of their diabolical plan. " The police,"
said he, " is instituted as much to correct and punish
malefactors, as to prevent their committing crimes ;
but on every occasion I would wish it to be understood,
that we hold ourselves under greater obligations to that
person who prevents one crime, than to him who pro-
cures the punishment of many." Conformably with

these instructions, I did not allow a single day to pass without seeing St Germain and his friend Boudin. As the blow they meditated was to procure them a considerable quantity of gold, I concluded that I might, without overacting my part, affect a degree of impatience about it. "Well," said I to them, every time we met, " and when is this famous affair to take place?"—" When!" replied St Germain, " the fruit is not yet ripe; when the right time comes," added he, pointing to Boudin, " my friend there will let you know." Already had several meetings taken place, and yet nothing was decidedly arranged; once more I hazarded the usual question. " Ah! ah!" said St Germain, " my good friend, now I can satisfy your natural curiosity; we have fixed upon tomorrow evening, and only waited for you to deliberate upon the best way of going to work." The meeting was fixed a little way out of Paris. I was punctual to the time and place, nor did St Germain keep me waiting. " Hark ye," said he, " we have reflected upon this affair, and find that it cannot be put into execution for the present. We have, however, another to propose to you; and I warn you, you must say at once, without any equivocation, ' yes' or ' no.' Before we enter upon the object of my coming hither, it is but fair I should let you into a little confidential story respecting yourself, which was told to me by one Carré, who knew you at la Force. The tale runs, that you only escaped its walls upon condition of serving the police as its secret agent!"

At the words ' secret agent,' a feeling almost approaching to suffocation stole over me, but I quickly rallied upon perceiving that, however true the report might be, it had obtained but little faith with St Germain, who was evidently waiting for my explanation or denial of it, without once suspecting its reality. My ever ready genius quickly flew to my aid, and without hesitation I replied, " that I was not much surprised

at the charge, and for the simple reason that I myself
had been the first to set the rumour afloat." St Germain stared with wonder. "My good fellow," said I,
"you are well aware that I managed to escape from
the police whilst they were transferring me from la
Force to Bicêtre. Well! I went to Paris, and stayed
there till I could go elsewhere. One must live, you
know, how and where one can. Unfortunately, I am
still compelled to play at hide and seek, and it is only
by assuming a variety of disguises that I dare venture
abroad, to look about and just see what my old friends
are doing; but in spite of all my precautions, I live in
constant dread of many individuals, whose keen eye
quickly penetrated my assumption of other names and
habits than my own; and who, having formerly been
upon terms of familiarity with me, pestered me with
questions I had no other means of shaking off, than by
insinuating that I was in the pay of the police; and
thus I obtained the double advantage of evading in my
character of 'spy,' both their suspicions and ill will,
should they feel disposed to exercise it in the procuring my arrest."

"Enough—enough," interrupted St Germain; "I
believe you; and, to convince you of the unbroken
confidence I place in you, I will let you into the secret
of our plans for to-night.—At the corner of the Rue
d'Enghien, where it joins the Rue Hauteville, lives a
banker, whose house looks out upon a very extensive
garden; a circumstance greatly in favour both of our
expedition and our escape after its completion. This
same banker is now absent, and the cash-box, in which
is a considerable sum in specie, besides bank notes, &c.
is only guarded by two persons—Well, you can guess
the rest. We mean to make it our own, by the law of
possession, this very evening. Three of us are bound
by oath to do the job, which will turn out so profit-
ably, but we want another; and now that you have
cleared your character and given scandal the lie, you

shall make the fourth. Come, no refusal!—we reckon on your company and assistance, and if you refuse, you are a regular set-down sneak."

I was as eager in accepting the invitation as St Germain could possibly be in giving it; both Boudin and himself seemed much pleased with my zeal. Who my remaining coadjutor was I knew not, but my surmises on the subject were soon settled by the arrival of a man, a perfect stranger to myself, named Debenne. He was the driver of a cabriolet, the father of a large family, and a man, who, more from weak than bad principles, had allowed himself to be seduced by the temptations of his guilty companions. Whilst a mixed conversation was going on between them, my thoughts were busily at work upon the best method of causing them to be taken in the very act they were then discussing. What was my consternation to hear St Germain, at the moment we all rose to pay our score, address us in these words:—

" My friends, when a man runs his neck into the compass of a halter, it behoves him to keep a sharp look out. We have this day decided upon playing a dangerous, but, as I take it, a sure game; and in order that the chance may be in our favour, I have determined upon the following measure, which I think you will all approve. About midnight, all four of us will obtain access into the house in question. Boudin and myself will undertake to manage the inside work, whilst you two remain in the garden, ready to second us in case of surprise. This undertaking, if successful, will furnish us with the means of living at our ease for some time; but it concerns our mutual safety, that we should not quit each other till the hour for putting our plan into execution."

This finale, which I feigned not to hear, was repeated a second time, and filled me with a thousand fears that I might not be able to withdraw myself from the affair, as I had intended. What was to be done? St Germain was a man of uncommon daring, eager for

money, and always ready to purchase it either with his
own blood or that of others; however, as yet it was
but ten o'clock in the morning; I hoped that,
during the long interval between that hour and midnight, some opportunity would present itself of dexterously stealing away and giving information to the police.   Meanwhile, I made not the slightest objection
to the proposition of St Germain, which was indeed
the best pledge we could separately have of the good
faith of the others.   When he perceived that we were
all agreed, St Germain, who, by his energy, his talents
for plotting and carrying his schemes into execution,
was the real head of the conspiracy, expressed his
satisfaction, and added further—" this unanimity is
what I like; and I beg to say, that, for myself, I will
leave nothing undone to merit the continuance of so
flattering a consent to my wishes and opinions."

It was agreed that we should take a hackney coach,
and proceed together to his house, situated in the Rue
St Antoine.   Arrived there, we ascended into his
chamber, where he was to keep us under lock and
key until the instant of departure.   Confined between
four walls, in close converse with these robbers, I
knew not what saint to invoke, and what pretext to
invent, to effect my escape.   St Germain would have
blown out my brains at the least suspicion; and how
to act, or what was to be done, I knew not.   My only
plan was to resign myself to the event, be it what it
might; and this determination taken, I affected to busy
myself with the preparatives for our crime, the very
sight of which redoubled my perplexity and horror.
Pistols were laid on the table, in order to have the
charges drawn and to be properly reloaded.   Whilst
they underwent a strict scrutiny, St Germain remarked
a pair which seemed to him no longer able " to do the
state any service;" he laid them aside—" Here," said
he, " these ' toothless barkers' will never do; whilst
the rest of you are loading and priming your batteries,
I will get these changed for others more likely to aid

our purpose. As he was preparing to quit the room,
I bade him remember that, according to our contract,
none of us could quit the place without being accompanied by a second. "Right—quite right," replied he;
" I like people not only to make, but to keep engagements; so come with me."—" But," said I, " these
other two gentlemen ?"—" Oh !" laughed St Germain, " they shall be kept out of harm's way till our
return;" so saying, he very coolly double-locked the
door upon them, and then taking me by the arm, led
me to a shop from which he generally supplied himself
with what he required for his various expeditions.
Upon the present occasion he purchased some balls,
powder, flints, exchanged the old pistols for new ones,
and then declaring his business completed, returned
with me to his house. On entering I felt a fresh thrill
of horror, from perceiving how earnestly and yet calmly
the wretch Boudin was occupied in sharpening two
large dinner-knives on a hone;—the sight froze my
blood, and I turned away in disgust.

Meanwhile the time was passing away; one o'clock
struck, and no expedient of safety had yet presented
itself. I yawned and stretched, feigning weariness, and
going into an apartment adjoining the one in which we
had assembled, threw myself on a bed, as if in search
of repose; after a few instants, I appeared still more
fidgetty with this indolence, and I could perceive that
the others were not less so than myself. " Suppose
we have a glass of something to cheer us," cried St
Germain. " An excellent idea!" I replied, almost
leaping for joy at the unexpected opening it seemed
likely to afford my scheme; " a most capital thought—
and by way of helping it, if you can manage to send to
my house, you may have a glass of Burgundy, such as
cannot be met with every day." All declared the
thought a most seasonable relief to the ennui which
was beginning to have hold of them, now that all
their work of preparation was at an end; and St Germain without further delay dispatched his porter to

Annette, who was requested to bring the promised
treat herself. It was agreed that nothing relative to our
plan should be uttered before her; and whilst my three
companions were indulging in rough jokes upon the
unexpected pleasure thus offered them, I carelessly
resumed my place on the bed, and whilst there traced
with a pencil these few lines—" When you leave this
place, disguise yourself; and do not for an instant lose
sight of myself, St Germain, or Boudin. Be careful
to avoid all observation; and, above all, be sure to
pick up anything I may let fall, and to convey it
as directed." Short as was this hurried instruction, it was, I knew, sufficient for Annette, who
had frequently received similar directions, and I felt
quite assured that she would comprehend it in its
fullest sense. It was not long before she joined us,
bringing with her the basket of wine. Her appearance
was the signal for mirth and gaiety. She was complimented by all; and as for myself, under the semblance
of thanking her for her ready attendance with an embrace, I managed to slip the billet into her hand:
she understood me, took leave of the company, and
left me far happier than I had felt an hour before.

We made a hearty dinner, after which I suggested
the idea of going alone with St Germain, to reconnoitre
the scene of action, in order to be provided with the
means of guarding against any accident. As this
seemed merely the counsel of a prudent man, it excited no suspicion; the only difference in his opinion
and mine, was, that I proposed taking a hackney-coach,
whilst he judged it better to walk. When we reached
the part he considered most favourable for scaling, he
pointed it out to me; and I took care to observe it so
well, that I could easily describe it to another, without
fear of any mistake arising. This done, St Germain
recollected that we had all better cover our faces with
black crape; and we proceeded towards the Palais Royal, for the purpose of buying some; and whilst he was
in a shop, examining the different sorts, I managed to

scrawl hastily on paper every particular and direction which might enable the police to interfere and prevent the crime. St Germain, whose vigilance never relaxed, and who had as much as possible kept his eye upon me with calm scrutiny, conducted me to a public-house, where we refreshed ourselves with some beer : quitting this place, we walked again homewards, without my having been enabled to dispose of the billet I had written; when, just as we were re-entering his odious den of crimes, my eye caught sight of Annette, who, disguised in a manner that would have effectually deceived every other but myself, was on the watch for our return. Convinced that she had recognized me, I managed to drop my paper as I crossed the threshold; and relieved, in a great measure, of many of my former apprehensions, I committed myself to my fate. As the terrible hour for the fulfilment of our scheme approached, I became a prey to a thousand terrors. Spite of the warning I had sent through Annette, the police might be tardy in obeying its directions, and might perhaps arrive too late to prevent the consummation of the crime. Should I at once avow myself, and, in my real character, arrest St Germain and his accomplices? Alas! what could I do against three powerful men, rendered furious by revenge and desperation? And besides, had I even succeeded in my attempt, who could say that I might be believed, when I denied all participation with them, except such as was to further the ends of justice. Instances rose to my recollection, where, under similar circumstances, the police had abandoned its agents, or confounding them with the guilty wretches with whom they had mingled, refused to acknowledge their innocence. I was in all the agony of such reflections; when St Germain roused me, by desiring I would accompany Debenne, whose cabriolet was destined to receive the expected treasure of money-bags, and was for that purpose to be stationed at the corner of the street. We went out together, and, as I looked around me, I

again met the eye of my faithful Annette, whose
glance satisfied me that all my commissions had been
attended to. Just then, Debenne enquired of me the
place of rendezvous. I know not what good genius
suggested to me the idea of saving this unhappy creature. I had observed that he was not wicked at heart,
and that he seemed rather drawn towards the abyss of
guilt by want and bad advice, than by any natural inclination for crime. I hastily assigned to him a post,
away from the spot which had been agreed on; and,
happy in having saved him from the snare, rejoined
St Germain and Boudin, at the angle of the boulevard
St Denis. It was now about half-past ten, and I gave
them to understand that the cabriolet would require
some time in getting ready; that I had given orders to
Debenne, that he should take his station in the corner
of the Rue du Faubourg Poissonnière, ready to hasten
to us at the slightest signal. I observed to them, that
the sight of a cabriolet, too near to the place of our
labours, might awaken suspicion; and they agreed in
thinking my precautions wisely taken.

    Eleven o'clock struck—we took a glass together in
the fauxbourg St Denis, and then directed our steps
towards the banker's habitation. The tranquillity of
Boudin and his infamous associate, had something in it
almost fiend-like: they walked coolly along, each with
his pipe in his mouth, which was only removed to
hum over some loose song.

    At last we arrived at the part of the garden wall it
had been determined to scale, by means of a large
post, which would serve as a ladder. St Germain demanded my pistols;—my heart began to beat violently,
for I fully expected, that, having by some ill chance
penetrated my real share in the affair, he meant that I
should answer for it with my life: resistance would
have been useless, and I put them into his hands; but,
to my extreme relief, he merely opened the pan, changed
the priming, and returned them to me. After having
performed a similar operation on his own pistols and

those of Boudin, he set the example of climbing the post; Boudin followed; and both of them, without interrupting their smoking, sprung into the garden: it became my turn to follow them : trembling, I reached the top of the wall; all my former apprehensions crowded back upon me. Had the police yet had time to lay their ambuscade? Might not St Germain have preceded them ? These and a thousand similar questions agitated my mind. My feelings were, however, wrought up to so high a pitch, that, in the midst of such a moment of cruel suspense, I determined on one measure, namely, to prevent the commission of the crime, though I sunk in the unequal struggle.   However, St Germain seeing me still sitting astride on the top of the wall, and becoming impatient at my delay, cried out, " Come, come, down with you." Scarcely had he said the words, than he was vigorously attacked by a number of men. Boudin and himself offered a desperate resistance. A brisk firing commenced—the balls whistled—and, after a combat of some minutes, the two assassins were seized, though not before several of the police had been wounded. St Germain and his companion were likewise much hurt. For myself, as I took no part in the engagement, I was not likely to come to any harm: nevertheless, that I might sustain my part to the end, I fell on the field of battle, as though I had been mortally wounded. The next instant I was wrapped in a covering, and in this manner conveyed to a room where Boudin and St Germain were; the latter appeared deeply touched at my death; he shed tears, and it was necessary to employ force to remove him from what he believed to be my corpse.

St Germain was a man of about five feet eight inches high, with strongly developed muscles, an enormous head, and very small eyes, half closed, like those of an owl; his face, deeply marked with the small pox, was extremely plain ; and yet, from the quickness and vivacity of his expression, he was by many persons considered pleasing. In describing his features, a strong resemblance would suggest itself to those of the hyena and wolf, particularly if the attention were directed to his immensely wide jaws, furnished with large projecting fangs; his very organization partook of the animal instinct common to beasts of prey; he was passionately fond of hunting; the sight of blood exhilarated him: his other passions were gaming, women, and good eating and drinking. As he had acquired the air and manners of good society, he expressed himself when he chose with ease and fluency, and was almost always fashionably and elegantly dressed; he might be styled a "well-bred thief." When his interest required it, no person could better assume the pleasant mildness of an amiable man; at other times he was abrupt and brutal. His comrade Boudin was diminutive in stature, scarcely reaching five feet two inches; thin, with a livid complexion; his eyes dark and piercing, and deeply sunk in his head. The habit of wielding the carving-knife, and of cutting up meat had rendered him ferocious. He was bow-legged; a deformity I have observed amongst several systematic assassins, as well as amongst many other individuals distinguished by their crimes.

I cannot remember any event of my life which afforded me more real satisfaction than the taking of these two villains. I applauded myself for having delivered society from two monsters, at the same time that I esteemed myself fortunate in having saved Debenne from the fate which would have befallen him, had he been taken with them. However, the share of self-satisfaction produced by the feeling of having been instrumental in rescuing a fellow-creature from destruction, was but a slight compensation for the misery I experienced at being in a manner compelled by the stern duties of the post I filled, either to send a fresh succession of victims to ascend the scaffold, or to mount it myself. The quality of 'secret agent' preserved, it is true, my liberty, and shielded me from the dangers to which, as a fugitive galley-

slave, I was formerly exposed; true, I was no longer
subjected to the many terrors which had once agitated
me : but still I was not pardoned; and until that happy
event took place, the liberty I enjoyed was but a
precarious possession, which the caprice of my em-
ployers could deprive me of at any moment.   Again,
I was not insensible to the general odium attached to
the department I filled.   Still, revolting as were its
functions to my own choice and mind, it was a necessary evil, and one from which there was no escape.
I therefore strove to reconcile myself to it by arguments such as these :—Was I not daily occupied in
endeavouring to promote the welfare of society ?   Was
I not espousing the part of the good and upright
against the bad and vicious ?   And should I by these
steps draw down upon me the contempt of mankind ?
I went about dragging guilt from its hidden recesses,
and unmasking its many schemes of blood and murder; and should I for this be pointed out with the
finger of scorn and hatred ?   Attacking thieves, even
on the very theatre of their crimes—wresting from
them the weapons with which they had armed themselves, I boldly dared their vengeance; and did I for
this merit to be despised ?   My reason became convinced ; and my mind, satisfied of the upright motives
which guided me, regained its calmness and self-com-
mand ; and thus armed, I felt that I had courage to
dare the ingratitude and obloquy of an unjust opinion
respecting me and my occupation.

CHAPTER XXVI.

I continue to frequent places of bad resort—The inspectors betray me—Discovery of a receiver of stolen goods—I arrest him
—Stratagem employed to convict him—He is condemned.

THE thieves, who had experienced a temporary panic
at the many arrests which had successively fallen,
with unexpected vengeance, on many of their party, were not long in re-appearing more numerous
and more audacious than ever.   Amongst their number were several fugitive galley-slaves, who, having
perfected in the Bagnes a very dangerous sort of trade
and ready invention, had come to exercise it in Paris,
where they soon rendered themselves dreaded by all
parties.   The police, exasperated at their boldness,
resolved upon putting an end to their career.   I was
accordingly commanded to seek them out ; and further
orders were given to me, to arrange a plan of action
with the peace-officers, by which they might be at
hand whenever I deemed it likely they could effect
the capture of any of these ruffians.   It may be easily
guessed how difficult my task must be : however, I
lost no time in visiting every place of ill fame, both in
the metropolis and its environs.   In a very few days
I had gained the knowledge of all the dens of vice
where I might be likely to meet with these wretches.
The barrier de la Courtille, those of the Combat and
de Menilmontant, were the places of most favourite
resort ;   they were, in a manner, their head-quarters ;
and woe to the agent who had shown himself there,
no matter for what reason ; he would assuredly have
had his brains beaten out.   The gendarmes were equally
in dread of this well-known and formidable association,
and carefully abstained from approaching it.   For my
own part, I felt less timidity, and ventured without
hesitation into the midst of this herd of miserable

beings. I frequented their society; I became to out-
ward semblance one of themselves; and soon gained
the advantage of being treated with so much confidence as to be admitted to their nocturnal meetings,
where they openly discussed the crimes they had
committed, as well as those they meditated. I managed so skilfully, that I easily drew from them the
particulars of their own abode, or that of the females
with whom they cohabited. I may go still further,
and assert, that so boundless was the confidence with
which I inspired them, that had any one of their
members dared to express the shadow of a suspicion
respecting me, he would have been punished on the
spot. In this manner I obtained every requisite information ; so that, when I had once indicated any fit
object for arrest, his conviction and condemnation
became matters of course. My researches ' intra
muros ' were not less successful. I frequented every
tennis-court in the environs of the Palais-Royal, the
Hotel d'Angleterre, the boulevards of the Temple;
the streets of la Vannerie, of la Mortellerie, of la
Planche Mibray; the market St Jaques, Petite Chaise;
the Rues de la Juiverie, la Calandre, le Châtelet; the
Place Maubert, and in fact the whole city. Not a
day passed in which I did not effect some important
discovery. Nothing escaped me, either relating to
crimes which had been committed, or were in contemplation. I was in all places; I knew all that
was passing or projecting; and never were the police
idly or unprofitably employed when set to work upon
my suggestions.

M. Henry openly expressed his surprise as well
as satisfaction at my zeal and success ; it was not so
with many of the peace-officers and sub-agents of
police, for, little accustomed to the hard duty and
constant watchfulness my plans induced, they openly
murmured. Some of them, in their anxiety to be
rid of the irksomeness of my direction, were cowardly enough to betray the secret of the disguise under

favour of which I had so skilfully manœuvred. This
imprudent act drew down upon them severe repri-
mands, without having the effect of making them more
circumspect, or more devoted to the public good.

It will be readily understood, that, associating as I
constantly did with the vilest and most abandoned,
I must, as a matter of course, be repeatedly invited to
join in their acts of criminal violence; this I never
refused at the moment of asking, but always formed
some plea for failing to attend the rendezvous for such
purposes. These men of crimes were generally so
absorbed in their villanous machinations, that the
most flimsy excuse passed current with them: I may
even say, that frequently it did not require the trouble
of an excuse to deceive them. Once arrested, they
never troubled themselves to find out 'by what means
it had been effected; and had they even been more
awake, my measures were laid too ably for them to
have arrived at the chance of suspecting me as the
author of it: indeed, I have often been accosted by some
of the gang to communicate the sorrowful tidings of
the apprehension of one of their number, as well as to
beg my advice and assistance in endeavouring to procure his release.

Nothing is more easy, when once on good terms
with the thief, than to obtain a knowledge of the persons to whom he disposes of his stolen property. I
was enabled to discover several; and the directions
with which I furnished the police were so unequivocal,
that they never failed to join their worthy companions
in the Bagnes. Perhaps the recital of the means I
adopted to rid Paris of one of these dangerous characters, may not be uninteresting to the reader.

For many years the police had had its eye upon
him, but as yet had not been able to detect him in any
positive act of delinquency. His house had undergone
repeated searches without any effect resulting from the
most diligent enquiry; nothing of the most trifling
nature could be found to rise in evidence against him.

Nevertheless, he was known to traffic with the thieves; and many of them, who were far from suspecting my connexion with the police, pointed him out to me as a staunch friend, and a man on whom they could depend. These assertions respecting him were not sufficient to effect his conviction; it would be requisite to seize him with the stolen articles in his possession. M. Henry had tried every scheme to accomplish this; but whether from stupidity on the part of the agents employed by him, or the superior address of the receiver of stolen property, all his plans had failed. He was desirous of trying whether I should be more successful. I willingly undertook the office, and arranged my plans in the following manner. Posted near the house of the suspected dealer in stolen property, I watched for his going out, and following him when he had gone a few steps down the street, addressed him by a different name to his own. He assured me I was mistaken; I protested to the contrary: he insisted upon it I was deceived, and I affected to be equally satisfied of his identity, declaring my perfect recognition of his person as that of a man who for some time had been sought after by the police throughout Paris and its environs. " You are grossly mistaken," replied he warmly. " My name is so and so, and I live in such a street." " Come, come, friend," said I, " excuses are useless. I know you too well to part with you so easily."—" This is too much," cried he; " but at the next police station I shall possibly be able to meet with those who can convince you that I know my own name better than you seem to do." This was exactly the point at which I wished to arrive. " Agreed," said I; and we bent our steps towards the neighbouring guardhouse. We entered, and I requested he would show me his papers: he had none about him. I then insisted upon his being searched, and on his person were found three watches and twenty-five double Napoleons, which I caused to be laid aside till he should be examined before a magistrate. These things had been wrapped in a handkerchief, which I contrived to secure; and after having disguised myself as a messenger, I hastened to the house of this receiver of stolen goods, and demanded to speak with his wife. She, of course, had no idea of my business or knowledge of my person; and seeing several persons besides herself present, I signified to her that my business being of a private nature, it was important that I should speak to her alone; and in token of my claims to her confidence, produced the handkerchief, and enquired whether she rocognised it? Although still ignorant of the cause of my visit, her countenance became troubled, and her whole person was much agitated as she begged me to let her hear my business. " I am concerned," replied I, "to be the bearer of unpleasant news; but the fact is, your husband has just been arrested, everything found on his person has been seized, and from some words which he happened to overhear, he suspects he has been betrayed; he therefore wishes you to remove out of the house certain things you are aware would be dangerous to his safety if found on the premises; if you please I will lend you a helping hand, but I must forewarn you that you have not one moment to lose."

The information was of the first importance; the sight of the handkerchief, and the description of the objects it had served to envelope, removed from her mind every doubt as to the truth of the message I had brought her, and she easily fell into the snare I had laid to entrap her. She thanked me for the trouble I had taken, and begged I would go and engage three hackney coaches, and return to her with as little delay as possible. I left the house to execute my commission; but on the road I stopped to give one of my people instructions to keep the coaches in sight, and to seize them, with their contents, directly I should give the signal. The vehicles drew up to the door, and upon re-entering the house, I found things in a high state of preparation for removing. The floor was strewed with articles of every description;

time-pieces, candelabra, Etruscan vases, cloths, cache-mires, linen, muslins, &c.   All these things had been taken from a closet, the entrance to which was cleverly concealed by a large press, so skilfully contrived that the most practised eye could not have discovered the deception.   I assisted in the removal, and when it was completed, the press having been carefully replaced, the woman begged of me to accompany her, which I did, and no sooner was she in one of the coaches, ready to start, than I suddenly pulled up the window, and at this previously concerted signal, we were immediately surrounded by the police.   The husband and wife were tried at the assizes, and, as may be easily conceived, were overwhelmed beneath the weight of an accusation, in support of which there existed a formidable mass of convicting testimony.

Some persons may perhaps blame the expedient to which I had recourse, in order to free Paris from a receiver of stolen property, who had been for a long time a positive nuisance to the capital.   Whether it be approved of or not, I have at least the consciousness of having done my duty; besides, when we wish to overreach scoundrels who are at open war with society, every stratagem is allowable by which to effect their conviction, except endeavouring to provoke the commission of crime.

CHAPTER XXVII.

Gueuvive's gang — A girl helps me to discover the chief—
I dine with the thieves—One of them takes me to sleep at his
house—I pass for a fugitive galley-slave—I engage in a plot
against myself—I wait for myself at my own door—A robbery
in the Rue Cassette—Great surprise—Gueuvive with four of
his men are arrested—The girl Cornevin points the others out
to me—A batch of eighteen.

NEARLY about the same time in which the event mentioned in the last chapter occurred, a gang had formed
itself in the Faubourg St Germain, which was more
particularly the scene of its exploits. It was composed of individuals who acted under the guidance of
a captain named Gueuvive, alias Constantin, shortened
by abbreviation into Antin; for the same custom exists
amongst thieves as amongst bullies, spies, and informers, of being called only by the last syllable of
the christian name. Gueuvive, or Antin, was a fencing
master, who after having served as bully to the lowest
prostitutes, and for the humblest wages, was completing in his present character the many vicissitudes
of his ill-spent life. It was well known that he was
capable of any action, however bad, and although
murder had never been proved against him, yet few
doubted his willingness to shed blood, if by so doing
he could reap the most trifling advantage. His mistress had been murdered in the Champs Elysées, and
suspicions were strongly directed against him as the
author of the crime. However this may be, Gueuvive
was a man of enterprising character, extreme boldness,
and possessed of the most unblushing effrontery; at
least, this was the estimate formed of him by his companions, amongst whom he enjoyed a more than
common celebrity.

For some time the attention of the police had been
directed to this man and his associates, but without

being enabled to secure any of them, although each day teemed with fresh accounts of their continued attacks upon the property of the citizens of Paris. At length it was seriously resolved to put an end to the misdeeds of these plunderers, and I received, in consequence, orders to go in search of them, and to endeavour to take them in the very fact. This last point was particularly insisted upon, as being of the utmost importance; I accordingly provided myself with a suitable disguise, and that very evening opened the campaign in the Faubourg St Germain, frequenting every place of ill-fame in it. About midnight, I went to the house of a person named Boucher, in the Rue Neuve Guillemain, where I took a glass of brandy with some common girls; and whilst sitting with them, I heard the name of Constantin pronounced at the table adjoining mine. I at first imagined he was present; but upon cautiously questioning one of the girls, she assured me he was not; although, added she, "he seldom fails being here every day to meet his numerous friends." From the tone in which she spoke I fancied I could perceive that she was perfectly conversant with the habits of these gentry, and in the hope of drawing further particulars from her, I invited her to sup with me. The offer was accepted, and by the time I had well plied her with liquor, she gave me the information I required, and with the more readiness, as from my dress, actions, and expressions, she had set me down in her own mind as one of the light-fingered brethren. We passed a part of the night together, and I did not quit her till she had fully explained to me the different haunts of Gueuvive.

The next day, at twelve o'clock, I repaired to the house of Boucher, where I again met my companion of the preceding night. I had scarcely entered when she saw me, and immediately addressing me, cried, "Now is your time if you wish to speak with Gueuvive: he is here;" and she pointed to an individual of from twenty-eight to thirty years of age, neatly dressed, although but in his waistcoat; he was about five feet six inches high, extremely good looking, fine black hair and whiskers, regular teeth, in fact, precisely as he had been described to me; without hesitation I addressed him, requesting he would oblige me with a little tobacco from his box. He examined me from head to foot, and inquired, " if I had served in the army ?" I replied, that I had been in an Hussar regiment, and soon over a glass of good drink we fell into a deep conversation upon military affairs.

Time passed whilst we were thus engaged, and dinner was talked of; Gueuvive declared that I should make one in a party he had been arranging, and that my company would afford him much pleasure. It was not very probable I should refuse: I accepted his invitation without further ceremony, and we went away together to the Barrière du Maine, where four of his friends were awaiting his arrival. We immediately sat down to the dinner-table, and as I was a stranger to all, the conversation was very guarded. However, a few cant words which occasionally escaped them, soon served to convince me that all the members of this charming society were cracksmen (thieves).

They were all very curious to hear what I did for my living, and I soon fudged a tale which satisfied them, and induced them not only to suppose I came from the country, but likewise that I was a thief on the look-out for a job. I did not explicitly state these particulars, but affecting certain peculiarities which betray the profession, I allowed them to perceive that I had great reasons for wishing to conceal my person.

The wine was not spared, and so well did it loosen every tongue, that before the close of the repast, I had learned the abode of Gueuvive, as well as that of his worthy coadjutor, Joubert, and the names of many of their comrades; at the moment of our separating I hinted that I did not exactly know where I should procure a bed, and Joubert immediately offered to give me a night's lodging with him, and conducted me to Rue St Jaques, where he occupied a back room on the second-floor, there I shared with him the bed of his mistress, the girl Cornevin.

We conversed together for some time, and before we fell asleep, Joubert overwhelmed me with questions; his object was to sift out my present mode of existence, what papers I had about me, &c. His curiosity appeared insatiable, and in order to satisfy it, I contrived either by a positive falsehood, or an equivocation, to lead him to suppose me a brother thief. At last, as if he had guessed my meaning, he exclaimed, " Come, do not beat about the bush any longer; I see how it is, you know you are a prig." I feigned not to understand these words; he repeated them; and I, affecting to take offence, assured him that he was greatly mistaken, and that if he indulged in similar jokes, I should be compelled to withdraw from his company. Joubert was silenced, and nothing further was said till the next day at ten o'clock, when Gueuvive came to awaken us.

It was agreed that we should go and dine at La Glacière. On the road Gueuvive took me aside and said, " Hark'ye, I see you are a good fellow, and I am willing to do you a service if I can; do not be so reserved then, but tell me who and what you are." Some hint I had purposely thrown out having induced him to believe that I had escaped from the Bagne at Toulon, he recommended me to observe a cautious prudence with my companions, " for though they are the best creatures living," said he, " yet they are rather fond of chattering."—" Oh," replied I, " I shall keep a sharp look out, I promise you; besides, Paris will never do for me, I must be off; there are too many sneaking informers about for me to be safe in it."— " That's true," added he, " but if you can keep Vidocq from guessing at your business, you are safe enough with me, who can smell those beggars as easily as a crow scents powder."—" Well," said I, " I can-

s 2

not boast of so much penetration, yet I think, too, that from the frequent description I have heard of this Vidocq, his features are so well engraved in my recollection, that I should pretty soon recognise him, if I came unexpectedly in his way."—" God bless you!" cried he, " it is easy to perceive you are a stranger to the vagabond: just imagine now, that he is never to be seen twice in the same dress; that he is in the morning perhaps just such another looking person as you; well, the next hour so altered, that his own brother could not recognise him, and by the evening, I defy any man to remember ever having seen him before. Only yesterday, I met him disguised in a manner that would have deceived any eye but mine, but he must be a deep hand if he gets over me; I know these sneaks at the first glance, and if my friends were as knowing as myself, his business would have been done long ago."—" Nonsense," cried I; " everybody says the same thing of him, and yet you see there is no getting rid of him."—" You are right," replied he, "but to prove that I can act as well as talk, if you will lend me a helping hand, this very evening we will waylay him at his door, and I warrant we'll settle the job, so as to keep him from giving any of us further uneasiness."

I felt curious to learn whether he really was acquainted with my residence, and promised readily to join his scheme, and accordingly, about the dusk of the evening, we each tied up in handkerchiefs a number of heavy ten-sous pieces, in order to administer to this scamp of a Vidocq a few effectual blows the moment he should issue from his house. Having fastened the money in a hard knot at the corner of our handkerchiefs, we set out; and Constantin, who seemed just in the humour for the task he had undertaken, led the way to the Rue Neuve St François, and stopped before a house, No. 14—my exact abode. I could not conceive how he had procured my address, and must confess the circumstance gave me great uneasiness, whilst it redoubled my wonder, that being so well acquainted with my dwelling, he should appear to have so little knowledge of my person. We kept watch for several hours, but Vidocq, as may be well imagined, did not make his appearance; Constantin, was highly enraged at this disappointment. "We must give it up for to-night," said he at length, "but the first time I meet the rascal, by heavens he shall pay doubly for keeping me waiting now."

At midnight we retired, putting off the execution of our project till the ensuing night. It was amusing enough to see me thus assisting in laying an ambuscade for myself to be caught in. The readiness with which I embarked in the scheme quite won the good-will of Constantin, who from this moment treated me with the greatest confidence, he even invited me to make one in a projected plan for robbing a house in the Rue Cassette. I agreed to join the party, but declared that I neither could nor would venture out in the night, without first going home for the necessary papers which would serve me in case of our scheme failing, and our getting into the hands of the police. "In that case," replied he, "you may as well just keep watch for us whilst we do the job." At length the robbery took place, and as the night was excessively dark, Constantin and his companions wishing to hurry faster than the absence of all light permitted them, had the boldness to take down a lamp from before a door, and to carry it before them. Upon their return home, this watchlight was placed in the middle of the room, whilst they seated themselves around it to examine and divide their booty; in the midst of their exultation at the rich results of their expedition, a sudden knocking was heard at the door: the robbers surprised and alarmed, looked at each other in silent dread. This was a surprise for which they were indebted to me. Again the knocking was heard. Constantin then by a sign commanding silence, said in a whisper, " 'Tis

the police; I am sure of it." Amidst the confusion
occasioned by these words, and the increased knocking
at the gate, I contrived, unobserved, to crawl under a
bed, where I had scarcely concealed myself when the
door was burst open, and a swarm of inspectors and
other officers of the police entered the room, a general search took place, even the bed where the mistress of Joubert slept did not escape : they struck their
sticks both over and under the bed which served as
my hiding-place without discovering me, but that, of
course, I was prepared for.

The commissioner of the police drew up a pro-
cès verbal, an inventory of the stolen property,
and it was packed off with the five thieves to
the prefecture. This operation completed, I quitted my hiding-place, and found myself alone with
the girl Cornevin, who was all astonishment at my
good fortune, the reason of which she was far from
suspecting. She urged me to remain where I was.
" What are you thinking of ? " said I. " Suppose
the police return ! No, no ; let me get away now
the coast is clear, and I promise to join you at
l'Estrapade." I sought my own house to procure the
repose I so greatly needed, and at the hour agreed on
went to fulfil my appointment with Cornevin, who
was expecting me. It was on her I depended to procure a complete list of all the friends and associates of
Joubert and Constantin ; and as I stood rather high
in her good graces, she soon furnished me with the
desired information ; so that in less than a fortnight,
thanks to an auxiliary I contrived to introduce
amongst the gang, I succeeded in causing them to be
arrested in the very commission of their crimes. There
were eighteen in all, who, with Constantin, were condemned to the gallies.

At the moment when the chain to which they belonged was about to set out, Constantin having perceived me, became perfectly furious, and broke out

into the most violent imprecations and invectives ; but, without feeling any offence at his gross and vulgar appellations, I contented myself with approaching him and saying coolly, " that it was very surprising how a man like him, who knew Vidocq, and could boast of the precious faculty of ' smelling out an informer as far off as a crow scents powder,' should have allowed himself to be done in that manner." This was a knock-down blow to Constantin; he could make no reply, but with an air of sullen confusion, turned away from me, and was silent.

CHAPTER XXVIII.

The agents of the police chosen from amongst liberated galley-
slaves, thieves, bullies and prostitutes—Theft tolerated—Degeneracy of the inspectors—Coalition of informers—They denounce
me—Destruction of three classes of thieves—Formation of a new
species—The brothers Delzève—How discovered—Delzève the
younger arrested—The perquisites of a préfet of police—I free
myself from the yoke of the peace officers and inspectors—My
life is in danger—A few anecdotes.

I was not the only secret agent of the police of safety:
a Jew named Gaffré was my coadjutor; he had been
employed before me by the police, but as our principles did not agree, we did not long go on with harmony together.   I perceived that he was a bad fellow,
and mentioned my opinion to the chief of the division,
who, having ascertained the justice of my report, expelled him, and ordered him to quit Paris.   Some
individuals without any other qualification than a
sort of low cunning acquired in prison, were likewise
attached to the police of safety, but they had no fixed employment, and were only paid according to the captures
they made.   There were also thieves who constantly
followed their profession, and whose presence was tolerated on condition of their giving up to justice the malefactors they might by chance fall in with; sometimes
it happened that for lack of other objects, they would
denounce their own comrades.   After these tolerated
thieves, came, in the third or fourth gradation, that
swarm of abandoned profligates who lived with girls
of infamous character.   This ignoble caste occasionally supplied important directions for the taking of
pickpockets and swindlers; generally, they came forward and offered the most useful information when
they were anxious to procure the release of their mis-
tresses who chanced to fall under the surveillance of
the police.   The women who lived with well-known

and incorrigible offenders were useful auxiliaries, constantly furnishing accounts which enabled the police to send off from time to time numbers of these lost creatures upon their travels to Bicêtre : this last class was indeed the very refuse of society, and yet up to the present period it had been impossible to dispense with its aid; for lengthened experience had, unfortunately, but too well shewn how impossible it was to depend on the zeal or intelligence of the inspecting officers. The intention of the administration was not to employ in the pursuit of robbers, unpaid men, but yet it was easy to profit by the assistance of those who from some interested motive only lent themselves to the police, with a proviso that they should remain behind the curtain, and enjoy certain immunities. M. Henry had, for some time, felt how dangerous it was to make use of these double-edged weapons, and had long contemplated measures for getting rid of them; and this had induced him to have me enlisted in the service of the police, which he was anxious to clear of all men decidedly robbers by profession. There are cures only to be effected by the aid of poison, and perhaps the leprosy of society can only be extirpated by similar means, but in this case the poisonous dose administered was too powerful, and the proof is, that nearly all the secret agents at this period were caught in the very act of committing crime, and many of them are still at the Bagnes.

When I entered the police, all these secret agents of both sexes were naturally leagued against me; and foreseeing that their reign was nearly at an end, they did all in their power to extend its period. I passed for a man inflexible and impartial; I would not permit that they should plunder in all quarters with impunity, and consequently they were my sworn foes. They spared no efforts to crush me. Useless endeavours! I braved the tempest as the time-rooted oak which scarcely stoops its head, despite the pitiless pelting of the storm.

I was denounced daily, but the voices of my calumniators were powerless, ineffectual. M. Henry, who had the préfet's ear, answered for my actions; and it was resolved that all denunciations against me should be immediately communicated to me, and that I should be allowed to refute them in writing. This proof of confidence gave me pleasure, and without rendering me more sedulous or attentive to my duties, it proved to me, at least, that my superiors had rendered me justice, and nothing in the world could have made me deviate from the plan of conduct which I had laid down.

In everything, enthusiasm is necessary if we would succeed. I did not hope to render the calling of a secret agent honourable, but I flattered myself with the idea of fulfilling its duties with honour. I was anxious to be esteemed upright, incorruptible, intrepid, and indefatigable; I wished to appear on all occasions prompt, adequate, and intelligent; and my successes conspired to give me the reputation I sought. Soon M. Henry took no steps without consulting me: we passed nights together in chalking out plans and means of repressing crimes and abuses, which were so efficacious that, in a short time the complaints of robberies were considerably diminished, because the number of robbers of all sorts was greatly reduced. I may even say, that there was a period, when the robbers of plate from houses, those who steal the luggage from coaches and carts, as well as pickpockets, gave no tokens of being in existence. At a later period, a new generation has sprung up, but they can never equal in dexterity Bombance, Marquis, Boucault, Compère, Bouthey, Pranger, Dorlé, La Rose, Gavard, Martin, and other first-rate rogues whom I reduced to a state of inaction. It was no intention of mine to allow their successors the opportunity of acquiring so much skill.

For about six months, I acted alone, excepting only a few common females who had devoted themselves

to the service, when an unforeseen occurrence emancipated me from all dependence on the peace officers,
who had, up to this time, so managed as to take upon
themselves all the merits of my discoveries. This circumstance proved greatly in my favour, as it completely
exposed the weakness and inefficiency of the inspectors, who complained, with much vehemence, that I
gave them too much to do. To come to the fact, I
shall begin the narration from its earliest commencement.

In 1810, robberies of a new kind and inconceivable
boldness suddenly awakened the police to the knowledge of the existence of a troop of malefactors of a
novel description.

Nearly all the robberies had been committed by lad-
ders and forcible entries; apartments on the first and even
second floor had been broken into by these extraordinary thieves, who, till then, had confined themselves
to rich houses; and it was evident that these robbers
must have had a knowledge of the localities, by the
method of their burglaries.

All my efforts to discover these adroit thieves were
without success, when a burglary which seemed almost impracticable was committed in the Rue Saint-
Claude, near the Rue Bourbon-Villeneuve, in an apartment in the second floor above the 'entresol,' in a house
in which the commissary of police for the district actually resided. The cord of the lantern which hung
at his house-door had served for a ladder.

A nosebag (a small bag in which corn is put for
horses to feed from when on the coach-stand) had
been left on the spot, which gave rise to a surmise that
the perpetrators might be hackney-coachmen, or at
least that hackney-coaches had been employed in the
enterprize.

M. Henry directed me to make my observations
amongst the coachmen, and I discovered that the nosebag had belonged to a man named Husson, who drove
the fiacre, No. 712. I reported this: Husson was ap-

T

prehended, and from him we obtained information concerning two brothers, named Delzève, the elder of whom was soon in the hands of the police, and on his interrogation by M. Henry, he made such important discoveries as led to the apprehension of one Métral, a room-cleaner (frotteur) in the palace of the empress Josephine. He was stated to be the receiver of the band, composed almost entirely of Savoyards, born in the department of Leman. The continuation of my search led to my securing the persons of the brothers Pissard, Grenier, Lebrun, Piessard, Mabou, called the apothecary, Serassé, Durand, &c. twenty-two in all, who were subsequently condemned to imprisonment.

These robbers were for the greater part messengers (commissionaires) room-cleaners, or coachmen; that is, they belonged to a class of individuals proverbial for honesty, and who from time immemorial had been celebrated for probity throughout Paris; in their district they were all considered as honest men, incapable of appropriating to themselves the property of another; and this opinion contributed to render them the more formidable, as the persons who employed them either in sawing wood or in any other kind of work, had no distrust of them, and gave them free ingress and egress everywhere, and at all times. When it was known that they were implicated in a criminal affair, they were not believed to be guilty; and I myself, for some time, hesitated in my opinion. However, evidence was adduced which was against them, and the ancient renown of the Savoyards, in a capital in which they had resided unsuspected for ages, was blasted never again to flourish.

During the year 1812 I had rendered to justice the principals of the band; but Delzève, the younger, had baffled all efforts to capture him, and bid defiance to the pursuits of justice, when, on the 31st of December, M. Henry said to me, " I think, if we manage well, we can get hold of Ecrevisse (Delzève's cognomen): tomorrow will be new-year's day, and he will be sure to visit the washerwoman, who has so often given him an asylum, as well as his brother; I have a presentiment that he will be there this evening or during the night, or certainly early in the morning."

I was of the same opinion; and M. Henry ordered me to go, with three officers, and place ourselves on the watch, near the washerwoman's house, who lived in the Rue des Gressillon, Faubourg St Honoré, in the Petite-Pologne.

I received this command with a satisfaction which is always, with me, a presage of good will. Attended by the three inspectors, I went, at seven o'clock in the evening, to the appointed spot. It was bitterly cold, the ground covered with snow, and never had winter been more severe.

We stationed ourselves in ambuscade; and, after many hours, the inspectors, nipped with cold and unable any longer to endure it, proposed that we should quit our station. I was half-frozen, having no covering but the light garment of a messenger. I made some remarks to them; and, although it would have been infinitely more agreeable to me to have retired, we determined to remain till midnight. Scarcely had the hour agreed on struck, than they claimed of me the fulfilment of my promise, and we quitted our post, which we had been ordered to keep till day-break.

We went towards the Palais Royal; a coffee-house was open, which we entered to warm ourselves, and having taken a bowl of hot wine, we separated, each to go to his own home. As I went towards mine, I reflected on what I was doing.—" What!" said I to myself, " so soon forget instructions which have been given to me; thus to deceive the confidence of my superior; it is an unpardonable baseness! My conduct not only seems reprehensible, but I think that it even deserves the most severe punishment." I was in despair at having complied with the wishes of the inspectors; and resolute in repairing my fault, deter-

mined to return alone to the post assigned, and pass
the night there, even if I died on the spot.   I then returned to the Pologne, and ensconced myself in a
corner, that I might not be seen by Delzève, in case
he should come.

For an hour and a half I remained in this position,
until my blood congealed, and I felt my courage weak-
ening, when suddenly a luminous idea shone upon me.
—At a short distance was a dunghill, whose smoke
betrayed a state of fermentation : this depôt is called
the " voirie " (lay-stall) : I ran towards it ; and
having made a hole in one corner, sufficiently deep to
admit me up to my waist, I jumped into it, and a comfortable warmth soon re-established the circulation of
my blood.   At five in the morning, I was still in my
lurking-place, where I did very well, except from the
fumes which invaded my nostrils.   At length the door
of the house, which was the one pointed out to me,
opened to let out a woman, who did not shut it after
her.   Instantly, and without noise, I leaped from the
dung-heap ; and entering the court looked about me,
but saw no light from any part.

I knew that Delzève's associates had a peculiar way
of whistling for him ; it was the coachman's whistle,
and known to me ; I imitated it ; and, at the second
attempt, I heard some one exclaim, " Who calls ? "

" It is the 'chauffeur' (a coachman from whom Delzève had learnt to drive) who whistles for l'Ecrevisse
(the crab)."

" Is it you ? " cried the same voice, which I knew
to be Delzève's.

" Yes ; the chauffeur wants you.   Come down."

" I am coming—wait a minute."

" It is very cold," I replied ; " I will wait for you
at the public-house at the corner ; make haste—do
you hear ? "

The public-house was already open ; for, on new-
year's day, they have custom betimes.   But I was not
tempted to drink ; and that I might trap Delzève, I

opened the side door, and then letting it shut with
violence, without actually going out, I concealed myself under a flight of steps. Soon afterwards Delzève
came down, and on perceiving him I jumped at him,
seized his collar, and holding a pistol to his breast,
told him he was my prisoner.   " Follow me," I said,
" and make the slightest signal at your peril ; besides,
I am not alone."

Dumb with surprise, Delzève made no answer, but
followed me mechanically. I fastened his hands, and
he was then incapacitated from either resisting or flying from me.

I hastened to convey him away, and the clock struck
six as we entered the Rue du Rocher; a hackney-
coach was passing, which I hailed, but the man seeing
me covered with dirt, hesitated, until I offered him
double hire; and led by that, he condescended to take
us up, and we were soon rolling over the pavement of
Paris. To make assurance doubly sure, I tightened
his wrist-cuffs, lest, having come to himself, he might
have rebelled; and although, in a personal conflict, I
should have been sure of victory, yet, as I contemplated
bringing him to confession, I was unwilling to have
any quarrel; and blows, which would have been inevi-
tably the result of rebellion, would decidedly have
produced this result.

Delzève felt aware of the impossibility of escape, and
I endeavoured to make him hear reason ; that I might
completely wheedle (amadouer) him, I offered him
some refreshment, which he accepted ; and the coachman having procured us some wine, we kept driving
about and drinking, without any determined plan.

It was still early, and persuaded that it would be
advantageous to prolong our tête-à-tête, I proposed to
Delzève, that we should go and breakfast in a place
where we could have a private room. He was then
quieted; and appearing hopeless of escape, accepted
my offer, and I took him to the Cadran Bleu ; but, before we got there, he had already told me many pieces

T 2

of important information as to the number of his accomplices still at large in Paris; and I felt convinced
that, at table, he would make "a clean breast of it"
(se deboutonnerait completement). I made him understand that the only way to propitiate the favour of
justice, was to confess all he knew; and to fortify his
resolution in this case, I used some arguments of a peculiar philosophy, which I have always employed with
success in consoling criminals; and, at length, he was
perfectly disposed to do all I wished, when the coach
reached the cook's shop. I made him go up stairs
first, and when I had ordered the breakfast, I told
him that, being desirous of eating my meal at my ease,
I must confine him as I wished. I agreed that he
should be left sufficiently unshackled to exercise his
arms at the game of knife and fork; and, at table, no
one could desire greater freedom. He was not at all
offended at the proposition, and I thus contrived it:—
with two napkins I tied each leg to the foot of his
chair, three or four inches from the bar, which prevented him from attempting to rise without the risk of
breaking his head by a fall.

He breakfasted with much appetite, and promised
to repeat before M. Henry all that he had confessed
to me. At noon we left the café, Delzève being well
primed with wine, and getting into a coach, quite
friends and on good terms with each other, we reached
the prefecture ten minutes afterwards. M. Henry
was then surrounded by his police-officers, who were
paying him the compliments of the new-year's day.
I entered and addressed this salutation to him:—"I
have the honour to wish you a happy and prosperous
year, and to present to you the redoubtable Delzève."

"This is, indeed, a new year's gift," said M. Henry
to me, when he perceived the prisoner, and then
turning to the officers of peace and security: "It
would be a desirable thing, gentlemen, that each of
you should have a similar present to offer to your
préfet." Immediately afterwards he gave me the

order for conducting Delzève to the depôt, saying, with much kindness: "Vidocq, go and take some repose; I am much satisfied with your conduct."

The apprehension of Delzève was productive of the highest testimonials of satisfaction to me, but at the same time it only augmented the hatred which the peace-officers and their agents cherished towards me; only one of them, M. Thibaut, rendered me the fullest justice.

Joining chorus with the thieves and malefactors, all the agents who were not successful as police-officers, assailed me with the utmost virulence. According to them, it was scandalous, abominable, to exercise my zeal in purging society of the evil-doers which troubled its repose. I had been a famous robber; there was no species of crime that I had not perpetrated: such were the reports which were widely spread, and generally accredited. Some perhaps believed them partly true; the thieves, at least, were persuaded that I had followed the vocation in which they worked; and in saying so they believed what they asserted. Before they were caught in my traps, it was necessary that they should think me one of themselves; and once taken, they considered me as a false comrade, but still not the less an "out-and-outer," (un grinche de la haute pégre) only that I plundered with impunity because I was necessary to the police: this was, at all events, the current tale in the prisons. The peace-officers and their satellites were not slow in giving all confirmation to such reports; and then perhaps, in becoming the echoes of the wretches who had cause to complain of me, they did not think that they lied so much as they really did; for, taking no pains to learn what had been the course of my early life, they were to a certain point excusable in thinking that I must have been a thief, since, from time immemorial, all the secret agents had followed that reputable means of getting a livelihood. They knew that such was the commencement of the lives of Goupil, Compère,

Florentin, Levesque, Coco-Lacour, Bourdarie, Cadet Herriez, Henri Lain, Cesar Vioque, Bouthey, Gaffre, Manigant; and, in fact, all who had preceded or were coadjutors with me. Nearly all the agents had returned to their old way of life, and as I appeared much more crafty, much more active, much more enterprizing than they, the conclusion was drawn, that being the most adroit of spies, was the result of having been the most expert of robbers. This error in reasoning I forgive; but the assertion that I continued daily to plunder, is an intentional calumny.

M. Henry, struck with the absurdity of such an imputation, replied to it by this unanswerable objection. He said, " If it be true that Vidocq commits daily robberies, it is an additional charge against your vigilance; he is alone, you are numerous; you say that he plunders, then how is it that you do not catch him in the fact? Unaided, he has contrived to secure many of your colleagues whilst in the commission of offences, and yet you, all of you, are unable to do so with him!"

The officers were somewhat puzzled how to reply, and thereupon kept silence; but as it was but too evident that the enmity they bore me would always lead them to cross my plans, the préfet of police determined on making me totally independent of them. From that moment I was free to act as I thought fittest for the public welfare. I now only received orders from M. Henry personally, and was amenable for my conduct to him only.

I would have redoubled my zeal had it been possible; and M. Henry did not fear that my exertions would fall off; but as he had already learnt that some persons had threatened my life, he appointed an auxiliary, who was charged with following me at a distance, and watching over me, to ward off any blows which might be aimed at me secretly. The isolated situation in which I was placed greatly favoured my success, and I apprehended a multitude of robbers, who would long have escaped

search had I not been emancipated from all interference from the police agents and inspectors. But
being so much in action, I became more known.   The
robbers swore they would get rid of me, and frequently I
narrowly escaped their blows; my physical strength, and
I may add, my courage, freed me victoriously from all
ambuscades, however craftily planned.   Many attempts,
in which my assailants always came off second best,
taught them that I was fully resolved to sell my life
most dearly.

CHAPTER XXIX.

I seek two celebrated thieves—The music mistress, or another
" mother of robbers"—A metamorphosis, which is not the last
—Scenes of hospitality—The false keys—Ramifications of an
admirable plot—Perfidy of an agent—The plan detected—Mother Noel accuses me of having robbed her—My innocence recognized—My female accuser sent to St Lazarre.

IT is very rare that a fugitive galley-slave escapes with
any intention of amendment ; most frequently the aim
is to gain the capital, and then put in practice the vicious
lessons acquired at the Bagnes, which, like most of
our prisons, are schools in which they perfect themselves in the art of appropriating to themselves the
property of another. Nearly all celebrated robbers
only become expert after passing some time at the galleys. Some have undergone five or six sentences before they become thorough scoundrels ; such as the
famous Victor Desbois, and his comrade Mongenet,
called Le Tambour (Drummer), who during various
visits to Paris comitted a vast many of those robberies
on which people love to descant as proofs of boldness
and address.

These two men, who for many years were sent away
with every chain, and as frequently escaped, were once
more back again in Paris ; the police got information
of it, and I received the order to search for them. All
testified that they had acquaintances with other robbers
no less formidable than themselves. A music mistress,
whose son, called Noel with the Spectacles (Noel
aux bèsicles) a celebrated robber, was suspected of
harbouring these thieves. Madame Noel was a well-
educated woman and an admirable musician; she was
esteemed a most accomplished performer by the middle
class of tradespeople, who employed her to give lessons
to their daughters. She was well known in the Marais
and the Quartier Saint-Denis, where the polish of her

manners, the elegance of her language, the gentility of her dress, and that indescribable air of superiority which the reverses of fortune can never entirely destroy, gave rise to the current belief that she was a member of one of those numerous families to whom the Revolution had only left its hauteur and its regrets.

To those who heard and saw her without being acquainted, madame Noel was a most interesting little woman; and besides, there was something touching in her situation; it was a mystery, and no one knew what had become of her husband. Some said that she had been early left in a state of widowhood; others that she had been forsaken; and a third affirmed that she was a victim of seduction. I know not which of these conjectures approaches nearest to the truth, but I know very well that madame Noel was a little brunette whose sparkling eye and roguish look were softened down by that gentle demeanour which seemed to increase the sweetness of her smile and the tone of her voice, which was in the highest degree musical. There was a mixture of the angel and demon in her face, but the latter perhaps preponderated; for time had developed those traits which characterise evil thoughts.

Madame Noel was obliging and good, but only towards those individuals who were at issue with justice; she received them as the mother of a soldier would welcome the comrade of her son. To ensure a welcome with her, it was enough to belong to the same "regiment" as Noel with the Spectacles; and then, as much for love of him and from inclination perhaps, she would do all in her power to aid, and was consequently looked upon as a "mother of robbers." At her house they found shelter; it was she who provided for all their wants; she carried her complaisance so far as to seek "jobs of work" for them; and when a passport was indispensably requisite for their safety, she was not quiet until by some means she had succeeded in procuring one. Madame Noel had many friends among her own sex, and it was generally in one of their names that the passport was obtained.　A powerful mixture of oxygenated muriatic acid obliterated the writing; and the description of the gentleman who required it, as well as the name which it suited his purpose to assume, replaced the feminine description.　Madame Noel had generally by her a supply of these accommodating passports, which were filled according to circumstances, and the wants of the party requiring such assistance.

All the galley-slaves were children of madame Noel, but those were the most in favour who could give her any account of her son; for them her devotion was boundless; her house was open to all fugitives, who made it their rendezvous; and there must be gratitude even amongst them, for the police were informed that they came frequeutly to mother Noel's for the pleasure of seeing her only; she was the confidante of all their plans, all their adventures, all their fears; in fact, they communicated all unreservedly, and never had cause to regret their reliance on her fidelity.

Mother Noel had never seen me; my features were quite unknown to her, although she had frequently heard of my name.　There was then no difficulty in presenting myself before her, without giving her any cause for alarm; but to get her to point out to me the hiding place of the men whom I sought to detect, was the end I aimed at, and I felt that it would be impossible to attain it without much skill and management. At first, I resolved on passing myself off as a fugitive galley-slave; but it was necessary to borrow the name of some thief, whom her son or his comrades had mentioned to her in advantageous terms.　Moreover, a little resemblance was positively requisite, and I endeavoured to recollect if there were not one of the galley-slaves whom I knew who had been associated with Noel with the Spectacles, and I could not remember one of my age, or whose person and features at all resembled mine.　At last, by dint of much effort

of memory I recalled to mind one Germain, alias
Royer, alias " the Captain," who had been an intimate
acquaintance of Noel's, and although our similarity was
very slight, yet I determined on personating him.

Germain, as well as myself, had often escaped from
the Bagnes, and that was the only point of resemblance between us: he was about my age, but a
smaller framed man; he had dark brown hair, mine
was light; he was thin, and I tolerably stout; his
complexion was sallow, and mine fair, with a very clear
skin; besides, Germain had an excessively long nose,
took a vast deal of snuff, which begriming his nostrils outside, and stuffing them up within, gave him a
peculiarly nasal tone of voice.

I had much to do in personating Germain; but the
difficulty did not deter me: my hair cut, *a là mode des
Bagnes,* was dyed black, as well as my beard, after it
had attained a growth of eight days; to embrown my
countenance I washed it with walnut liquor; and to
perfect the imitation, I garnished my upper lip thickly
with a kind of coffee grounds, which I plastered on by
means of gum arabic, and thus became as nasal in my
twang as Germain himself. My feet were doctored
with equal care; I made blisters on them by rubbing
in a certain composition of which I had obtained the
recipe at Brest. I also made the marks of the fetters;
and when all my toilet was finished, dressed myself
in the suitable garb. I had neglected nothing which
could complete the metamorphosis, neither the shoes
nor the marks of those horrid letters G A L. The
costume was perfect; and the only thing wanting was
a hundred of those companionable insects which people
the solitudes of poverty, and which were, I believe,
together with locusts and toads, one of the seven plagues
of old Egypt. I procured some for money; and as
soon as they were a little accustomed to their new domicile, which was speedily the case, I directed my steps
towards the residence of madame Noel, in the Rue
Ticquetonne.

I arrived there, and knocking at the door, she opened it: a glance convincing her how matters stood with me, she desired me to enter, and on finding myself alone with her, I told her who I was. " Ah, my poor lad," she cried, "there is no occasion to tell me where you have come from; I am sure you must be dying with hunger ?"—" Oh yes," I answered, "I am indeed hungry; I have tasted nothing for twenty-four hours." Instantly, without further question, she went out, and returned with a dish of hog's puddings and a bottle of wine, which she placed before me. I did not eat, I actually devoured ; I stuffed myself, and all had disappeared without my saying a word between my first mouthful and my last. Mother Noel was delighted at my appetite, and when the cloth was removed she gave me a dram. " Ah, maman," I exclaimed, embracing her, "you restore me to life; Noel told me how good and kind you were:" and I then began to give her a statement of how I had left her son eighteen days before, and gave her information of all the prisoners in whom she felt interested. The details were so true and well known, that she could have no idea that I was an impostor.

" You must have heard of me," I continued; " I have gone through many an enterprize, and experienced many a reverse. I am called Germain, or the Captain ; you must know my name ?"

" Yes, yes, my friend," she said, " I know you well; my son and his friends have told me of your misfortunes; welcome, welcome, my dear captain. But heavens ! what a state you are in; you must not remain in such a plight. I see you are infested with those wretched tormenting beasts who——; but I will get you a change of linen, and contrive something as a comfortable dress for you."

I expressed my gratitude to madame Noel ; and when I saw a good opportunity, without giving cause for the slightest suspicion, I asked what had become of Victor Desbois and his comrade Mongenet. " Desbois and

Le Tambour ? Ah ! my dear, do not mention them, I beg of you," she replied; "that rogue Vidocq has given them very great uneasiness; since one Joseph (Joseph Longueville, an old police inspector), whom they have twice met in the streets, told them that there would soon be a search in this quarter, they have been compelled to cut and run, to avoid being taken."

" What," cried I with a disappointed air, " are they no longer in Paris ? "

" Oh, they are not very far distant," replied mother Noel; "they have not quitted the environs of the ' great village' (Paris) ; I dare say we shall soon see them, for I trust they will speedily pay me a visit. I think they will be delighted to find you here."

" Oh, I assure you," said I, " that they will not be more delighted at the meeting than myself; and if you can write to them, I am sure they would eagerly send for me to join them."

" If I knew where they were," replied mother Noel, " I would go myself and seek for them to please you; but I do not know their retreat, and the best thing for us to do is to be patient and await their arrival."

In my quality of a new comer, I excited all madame Noel's compassion and solicitude, and she attended to nothing but me. " Are you known to Vidocq, and his two bull-dogs Lévesque and Compère ?" she enquired.

" Alas ! yes," was my reply; " they have caught me twice."

" In that case then, be on your guard : Vidocq is often disguised; he assumes characters, costumes, and shapes, to get hold of unfortunates like yourself."

We conversed together for two hours, when madame Noel offered me a foot bath, which I accepted; and when it was prepared, I took off my shoes and stockings, on which she discovered my wounded feet, and said with a most commiserating tone and manner. " How I pity you; what you must suffer ! Why did you not tell me of this at first, you deserve to be scolded for it." And whilst thus reproaching me, she examined my feet; and then pricking the blisters, drew a piece of worsted through each, and anointed my feet with a salve which she assured me would have the effect of speedily curing them.

There was something of antique custom in these cares of kind hospitality; and all that was needed to the poetry of the action was, that I should have been some illustrious traveller, and madame Noel a noble stranger. The bath concluded, she brought me some clean linen; and as she thought of all that was needful, added a razor, recommending me to shave. " I shall then see," she added, " about buying you some workman's clothes, as that is the best disguise for men who wish to pass unnoticed; and besides, good luck will turn up, and then you will get yourself some new ones."

As soon as I was thoroughly cleansed, mother Noel conducted me to a sleeping room, a small apartment which served as the workshop for false keys, the entrance to which was concealed by several gowns hanging from a row of pegs. " Here," said she, " is a bed in which your friends have slept three or four times; and you need not fear that the police will hunt you out; you may sleep secure as a dormouse."

" I am really in want of sleep," I replied, and begged her permission to take some repose, on which she left me to myself. Three hours afterwards I awoke, and on getting up we renewed our conference. It was necessary to be armed at all points to deceive madame Noel; there was not a trick or custom of the bagnes with which she was not thoroughly informed; she knew not only the names of all the robbers whom she had seen, but was acquainted with every particular of the life of a great many others; and related with enthusiasm anecdotes of the most noted, particularly of her son, for whom she had as much veneration as love.

" The dear boy, you would be delighted to see him ?" said I.

" Yes, yes, overjoyed."

"Well, it is a happiness you will soon enjoy; for Noel has made arrangements for an escape, and is now only awaiting the propitious moment."

Madame Noel was happy in the expectation of seeing her son, and shed tears of tenderness at the very thoughts of it. I will own that I was affected, and for a moment wavered if for once I would not betray my duties as a police agent; but when I reflected again on the crimes committed by the Noel family, and considered what was due to the interests of society, I remained firm and determined in my resolution to go through with my enterprise at all risks.

In the course of conversation, mother Noel asked me if I had any affair (plan of robbery) in contemplation; and after having offered to procure me one, in case I was not provided, she questioned me on my skill in fabricating keys. I told her I was as adroit as Fossard. "If that be the case," she rejoined, "I am easy, and you shall be soon furnished; for as you are so clever, I will go and buy at the ironmonger's a key which you can fit to my safety lock, so that you will have ingress and egress whenever you require it."

I expressed my feelings of obligation for so great a proof of her kindness; and as it was growing late, I went to bed reflecting on the mode of getting away from this lair without running the risk of being assassinated, if perchance any of the villains whom I was seeking, should arrive before I had taken the necessary precautions.

I did not sleep, and arose as soon as I heard madame Noel lighting her fire; she said I was an early riser, and that she would go and procure me what I wanted. A moment afterwards she brought me a key not cut into wards, and gave me files and a small vice, which I fixed on my bed; and as soon as my tools were in readiness, I began my work in presence of my hostess, who seeing that I was perfectly conversant with the business, complimented me on my skill; and what she most admired was the expedition of my work, for in fact, in

less than four hours, I had perfected a most workman-
like key, which I tried, and it fitted almost accurately.
A few touches of the file completed the instrument;
and, like the rest, I had the means of unobstructed
entrance whenever I wished to visit the house.

I was madame Noel's boarder; and, after dinner, I
told her I was inclined to take a turn in the dusk, that
I might find whether " a job " I contemplated was yet
feasible, and she approved the suggestion, at the same
time recommending me to use all caution. " That
thief of a Vidocq," she observed, " is a thorn in one's
path; mind him;—and, if I were you, before I made
any attempts, I would wait until my feet were well."
" I shall not go far," I replied; " nor stay away long."
This assurance of a speedy return seemed to quiet her
fears. " Well then, go," she said; and I went out
limping.

So far all succeeded to my most sanguine wishes;
it was impossible to stand better with mother Noel;
but, by remaining in her house, who would guarantee
that I should not be knocked on the head? Might not
two or three galley-slaves arrive together, recognize
me, and attack me? Then farewell to all my plottings; and it was incumbent, that, without losing the
fruit of my friendship with mother Noel, I should prepare myself for the contingent danger. It would have
been the height of imprudence to have given her cause
to think that I had any motives for avoiding contact
with her guests, and I consequently endeavoured so
to lead her on, that she should herself suggest to me
the necessity of quitting her house; that is, that she
should advise me no longer to think of sleeping in her
domicile.

I had observed that madame Noel was very intimate
with a fruit-seller who lived in the house, and I sent
to this woman one of my agents named Manceau,
whom I charged to ask her secretly, and yet with a
want of skill, for some accounts of madame Noel. I
had dictated the questions, and was the more certain

that the fruit-woman would not fail to communicate the particulars, as I had desired my man to beg her to observe secrecy.

The event proved that I was not deceived;—no sooner had my agent fulfilled his mission, than the fruit-woman hastened to madame Noel with an account of what had passed; who, in her turn, lost no time in telling me. On the look-out at the steps of the door of her officious neighbour, as soon as she saw me, she came to me, and, without further preface, desired me to follow her, which I did; and, on reaching the Place des Victoires, she stopped, and looking about her to be assured that no one was in hearing, she told me what had passed:—" So," said she, in conclusion, " you see, my poor Germain, that it would not be prudent for you to sleep at my house; you must even be cautious how you approach it by day." Mother Noel had no idea that this circumstance, which she bewailed so greatly, was of my own planning; and, that I might remove all suspicion from her mind, I pretended to be more vexed at it than she was, and cursed and swore bitterly at that blackguard Vidocq, who would not leave us at peace. I deprecated the necessity to which I was reduced, of finding a shelter out of Paris, and took leave of madame Noel, who, wishing me good luck and a speedy return, put a thirty-sous-piece into my hand.

I knew that Desbois and Mongenet were expected; and I was also aware that there were comers and goers who visited the house, whether madame Noel was there or not; and she was often absent, giving music lessons in the city. It was important that I should know these gentry; and to achieve this, I disguised several of my auxiliaries, and stationed them at the corners of the street, where, mixing with the errand boys and messengers, their presence excited no suspicion.

These precautions taken, that I might testify all due appearance of fear, I allowed two days to pass before

I again visited madame Noel; and this period having elapsed, I went one evening to her house, accompanied by a young man, whom I introduced as the brother of a female with whom I had once lived; and who, having met me accidentally in Paris, had given me an asylum. This young man was a secret agent, but I took care to tell mother Noel that he had my fullest confidence, and that she might consider him as my second self; and, as he was not known to the spies, I had chosen him to be my messenger to her whenever I did not judge it prudent to show myself. " Henceforward," I added, " he will be our go-between, and will come every two or three days, that I may have information of you and your friends."

" I'faith," said mother Noel, " you have lost a pleasure; for, twenty minutes sooner, and you would have seen a lady of your acquaintance here."

" Ah! who was it ?"

" Mongenet's sister."

" Oh! indeed; she has often seen me with her brother."

" Yes; when I mentioned you, she described you as exactly as possible ;—' a lanky chap,' said she, ' with his nose always grimed with snuff.' "

Madame Noel deeply regretted that I had not arrived before Mongenet's sister had departed; but certainly not so much as I rejoiced at my narrow escape from an interview which would have destroyed all my projects; for, if this woman knew Germain, she also knew Vidocq; and it was an impossibility that she could have mistaken one for the other, so great was the difference between us! Although I had altered my features so as to deceive, yet the resemblance which, in description, seemed exact, would not stand the test of a critical examination, and particularly the reminiscences of intimacy. Mother Noel then gave me a very useful warning, when she informed me that Mongenet's sister was a very frequent visitor at her house. From thenceforward I resolved that this female should never catch a glimpse of my countenance; and, to avoid meeting with her, whenever I visited madame Noel, I sent my pretended brother-in-law first, who, when she was not there, had instructions to let me know it, by sticking a wafer on the window. At this signal I entered, and my aide-de-camp betook himself to his post in the neighbourhood, to guard against any disagreeable surprise. Not very far distant were other auxiliaries, to whom I had confided mother Noel's key, that they might come to my succour in case of danger; for, from one instant to another, I might fall suddenly amongst a gang of fugitives, or some of the galley-slaves might recognize and attack me, and then a blow of my fist against a square of glass in the window was the signal which was to denote my need of assistance, to equalize the contending parties.

Thus were my schemes concerted, and the finale was at hand. It was on a Tuesday, and a letter from the men I was in quest of, announced their intended arrival on the Friday following; a day which I intended should be for them a black Friday. At the first dawn I betook myself to a cabaret in the vicinity, and, that they might have no motive for watching me, supposing, as was their custom, that they should traverse the street several times up and down before they entered Madame Noel's domicile, I first sent my pretended brother-in-law, who returned soon afterwards, and told me that Mongenet's sister was not there, and that I might safely enter. " You are not deceiving me?" said I to my agent, whose tone appeared altered and embarrassed, and fixing on him one of those looks which penetrate the very heart's core, I thought I observed one of those ill-suppressed contractions of the muscles of the face which accompany a premeditated lie: and then, quick as lightning, the thought came over me that I was betrayed; that my agent was a traitor. We were in a private room, and, without a moment's hesitation, I grasped his throat with violence, and told him, in presence of his comrades, that I was informed of his perfidy, and that if he did not instantly confess all, I would shoot him on the spot. Dismayed at my penetration and determined manner, he stammered out a few words of excuse, and falling on his knees, confessed that he had discovered all to mother Noel.

This baseness, had I not thus detected it, would probably have cost me my life, but I did not think of any personal resentment; it was only the interest of society which I cared for, and which I regretted to see wrecked when so near port. The traitor, Manceau, was put in confinement, and, young as he was, having many old offences to expiate, was sent to Bicêtre, and then to the isle of Oleron, where he terminated his career. It may be conjectured that the fugitives did not return again to the Rue Ticquetonne; but they were, notwithstanding, apprehended a short time afterwards.

Mother Noel did not forgive the trick I had played her; and, to satisfy her revenge, she, one day, had all her goods taken away; and when this had been effected, went out without closing her door, and returned crying out that she had been robbed. The neighbours were made witnesses, a declaration was made before a commissary, and mother Noel pointed me out as the thief; because, she said, I had a key of her apartments. The accusation was a grave one, and she was instantly sent to the prefecture of police, and the next day I received the information. My justification was not difficult, for the préfet, as well as M. Henry, saw through the imposture; and we managed so well, that mother Noel's property was discovered, proof was obtained of the falsity of the charge, and, to give her time for repentance, she was sentenced for six months to St Lazarre. Such was the issue and the consequences of an enterprize, in which I had not failed to use all precaution; and I have often achieved success in affairs, in which arrangements had been made, not so skilfully concerted or so ably executed.

CHAPTER XXX.

The police-officers sent in pursuit of a celebrated robber—They
are unable to discover him—Great anger of one of them—I
promise another new-year's gift to the préfet—The yellow curtains and the hump-backed female—I am a good citizen—A
messenger puts me on the right scent—The chest of the prefecture of police—I am a coal-man—The fright of a vintner and
his wife—The little Norman in tears—The danger of giving Eau
de Cologne—Carrying off of mademoiselle Tonneau—A search—
The thief takes me for his mate—Thieves laugh at locksmiths—
The jump from the window—The ,effects of a long slide, or
broken stitches.

IT has been seen how greatly I was thwarted by the
infidelity of an agent, and I have long since learnt that
there is no secret well kept but that which we tell to
nobody; and sad experience more and more convinced
me of the necessity of acting alone in all my operations, when I could do so; and I pursued this mode,
as will be seen on a very important occasion.

After having undergone several sentences, two fugitives of the isles, named Goreau and Florentin, called
Chatelain (governor), of whom I have already spoken,
were detained at Bicêtre, as incorrigible robbers.
Weary of confinement in these cells, where they were
buried alive, they sent to M. Henry a letter, in which
they offered to give such information as should lead to
the apprehension of several of their comrades, who
were daily perpetrating robberies in Paris. Fossard,
sentenced for life, who had frequently escaped from
the Bagnes, was the one marked out as the most dangerous. " He was," they wrote, " unequalled for intrepidity, and must be attacked with caution; for,
always armed to the teeth, he had resolved on blowing
out the brains of that police-agent who should be
hardy enough to attempt to apprehend him."

The heads of the police asked nothing better than
to free the capital from such a daring thief, and their

first idea was to employ me in discovering him; but the informers having suggested to M. Henry that I was too well known to Fossard and his concubine not to defeat an operation which must be most delicately effected, it was decided that the affair should be intrusted to the skill of some police-officers. To them therefore were given all the necessary instructions to regulate their searches; but, either they were not lucky, or they did not especially approbate a rencontre with Fossard, who was 'armed to the teeth,' for he continued his exploits, and the numerous complaints to which his activity gave rise, announced, that in spite of their apparent zeal, these gentlemen, as usual, made more noise than work.

The result was, that the préfet, who preferred doings to sayings, sent for them one day, and reprimanded them in a manner which must have been severe, to judge by the discontent which they could not help testifying.

They had just received this official proof of disapprobation, when I happened to meet, in the market of Saint-Jean, M. Yvrier, one of the officers in question, whom I saluted, and he thereupon accosted me, almost bursting with rage, saying, " Ah! there you are, Mr Do-so-much; you are the cause of our having been reprimanded about that Fossard, the fugitive galley-slave, who they say is in Paris. If we are to believe monsieur le préfet, there is no one but you who can do anything. If Vidocq, he said to us, had been ordered to this business, we should have had this fellow apprehended long ago. Well, then, let us see, M. Vidocq; set your wits to work to find him, you who are so very clever, and prove that you have all the talent that they say you have."

M. Yvrier was an old man, and it was respect for his age which checked my reply to his impertinence; and although I was wounded by the tone of his address, I did not care to show it, contenting myself with replying, that I had not then the leisure to occupy myself about Fossard, that he was a capture I should reserve till the first of January, that I might have a suitable new year's gift for M. le préfet, as the previous year I had brought the famous Delzève.

"Go on your own way," replied M. Yvrier, irritated at this boast; "the event will show what you are, a presumptuous fellow, who creates difficulties to show his skill in surmounting them;" and he left me, grumbling out from between his teeth some other epithets and qualities which I neither understood nor heeded.

After this scene, I went to M. Henry's private room, to whom I related it. "Ah! they wince—they are angry, are they?" said he, laughing; "so much the better; it proves that they defer to your ability. I see," added M. Henry, "that these gentlemen are like the eunuchs of a seraglio; they cannot do themselves, and would not allow others to be doing." He then gave me the following particulars :—

"Fossard lives in Paris, in a street leading from "the market-place to a boulevard that is somewhere "between the Rue Comtesse d'Artois and the Rue "Poissonnière, passing by the Rue Montorgueil and the "Petit-Carreau: on what story his apartments are is "unknown; but the windows may be recognised by "having yellow silk curtains and other curtains of em- "broidered muslin. In the same house resides a little "hump-backed woman, a seamstress, and intimate with "the female who lives with Fossard."

These particulars were, it may be seen, not sufficiently definite to lead at once to the spot we wished to discover.

A hump-backed woman and yellow curtains with others of embroidered muslin, were not certainly to be found readily in the extent of ground which was to be explored. Perhaps such a combination might be found more than once in the limits prescribed. How many humps, old as well as young, are there not to be found in Paris? And who could count all the yellow curtains? In fact, the data were excessively

vague, and yet the problem was to be solved; and I
determined to try, if by dint of all my acumen and
research, my good genius would not direct my finger
to the very spot I sought.

I was in doubt as to what steps I should first take;
but as I had generally found that, in all my undertakings, it was principally from females that I gleaned
my information, whether women or girls, I soon determined on the disguise which was best adapted for
my purpose. It was apparent that I must assume the
guise of a very respectable gentleman, and, consequently, by means of some false wrinkles, a pig-tail,
snowy white ruffles, a large gold-headed cane, a three-
cornered hat, buckles, breeches and coat to match,—
I was metamorphosed into one of those good
sexagenarian citizens, whom all old ladies admire.
I had the precise appearance and air of one of those
rich old boys of the Marais, whose rubicund and jolly
countenance proves the ease of his circumstances, and
the desire to bestow charity on those who need it, by
way of a recompense to fortune. I was very sure that
the hump-backed women would set their caps at me;
and I had the appearance of so good a man, that it
was impossible they would make any attempts at
deceiving me.

Thus disguised, I went into the streets, gazing upwards to discover all the curtains of the prescribed
colour. I was so much occupied with this investigation that I was entirely lost to all around me. Had I
been a little less substantial looking I might have
been taken for a metaphysician, or perhaps for a poet
who was seeking a couplet in the region of the
chimney-pots; twenty times I narrowly escaped the
cabriolets; on all sides the cry of " Gâre! gâre!"
(mind, mind) assailed me, and then, on turning round,
I was under the wheel, or else close beside a horse;
sometimes, whilst I was wiping the dirt from my
sleeve, a lash of a whip came across my face, or, if the
driver were less brutal, it was some such salutation as

this:—" Out of the way, old dunny-head," or else,
" Come, what are you at, old stupid?"

My work was not to be completed in a single day,
even as far as the yellow curtains went, I marked
down more than one hundred and fifty in my memorandum book, which gave choice enough in all conscience. Had I not, as the saying is, worked for the
king of Prussia?—(i. e. unavailingly.) Might not the
curtains, behind which Fossard was concealed, have
been taken down and replaced by white, red, or green
ones? However, if chance was against me, she might
yet throw out some favourable hint for my guidance;
and I took courage, although it is a somewhat painful
task for a sexagenarian to ascend and descend a hundred and fifty staircases, consisting at least of seven
hundred and fifty stories, to take more than thirty
thousand steps, or twice the height of Chimborazo;
but as I felt my breath good, and my legs strong, I
undertook the task, sustained by the same hope as
that which impelled the Argonauts to sail in quest of
the golden fleece. It was my hump-backed lady that
I sought; and in my ascents, in how many landing-
places have I not stood centinel for hours together, in
the persuasion that my lucky star would shine upon
her. The heroic Don Quixote was not more ardent
in the pursuit of his Dulcinea. I knocked at the doors
of all the seamstresses; I examined them one after
another, but no humps; they were all perfectly formed;
or if by chance they had a projection, it was not a
deviation of the spine, but one of those temporary
exuberances which resolve themselves into maternity.

Thus passed several days without presenting to my
longing eyes the object of my search, and I was
heartily tired of my job, for every night my back
ached past bearing, and yet the work was to be re-
commenced the next morning. I dared ask no questions; for although then some charitable soul might
have put me on the right scent, yet I might get into

danger; and at last, fatigued with this unsatisfactory mode of search, I determined to adopt another.

I have remarked, that hump-backed women are generally very inquisitive, and great chatterers; they are generally the news-distributors of the district, and if not, they are then the registers of petty slanders, and nothing passes with which they are not acquainted. Impressed with this idea, I concluded that, under pretext of getting her little requisites supplied, the unknown humpy lady, who had already cost me so much trouble, would not fail, any more than many others, to come and have her wonted gossip at the milkman's, the baker's, the fruiterer's, the mercer's, or the grocer's. I resolved therefore to station myself at the doors of several of these chattering shops, and as every humpy woman, anxious for a husband, makes a great parade of her abilities as a clever caterer, I was persuaded that mine would be on foot early in the morning, and that I ought, to see her, to station myself at an early hour at my post of observation, and accordingly I went there at daybreak.

I first employed myself in considering how best to take my measures. To what milk-woman would a hump-backed lady give the preference? Certainly, to her who had most gossip, and sold cheapest. There was one at the corner of the Rue Thevenot, who seemed to me to combine these two qualities; she had about her a great number of small cans, and from the midst of her circle did not cease to talk and serve, serve and talk. Her customers babbled away to their hearts' content, and she chattered as indefatigably as her customers; but this was not of any consequence to me; I had pitched upon an admirable and likely spot, and was determined not to lose sight of it.

On going to my second watch in the evening, I impatiently awaited the arrival of my female Esop, but there were only young girls, well made, slender, with good figures, easy appearance, neatly attired, and not one of them that was not as straight and upright as the letter I. I was beginning to despair, when at length my star beamed in the horizon; I saw the Venus, the prototype of all humped women! Ye gods! how handsome she appeared; and how splendid was the contour of that prominent feature for which I had so anxiously watched,—her adorable hump! I gave myself time to contemplate this protuberance, which naturalists should, I think, take into consideration, and enumerate an additional race in the human species. I thought I was gazing on one of those fairies of the middle age, in whom a deformity of this kind was 'a double charm.' This supernatural being, or rather extra-natural, approached the milk-woman, and having gossiped for some time, as I had anticipated, she took her cream; she then entered the grocer's; then paused a moment at the tripe-shop, where she procured some lights, probably for her cat; and then, her stores provided, she turned off in the Rue du Petit Carreau, down the gateway, to a house of which the ground-floor was occupied by a working turner. I cast my eyes instantly on the windows, but, alas! no yellow curtains met my longing lingering look. I however made the reflexion which had before suggested itself, that curtains, of whatever shade, have not the immobility of an original hump; and I resolved not to retire until I had some converse with the enchanting little lump of deformity, whose appearance had so truly enchanted me. I surmised, that in spite of my disappointment with regard to one of the main circumstances described for my guidance, yet that a conversation would elicit some useful information to lighten my path.

I determined to ascend the stair-case; and on getting up to the first landing-place, enquired for "a little lady rather deformed."—"Oh, it is the seamstress you want," was the reply, attended by a significant grin.

" Yes, the seamstress I want; a person who has one
shoulder somewhat higher than the other." Again I
was laughed at, and her apartment pointed out as on
the third story. Although her neighbours were very
complaisant, I was rather nettled at their chuckling
and laughing; it was exceedingly unpolite : but such
was my tolerance, that I freely pardoned the expression of their mirth; and ,was not that commendable in
me? It preserved the character I had assumed. The
door was shown to me ; I knocked, and it was opened
by my darling little Humpa herself; and after fifty
apologies for the visit, I begged her to give me a few
moments' audience, adding, that I had personal business
to discuss with her.

" Mademoiselle," said I, with a solemn tone, after
she had seated me opposite to herself, " you are ignorant of the motive which has led me hither; but when
you shall know it, perhaps the step I have taken will
excite your interest."

The hump-backed damsel thought that I was going
to make an open avowal; the colour rushed to her
cheeks, and her look became animated, although she
cast her eyes on the ground. I continued :

" Doubtless, you will be astonished that at my age
one can be as deeply enamoured as at twenty years
old."

" Ah, sir, you are still young," said the amiable
Humpina, whose mistake I would not allow to be
prolonged.

" Why, pretty well for that," I added, " but it is
not of that I would speak. You know that in Paris
it is not an uncommon thing for a man and woman
to live together without the benediction of holy
Mother Church."

" What do you take me for, sir, to make such a
proposal to me?" cried the little Humpetta, without
giving me time to finish my sentence. I smiled at her
mistake, and continued : " I have no intention to make
any snch proposition; I only request that you will

have the goodness to give me some information respecting a young lady, who, I am told, lives in this house with a gentleman who passes for her husband." —" I know nothing at all about it," answered my little lady, very snappishly

I then gave her a tolerably accurate description of Fossard, and the demoiselle Tonneau, his lady.

"Ah, I know now," said she; "a man of your figure and size, about thirty or five-and-thirty years of age, a good-looking gentleman: the lady, a pretty brunette, beautiful eyes, lovely teeth, charming mouth, superb eyelashes, dark brows, nose a little turned up, with a most engaging and modest demeanour. They did live here, but they have removed." I entreated her to give me their new address; and on her reply, that she did not know it, I weepingly besought her to aid in the recovery of an ungrateful creature, whom I still fondly, dotingly loved, despite her perfidy.

The seamstress was touched. The tears I shed moved her tender heart; and feeling that I gained ground, I became more and more pathetic. "Ah! her infidelity will cause my death: pity, commiserate a wretched husband; I conjure you, do not conceal from me her retreat, and I shall owe you more than life."

Your hump-backed women are compassionate; moreover, a husband is, in their eyes, so inappreciable a treasure; and as they are not possessed of one, they cannot imagine how any one can be unfaithful; and thus my seamstress held adultery in utter abhorrence. She sincerely pitied me, and said she would do all in her power to serve me. "Unfortunately," she added, "their goods having been removed by porters not belonging to the district; I am completely ignorant of where they have gone, or what has become of them; but would you like to see the landlady?" As I had no doubt of her sincerity, I went to see the landlady, but all I learnt from her was, that they had paid for the term agreed on, and had not left any tidings of their new abode.

Except having discovered Fossard's old lodging, I was no forwarder than at first; but I would not abandon the quest without exhausting every chance and enquiry that could suggest itself. Usually, the porters of the various districts knew each other; and I interrogated those of the Rue du Petit Carreau, to whom I introduced myself as a wronged husband; and one of them pointed out to me a comrade who had aided in the removal of my rival's goods and chattels.

I saw this individual, and told him my concerted story; but he was a cunning chap, and intended to trick me. I pretended not to perceive it; and, as a recompense for promising that he would conduct me the next day to the place where Fossard had pitched his tent, I gave him two five-franc pieces, which were spent the same day at the Courtille, in company with the lady he 'protected.'

This interview was on the 27th of December, and we were to meet again the next day; and to fulfil my assertion of the 1st of January there was not much time to lose. I was punctual at the rendezvous; and the porter, whom I had caused to be watched by some agents, was also to the time and place. Some more five-franc pieces changed masters from my purse to his, and I paid for his breakfast. We then started, and we arrived at a very pretty house, at the corner of the Rue Duphot and that of Saint Honoré. "Now," said he, "we must ask the vintner just by if they are still here." He wanted me to regale him again. I did not refuse; and we entered the shop, where we emptied a bottle of good wine: I then left him, fully assured of the residence of my pretended wife and her seducer. I had no farther occasion for my guide, and dismissed him with a mark of my gratitude; but to be sure that he did not betray me, in the hope of being doubly paid, I ordered the agents to watch him closely, and to prevent his returning to the vintner's. As well as I remember, to preclude all possibility of his so doing, they put him in the guard-house : in such cases we are not over particular; and, to be sincere, it was I who put him in the stone doublet, which was but a just retaliation. " My friend," I said to him, " I have left with the police a note of five hundred francs, destined to reward the man who shall successfully aid me in recovering my wife. It is now yours; and I will give you a note which will enable you to secure it ;" and I gave him a small note to M. Henry, who, on perusal, said to a police-officer, " Conduct this gentleman to the chest." The chest was, in this instance, the Sylvestre-Chamber (a place of confinement) where my friend, the porter, had a little leisure for salutary reflection.

I was not certain of Fossard's residence, but yet relied on the indications given to me, and I was provided with the necessary power for his apprehension. Then the " richard du Marais" (the rich old man of the Marais) was suddenly metamorphosed into a coal-man; and in this costume, under which neither the mother who bore me, nor any of the agents of the police who saw me daily, could have recognised me, I employed myself in studying the ground on which I should so shortly be compelled to manœuvre.

The friends of Fossard—that is, his denouncers— had advised that the agents employed in his apprehension should be warned that he was always provided with a dagger and pistols, one of which latter, with double barrels, was concealed in a cambric handkerchief which he always held in his hand. This information called for precaution; and, besides, from the known desperation of Fossard's character, it was certain that to avoid a confinement worse than death, he would not hesitate about a murder. I felt no anxiety to become his victim; and thought that it would sensibly diminish my chance of peril, if I came to a previous understanding with the vintner whose tenant Fossard

was. The vintner was a good fellow enough,* but the
police is always in such ill odour, that it is no easy
matter to procure the assistance of honest men. I determined to bring him over to my side, by making it
much to his interest to do so. I had visited his house
several times in my double disguise, and had leisure to
make myself acquainted with all the localities, and to
become acquainted with the sort of visitors who came
there. I then went in my usual dress, and accosting
the man, told him I wished to speak with him in private. He took me into a small private room, when I
thus addressed him :—

"I have to inform you, from the police, that a plan
is formed to rob your house ; the thief who has devised
the means, and who probably intends perpetrating the
robbery himself, lodges in your house ; the female who
lives with him comes sometimes behind your counter,
sees your wife, and whilst conversing with her, has contrived to get the impression of the key which opens
the door by which the proposed entry is to made. All
is arranged; the alarum is to be cut with nippers whilst
the door is a-jar; once inside, they will ascend quickly
to your chamber; and if they have any suspicion that
you are awake, as it is a perfect ruffian who concerts
the project, there is no need for me to tell you what
will ensue——." " They will cut our throats," said
the alarmed vintner, and then called his wife to communicate the intelligence.—" Oh, my love, what a
world we live in—trust nobody ! That madame Hazard
who seemed too good to have a sin to confess—would
you believe it—actually contemplates the cutting of our
throats ! This very night they will come and settle the
business."—" No, no, be quiet," I replied, " not this
night; the till is not full enough, they wait until the
fitting time ; but if you are discreet and will second me,
we will defeat them."

* He now lives at Rue Neuve-de-Seine. It was at his door
that " La belle Ecaillère" was assassinated.

Madame Hazard was mademoiselle Tonneau, who had assumed the name by which Fossard was known in the house; and I desired the vintner and his wife, who were gladly led by me, to treat their lodgers as usual. It need not be asked how willingly they followed my instructions; and it was agreed between us that to see Fossard go out, and to be able to decide on the best time to seize on him, I should ensconce myself in a small closet under the stairs.

At an early hour on the 29th of December, I betook myself to my station; it was desperately cold, the watch was a protracted one, and the more painful as we had no fire; motionless, however, and my eye fixed against a small hole in the shutter, I kept my post. At last, about three o'clock, he went out; I followed, gladly, and recognized him; for up to that period I had my doubts. Certain now of his identity, I wished at that moment to put into execution the order for his apprehension; but the officer who was with me said he saw the terrible pistol. That I might authenticate the fact, I walked quickly and passed Fossard; and then returning, saw clearly that the agent was right. To attempt to arrest him would have been useless, and I resolved to defer it; and on recalling to mind that a fortnight before I had flattered myself with the prospect of apprehending Fossard on the 1st of January, I was not displeased at the delay; but till then my vigilance was not to be relaxed for a single instant.

On the 31st of December, at eleven o'clock, when all my batteries were charged and my plans perfect, Fossard returned, and without distrust ascended the staircase shaking with cold; and twenty minutes after, the disappearance of the light indicated that he was in bed. The moment had now arrived. The commissary and gendarmes, summoned by me, were waiting at the nearest guard-house until I should call them, and then enter quietly; we deliberated on the most effectual mode of seizing Fossard without running the risk of being killed or wounded; for they were persuaded that unless surprised, this robber would defend himself desperately.

My first thought was to do nothing till day-break, as I had been told that Fossard's companion went down very early to get the milk; we should then seize her, and after having taken the key from her, we should enter the room of her lover; but might it not happen, that contrary to his usual custom, he might go out first? This reflexion led me to adopt another expedient.

The vintner's wife, in whose favour, as I was told, M. Hazard was much prepossessed, had one of her nephews at her house, a lad about ten years of age, intelligent beyond his years, and the more desirous of getting money as he was a Norman. I promised him a reward on condition that, under pretence of his aunt's being taken suddenly ill, he should go and beg madame Hazard to give him some Eau de Cologne. I desired the little chap to assume the most piteous tone he could; and was so well satified with a specimen he gave me, that I began to distribute the parts to my performers. The dénouement was near at hand. I made all my party take off their shoes, doing the same myself, that we might not be heard whilst going up stairs. The little snivelling pilot was in his shirt; he rang the bell—no one answered; again he rang :— " Who's there," was heard.—" It is I, madame Hazard; it is Louis: my poor aunt is very bad, and begs you will be so very obliging as to give her a little Eau de Cologne—Oh! she is dying !—I have got a light."

The door was opened; and scarcely had mademoiselle Tonneau presented herself, when two powerful gendarmes seized on her, and fastened a napkin over her mouth to prevent her crying out. At the same instant, with more rapidity than the lion's when darting on his prey, I threw myself upon Fossard; who, stupified by what was doing, and already fast bound and confined in his bed, was my prisoner before he could make a single movement, or utter a single word. So great was his amazement, that it was nearly an hour before he could articulate even a few words. When a light was brought, and he saw my black face and garb of a coalman, he experienced such an increase of terror, that I really believe he imagined himself in the devil's clutches. On coming to himself, he thought of his arms, his pistols and dagger, which were upon the table; and turning his eyes towards them, he made a struggle, but that was all; for, reduced to the impossibility of doing any mischief, he was passive, and contented himself with " chewing the cud of sweet and bitter fancy."

On searching the domicile of this formidable brigand, a great quantity of jewels were found; diamonds, and cash to the amount of eight or ten thousand francs. Fossard having recovered his spirits, told me, that under the marble of the chimney-piece were ten notes, of a thousand francs each. " Take them," said he; " we will divide, or you shall take as much as you please." I took the notes, and getting into a fiacre, we soon reached M. Henry's office, where we deposited the booty found in Fossard's apartment. On making out the inventory, when we came to the last item, the commissary who had accompanied me in the enterprize, said, " It now only remains to conclude the procès-verbal."—" Stay one moment," I cried, " here are ten thousand francs which the prisoner has handed over to me." I displayed this sum, to the great regret of Fossard, who gave me one of those looks which would say, " this is a turn I will never forgive."

Fossard entered early on a career of crime. Born of reputable parents, he had received a good education ; his friends had done all in their power to divert him from his vicious courses, but, in spite of good advice, he had thrown himself headlong into the vortex of bad company. He began by stealing trifling articles; but soon after, having acquired a decided taste for such pursuits, and blushing, no doubt, at being confounded with ordinary robbers, " petty-larceny knaves," he adopted what the gentlemen style a " distinguished line." The famous Victor Desbois and Noel with the

Spectacles, who now honour the Bagne at Brest with
their distinguished presence, were his associates; and
they committed together those robberies which led to
their imprisonment for life. Noel, whose talents as
a musician, and in his quality of teacher of the
piano-forte, got access to all the rich houses, took impressions of the keys which Fossard then fabricated.
It was an art in which he defied Georget and all the
locksmiths in the world to surpass him; however complicated the lock, however ingenious and difficult the
secret, nothing resisted the efforts of his skill.

It may be easily conceived what advantage he made
of such a pernicious talent; being, moreover, a man who
could insinuate himself into the company of honest
persons, and then dupe them. Besides, he was a close
and frigid character, to which he added courage and
perseverance. His comrades regarded him as the
prince of thieves; and, in fact, amongst the " tip-top
cracksmen" (grinches de la haute pegre), that is, in
the aristocracy of robbers, I never knew but Cognard,
Pontis, Comte de St Hélène, and Jossas (mentioned
in the first volume of these Memoirs), who were at all
comparable with him.

After I had reinstated him at the Bagne, Fossard
often attempted to escape. Some liberated prisoners who have lately seen him, have assured me that
he only longs for liberty, that he may avenge himself
on me. They say, he has threatened to kill me. If
the accomplishment of this kind intention depended
solely on him, I am sure he would keep his word, if it
were only to give a proof of his intrepidity. Two
circumstances that have been told me, will give some
idea of the man.

One day Fossard was about to commit a robbery in
an apartment on the second story: his comrades, who
were watching without, were stupid enough to allow
the proprietor to ascend the staircase; and he, on
putting the key into the door, opened it, went through
several rooms, and on getting to an inner closet, saw

the thief at work; but Fossard, putting himself on the defensive, escaped. A window was open near him, and, darting out of it, he fell into the street without injury, and disappeared as swift as lightning.

Another time, whilst he was escaping, he was surprised on the tiles of Bicêtre, and fired at. Fossard, never disconcerted, continued to walk along without stopping or hastening his steps, and getting to that side which looks into the fields, he slid down. The fall was enough to have broken a hundred necks,. but he received no hurt; only the slide was so rapid, that his clothes were rent in shreds.

CHAPTER XXXI.

A general clearance at la Courtille—The white cross—I am
called a spy—The popular opinion concerning my agents—
Summary of the results of the Brigade de Sureté—Biography
of Coco-Lacour, M. Delavau, and the Trou-Madame—The
grant of my pardon—Retrospective glance over these Memoirs
—I can speak, I will speak.

AT the period of Fossard's arrest, the brigade of security was already formed; and, since 1812, when it
was first established, I had ceased to be a secret agent.
The name of Vidocq had become popular, and many
persons identified me as the person thus known. The
first expedition which had introduced me to notice,
had been directed against the principal places of rendezvous in la Courtille. One day, M. Henry having
expressed an intention of making a general search at
Denoyez's house, that is, a pot-house the most frequented
by riotous persons and rogues of every denomination;
M. Yvrier, one of the police-officers present, observed,
that to put this measure in execution, nothing less
than a battalion was necessary. " A battalion," I
cried out instantly; " why not the great army? As
for me," I added, " give me eight men, and I will
answer for success." We have already had a specimen of the acerbity of M. Yvrier's temper, and, on
this occasion, his face actually blazed with rage, and
he asserted that it was all empty talk.

Be that as it might, I maintained my proposition,
and received my orders to proceed at once to the enterprize. The crusade which I was about to enter
upon, was directed against thieves, fugitives, and many
deserters from the colonial regiments. Having provided myself with an ample supply of manacles, I set
forth with two auxiliaries and eight gendarmes; and,
on reaching Denoyez's, I entered the public room, followed by two of my attendants. I commanded the

musicians to be silent, and they obeyed me; but instantly a cry arose, which soon became general—" to
the door, to the door." There was no time to hesitate, and it was necessary to repress the most forward
of the party before they became so violent as to proceed to blows. I immediately produced my authority,
and, in the name of the law, ordered every one, females excepted, to leave the room. Some murmurs
were heard at this injunction, but, after a few minutes,
the most riotous surrendered and began to depart. I
then stationed myself in the passage, and, as I recognized one or more of the individuals whom I sought,
I marked a cross on their backs with white chalk,
which was a pre-concerted signal, to point out to the
gendarmes, who were in attendance without, to seize
them and fetter them as they went out. In this manner we secured thirty-two of these noted offenders, of
whom we formed a string, which was conducted to the
nearest guard-house, and thence to the prefecture of
police.

The boldness of this coup-de-main made much noise
amongst the persons who frequent the barrier; and,
in a short time it was reported amongst all the thieves
and blackguards of Paris, that there was a spy amongst
them, called Vidocq. The most notorious threatened
to " do for me" on the first opportunity, and some of
them attempted it, but were defeated most wofully;
and the repulses they met with begot for me such an
extensive renown, that it was at length equally spread
over all the individuals of my brigade; and there was
not a stripling amongst them who had not the reputation of Alcides himself; and, to such a pitch was this
idea carried, that, forgetting occasionally of whom
they were discoursing, I experienced a sentiment almost amounting to fear, when the people, without
knowing who I was, conversed, in my presence, of me
or my agents. We were colossal in stature, and the
" old man of the mountain" was not more terrible; his
emissaries, the Seids, were not more devoted or more to

to be dreaded. We broke legs and arms unsparingly; nothing resisted us; and we were everywhere. I was invulnerable; and some asserted, that I was enveloped in armour from head to foot; which may be said, perhaps, to be true, when one is not reputed a coward. The formation of the brigade soon followed the expedition of la Courtille. I had at first four agents, then six, afterwards ten, and finally twelve. In 1817, I had no more; and yet, with this handful of men, from the first of January to the thirty-first of December, I effected 772 arrests and 39 perquisitions or seizures of stolen property.

The following table, which is a recapitulation of the arrests during the year 1817, shows the importance of the operations of the " Brigade de Sûreté :"—

Assassins or murderers	15
Robbers or burglars	5
Ditto with false keys, &c.	108
Ditto in furnished houses	12
Highwaymen	126
Pickpockets and cut-purses	73
Shoplifters	17
Receivers of stolen property	38
Fugitives from the prisons	14
Tried galley-slaves, having left their exile	43
Forgers, cheats, swindlers, &c.	46
Vagabonds, robbers returned to Paris	229
By mandates from his excellency	46
Captures and seizures of stolen property	39
Total	811

From the moment that the robbers knew that I was to exercise the functions of principal police agent, they gave themselves up for lost; and what most disturbed them was to see me surrounded by men who, having lived and " worked" with them, knew them thoroughly.

The captures I made in 1813 were not so numerous as in 1817, but quite sufficient to increase their alarm. In 1814 and 1815, a gang of Parisian robbers freed from the English prison ships, returned to the capital, where they were not slow in resuming their former avocations : they had none of them ever seen me, nor had I seen them ; and flattering themselves with the hope of eluding my vigilance, they commenced their campaign with surprising activity and audacity. In one single night there were in the faubourg St Germain, ten robberies by forcible entry ; during more than six weeks nothing was talked of but such hardy exploits as these. M. Henry, despairing of any mode of repressing this system of robbery, was constantly on the watch; and I could discover nothing. At length, after many ambuscades and much vigilance, an experienced thief whom I apprehended, gave me some information; and in less than two months I placed in the grasp of justice a band of twenty-two thieves, one of twenty-eight, a third of eighteen, and some others of twelve, ten, or eight; not to say anything of the single ones, and the many "fences" (receivers), who were all forwarded to increase the population of the bagnes. It was at this period that I was authorised to augment my brigade with four new agents, chosen from amongst those thieves who had the advantage of knowing the new importation of robbers before their departure.

Three of these veterans, named Goreau, Florentin, and Coco-Lacour, who had been long confined at Bicêtre, earnestly prayed to be employed; they said they were entirely reformed, and swore they would henceforward live honestly by the produce of their labours, that is, upon the salary allotted to the police officers. They had been steeped in crime from infancy ; and I thought that if their determinations of reformation were sincere, none could render me more important services than themselves, and I thereupon applied for their pardon; and although I was told of the chance of

their return to evil courses, particularly the two last,
yet by dint of solicitations and representations founded
on the utility they could be to me, I obtained their
freedom.   Coco-Lacour, against whom the greatest
prejudice existed, because when a secret agent, he had
been accused (rightly or wrongfully is a question) of
stealing the plate of the inspector-general Veyrat, is the
only one who has given me no cause to repent of having
in some degree become answerable for his conduct.
The two others soon compelled me to expel them; and
they have since been condemned at Bourdeaux. As
for Coco, I thought he would keep his word, and I was
not deceived. As he was very intelligent, and had some
knowledge of his business, I made him my secretary.
Subsequently, in consequence of some remonstrances I
made him, he gave me in his resignation, as did two of
his comrades, Decostard, called Procureur, and another
named Chrétien.   Coco-Lacour is now the chief police
agent; and until he publishes his Memoirs, it may not
be uninteresting to show the vicissitudes through which
he has passed in attaining the post which I so long
filled.   There are many palliatives for his course of life;
and in his radical reformation from capital crimes, are
shewn potent reasons why we should never despair of the
return of a man of perverted courses of life to the paths
of rectitude.   The documents from which I shall extract the principal features of the history of my successor, are most correctly authentic.   Here we have
the first traces of his existence left at the prefecture of
police.   I open the " Registres de sureté," and thus
transcribe :—

  " LACOUR, Marie-Barthelemy, aged eleven years, re-
siding Rue du Lycée; sent to the Force 9th Ventose,
year 9, charged with an attempt at robbery: eleven
days afterwards sentenced to a month's imprisonment
by the Correctional Tribunal.

  " The same, apprehended 2nd Prairial following, and
again sent to the Force accused of stealing lace in a

shop. Set at liberty the same day by the judicial police magistrate of the 2nd arrondissement (division).

" The same, sent to Bicêtre 23d Thermidor, year 10, by order of M. le préfet; discharged 28th Pluviose, year 11.

" The same, sent to Bicêtre 6th Germinal, year 11, by order of the préfet; remanded to the gendarmerie 2nd Floréal following, to be conveyed to Havre.

" The same, aged 17 ; a notorious pickpocket, and already frequently in custody as such ; sent to Bicêtre in July 1807, to serve (voluntarily) in the colonial corps, and remanded 31st of the same month to the gendarmerie, to be conveyed to the fixed destination. Escaped from the Isle of Rhé the same year.

" The same Lacour called Coco (Barthelemy), or Louis Barthelemy, aged 21; born at Paris, a porter, living faubourg St Antoine, No. 297. Sent to the Force 1st December 1809, accused of theft. Sentenced to two years imprisonment by the Correctional Tribunal on the 18th of January 1810, and then handed over to the minister of the marine department as a deserter.

" The same, sent to the Bicêtre 22nd January 1812, as an incorrigible thief. Sent to the prefecture 3d of July 1816."

The youth of Lacour presents a sad picture of the dangers of a bad education. All I can say is, that since his liberation he has shown every symptom of an excellent natural disposition. Unfortunately, his parents were poor ; his father, a tailor and porter in the Rue du Lycée, did not bestow any thought or care on the guidance of his early years, on which so frequently depends the destiny of most men. I believe, besides, that he was left an orphan at a very tender age; but certainly he grew up, nursed on the knees of his neighbours the courtezans and milliners of the " Palais Egalité ;" and as they found him a nice little fellow, they were prodigal of their favours and caresses ; they, at the same time, instilled into him what they termed " acuteness." These were the ladies who took care of his infancy, and with whom he was constantly to be found. He was "the ladies' toy, the charming boy;" and when the duties of their calling took them away from a leisure of so much innocence, little Coco went into the garden, and played with the throng of black-guards, who, between the games of hockey and peg-top, kept a school of initiation into the mysteries of sleight of hand. Nourished by prostitutes, and taught by pickpockets, there is no need to descant at length on the ' trade ' in which he acquired an early proficiency. The road he travelled was a dangerous one. One female, who perhaps thought herself entitled to give a better direction to his 'studies,' invited him to her house; her name was Marechal, who kept a notorious house in the Place des Italiennes. There Coco was well nurtured ; but complaisance was the only moral quality which his hostess sought to develope, and very complaisant he became : he was at everybody's beck and call, and made himself subservient to the minutest wants of the establishment, whose every detail was perfectly familiar to him. However young, Lacour had his days and hours for walking abroad, and it appears that he did not pass them idly; for before he attained his twelfth year, he was quoted as one of the greatest adepts at stealing lace, and in a very little time his frequent arrests would have procured for him the first rank amongst the shoplifters, called knights of the post (chevaliers grimpants). Four or five years detention at Bicêtre, where he was confined, as a dangerous and incorrigible thief, did not amend him ; but there he learned the trade of a cap-maker, and received other instruction.

Insinuating, plastic, with a soft voice, and a face effeminate but not handsome, he took the fancy of a M. Mulner, who, sentenced to sixteen years of hard labour, had obtained permission to await the expira-tion of his sentence at Bicêtre. This prisoner, who was brother to a banker at Anvers, was a man of good education; and to divert his thoughts, took Coco under his care, and must have aided his studies with much attention, as in a short time Coco could speak and write his own language in a tolerably correct manner. The good graces of M. Mulner were not the only advantage which Lacour derived from an agreeable exterior. During the whole of his imprisonment, a female, called Elisa l'Allemande, (German Eliza) who was enamoùred of him, bestowed all possible favours on him; but this girl, to whom he owes life itself, has, according to report, experienced only ingratitude from him in return.

Lacour is a man whose height does not exceed five feet two inches;* he is fair and bald-headed, with a mean, nay, almost servile look; his eyes blue, but dull; a care-worn countenance, and nose slightly rubicund at the tip, which is the sole part of his face that is not as pale as a corpse. He is passionately fond of dress and trinkets, and makes a great show of chains and gewgaws of all sorts: in his conversation he affects great refinement, and makes use of fine words upon every occasion. It is impossible to be more polite, nor more humble; but at the first glance it is perceptible that his manners are not those of well-bred society; they are rather those derived from the genteel part of the inmates of prisons, and those places which Lacour has frequented. He has all the suppleness of loins needful to keep a man in place; and moreover has a wonderful aptitude for genuflexion. Tartuffe himself, and the resemblance is striking in more than one particular, could not acquit himself more satisfactorily.

Lacour having become my secretary, could not be made to understand, that, to preserve the decorum of his post, his lady companion, who had turned fruiteress and washerwoman, after giving up a certain other employment, would do well to choose a business somewhat more respectable. A discussion on this subject

* Nearly 5 feet 8 inches English measure.

occurred between us, and rather than yield the point, he resigned his situation. He became a pedlar, and sold pocket-handkerchiefs in the streets; but soon, as fame reports, he became a church-goer, and enrolled himself beneath the banner of the Jesuits, and thence grew into the "odour of sanctity" with MM. Duplessis and Delavau. Lacour has all the devotion which could recommend him in their eyes. One fact I can testify, that at the period of his marriage, his confessor, who deemed a heavy penance necessary, inflicted one upon him of a most rigorous nature, which he endured to the fullest extent. For a month, rising at dawn of day, he went with bare feet to the Rue Sainte-Anne au Calvaire, the only place where he was to meet his wife, who was also expiating offences committed.

After the appointment of M. Delavau, Lacour had an accession of religious fervour; he lived then in Rue Zacharie, and although his parochial church was that of Saint Severin, yet he went to mass every Sunday at Notre-Dame, where chance (of course) always placed him in front of the new préfet and his family. That Lacour was so thoroughly reformed must be a matter of congratulation; but it is to be lamented that it did not commence twenty years earlier; but better late than never.

Lacour has very mild manners, and if he did not get dead drunk occasionally, we should think that he had no other passion than a great love of fishing. He throws his line in the vicinity of the Pont Neuf, and frequently devotes whole hours to this silent enjoyment. Constantly near him is a female, who gives him from time to time the worm with which to bait his hook; it is madame Lacour, formerly celebrated for offering other baits still more captivating. Lacour was enjoying this innocent recreation, the taste for which he partakes with his 'Britannic majesty,' and the poet Coupigny, when honors came in quest of him. The messengers of M. Delavau found him under the Arche-Marion, and took him, line in hand, as the officers of the Roman senate took Cincinnatus from his plough. There are always in the lives of great men, deeds of similarity, and perhaps madame Cincinnatus also sold dresses for the accommodation of the young ladies of her time. This is now the trade of the legitimate better moiety of Coco-Lacour. But " something too much of this." I have said enough about my successor, and now to return to the history of the ' Brigade de Sureté.'

It was in the course of the years 1823 and 1824 that it received its greatest increase of numbers, the amount of agents of which it was then composed being, on the proposition of M. Parisot, extended to twenty, and even twenty-eight, including eight individuals supported by the profits of gambling tables, which the préfet authorised them to keep in the public streets.

When millions (francs) were allowed for the expenses of the police, it is scarcely conceivable how recourse can be had to such pitiful measures From the 20th of July to the 4th of August, the gambling-tables held under the authority of M. Delavau produced 4,364 francs 20 cents. This was the money of mechanics and apprentices, who were thus inoculated with a lust for the most destructive of all passions. It will scarcely be believed, that a functionary, a magistrate professedly so religious, could lend himself to such immorality ; but the perusal of the following document will remove all doubts :—

" PREFECTURE OF POLICE.

" Paris, 13 Jan. 1823.

" We, councillor of state, préfet of police, &c. ordain as follows :—

" To include from this date, the Sieurs Drissenn and Ripaud, formerly authorized to keep in the public streets a gaming-table of ' trou-madame,' in the par-

ticular 'Brigade de Sureté,' under the orders of Sieur
Vidocq, chief of this brigade.

"They shall continue to keep the gambling-table,
but six other persons shall be added to their numbers,
who shall also perform the services of secret agents.

" The councillor of state, préfet, &c.

                    (Signed)   " G. DELAVAU.

" Copied by the secretaire-general.

                              " L. DEFOUNGERES."

It was with a troop so small as this that I had to
watch over more than twelve hundred pardoned convicts, freed, some from public prisons, others from
solitary confinement: to put in execution, annually,
from four to five hundred warrants, as well from the
préfet as the judicial authorities; to procure information, to undertake searches, and obtain particulars
of every description; to make nightly rounds, so perpetual and arduous during the winter season; to assist
the commissaries of police in their searches, or in the
execution of search-warrants; to explore the various
rendezvous in every part; to go to the theatres, the
boulevards, the barriers, and all other public places,
the haunts of thieves and pickpockets. What activity
must be exercised when only twenty-eight men were
appointed for such details on so vast a space, and at
so many points at once! My agents had almost the
talent of ubiquity, and I, to keep alive the spirit of
emulation and zeal amongst them, incited them by
unremitting exertions. In no expedition, however
perilous, did I spare myself; and if the most notorious
criminals have been brought to justice by my vigilance,
I may say, without boasting, that the most daring were
the capture of my own hands, the prize of my bow and
spear. As principal agent of ' La police particuliere
de sureté,' I might, as chief, have kept quiet at my
office in Rue Sainte-Anne: but more actively, and
moreover, more usefully employed, I only went there

to give my orders for the day, to receive reports, or
to give audiences to persons who, having been robbed,
came to me with their complaints, trusting to having
the thieves detected.

Up to the moment of my quitting office, the police
of safety—the only requisite police, that which should
have received the greater portion of the funds allowed
by the budget, because it is on it principally that
reliance has been placed—the police of safety, I say,
has never employed more than thirty men, nor cost
more than 50,000 francs per annum, from which five
were allotted to me.

Such have been, at the utmost, the effective force
and the expense of the Brigade de Sureté: with so
small a number of auxiliaries, and means so limited,
I have maintained security in the bosom of a capital,
populated by nearly a million of inhabitants. I have
broken up all the associations of malefactors; I have
prevented their reunion; and during the year since I
have left the police, if no new gangs have been formed,
although robberies have increased, it is because all
the 'first-rate professors' have been confined at the
Bagnes, when I had the commission to pursue them,
and the power to repress them.

Before my time, strangers and country people
looked on Paris as a den of infamy, where it was
requisite to keep incessantly on the alert; and where
all comers, however guarded and careful, were sure
to pay their footing. Since my time, there was no
department, taking the year round, in which more
crimes, and more horrible crimes, were perpetrated
than in the department of the Seine; now there is
none in which fewer guilty offenders have remained
unknown, or fewer crimes remained unpunished. In
truth, since 1814, the continued vigilance of the
national guard has powerfully contributed to such
results. Never was the watchfulness of a national
guard more requisite, and more efficient: but still it
must be allowed that, at the period when the com-

pulsory enlistment of our troops, and the desertion of
foreign soldiers poured out upon our metropolis, a
crowd of bad characters, adventurers, and needy
persons of all nations, in spite of the presence of the
national guard, much work was still to be performed
by the brigade of safety and their chief. And we did
much; and if I feel pleasure in paying to the national
guard the well-earned tribute of their merits,—if from
the experience I had during their existence, and since
their disbanding, I declare that Paris without them
cannot be in safety, it is because I have always found
in them an intelligence, an anxiety to assist, a perfect
desire to act in concert for the public good, which
I have never observed in the gendarmes, who
manifest their zeal, for the most part, by acts of
brutality, after the actual danger has passed. I
have left for the present police of safety an infinity
of precedents, and the traditions of my enterprizes
will not soon be forgotten: but whatever may be
the abilities of my successor, as long as Paris shall
be destitute of its civil guard, no measures will reduce to a state of inaction the generation of malefactors, which will spring up from the instant that
a watch ceases to be kept, at all hours, and in all
quarters. The chief of the police cannot be at
all points at once, and each of his agents has not the
hundred arms of Briareus. On looking over the
columns of the daily journals, we are alarmed at the
enormous quantity of violent burglaries nightly committed, and yet the journals do not detail nine-tenths
of those that occur. It appears that a gang of galley-slaves has recently established itself on the
banks of the Seine. The shopkeepers, even in the
most frequented and most populous streets, cannot
sleep in safety: the Parisian is afraid to leave his
apartments for a short excursion into the country:
we hear of nothing but breakings in, doors opened
with false keys, apartments plundered, &c.; and yet we
are in the season of the year most favourable for the

lower orders. What must we then expect, when winter comes on, and when, by the interruption of labour, misery will add to her numbers? For, in spite of the assertions of some persons about the king, who are desirous of remaining in ignorance of all that passes around them, misery will engender crime; and misery in a society which is ill combined, is not a scourge from which we can always shield ourselves, even when indefatigably industrious. The moralists of a time when the population was secure, might have been able to assert, that the idle only are liable to die of hunger; but now all is changed, and if we make observations, we shall soon be convinced, not only that there is not employment sufficient for everybody, but, moreover, that the pay for certain labour is not sufficient to satisfy the first demands of nature. If circumstances occur as severe as many anticipate, when trade is languishing, so that industry is exerted vainly in seeking a market for its productions, and that she is impoverished in proportion as she creates, how can so great an evil be remedied? Certainly, it is better to support the necessitous than to think of repressing their despair; but in the impossibility of doing better, and the crisis so near at hand, is it not adviseable, in the first instance, to strengthen the arms of public order? And what guard is preferable to the continual presence of the civic body, who watch and act perpetually under the auspices of legality and honour? Shall we substitute for an institution so noble, so admirable, a changeable police, whose numbers can be extended or curtailed at pleasure? Or, shall we have a legion of agents, who will be discharged the moment they are thought past service? It is generally known that the police of safety is recruited even at the present time from the prisons and Bagnes, which are a sort of preparatory school for spies on robbers, and the nursery whence they must be drawn. Employ these people in numbers, and seek to send them back again when they have acquired the know-

z 2

ledge of the plans of the police; they will return to
their old trade, and with additional prospect of success. All trials, when I have made them with my
auxiliaries, have proved to me the truth of such an
assertion. Not but that some of the members of my
brigade (and it was entirely composed of individuals
who had undergone sentences of punishment) were
incapable of doing an action contrary to honesty; I
could quote the names of many to whom I should not
have hesitated to confide money to any amount without an acknowledgement for it—without even counting
it; but those who were thus thoroughly reformed were
in the distinguished minority: and this would not bear
out an assertion, (with all respect for the profession)
that there were amongst them fewer honest men in
proportion, than are to be found in the other classes
to which it is deemed honourable to belong. I have
seen amongst notaries, money-brokers, and bankers,
many faithless agents who have seemed to rejoice in
the infamy with which they were covered. I have
seen one of my subalterns, a freed galley-slave, blow
out his brains, because he had lost at the gaming-table
five hundred francs, of which he was only the de-
pository. Can many similar suicides be pointed out
in the annals of the Exchange ? And yet——but it is
not our business to apologise here for the brigade of
safety, in a point of view totally foreign to its service.
It was the inconvenience of large bodies of spies that
I proposed to make evident ; and inconvenience results
from all that I have said, without mentioning its dangerous effect on the morals of the people, who become
thereby familiarised with the idea, that every sentence
undergone is a noviciate or introduction to a certain
mode of existence, and that the police is only the
invalid squadron of the galleys.

It is perhaps from the period of the formation of
the Brigade de Sureté that the interest of these
Memoirs really commences. It may be thought that
I have expatiated somewhat too much at large on my

personal affairs, but it was a necessary preliminary
that I should impart a knowledge of the vicissitudes
through which I have passed to become the Hercules
for whom was reserved the purging the earth of dire
monsters, and cleansing out the Augean stable. I did
not reach the eminence in a single day, but have
furnished a long career of observation and painful
experience. Soon,—and I have given some trifling
specimens of my means to do so,—I will detail my
labours, the efforts I have made, the perils I have
confronted, the plots and stratagems to which I have
had recourse, to fulfil the utmost of my duty, and to
render Paris the safest residence in the world. I will
unfold the expedients resorted to by the thieves, and
the signs by which they may be detected; I will
write of their manners and their habits; I will explain
their language and their costume, according to the
peculiarities of each; for thieves have a costume
adapted to the enterprizes in which they are engaged.
I will propose infallible measures for the destruction
of all rogueries, and putting a stop to the destructive
skill of all those swindlers, cheats, impostors, &c. &c.
who, in spite of Sainte Pelagie, and despite the
useless and barbarous custom of personal arrest
(contrainte par corps), daily cheat to the extent of
millions (francs). I will lay open all the modes and
tactics practised by all these scoundrels to catch their
'gudgeons.' I will do 'all this, aye, more;' I will
mention by name the principal of them, and thus
brand them in the forehead with a distinguishing
mark. I will class the different grades of malefactors,
from the murderer to the pickpocket, and form of
them lists more useful than those of La Bourdonnaie
for the use of the proscribers of 1815; for mine will,
at least, have the advantage to pointing out at the
first glance, the persons and places to whom mistrust
should be attached. I will expose to the eyes of the
honest man, all the snares laid to catch him; and I
will note down, for the use of the criminal accuser,

the various modes of escape by which the guilty but too often succeed in setting at defiance the sagacity of the judge.

I will display to the glare of noon-day the faults of our criminal informations, and the still greater errors of our penal code, so absurd in many of its enactments. I will ask for alterations, revisions; and what I ask will be conceded: because reason, come from where she may, is always sooner or later understood. I will offer important ameliorations in the regulations of prisons and bagnes; and as I compassionate more deeply than another can, the sufferings of my old companions in misery, condemned or pardoned, I will probe the wound to the bottom; and shall, perhaps, be the happy man who will offer to a philanthropic legislator the only remedies which it is possible to apply, and which alone will be not temporising but effective. In delineations, as varied as novel, I will give original traits of many classes of society, destitute as yet of all civilization; or rather which have emanated from her and infest her, attended by all that is hideous and infamous. I will mould with fidelity the physiognomy of these " paria castes ;" and I will so contrive, that the necessity of some institutions to purify them, as well as to regulate the manners of a portion of the people, shall result; for having had closer and more frequent opportunities of studying them than any other person, I can give a more exact account of them. I will satisfy curiosity on more heads than one; but that is not the end I aim at. Corruption must be lessened by it, the blemishes on propriety must be more rare, prostitution must cease to be the consequence of certain peculiarities of situation ; and those nameless depravities so abhorrent, that those who have abandoned themselves to them have been placed out of the pale of the law as a punishment for their outrage on morals, as well as for the protection of the correct portion of society, should disappear, or cease to be, by their infamous publicity, a perpetual object of just offence to the man who obeys and re-

spects the law of nature. This is the apex of crime;
and to root it out, the highest stations of society must
be assailed. Persons of exalted rank are tainted with
this leprosy, which has lately spread to a dreadful
extent. At the sight of venerated names in the list of
the modern Sardanapali, we can but shudder at the
frailty of humanity; and yet this list makes mention only
of those who have been reduced to the necessity of
sending for the police, or allowing them to interfere in
the disgraceful scenes which they brought on by their
own turpitude.

It has been publicly stated that I shall not speak of
the political police: I shall speak of all police now ex-
isting, from that of the jesuits to that of the court;
from the police of the ' ladies of the pavé' (bureau des
mœurs) to the diplomatic police (a system of espionage
established by the powers of Russia, England, and
Austria); I will show up all the wheel-work, great and
small, of those machines which are always set in motion,
not for the sake of the general weal, but for the service
of him who introduces the drops of oil; that is to say,
for the benefit of the first comer who dispenses the
cash of the treasury: for when we mention political
police, we mention an institution created and maintained
by a desire of enriching certain persons at the expense
of a government whose alarms it perpetually excites.
When we talk of a political police, we talk of the necessity of being incribed in the budget of secret expenses;
—the necessity of giving a concealed destination to
funds visibly and often illegally levied (such as the tax
on prostitutes, and a thousand other trifling imposts);
—the necessity for certain administrators to create important wants, asserted to be for state exigencies;—the
necessity, in fact, of extortions for the profit of a vile
herd of adventurers, intriguers, gamblers, bankrupts, pil-
ferers, &c. Perhaps I shall be fortunate enough to
point out the inutility of those perpetual agents destined
to prevent attempts which are " few and far between,"
—crimes which they have never foreseen,—plots which

they have never detected when they were real, or only discovered when they themselves had concocted them. I will develope all these things without disguise, without fear, without temper; I will tell the whole truth, whether I speak as a witness or as an actor.

I have always held political spies in the most profound contempt, and for two reasons : first, if they never fulfil their orders, they are rogues ; and if they do fulfil them, as soon as it becomes a personal matter, they are wretches. Yet, my functions frequently placed me in contact with the majority of these hireling spies ; they were all known to me directly or indirectly, and I shall name them all. I can do it; I have not shared their infamy; I have only seen the mine and countermine somewhat nearer than any other person. I know what are the resources of the polices and counterpolices. I have learnt, and will communicate the means of ensuring their services; how to play them off, to disturb their treacherous and malevolent plottings, and even mystify them. I have observed all, understood all; nothing has escaped me; and those who gave me my cue for hearing and understanding all, were not false brethren; for, as I was at the head of one of the portions of police, they might think I was a bird of their feather. Did we not all grind at the same mill ?

I may be believed or not; but so far I have made some confessions so humiliating, as to leave no doubt that if I had belonged to the political police, I should unhesitatingly avow all. The journals, which are not always well-informed, have asserted that they had frequently discovered me in different enterprises; that I and my brigade were in action during the troubles of June; during the missions; at the burial of General Foy; at the anniversary of the death of young Lallemand; at the schools of law and medicine, when certain questions were agitated. It would be easy to assert that I was wherever a multitude assembled; but what would be the fair inference ? Why, that I was seeking for

thieves and pickpockets where they were carrying on
their trade. I was on the look-out for cut-purses,
friends or not of " La Charte;" but I defy any one to
say that any one of my agents could be detected in
uttering a seditious cry. There is no point of relation between a political spy and a police spy. Their
attributes are totally distinct: the one only needs the
courage to apprehend an honest man, who rarely
makes any resistance. The courage of the other is
wholly different, and rogues are not so tractable.

There was a report which for some time was very
prevalent, namely, that recognized by a water-carrier
in the midst of a group of students who would not
attend to the lessons of M. the professor Recamier, I
was nearly killed by them. I here declare that the
statement was utterly unfounded. A spy was certainly pointed out, menaced, and even ill-treated. It
was not I, and I confess I was not sorry for it; but
had I been amongst the young men who were active
in this fray, I should instantly have declared my name:
they would soon have known that Vidocq never meddled with respectable young men, who did not carry
on business in the " purse and watch line." Had I
been amongst them, I would have conducted myself
so as not to have drawn down any disagreeables on
my head; and it would have been generally understood that my duty did not consist in exciting individuals already too much exasperated. The man who
saved himself in a court, and thus escaped their vengeance, was Godin, a peace-officer. Besides, I repeat
it, neither the seditious cries, nor the other evidences
of opinion, were of consequence to me; and had any
one pointed out to me the most seditious of the party,
I should not have considered it any part of my duties
to have noticed him. The political police is in regular
troops, and has always volunteers on grand occasions,
paid or unpaid, ready to second its designs. In 1795
the Septembrizers were let loose; they came from
under-ground, and returned there again after the mas-

sacres. The window-smashers, who, in 1817, were the preluders to the carnage of the Rue Saint Denis, were not, I believe, belonging to the 'Brigade de Sureté.' I appeal to M. Delavau; I appeal to the director Franchet:—the freed convicts are not the worst inhabitants of Paris; and in more cases than one, have evinced that they will not stoop to all that is required of them. My post, as far as concerns political police, was limited to the execution of some warrants of the attorney-general and the ministers; but these warrants would have been enforced without me; and, besides, they had decided legal authority. And besides, no human power, no prospect of reward, could have induced me to act conformably to principles and sentiments not my own: and my veracity will not be impugned, when I state the motives that induced me voluntarily to resign the post I had filled for fifteen years;—when I explain the source and the reason of the ridiculous tale, according to which I was to have been hanged at Vienna, for an attempt to assassinate the son of Napoleon;—when I shall have told to what jesuitical plot is to be assigned the false story of the apprehension of a thief, who was stated to have been lately seized at the back of my carriage, at the moment I was passing Place Baudoyer.

In drawing up these Memoirs, I at first limited myself to arrangements and restrictions prescribed by my personal situation, which were prudential. Although pardoned since 1818, I was not out of the reach of administrative rigour: the letter of pardon which I have obtained, instead of a revision which would have freed me, was not drawn out; and it might be that the "powers that be," still bearing the license of absolute control over me, might make me repent these disclosures, which do not however exceed the bounds of our constitutional liberty. Now that at the solemn audience of the first of last July, (1828,) the court of Douai proclaimed that the rights which had been taken from me by an error of justice, were at length restored to me, I will omit nothing, I will disguise nothing which it is fitting to say; and it shall still be for the service of the state and the public, that I will be indiscreet: this intention will be evident in every subsequent page. That I may perform it in a way which will leave me nothing to desire, and not to deceive the general expectation in any way, I have imposed on myself a task very painful for a man more accustomed to do than to narrate, that of revising the greater part of these Memoirs. They were terminated, and I might have given them as they were; but, in addition to the inadequacy of a careless style, the reader would therein detect the mark of a strange influence which I must have submitted to unwillingly. Distrusting myself, and little accustomed to the requisites of the literary world, I had submitted my work to the revision of a soi-disant man of letters. Unfortunately, in this censor, whose private orders I was far from suspecting, I met with one who, for a bribe, had undertaken to emasculate my manuscript, and only to present me under the most odious colours; to pervert my meaning, and deprive all I wished to say of its due importance. A very severe accident, the fracture of my right arm, which I was on the point of having amputated in consequence, was a favourable occurrence in aid of the perpetration of such a project; and therefore all haste was made to profit by the period of my excessive sufferings. The first volume and part of the second were already printed, when all this intrigue was discovered. To render it perfect, I must have re-commenced, at a fresh expense; but to that time only my private adventures were detailed; and although I am drawn in the most unfavourable colours, I hope that in spite of the expressions and bad arrangement, since the facts are told, the just estimation will be set on them, and the most correct inferences drawn. All that portion of the narrative which only relates to my private life, I have allowed to remain. I had the right to subscribe to a sacrifice of my self-love; a

A A

sacrifice which I make, at the risk of being taxed with immodesty, for a confession, the motives of which have been dissembled or perverted: it marks the limit between what I ought to preserve and what to destroy. After my enlistment amongst the pirates at Boulogne, it will be perceived easily that it is I who hold the pen. This prose is such as M. Baron Pasquier was pleased to approve, for which he had even a predilection which he did not conceal. I ought to remember the eulogiums he passed on the abridged reports which I addressed to him : be that as it may, I have repaired the injury as far as was in my power, and in spite of the increase of labour which has fallen to my lot in the direction of a large working establishment which I have formed, resolved my Memoirs shall be really " the police stripped and exposed to the public," I have not hesitated to undertake, in addition, the narration of all that relates to the police. The necessity of such a labour must cause some delays, but it will justify them at the same time, and the public will not be the losers. Formerly, Vidocq, under sentence of justice, could only speak reservedly; now it is Vidocq, the free citizen, who freely narrates " the truth, the whole truth, and nothing but the truth."

END OF THE SECOND VOLUME.

LONDON

PRINTED BY C. AND W. REYNELL, BROAD ST. GOLDEN SQ.

Literature of Mystery and Detection

AN ARNO PRESS COLLECTION

Adams, Samuel Hopkins. **Average Jones.** [1911]

Allen, Grant. **An African Millionaire.** 1897

Arkwright, Richard. **The Queen Anne's Gate Mystery.** 1889. Two volumes in one

Benson, E[dward] F[rederic]. **The Blotting Book.** 1908

[Burgess, Gelett]. **The Master of Mysteries.** [1912]

Canler, [Louis]. **Autobiography of a French Detective From 1818 To 1858.** 1862

Claretie, Jules. **The Crime of the Boulevard.** [1897]

Collins, Wilkie. **The Queen of Hearts.** 1859

Farjeon, B[enjamin] L[eopold]. **Devlin the Barber.** 1888

[Felix, Charles]. **The Notting Hill Mystery.** [1862]

Gaboriau, Emile. **File No. 113.** 1900

Gaboriau, Emile. **The Widow Lerouge.** 1873

Green, Anna Katherine. **The Filigree Ball.** [1903]

Griffiths, Arthur [George Frederick]. **The Rome Express.** 1907

Gulik, R[obert] H[ans] van. **Dee Goong An:** Three Murder Cases Solved by Judge Dee. [1949]

Haggard, H. Rider. **Mr. Meeson's Will.** 1888

Hawthorne, Julian. **David Poindexter's Disappearance and Other Tales.** London, 1888

Hume, Fergus [Wright]. **The Mystery of a Hansom Cab.** [n. d.]

James, Henry. **The Other House.** 1896

Leblanc, Maurice. **The Exploits of Arsène Lupin.** [1907]

Leighton, Marie Connor and Robert Leighton. **Michael Dred, Detective,** 1899

Leroux, Gaston. **The Mystery of the Yellow Room.** 1908

Lowndes, [Marie Adelaide] Belloc. **The End of Her Honeymoon.** 1913

Lynch, Lawrence L. (pseud. of Emma Murdoch Van Deventer). **Dangerous Ground.** 1885

Meade, L. T. (pseud. of Elizabeth Thomasina Smith) and Clifford Halifax. **Stories From the Diary of a Doctor.** 1895

Moffett, Cleveland. **Through the Wall.** [1909]

Morrison, Arthur. **Martin Hewitt, Investigator.** [1894]

O. Henry (pseud. of William Sidney Porter). **The Gentle Grafter.** 1908

Orczy, [Emmuska]. **Lady Molly of Scotland Yard.** [1926]

Payn, James. **Lost Sir Massingberd.** [n. d.]

Pemberton, Max. **Jewel Mysteries I Have Known.** [1894]

Pidgin, Charles Felton and J. M. Taylor. **The Chronicles of Quincy Adams Sawyer, Detective.** 1912

Pinkerton, Allan. **The Expressman and the Detective.** 1875

Post, Melville Davisson. **The Strange Schemes of Randolph Mason.** [1896]

Reeve, Arthur B[enjamin]. **The Silent Bullet.** 1912

Shiel, M[atthew] P[hipps]. **Prince Zaleski.** 1895

[Simms, William Gilmore]. **Martin Faber, The Story of a Criminal; and Other Tales.** 1837. Two volumes in one

Speight, T[homas] W[ilkinson]. **Under Lock and Key.** 1869. Three volumes in one

Stevenson, Burton E[gbert]. **The Mystery of the Boule Cabinet.** 1921

Trollope, T[homas] Adolphus. **A Siren.** 1870. Three volumes in one

[Vidocq, Eugène François]. **Memoirs of Vidocq. Principal Agent of the French Police Until 1827.** 1828/1829. Four volumes in two

Warren, Samuel. **Experiences of a Barrister, and Confessions of an Attorney.** 1859. Two volumes in one

"Waters" (pseud. of William Russell). **The Experiences of a French Detective Officer** .[185?]

Whyte-Melville, G[eorge] J[ohn]. **M. Or N.** 1869. Two volumes in one